COLD
WARRIORS

COLD WARRIORS

The Navy's Engineering and Diving Support Unit

Roy R. Manstan

authorHOUSE®

AuthorHouse™ LLC
1663 Liberty Drive
Bloomington, IN 47403
www.authorhouse.com
Phone: 1-800-839-8640

Published by AuthorHouse   05/29/2014

ISBN: 978-1-4918-6957-4 (sc)
ISBN: 978-1-4918-6955-0 (hc)
ISBN: 978-1-4918-6956-7 (e)

Library of Congress Control Number: 2014904395

(Richard Thibeault)

Dennie "Mac" McClenny
1924-2014
From the Greatest Generation
United States Navy
Active Duty Service—1942-1966
Civilian Service—1966-1989

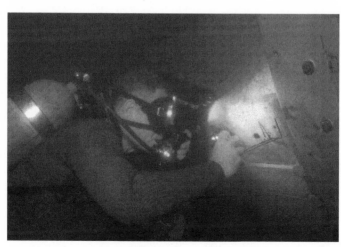

(Roy Manstan)

They shall beat their swords into plowshares and their spears into pruning hooks. Nation shall not lift up sword against nation; neither shall they learn war any more.

—Isaiah 2:4

The regard we ought to have for unborn posterity, yea every thing that is dear and sacred, do now loudly call upon us, to use our best endeavours to save our country: We must *beat our plow-shares into swords, and our pruning hooks into spears,* and learn the art of self-defense against our enemies.

—Samuel West, in a sermon preached before the
Massachusetts General Assembly, May 29, 1776,
on the eve of the Declaration of Independence.
[West's emphasis]

CONTENTS

PREFACE
An ounce of truth

The Cold War was defined by a massive emphasis on technology—the threat of a nuclear confrontation was real. Much of the threat, and the solution, were embodied in the silent service. Submarine and antisubmarine warfare dominated America's strategy of maritime superiority, and it fell to the Cold Warriors—civilian and military—to keep one step ahead of the ever-expanding capabilities of the Soviet Union. But the urgency demanded action from the intellectual and physical risk takers at the Navy's research institutions. The pages that follow look back at one of these: the U.S. Navy Underwater Sound Laboratory in New London, Connecticut, and its successors. You will not read about those at the top—not the admirals and captains, not the civilian executives and managers, nor the politicians—you will see the evolution of an organization that embraced risk among its staff, and in the face of the Soviet threat, allowed the risk takers to do what they do best.

This book describes the more than half-century history of one such group where risk comes with the job: a team of Navy trained civilian divers, formed during the Cold War, and who still carry on the tradition of excellence under pressure. Because it is written by and about Navy divers, however, there are two important considerations the reader must be mindful of before proceeding.

First, there will be an occasional outburst of unsavory language. With a desire for authenticity, it is necessary to include certain four-letter words in their various forms that, within the context of the dialogue, can be used as verbs, nouns, adjectives, or adverbs. In real conversations among Navy divers such words appear with unconstrained abandon, yet in social situations among human beings most of us have built-in filters that remove these words as a sentence spills out. Thus, the dialogue within this book (hopefully read by human beings and not just Navy divers) only includes these words when their original use emphasized a particular point, or if their removal compromises the meaning of the sentence.

Second, Navy divers have a genetic need to tell sea stories—a centuries-old maritime tradition: "With hard labor, the machine might be impelled at the rate of 3 knots an hour . . ." was how Ezra Lee related the speed of David Bushnell's wooden submarine *Turtle* in a letter written in 1815, four decades after his attempt to sink the British flagship *Eagle* with Admiral Lord Richard "Black Dick" Howe on board (his nickname a reference to the dark side of his personality, and not to his anatomy). As the war came to a close, Lee no doubt joined his buddies at the local tavern in Lyme, Connecticut, to down a draught or two and swap war stories. His sober recollections of how he approached *Eagle* probably began something like this: "For a few hours, I struggled to maintain headway at a knot and finally . . ." But by the third round, the speed of the *Turtle* had tripled: "It was a dark and stormy night . . . British to the right o' me . . . British to the left o' me . . . Hour after hour, I cranked Bushnell's infernal machine, making at least three knots, and finally . . ." When Ezra Lee wrote his letter nearly forty years later, he remembered the ale-enhanced version.

So, other than sitting in a bar reminiscing, where does a modern-day Ezra Lee turn to for "facts" when compiling stories about the Cold War? While all of us old timers consider our memories infallible, there have been times when two infallible memories (my own included) have provided somewhat different accounts of events. Thus, a history book has to rely on "fact checking," which contemporary published accounts can provide to confirm or deny that infallibility. Of all the reference material consulted while researching this book, the most interesting and insightful source was the Underwater Sound Laboratory publication ECHO—particularly during the ten years from 1958 to 1967, the year I arrived in New London and joined the Sound Lab. This weekly newsletter and its successor publications provided summaries of the projects and, more important, the people who created the technologies that helped bring about the demise of the Soviet Union.

Nonetheless, there were many conversations and dozens of emails from retirees that provided vivid color to the ECHO's black-and-white print, adding details that the space-limited editors deleted. And so, when writing all of the chapters that follow, I have mixed together each conversation and email—some providing a splash of red, from others a splash of yellow, with yet others tossing in a touch of green or a swirl of blue—and the result may take on the appearance of a 1960s tie-dyed T-shirt.

Readers of this book, however, can be confident in the accuracy of the historical narrative, all well documented; the sea stories (designated as such by the pound-sign, #) will require a bit of latitude. Bottom line: sea stories and wine go well together and improve with age; some of what you will read has aged significantly. For anyone who has purchased this book and is concerned about their authenticity, I include the following money-back guarantee: "There is *at least* an ounce of truth in every one-pound story."

Figure 1. USS *Nautilus* (SSN-571), launched on January 21, 1954, signaled the beginning of a nuclear-powered submarine fleet that would forever change the nature of naval warfare. (*Submarine Force Library and Museum*)

PROLOGUE
"The only easy day was yesterday!"

... a reality our instructors repeated every morning ...

Becoming a Navy diver requires a high level of physical and mental tenacity, traits that had to be constantly called upon throughout the long weeks of training. The instructors were relentless, yet professional and dedicated to giving us the skills that would keep us alive. Each morning's recollection of the "easy day" was a wake-up to what was about to happen and what we would face each day that followed. The end-point—the target of all this effort—had to have a focus and a purpose. For those of us coming of age in the 1960s, it was the growing and spreading threat of Soviet communism. Keeping a Cold War from turning very hot became a silent but intense war that would call on a new breed within the military and their civilian partners—the Cold Warrior.

On January 21, 1954, a revolution in undersea warfare slid down the ways at Electric Boat in Groton, Connecticut (figure 1). The devastation wrought on the world's navies and merchant fleets by submarines during two world wars had just been superseded by a new and awesome technology: the nuclear-powered submarine. The Soviets had been expanding their submarine fleet, relying on the well-established diesel-electric-powered vessel. With the launch of USS *Nautilus* (SSN-571), the United States could rightly claim superiority beneath the sea. The Soviets raced to develop their own nuclear powered submarine, and a realization swept across the technological world that "the only easy day was yesterday!"

This book is about finding solutions when there were, and still are, no easy days ahead. The Cold War drew a generation of individuals from America's diverse population willing to take both physical risk and intellectual risk. But the intensity of the technological race demanded that every individual understood the importance of his or her role along the path to the prize, where every hurdle, which had to be jumped, was accomplished by *teamwork*. This book tells the stories of one such team—but it is also about the evolution of *any* organization responsible for creating an environment where solutions are mandatory, risk is a way of life, mediocrity must stand aside, and excellence is the result.

SHOCK AND AWE

Many of the parents and grandparents of the Cold Warriors lived through World War I, a four-year conflict of true "shock and awe," which exhausted survivors termed the War to End All Wars—an expression of hope that was shattered only two decades later with the onset of World War II. These long, tedious wars resulted in the loss of millions of soldiers, sailors, and civilians. The end of World War II brought relief from the anxieties of the first half of the twentieth century—that relief would be short lived. A stark realization emerged that with the atomic bomb and the rush to develop the capability of a "first strike," millions of lives could now be incinerated at the speed of light.

Every year, on the third Saturday in September, retirees from the Navy's Underwater Sound Laboratory gather for an afternoon filled with memories as well as a collective sigh of relief. Everyone there is a product of the development of nuclear technology. Some began their careers under the mushroom cloud that brought an abrupt end to World War II, while many of us were born under that cloud, watched neighbors build fallout shelters, and were taught to crawl under our desks if the sirens blew, all while countries anxious to join the atomic age carried out weapon tests in the atmosphere.

A TRIAD OF DETERRENCE

The so-called super powers vied for dominance with an ever-escalating rush to create a bigger, more powerful nuclear weapon and the means to deliver it. By 1949, the Soviets had detonated their first atomic bomb. In response, the United States developed the hydrogen bomb and in 1952 demonstrated its destructive power. This nuclear superiority only lasted a year, when the Soviets followed with their hydrogen bomb in 1953.

In John Piña Craven's book *The Silent War* (2001), he describes a "triad of deterrence," where the Army, Air Force, and Navy each have a role in the delivery of a nuclear bomb or missile.[1] The Army would take on the Intermediate-Range Ballistic Missile (IRBM), and the Soviets responded with their own mobile, tactical missiles. The Air Force was tasked to develop the Intercontinental Ballistic Missile (ICBM) with stationary, hardened silos, and soon the Strategic Air Command (SAC) would operate air bases with the B-1 bomber. The Soviet response came quickly, demonstrating their ability to launch a missile with their first tests of an ICBM in August 1957, punctuated that same year when Sputnik began orbiting overhead.

It was the Navy, however, that would need to evaluate the type of platform that could perform its role in the triad. The first thought of attempting to launch a liquid-fueled Jupiter missile from a surface vessel was quickly dismissed. A surface ship was a relatively easy target, and missile accuracy was highly dependent on stability during launch, an impossible requirement on the high seas. By the end of 1956, after two years of experience with *Nautilus*, serious consideration was given to developing a submarine-launched nuclear weapon, dubbed the Polaris fleet ballistic missile (FBM).

Beginning in 1958, the concept of submarine-launched missiles was already being tried when Regulus cruise missile launch capability was added to four conventional-powered submarines including the World War II fleet boat USS *Tunny* (SS-282 became SSG-282), and on the nuclear USS *Halibut* (SSGN-587). These submarines, however, had to surface in order to launch Regulus, a precarious and vulnerable operation. Long after Regulus was discontinued in 1964, a cruise missile once again became part of the Navy's submarine armament when the submerged vertical-launched Tomahawk cruise missile was back fitted into older SSBN Polaris launch tubes.

By 1959, after a monumentally ambitious effort, the first of an eventual fleet of nearly sixty ballistic missile submarines was commissioned USS *George Washington* (SSBN-598). On July 20, 1960 this same vessel conducted the first successful underwater launch of a Polaris missile, establishing the Navy's role in the nuclear-deterrence triad. Four months later *George Washington* went to sea for its initial strategic patrol, carrying sixteen Polaris missiles with their nuclear payload (figure 2).

Figure 2. *Above:* USS *George Washington* (SSBN-598) carried sixteen fleet ballistic missiles with nuclear warheads. Their hidden presence beneath the world's oceans ensured America's strategy of deterrence throughout the Cold War. (*Navsource.org*)

Right: Launched from beneath the sea, the A-1 Polaris missile and its later versions helped maintain this country's maritime superiority. (*Courtesy Lockheed-Martin*)

Most of the decision makers at that time, both political and military, had experienced the ravages of a world war and understood the implications of an all-out nuclear confrontation. These rational minds prevailed over the few, albeit vocal, proponents of a first strike to end the Communist threat once and for all. It was thought that a corresponding rationale existed among the Soviets, and that for the Cold War to remain cold the United States and the Soviet Union would engage in a race to design for deterrence.

This strategy was put to the test in October 1962, with the arrival of nuclear missiles on the island of Cuba. In the potentially lethal game of deterrence, Soviet premier Nikita Khrushchev had played his card. Only ninety miles from the United States, President John F. Kennedy considered this to be beyond the rules of the game, and more provocative and threatening than could be tolerated. Thus began a brief time when anxiety over a potential first strike by the Soviets escalated, eliciting an equally provocative threat as Kennedy put the Strategic Air Command on alert and deployed the small but lethal fleet of eight SSBN submarines, each with the capability to launch sixteen Polaris missiles with their nuclear warheads aimed at Soviet targets. Their potential effectiveness had only recently been demonstrated on May 6, 1962, when USS *Ethan Allen* (SSBN-608) launched a Polaris missile that detonated over the Pacific Ocean in what would be the last atmospheric test of a nuclear warhead. Khrushchev relented, and the Soviet missiles were removed from our doorstep. We all breathed that collective sigh of relief. (Figure 3)

Figure 3. *Above:* This Golf II-class submarine is typical of the early Soviet ballistic missile boats that, by the 1960s, were deployed in response to our increasing fleet

of SSBN submarines. *Below:* During the Cuban missile crisis in 1962, Soviet Premier Nikita Khrushchev sent four of these Foxtrot-class submarines to face the U.S. blockade of the island. Although powered by conventional diesel-electric propulsion, these submarines carried nuclear-tipped torpedoes. (*Department of Defense Photos*)

The fleet ballistic missile submarine had demonstrated the effectiveness of a deterrent, tipped with stealth and uncertainty. It would be difficult to conceal the whereabouts of land- and air-based weapons, and their existence would be among an adversary's targets during a first strike. It was the submarine, therefore, that would command the most effective element in the triad of deterrence. Its strategic value was not lost on the Soviets and they rushed to compete.

SWORDS INTO PLOWSHARES

Not everyone, however, was a proponent of a nuclear Navy. In 1980, two brothers, Daniel and Philip Berrigan, both Catholic priests, established the anti-nuclear Plowshares Movement. Their members protested the involvement of government and industry in nuclear weapons development— when the group entered General Electric's missile facility in King of Prussia, Pennsylvania, damaging several pieces of equipment, the incident was followed by a lengthy court case and convictions. Nuclear submarines were no less of a target. The commissioning ceremony for submarines launched from Electric Boat Division of General Dynamics would often be held at the Naval Underwater Systems Center in New London. A typical scene during a 1980s commissioning was the appearance on the Thames River of a fast-moving Zodiac inflatable boat carrying several nuns. The boat would cross the security barrier and, in a symbolic gesture of beating swords into plowshares, the nuns began beating the side of the submarine with hammers.

But the Soviets were hard at work sharpening their swords and the tips of their spears. While the peace movements of the Cold War were determined, heart-felt, and sincere, a strategy of deterrence would require an equally determined effort. Remaining one step ahead of the Soviets would emphasize technology. For the half century following World War II, the Navy accelerated its participation in the Cold War with what John Merrill referred to as a "slide rule strategy," where the pace of technological advance accelerates only when there is a marriage between the operational Navy and its civilian scientists and engineers.[2] For most Americans, keeping the peace meant the submarine would remain front and center.

ORIGINS OF SUBMARINE WARFARE

The roots of submarine warfare reach deep into American history, as far back as 1776, during the opening months of the Revolutionary War, when a tiny one-man submarine attempted to sink the British flagship HMS *Eagle* anchored in New York harbor.[3] David Bushnell's *Turtle* was a well conceived vessel, described by contemporary observer and Bushnell friend Colonel David Humphreys as "a *Machine* altogether different from any thing devised by the art of man."[4]

The potential of a mode of naval warfare that pushed far beyond the technology available to David Bushnell continued to be tested throughout the following century. Yet the technological advances brought on with the industrial revolution were still insufficient to convert visionary ideas into reality. Reality and its evil twin lethality, however, all changed at the dawn of the twentieth century as submarine warfare matured during two world wars. The success of the German U-boat was a combination of naval strategy, engagement tactics, and superior design, while the technology devised by the Allied Powers—during both World Wars—to counter the threat continually pushed the limits of engineering.

With the introduction of a nuclear-capable adversary, the Navy could no longer depend on brute force technology; the stakes of the Cold War were high, and deterrence would be based on gaining and maintaining the upper hand. It would take the best and brightest; it would require ingenuity and a willingness to take intellectual and physical risks; and it would fall to the Navy laboratories to understand and adapt to the undersea battlespace. At the forefront was the U.S. Navy Underwater Sound Laboratory known officially as USN/USL, NUSL, or simply USL; and the "Sound Lab" by those of us who worked there.

USN/USL . . . NUSC . . . NUWC

Established at the beginning of World War II as the New London Laboratory of the Columbia University Division of War Research, its initial mission was to develop antisubmarine warfare (ASW) technologies against the German U-Boat. As the war moved toward closure, research and operations in New London were transitioned from a Navy-supported university function to a component of the Navy Department—the U.S. Navy Underwater Sound Lab under the Bureau of Ships (BUSHIPS). After a quarter century, in 1970, USN/USL merged with Rhode Island's Naval Underwater Weapons Research and Engineering Station (NUWRES) to form the Naval Underwater Systems Center (NUSC), headquartered in Newport but retaining the New London Laboratory (NUSC/NL). By this time, BUSHIPS had been reestablished as the Naval Ships Systems Command (NAVSHIPS). In 1974, NAVSHIPS merged with the Naval Ordnance Systems Command to form today's Naval Sea Systems Command (NAVSEA). By 1992, with another extensive reorganization of Navy laboratories, NUSC was established as a Division within NAVSEA called the Naval Undersea Warfare Center (NUWC). Five years later, a Base Realignment and Closure Commission (BRAC) would close and move the New London facilities to Newport, where NUWC continues its undersea warfare mission.

For the reader, acronyms are like a language of their own, and the Navy has been particularly adept at creating them. But there are three acronyms defined in the previous paragraph for which I feel compelled to provide this additional emphasis from the start, as these have the appearance of being used at random. I use the terms *Sound Lab* and *USN/USL* frequently, as they are synonymous and represent the first of three post-World War II time periods. When you see the acronym NUSC (or occasionally NUSC/NL), the information relates to activities that occurred between 1970 and 1992, at which time this narrative (and the Navy) replaces NUSC with NUWC. Acronyms are often expressed phonetically, rather than as a series of letters—thus USN/USL is pronounced as a word: us'n-us'l; NUSC rhymes with tusk; NUWC sounds a bit like new'-ik.

A WAR IN WHICH TECHNOLOGY IS KING

Soon after we entered the twenty-first century, on September 11, 2001, the world experienced the opening salvo in what has become known as the Global War on Terror. The World Trade Center was attacked by an enemy that employed the tactic of asymmetric warfare—using a small but very lethal group of individuals whose goal was to exact the maximum damage on a country with a vastly superior military capability. A half century earlier, however, there was nothing asymmetric about our antagonist. The Cold War was also a global war, but this time dominated by technology; each side with individuals and agencies that could rapidly send their fleets out onto and under the oceans armed with the awesome power of a nuclear strike.

The stakes were high—Soviet submarines prowled in a real battlespace and it would take real data and real science to maintain the advantage; creating a virtual battlespace with inspired opinion and speculation was not going to be enough to win the war. It would be the intellectual risk takers and the physical risk takers—those Cold Warriors walking the halls of the U.S. Navy Underwater Sound Lab—who would quietly enter that real battlespace, gathering scientific data needed to create the tools for a Cold War strategy.

It was an abundance of "kick-ass" energy in New London that sent field teams over the oceans on a project called AMOS, while others explored the mysteries of the arctic, living in camps on ice islands in the 1950s. Throughout the 1960s, scientists dove into the deep ocean in submersibles—the bathyscaphe *Trieste*, Cousteau's *Diving Saucer*[5], *Deepstar 4000, Alvin, Star III*, and the Perry *Cubmarine*, all carrying individuals who knew that knowledge and risk go hand in hand. Field teams would live and work at an oceanographic research station, twenty-five miles off Bermuda called Argus Island, and in 1964, hosted the Sealab habitat where the Navy conducted saturation diving experiments.

But it was sonar—and the science of underwater sound—that dominated the mission of the Underwater Sound Lab. Adventurous field teams became involved with projects that were often international in scope. During one of the periodic staff briefings held at the Sound Lab's Christopher Columbus Auditorium, Fernand "Fred" Deltgen described his experiences in Africa at Lake Tanganyika,[6] a very long deep-water lake where the Lab planned to conduct acoustic testing—at that moment I knew I was working at the right place. The research and the people who surrounded me were focused on creating the best sonar possible, and each project carried its own name. There was Fishbowl, Ocean Acre, SNAP 7-E, Artemis, AMOS, and ANZUS Eddy, Colossus and Cormoran, Sanguine and Seaguard. Engineers went to sea with FLIP, BRASS, AFAR and MACS—this list only scratches the surface of decades of successful field work, all documented and archived at the Sound Lab's phenomenal reference library and available to young engineers curious about the "how and why" of the Navy's principal ASW research lab. What I soon learned, however, was that reading books and listening to sea stories only helps understand what *was* possible . . . knowing what *is* possible required becoming a participant.

USN/USL was composed of a mix of farsighted scientists, aggressive engineers, technically astute technicians, and creative machinists, all supported by an administrative staff that couldn't do enough to facilitate our mission. The organization that encourages these individuals, even at its own peril, is inevitably assured success and deserved of praise; those that discourage risk taking are soon forgotten. But the Sound Lab will not be forgotten, nor will the efforts of its dedicated staff—efforts that covered the world's oceans, efforts necessary to match the global intentions of the Union of Soviet Socialist Republics, the USSR.

THE TIP OF THE SPEAR

Nuclear submarines would dominate the Navy's role in the triad of deterrence, and sonar would keep the tip of the spear pointing at the heart of the Soviet bear. But the Cold War eventually came to a close, and within a few years, research and development of the Navy's undersea warfare systems became consolidated in Newport. The long histories of submarine and antisubmarine warfare technology at both locations—Newport and New London—is far beyond the scope of this book and has been covered in detail by authors John Merrill and Lionel Wyld, who enjoyed distinguished careers at the Naval Underwater Systems Center.[7]

Our story, however, is about a small team of engineers and technicians, created in response to the Cold War, from the staff of the U.S. Navy Underwater Sound Laboratory and its successors—a team with a unique and unusual collective personality. Known today as the NUWC Engineering and Diving Support Unit (EDSU), this team originated in the late 1950s when the *Underwater* Sound Lab recognized the need to have a few of its engineering staff trained to participate in its *underwater* research. In 1958, Sumner "Joe" Gordon became the first USN/USL engineer to become a Navy qualified diver, just four years after the Navy began the systematic training of its "underwater swimmers" in the use of scuba. For the next two and a half decades, a small number of USN/USL and NUSC engineers and technicians would train at the Groton submarine base and the Navy Diving and Salvage Training Center (NDSTC) in Panama City, Florida, forming a field team simply known as "the divers."

Then, in 1984, the Navy initiated a review of the role a civilian dive team had within the Research, Development, Test, and Evaluation (RDT&E) mission at NUSC. A decision was made to formalize the function and place "the divers" under the Command Support Department. Membership in what would soon became the NUSC Scientific Diving Team (SDT) remained a collateral duty, but one individual would be appointed as the SDT Diving Officer, whose responsibilities would include managing day-to-day operations and answering directly to the Officer in Charge (OIC) of the New London Laboratory. I became one of "the divers" in May 1974, serving as diving officer and diving program manager from September 1986 until retirement in January 2006. In an effort to minimize confusion, I will refer to "the Sound Lab divers" or "the NUSC divers" until December 31, 1996. On that date the curtain fell on the New London Laboratory and we formally became the Engineering and Diving Support Unit (EDSU) at NUWC in Newport under the Test and Evaluation Department.

After more than a half century, the Navy's undersea warfare mission continues to find the EDSU working on and under the waterfront. But the EDSU is only one of many small groups within all naval warfare centers whose men and women dedicate their careers to providing the warfighter with the most sophisticated tools possible. Field engineering is a lifestyle in which knowledge is king and creativity his right hand. Our story—that of the EDSU—is intended to highlight by example, the role played by groups like ours; Cold Warriors who worked behind and beneath the scene. As I have said many times, we are not the tip of the spear. Our job is to keep the tip of the spear sharp.

ON THE PROJECT

Only thirty-nine individuals among the thousands who had long successful careers at USN/USL, NUSC, and NUWC would accept and complete the challenge of becoming a qualified Navy diver. Throughout this long history, another fourteen previously qualified divers would join the team—some on active duty assigned to the Lab, and some prior military, now civilian employees. Our team (see appendix) was created to support the development of undersea warfare systems in New London and now in Newport. With these new systems, ships and submarines could take on much more complex missions against any potential adversary; but retaining that high-tech capability was essential. Expertise comes from experience. Our dive team—or any field engineering team, for that matter—has become intimately familiar with each of these systems and will bring that expertise to the waterfront when called; in our case, to the active duty divers whose day to day mission is what the Navy refers to as underwater ship husbandry. When a Navy diver is sent down to accomplish an assignment, he communicates to his topside team that he is ready to proceed with three words: "On the project." For more than a half century, our divers have been "on the project" thousands of times.

History speaks volumes, so as a mentor often exclaimed, "Pay attention, dammit!" (You'll see this quote again.) There is the old adage that we study history so that we don't repeat the mistakes of the past, but a historical perspective—and the goal of this book—will make very clear how and why people respond to difficult challenges. I summarize the long evolution of submarine warfare, emphasizing the need for risk takers, both individual and organizational, who stepped front and center to face a technological adversary embodied in the Soviet Union. The willingness of these Cold Warriors to accept risk, while stopping the spread of communism, was inspired by mentors and role models from "the greatest generation," who had faced daunting challenges during World War II. They, in turn, were inspired by the previous generation, which endured the War to End All Wars, and whose parents were a product of an industrial revolution that struggled to affect the outcome of the Civil War.

None of this was easy, yet these past generations were always ready and willing to be "on the project"—whether above, on, or under the water—never shrinking from the risks and dangers of their adversaries. Looking back on our predecessors and how they met their challenges, helps us understand why we did the things we did to win the Cold War.

In recent months, Russia's power brokers—remnants from the Soviet Union—have reverted to the strong-arm tactics of the Cold War. Tensions between the "East" and the "West" escalated with the annexation of Crimea into the Russian Federation, through a treaty of accession signed in Moscow on March 18, 2014. These events are a reminder to the current and next generation that your challenges will be no more or less difficult than what was experienced by those of us who preceded you; your ability to respond may only be limited by the policies and structure of the organization behind you. So this book is intended to send a message to the movers and shakers of *any* organization that strives to lead the pack:

"Don't let the tail wag the dog. It's the dog's nose that finds the bone, not its other end."

Front row: Haver, Cook, Schmidt, Buchet, Manstan, Thompson. Second row: O'Grady, Easley, Keller, Cropper, Sharp. Third row: Jackson, Burgess, Pless. Back row: Instructors Clark, Schmidt, Willis, Downey, Moon, Simlich.

Figure 4. *Above:* Navy scuba class, May 31, 1974. (*US Navy Photo; Courtesy Roy Manstan*) *Right:* The submarine escape training tower where all scuba trainees were required to successfully perform a free ascent. (*Submarine Force Library and Museum*)

CHAPTER 1
Lower than Whale Shit

After a few introductory remarks from the diving officer, Lieutenant G.F. Heeger, our orientation was turned over to the training team.

"Gentlemen!"

"My name is Downey . . . Chief Downey. Welcome to the Navy's submarine escape training facility, where you will receive the required instruction leading to qualification in scuba. Those of you who graduate will be eligible to wear the pin designating this qualification. You will be as proud to wear this as we are to present it to you. Standing to my right are your instructors, who you will come to love more and more each day."

"During this course, we leave our rank at the door. You will address us as 'Instructor.' The exception to this rule is the one person here who will be your only friend for the duration of your stay at this school."

All of the instructors were dressed in their khakis except for an individual standing at the entrance to the classroom wearing his dress uniform. "This, gentlemen, is Master Diver Einhellig. He will be happy to meet with you if and when you decide to check out and will make that process simple and quick. You will address him as 'Master Diver!!!'"

Chief Downey then set the tone.

"You, however, are lower than whale shit on the bottom of the ocean and will remain that until graduation. I see among you a lieutenant, an ensign, and," Downey looked in my direction, "a civilian retread. I repeat. You are *all* whale shit! Look at the person on either side of you. History has shown us that at least one of you will not be sitting here by the end of this course." Downey was right. We had a large class—thirty-two of us on day one. Fourteen would graduate. (Figure 4)

Chief Downey then introduced each instructor, who nodded to us as his name was called. The mood was tense. There were no smiles.

"Instructor Simlich . . ."

"Instructor Willis . . ."

"Instructor Moon . . ."

"This is Instructor Schmidt. As your diving med tech, you may address him as 'Instructor' or 'Doc' Schmidt."

"Finally, this is Instructor Clark. He is an instructor in training and will be even more enthusiastic assisting you with your progress."

"Good God," I thought, "what have I gotten myself into . . . and for a second time!" Downey referred to me as a "retread." It had been a year since I sat in this same classroom. Scuba training is the first step that all Navy divers must complete before advancing on to other diving specialties. I had lasted only one week in May 1973, when, during a run, I landed in a rain-filled pothole and hyper extended my knee. It would be two months on crutches and physical therapy, and ten months of training. Now I was back for a second try—prepared but fully aware what was coming next, cringing when Chief Downey proclaimed to the class: "The only easy day was yesterday."

But why would any sane, well-educated engineer, working under the guidance of other sane, even better-educated engineers, venture into a world that by its very nature is filled with risk—and for a second time? Dropping out of dive school forced me to face the awful truth that I was not in control of my future. I returned to my cubicle, set the crutches against the wall, and was handed my next design task. A month after dropping out I completed my graduate work, receiving a Masters degree in mechanical engineering from the University of Connecticut. Yet the disappointment at failing to complete the scuba training far exceeded any satisfaction gained from receiving the degree. I knew right then that my career path would have to eventually include diving for the Navy. I was born to be a field engineer—not tied to a cubicle.

The morning I checked out, the Master Diver said I would be welcomed back, but that I would need to be better prepared and in much better physical condition than what he had observed during my short stay. He didn't know if I was mentally up to the task but would be willing to give me another chance. My office overlooked the Thames River, where I could watch the submarine base dive boat carrying my classmates out into Long Island Sound. It was one of those "take a deep breath" moments, and I swore to make it back. While the projects were interesting, and I liked and respected the people around me, they all questioned my sanity. No one understood what I meant when I tried to explain that diving would help me regain my rapidly disappearing sanity. I was losing sight of the reason I joined the Sound Lab in the first place.

A TEENAGER IN THE 1960s

I had been a typical high school kid, stumbling through my early teenage years listening to Elvis and wearing a James Dean haircut. I liked to tinker with a Model A Ford and was curious about everything that crossed my path. On weekends I would join my family hunting for Indian artifacts. When it finally came time to decide what would be next, I was certain I would become Indiana Jones (long before Steven Spielberg and George Lucas invented their fictional character), and by the end of my junior year I had been accepted to Yale University's anthropology department. While my parents were quite proud of me, there was soon to be a reality check. My dad was a postal worker, and we lived comfortably from payday to payday. They encouraged me to be creative, but I knew that I might have to set somewhat less lofty career goals. I was pretty good in math, and liked mechanical things, so as my senior year progressed an engineer I would become—Indiana Jones would have to explore without me.

Bowing to collegiate peer pressure, I staggered through my early college years (often under the influence of frequent fraternity parties) until once again we all had to face that same question: What's next? Two years of mandatory ROTC immortalized in the 1978 movie *Animal House*, an all-too-accurate portrayal of 1960s college and fraternity life, convinced me that I wasn't a good candidate for an Army career. I was, however, intrigued by military technology, and that of the Navy's in particular. Raised along the Connecticut shore, being in and around the water was a part of daily life. I lived less than a mile from the homestead of David Bushnell, a local Revolutionary War hero, who invented the world's first submarine used in naval combat. Okay, so to Hell with Indiana Jones! I would become a modern-day David Bushnell. Then I began reading (a risky behavior for those with overactive imaginations) about William Beebe's 1934 descent to 3,028 feet in his bathysphere. Then there was Auguste and Jacques Piccard and their bathyscaphe, reaching a depth of 35,800 feet while exploring the Marianas Trench in 1960. It was during my senior year, in 1967, when I discovered Jacques Cousteau and his "Aqualung."

MENTORS AND ROLE MODELS

As graduation approached, there was a career decision I had to make—one I'm sure that many of my engineer colleagues also faced. Would we take lucrative positions in private industry, or one of those low-paying government jobs? Anyone who has stepped into their twenties with mouth open and glazed-over eyes has an insatiable desire for independence, for a fast car, for booze and babes. It sometimes takes advice from old-timers (like me, now) who had to make similar choices decades earlier.

I met Guy and Jane Williams during my summer job delivering mail from the Old Saybrook Post Office. Guy was a fine gentleman who had a long career in federal service, and had transferred to the Underwater Sound Laboratory from the Naval Electronics Lab (NEL) in San Diego. He was married to a delightful and very unique Southern Belle, Jane, who was determined to save me from a career at the post office. One summer evening they invited me to their home and encouraged me to consider joining the Sound Lab. I explained my interest in oceanographic research and in deep-submergence vehicles in particular. I was stopped cold, not knowing what to say next when Guy responded: "You mean, like the bathyscaphe? I know those guys!"[8] (Figure 5)

Figure 5. The bathyscaphe *Trieste* is lifted from the water after one of its deep dives. (*Naval History and Heritage Command*)

4

Jacques Piccard??!! The bathyscaphe??!! I learned that evening that Guy and Jane were close personal friends with three generations of the Piccard family. While at NEL, Guy had been involved with the Marianas Trench expedition. He had been presented with a piece of the Plexiglas window that cracked when the bathyscaphe *Trieste* reached the bottom. I held this artifact from a moment in history when Jacques Piccard and Navy Lieutenant Don Walsh dropped to the deepest spot on the Earth, where their fragile sphere and this window had been subjected to pressure of more than 16,000 pounds per square inch, a record that can't be broken.

In my senior year, during one of my visits to the Williamses' home, I told them that I had interviewed with Westinghouse and then at Electric Boat, where a grade school friend's dad was an engineer (I had been invited to see the launch of the second nuclear sub, USS *Seawolf* (SSN-575), in 1955). Westinghouse was building deep submersibles, including the *Deepstar 4000*; Electric Boat was working with the Reynolds Company on the *Aluminaut*, and had launched a series of three of its Submarine Test And Research (Star) submersibles—*Star II* and *Star III* were both christened and launched at USN/USL on May 3, 1966—all of which were being used for exactly the type of work I had wanted.[9] I was anxious to graduate and move on.

Guy was very patient and listened with interest, probably to determine if I was sincere or if these were just the ramblings of a confused college student. Nonetheless, he and Jane both encouraged me to consider interviewing at the Sound Lab, which, of course, I did. Guy introduced me to many of his coworkers, all of whom were delighted to talk to a young enthusiastic engineer and expressed interest in having me join the Sound Lab staff. We spoke with Walt Whitaker, a mechanical engineer who had been involved with the installation of the oceanographic research facility Argus Island in 1960. Walt had been responsible for placing the SNAP-7E nuclear-powered acoustic beacon in fifteen thousand feet of water off Bermuda in 1964. I was then introduced to Lou Maples, who had also been a part of the SNAP-7E team and was now the USN/USL program manager for the *Deepstar 4000* project.[10]

We visited several of Guy's colleagues, who were all involved in an impressive assortment of projects. What also caught my attention was how happy everyone seemed to be. Morale was high, and everyone took pride in the organization. No one complained or warned me about underlying issues at the Lab or with the "bureaucrats" that ran the place, who, I would later learn, had all begun their careers with "real jobs," ones that sent them into the field and off-shore.

Later, Guy left me with a final thought. "We've been working with EB and Westinghouse for several years, and have used their submersibles. Consider this, however. If you join, for example, Westinghouse, where they are building a submersible that can go much deeper than their *Deepstar 4000*, you will find that a great challenge. But—," Guy paused briefly to emphasize the point "—I guarantee that their oceanography program will be short lived, and you will soon be designing refrigerators instead of submarines." He was even less enthusiastic about working at Electric Boat.

Guy, and Jane as well, had been simply offering their perspective based on a personally satisfying, life-long career. If, they worried, I bought into the enthusiastic and lucrative proposal from Westinghouse, where I salivated at the sight of their submersibles, instant gratification could quickly turn into buyer's remorse. So I thanked Guy and Jane, sent letters of appreciation to Westinghouse and Electric Boat, contacted the Sound Lab, and bid farewell to college life.

The Sound Lab provided a remarkable assemblage of dedicated individuals, whom I looked to as role models and from which I found a few who became true mentors. I remained friends with Guy and Jane throughout their lives, and deep inside will always remember and appreciate their interest in some young clueless kid. I hope this book will "pay it forward."

U.S. NAVY UNDERWATER SOUND LABORATORY

A few days after graduation in June 1967, I checked in at the U.S. Navy Underwater Sound Lab (figure 6), visiting the security and personnel offices in Building 41 just inside the gate. The process was efficient. The people I met while signing in were welcoming and friendly, but were also professional with little time allotted for idle conversation. Within minutes, all of your physical senses engaged at once to inform your intellect that the wheels of a complex military machine within the chain-link fence were turning at a fast pace; and you knew, as the personnel representative handed each document to you for your perusal and signature, that civilian life was about to change.

Figure 6. Aerial view of the U.S. Navy Underwater Sound Laboratory taken at the time of the opening of Building 80, the H-shaped structure near the center of the photograph, built in 1962 to accommodate an influx of young engineers. The New London facilities would soon expand as the technological demands of the Cold War increased. The dog-leg section of the old wooden pier (far right) was soon removed and replaced with a modern concrete pier, and the semi-circular cove in the foreground was filled to provide more parking. A portion of the New London shoreline is visible at the top. (*USN/USL; Courtesy Bernie Cole*)

The most memorable document, one that has long since been eliminated, was a simple statement that as a condition of employment at the Underwater Sound Lab, I would agree to go to sea if the need arose. "Go to sea if there was a need? My God," I thought, "that's why I was there!" It didn't take long for me to read, swear to, and sign everything in sight.

Here was an organization that understood its existence was predicated on the ability of its staff to charge ahead. Management, as I would learn, thrived on the accomplishments of risk takers with scientific curiosity and engineering insights—traits that could also be found in the machinists and technicians, who were an integral part of the technological machine.

I was joining a unique staff numbering about twelve hundred, and I was surrounded by role models. Whether I was in the shop bouncing ideas off a lathe operator or in a meeting with PhDs, everyone had a back story. It was intimidating, yet exhilarating to a fledgling engineer—but could I keep up? One thing I quickly learned was that the Underwater Sound Lab thrived on a culture based on the team concept. You were expected to carry your share of the weight, but everyone was committed to the end result, and the organization was designed to bend to facilitate, rather than hinder, progress toward its mission. Yes, over the years I would encounter individuals, grumpy and obstinate, who lived and loved the bureaucratic life and would toss administrative process into the path of progress. But at USN/USL, risk takers—young and old—were welcomed!

With that final signature, I was now on the staff of the Underwater Sound Lab, a rather unassuming title for an organization whose mission was to provide the Navy with technology designed to detect and destroy enemy submarines. But the mission had evolved from Harvard and Columbia, two academic institutions tasked during the early days of World War II to develop the sonar needed to permanently neutralize German and Japanese submarines threatening Allied fleets in the Atlantic and Pacific. After the war, when the Navy took on the direction of the New London facilities, the laboratory spirit of the staff remained embodied in the name "Underwater Sound Laboratory."

There was a new threat now. Soviet and American nuclear submarines competed for strategic advantage across the globe. To keep one step ahead in the technological war, the Navy depended on their civilian laboratories for that "slide rule strategy." What I began to learn, however, was that there was nothing new about the concept of submarine warfare—the technology had changed, but these "infernal machines" had a long history, and I was about to become a participant.

Figure 7. *Above:* Drawing of CSS *H.L. Hunley* by R.G. Skerrett, 1902. (*Naval History and Heritage Command*) *Below: Hunley,* discovered in 1995 and raised five years later, is shown in its cradle at the Warren Lasch Conservation Center, North Charleston, SC. (*Friends of the* Hunley)

CHAPTER 2
Submarine Warfare, Offensive and Defensive

This chapter title is the same as the book title by Navy Lieutenant Commander J. S. Barnes.[11] What seems at first glance remarkable about his 230-page book is that it was published in 1869. Yet what Barnes brings to our attention is the realization that naval warfare was taking a huge technological leap. The Civil War, as with any conflict, brought out an inventive spirit on both sides. Born on the thrust of a developing industrial revolution, centuries-old concepts were now technologically feasible. Both the North and South indulged in that competition for superiority as thousands of troops engaged in bloody battles, yet technology entered onto an even more creative battlefield—on and under the sea.

It was the afternoon of March 8, 1862, when naval surface warfare saw its future emerge off Hampton Roads, Virginia, as the ironclads USS *Monitor* and CSS *Virginia* battered each other during a four-hour struggle, both eventually retiring from the battle to lick their wounds, neither one a winner nor a loser. Although marginally seaworthy, *Monitor* was an entirely new concept, with a flat low-profile deck and little freeboard, mounting a pair of massive eleven-inch Dahlgren cannons within a cylindrical turret. *Virginia* was previously the steam frigate USS *Merrimack*, a wooden vessel scuttled and burned to keep it from being captured, later salvaged and converted to an ironclad by the Confederacy. These armored vessels and the development of the steam engine-powered propeller signaled the beginning of the end of the Age of Sail.

While both sides also looked beneath the sea for methods to engage their navies, it was the Confederacy that took 1860s technology and engineering as far as its limited material resources would allow. When Admiral David G. Farragut shouted "Damn the torpedoes, full speed ahead!" he was referring to underwater mines. The word "torpedo" was used in the nineteenth century to describe an explosive device, typically submerged and waiting to contact an unsuspecting warship—what we now define as a mine. Spar torpedoes were a similar device but attached to a long rod—the spar—extending out from a small attacking vessel. The South had employed this technology on its David-class semi-submersible torpedo boats, but the most spectacular attack occurred on February 17, 1864, by CSS *Hunley* (figure 7), a true submarine that drove its spar torpedo into the side of USS *Housatonic*, sending it to the bottom within minutes. *Hunley*'s story ended when it sank with all hands before reaching the safety of Charleston.

In *Submarine Warfare in the Civil War*, Mark Ragan (2002) provides an in-depth view of the incredible array of submarine designs that were being proposed during the Civil War.[12] Ragan describes the individuals who were responsible for the design of *Hunley* as visionary, talented engineers and artisans. For two years, New Orleanians Horace Hunley, James McClintock, and Baxter Watson had been collaborating on submarine concepts, including *Pioneer*, launched in March 1862 and tested in Lake Pontchartrain. They hoped to include a revolutionary new power source as a propulsion system that would free a crew from having to manually turn the propeller. Ragan includes a letter to the Confederate War Department where Watson "claimed that an engine of 'electro-magnetism' capable of powering a small submarine could in fact be purchased in New York City at a cost of $5000." Electric motors were truly in their infancy, and it took an engineer's vision to consider their potential application for cranking a submarine propeller. Ragan quotes McClintock, who, in 1902, wrote that "there had been much time and money lost in efforts to build an electro-magnetic engine for propelling the boat." After their futile efforts to produce an electric motor, the inventors then tried, also unsuccessfully, to incorporate a steam engine before returning to the use of human sweat.

When Barnes published his book in 1869, the "submarine warfare" technologies used by the South were just beginning to be evaluated and considered by the U.S. Navy. But *Hunley* was lost, and with it the true details of its mission—yet Barnes understood the potential. He noted that "to be effective, boats must be built specially designed for the purpose, and men must be trained and accustomed to their employment. Who can doubt but that . . . great improvements will hereafter be made in them as have marked the progress of invention in other engines of war?"[13]

1775

It was the American Revolution, however, that inspired the first truly "engineered" submarine—a tiny one-man vessel launched in the summer of 1775 by David Bushnell, and used in three attempts against British warships in New York Harbor and the Hudson River in 1776.[14] Known only as Bushnell's "machine," this famous vessel would eventually be given the name *Turtle* by one of David Bushnell's close friends and General George Washington's aide-de-camp, Colonel David Humphreys.[15]

I say "engineered" because Bushnell, a graduate of Yale, applied his knowledge of science to the solution of every system essential for creating a vessel and its weapon and which was capable of covertly navigating to its target at night, submerging, attacking, and (most important) surviving the attack. It was, as Barnes had proclaimed necessary for a submarine to be successful, "built specially designed for the purpose." What Bushnell must have understood was that the pilot, initially his brother, Ezra, would be entering a world totally contrary to human survival: if his "submarine vessel" flooded, the obvious consequence would be death. He had to create operational systems that minimized risk—a responsibility that twenty-first-century engineers face whether designing human systems for inner or outer space. Survival depends wholly on engineered solutions. There is no place for wishful thinking.

Although *Turtle* was unsuccessful in its mission, the vessel performed as a submarine, exactly as designed. Bushnell was a visionary thinker, but pragmatic in the execution of his ideas. Washington proclaimed "Bushnell's projects for the destruction of ships" to be "an effort of genius, but that too many things were necessary to be combined to expect much from the issue against an enemy who are always upon guard."[16]

Bushnell was a child of an industrial revolution that was just growing out of infancy. Complex mechanical devices were being produced, and the application of steam power was beginning to find a future. Bushnell's foray into the world of submarine warfare caught the attention of nineteenth century visionary engineers, Robert Fulton and Horace Hunley among them, who could only imagine the effect that a clandestine operation by a few courageous submariners would have on naval warfare if they were successful at destroying a massive warship with a crew of hundreds.

1875

Exactly one hundred years after Bushnell first launched his "submarine vessel," Lieutenant Francis M. Barber, an instructor at the Naval Torpedo Station in Newport, Rhode Island, paid tribute to Bushnell's engineering genius in one of a series of lectures he was giving students assigned to the Torpedo Station.[17] Barber's "Lecture on Submarine Boats and their Application to Torpedo Operations" outlined the history of the development of the "submarine torpedo boat" and gave particular attention to *Turtle* (figure 8). "I have been thus particular in my description of this invention, as it seems, notwithstanding its failures, to have been the most perfect thing of its kind that has ever been constructed, either before or since the time of Bushnell; and considering the disadvantages under which he must have labored at the time, (it occupied him from 1771 to 1775 to complete it,) it would seem that he has well earned the title 'Father of Submarine Warfare.'"

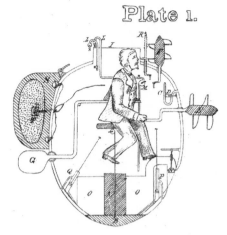

Plate 1.

Figure 8. *Above:* In 1875, LT Francis Barber created this rendition of David Bushnell's *Turtle*, the world's first submarine used in naval combat, September 6, 1776. (*Barber 1875*) *Below:* A replica of *Turtle* rests on the shiplift facility at the Mystic Seaport Museum after completing its operational testing, May 2008. (*Jerry Roberts*)

Barber also described the ideas of yet another visionary submarine designer who would, by the turn of the twentieth century, provide the world with the first practical naval submarine. In 1875, John P. Holland proposed his initial concept to the Navy Department in Washington, DC. It was a one-man "wet" submarine where the operator, wearing diving equipment supplied from air flasks within the hull, cranked the propeller with a foot-operated treadle. It is unlikely that the design was ever built, as Holland received little encouragement. The Navy Department soon forwarded Holland's design to Captain Edward Simpson, commanding officer at the Torpedo Station, for his review. Simpson's response was short, concluding that "the whole scheme was impractical . . . no one would go down in such a craft and the inventor should drop the whole thing."[18] Barber was a bit more favorable in his lecture: "In [Holland's] case, the lines of the boat are such as to obtain a much greater speed than Bushnell's, and the arrangement for respirator is very ingenious; but the operator would seem to be required to perform more operations than one man could attend to, especially as he is entirely surrounded by water."[19]

It is obvious (at least to me) that Captain Simpson didn't ask any Navy divers if they would consider "going down in such a craft." Had Holland been contracted by the Navy to build an experimental version of his human-powered submarine, the concept of divers conducting clandestine warfare from a free-flooding "wet" submarine would have preceded by sixty-five years, that practiced by combat swimmers during World War II. Simpson's lack of foresight might be excused considering the infancy of diving technology in 1875. Yet today, with access to modern scuba equipment, colleges and high school students compete in a biennial international "Human Powered Submarine" race. Students are challenged to design, build, and operate a free-flooding submarine in which the operator, just as suggested by Holland, breathes from a supply of compressed air.[20]

Holland would continue to promote his ideas, and by the turn of the century had finally developed and successfully sold to the Navy USS *Holland* (SS-1), which was commissioned in 1900. Within just a few years, Holland's new found success led to his vessel entering the fledgling submarine fleets of Britain, Russia, and (with then-retired Francis Barber acting as Holland's agent) Japan.

ENGINEER IN CHIEF, UNITED STATES NAVY

Although there was cautious skepticism among naval brass, one outspoken admiral was willing to publically proclaim that naval warfare would never be the same. Holding the turn-of-the-century title "Engineer in Chief, United States Navy," Rear Admiral George W. Melville published the article "The Submarine Boat: Its Value as a Weapon of Naval Warfare" in *The Annual Report of the Smithsonian Institution for the Year Ending June 30, 1901.* Melville's article, written in 1902, must have slipped into the publisher's hands just before going to press. His observations, as relevant today as they were over a century ago, give insight, through the eyes of the Navy's chief engineer, to the technological potential of submarine warfare: "As few things are impossible, the submarine may be developed in time to a state of efficiency and reliability that will cause a revolution in the composition of fleets."[21]

Melville warned that "under no circumstances should the opinion be permitted to prevail that any one design of boat is an accomplished fact, and that no further development is possible." As the Navy's chief engineer, it is not surprising that he proclaimed "the advances made in making the submarine boat more efficient have been almost altogether along engineering lines. It is because the capabilities of the engineer are progressively increasing that still further advance will be made in the development of the submarine boat," adding later that the "submarine may not only involve a change in naval

Figure 9. *Above:* Post card view of USS *Holland* (SS-1) underway near Newport, Rhode Island. (*Roy Manstan collection*) *Below:* The starboard bow of *Holland* on the ways in 1900. (*National Archives*)

construction, but a revolution in naval tactics," his comments written when the Navy operated a single submarine—USS *Holland*. (Figure 9)

How right he was. World War I was only twelve years away, and, he warned: "The naval battles of the future will be won by the nation which has made preparation for a conflict, and has supplied itself with every possible weapon of war." Germany had prepared—America, England and the rest of Europe had not. The Imperial German Navy would enter the war with a submarine design and construction program capable of winning more than just the battle.

WORLD WAR I

Tension had been building across Europe, erupting with a singular event on July 28, 1914. The assassination of the heir to the Austro-Hungarian throne, Arch Duke Franz Ferdinand, by a Serbian dissident was the trigger that fired the first bullet of many millions more in a four-year war, which rapidly spread across the continent. This European conflict became a world war, with American intervention in 1917.

Germany had been developing its war machine quietly for several decades after its decisive win during the Franco-Prussian War in 1871. The turn of the century ushered in technologies intended to conquer the air, land, and sea. By 1903, the Wright brothers had demonstrated that motorized aerial flight was possible, and Henry Ford was on the verge of mass production of his Model T. The value of these well-engineered inventions, generally intended for the benefit of mankind, was not lost on military strategists, and it took little effort to adapt revolutionary technologies for tactical use on and above the battlefield.

Conventional ground war pit hundreds of thousands of troops in a devastating conflict; nineteenth-century tactics staggered under the destructive power of twentieth-century technologies brutally introduced onto the battlefield. Cavalry raced across open fields, and trench warfare saw bayonet charges in which masses of troops emerged and struggled through barbed-wire defenses. Thousands fell to the recently perfected machine gun. Mustard gas settled into the trenches suffocating thousands more. A newly mechanized army simply made an end run around the heavily fortified Maginot Line, battered and pulverized by long-range artillery.

There was also a revolution in naval warfare, which, as Rear Admiral Melville had predicted, was embodied in the submarine—a technology that from its very origins was intended as a covert weapon delivery system. A century and a half prior to Bushnell's *Turtle*, a Dutch inventor, Cornelius Drebbel, working in England, experimented with an oar-driven submersible vessel. A contemporary observer, the Reverend John Wilkins, wrote in 1648 that Drebbel's "ark for submarine navigation" would be "of great advantage against a Navy of enemies, who by this means may be undermined in the water, and blown up."[22]

The Imperial German Navy, at first skeptical about the usefulness of the submarine, didn't acquire its first until 1906 as they considered these small vessels only applicable for coastal defense and of little strategic value. In his 1902 article, Melville described a conversation he had had with a German official visiting New York who informed him "that the Americans had done very well in going slowly in building such boats [but] that the German Admiralty had done better, for they had refused to build any."

That attitude would soon change. A French-designed submarine capable of long-distance operations was being constructed at the Kiel-Germania shipyard for Russia. With their interest piqued, Germany shed its earlier objections and moved quickly to acquire its own ocean-capable flotilla. By August 1914, Germany had twenty-eight submarines commissioned, with sixteen under construction. Its *Unterseeboote*, soon known as the infamous U-boat, emerged as an integral component of its strategy to win the war by controlling the sea routes, isolating Britain and Europe from resupply by sympathetic and presumably (though, in fact, not totally) neutral nations (figure 10). The U-boat would be an effective threat throughout a half century and two world wars, responsible for the sinking of 8,209 Allied merchant vessels, and grossing 27,200,678 tons.[23]

Figure 10. At the beginning of the war, Germany had twenty-eight submarines in service. This photo, taken at the harbor in Keil, shows a significant portion of Germany's two operational flotillas. In May, 1915, *U-20* (front row) sank the Cunard Line's *Lusitania*. (*Library of Congress*)

The emergence of the U-boat resolved any questions posed by doubters whom Melville was addressing in 1902: "There is practically no conflict of opinion in the Navy as to the value and efficiency of the battle ship. The same general testimony will be cheerfully paid to the work of the submarine when it is developed to a state where it is an efficient and reliable weapon of war . . . The possibilities are only limited by the imagination of the reader." Soon after the opening days of World War I, the U-boat and submarines of the Allied navies demonstrated their worth as naval combatants. Engineers now had to face the need to design a counter technology that could deny the maritime superiority and predatory capability of an enemy with this "efficient and reliable weapon of war."

WHEN SIZE MATTERED

Throughout history, size determined the winner in naval engagements. A broadside from a First-Rate Man-of-War carrying as many as one hundred cannons could disintegrate a smaller opponent. As the Age of Sail came to a close with the arrival of the Ironclads, admirals depended on maneuvering heavily armed and armored battleships and dreadnaughts into favorable positions to engage the enemy, and blast away with their massive firepower. A nation's influence on world affairs was determined by its dominance over the oceans, hence its ability to control international commerce. As the twentieth century dawned, and America transitioned from an agricultural to an industrial country, President Theodore Roosevelt sent the Great White Fleet on a worldwide cruise to proclaim this country's entrance onto the world stage—yet only seven years later, in 1914, the submarine stepped onto the stage and changed the script forever.

Size no longer mattered. Submerged and invisible, a tiny vessel patrolling the sea routes could now send a battleship to the bottom with a single shot from its torpedo tube. Merchant fleets, unarmed and unprotected, were vulnerable, and international trade could now be seriously disrupted by the threat of submarine attack. After 140 years, David Bushnell's vision was now a reality.

Naval strategists faced a dilemma as to how to counter this threat. Merchant ships had always simply left port as schedules and weather dictated. A chance encounter on the vast high seas with an enemy naval vessel, privateer, or pirate, was simply a matter of bad luck. The assumption was that if enough ships went out carrying their cargo, most would make a successful passage and a few losses would have minimal impact on the supply of materials.

This philosophy dominated naval planners during the early years of World War I: just build merchant ships faster than the U-boats could sink them, and the flow of supplies would continue. The unrestricted campaign against shipping, however, presented the decision makers with tactics for which they had no prior experience, and no insight into the most efficient way to neutralize the U-boat. It was a brute force method—try your best to locate them, chase them down, and either run them over or drop as many depth charges as you could carry. Unless you encountered one on the surface, naval gun fire was of no value.

THE CONVOY

Admiral Sir John Jellicoe, Britain's First Sea Lord during World War I, strongly objected to a system in which ships would assemble and transit in a group, or convoy. He believed that his antisubmarine resources should be allocated to search and destroy missions. The Admiralty preferred engaging what was then referred to as the "thousands scheme"—thousands of patrol craft would search for submarines, while areas infested with U-boats would be protected by deploying thousands of mines and thousands of nets. The nets carried surface floats that would indicate if a submarine had been snared, a visual signal for a destroyer to rush in with its depth charges.[24]

The British Royal Navy employed hydrophone flotillas, multiple small vessels that hung listening devices over the side in hopes of hearing the sounds of a patrolling submarine. Spotters in planes and dirigibles searched from the sky, but there was little chance of finding a submarine moving well below the surface. A U-boat could remain submerged during the day, operating on its batteries, only surfacing at night to recharge under cover of darkness.

Yet merchant ships were on their own, leaving port individually and at random intervals. Once off shore and beyond any possible naval protection, these vessels simply became targets, picked off at alarming rates by a very small number of submarines that bypassed the mine fields and nets. It was almost inevitable that among the hundreds of merchant vessels which ventured out to sea, some would pass through an area where a submarine lurked uninhibited by British warships.

Although the Admiralty had seen proposals for sending merchant ships in groups, with some protection from naval escort vessels, there were overwhelming objections to the effectiveness of these plans. Convoys, it was generally thought, would present an even larger target, and the participating vessels, all transiting at different speeds, would find it impossible to remain together; besides, there were too few cruisers and destroyers available for duty as escorts.

What was overlooked, however, was that because there was a limited number of U-boats patrolling a vast ocean, a chance encounter with a convoy was the same as a chance encounter with a particular vessel transiting alone. If there were ten ships in a convoy, a submarine would have only one chance to spot them, whereas there would be ten potential encounters if the vessels were each transiting alone. This simple math, however, did not win the argument.

The proponents also argued that once a torpedo was fired, an escort destroyer could follow its trail to the source and either ram the submarine if on or near the surface or saturate the area with depth charges. The simple fact is that a submarine might only have an opportunity to fire a single torpedo before it would change from hunter to hunted, allowing the convoy to proceed out of danger. With their somewhat limited range, U-boats tended to remain within the coastal sea lanes where a convoy would require the most protection. After passing beyond a longitude of about 15° west, the outbound convoy vessels could now disperse, and the escort ships would wait for incoming vessels to assemble.

Faced with appalling losses to merchant shipping, the Admiralty finally agreed to initiate the convoy system and allocate the needed antisubmarine resources. The effect was immediate, as the statistics soon demonstrated. During the winter of 1917, of the nearly 9,000 ships that transited in convoys between England and the coast of France, less than 30 were lost to U-boat predation. Another amazing statistic is that of the 83,958 ships participating in coastal and ocean convoys between February 1917 and October 1918, 260, or 0.3 percent, were lost to U-boats, whereas during a similar period U-boats sank 1,757, or 3.6 percent, of 48,861 ships that sailed alone—in percentages, a factor of more than ten.[25]

AMERICA ENTERS THE WAR—APRIL 6, 1917

The previous years had been a series of protests and promises. American diplomats complained about attacks on merchant ships and the lack of concern for their civilian crews. Germany, desperately trying to keep America out of the war, responded by providing assurances that its submarine captains would take more care in only targeting ships carrying war materials and that were not from neutral countries.

Faced with shifting policies, U-boat captains struggled to conduct their attacks in accordance with directives from Germany. The first encounter with a merchant ship, the British steamer *Glitra*, occurred on

October 20, 1914. *U-17* sent over a boarding party, put the crew in life boats and, after sinking their vessel (scuttled by the boarding party to avoid using a valuable torpedo), towed the crew to the coast of Norway. There was certainly no room in these early submarines to take surviving crews on board. Many encounters, however, were far from shore, making it impossible to tow life boats and expose the U-boat to attack. It was war, and survivors were on their own. In 1915, the policy of unrestricted submarine warfare was in full force; by spring, during a three-month period 115 merchant vessels were sunk—half were torpedoed without warning.

On May 7, 1915, *U-20* spotted the Cunard Line's *Lusitania* approaching the Irish coast. While there were conflicting reports on the incident at the time it occurred, it is now generally accepted that *Lusitania* was sunk with a single torpedo, and that a second explosion, which helped send the 787-foot-long liner to the bottom in less than twenty minutes, was from the detonation of ammunition being shipped to Britain. Whether U-boat captain Walther Schwieger acted according to the rules of engagement in an attack on a ship carrying civilians as well as war materials is debatable. The incident that took nearly 1,200 lives, including 128 Americans, was a stark early example of the destructive potential of the submarine, and a wake-up call to America.

After several similar incidents, American protests resulted in a lessening of the offensive against merchant vessels during much of 1916. But with the British blockade tightening and winter approaching, Germany felt justified in resuming its unrestricted U-boat campaign, declaring all of the waters surrounding Britain to be a war zone. The cycle of promises kept and broken characterized the U-boat strategy.

As pressure mounted for American intervention, the gears of the military machine began to turn. The importance of this new weapon, the submarine, was not lost on U.S. naval planners, who watched with concern the effectiveness of the U-boat. Finally, tired of the abuse of international law and the ever-increasing loss of American shipping, as well as Germany's proposal to ally itself with Mexico and Japan against the United States, President Woodrow Wilson declared war on April 6, 1917. This action provided two primary influences on the war: the infusion of troops and supplies for the ground war, and the introduction of the escorted convoy system.

America's response to the U-boat was centered on one geographic area located along Connecticut's Thames River. On the Groton side, the New London Ship and Engine Company (NELSECO or NLSECO) provided diesel engines for submarines built by parent company Electric Boat at its various shipyards (the Groton facility would not begin submarine construction until well after the war). A few miles upriver, the Navy converted an underutilized coaling station into a base for the Atlantic Submarine Flotilla (figure 11). Secretary of the Navy George von L. Meyer had created this

Figure 11. *Above:* During World War I, the submarine base along the Thames River in Groton, Connecticut, was home to the Atlantic submarine flotilla. (*Submarine Force Library and Museum*) *Below:* This photograph, and above, were taken in January 1918, showing the significant ice that formed in the river. (*Naval History and Heritage Command*)

submarine flotilla in March 1912, with Lieutenant Chester W. Nimitz in command. On October 18, 1915, three submarines—*G-1* (SS-19a), *G-2* (SS-27), and *G-4* (SS-26)—arrived at the base accompanied by their tender, the monitor USS *Ozark* (BM-7). These were followed by *D-1* (SS-17), *D-3* (SS-19), and *E-1* (SS-24) with USS *Tonopah* (BM-8). On November 1, USS *Fulton* (AS-1) joined the flotilla as the first vessel built specifically as a submarine tender.

A submarine school was established in January 1917 at the Groton base, where crews learned the operation of their formidable weapon. The submarine school has continued unabated throughout the twentieth century and into the twenty-first, and was instrumental in providing submarine crews during World War II and for the Cold War nuclear fleet.

Also in 1917, the need to develop an effective counter to the U-boat resulted in the creation of an antisubmarine warfare research facility directly across the river from Electric Boat's NELSECO shipyard, which became the genesis of future scientific and engineering efforts embodied in the U.S. Navy Underwater Sound Laboratory.

NAVY EXPERIMENTAL STATION, NEW LONDON

As 1916 came to a close and Germany's unrestricted warfare against merchant vessels escalated, efforts of America's scientific and engineering talent to counter the U-boat also escalated. Earlier that year, in April, President Wilson was approached by the National Academy of Sciences with a proposal to tackle urgent issues concerning military technology. Two months later, encouraged by Wilson, the NAS created a National Research Council to coordinate input from universities, industry, and government. In February 1917, at the request of the Navy, the NRC formed the Special Board of Antisubmarine Devices to develop a method to detect the distinctive sounds submarines generate while operating submerged. This Board met at the Mohegan Hotel in New London to discuss the technical issues, and to review a particularly interesting French design.

The U.S. government owned several buildings along the New London waterfront at the site of Fort Trumbull, near the mouth of the Thames River. In 1910, Fort Trumbull became the home of the U.S. Revenue Cutter Service, and in 1914 the fort was designated as its officer's academy. A year later, the Cutter Service merged with the U.S. Lifesaving Service to form the U.S. Coast Guard. There was, however, plenty of room to support the ideas and experimental work proposed by the NRC scientists, who represented, and were initially funded by, several academic institutions.

Franklin Delano Roosevelt was the Assistant Secretary of the Navy throughout World War I and under his direction was able to extend a funding line of $300,000 to support submarine detection research. With the funding, however, the Navy also took control over the work being conducted along the waterfront, and on October 12, 1917, the facilities became the Navy Experimental Station (NES), New London.[26] (Figure 12)

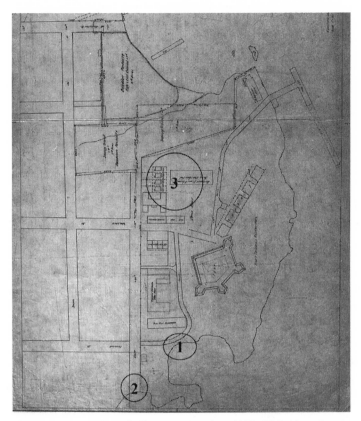

Figure 12. Fort Trumbull, New London 1918. This drawing is oriented to match the 1962 aerial photo shown in Figure 6. Curtis airboats were launched in South Cove ("**1**"), while the Navy Experimental Station engineering staff occupied a building (not shown) in the area marked "**2**." The Coast Guard was located just to the north of the fort ("**3**"). The pier was used by all of the Fort Trumbull occupants. (*Fort Trumbull State Park*)

Led by Dr. Harvey C. Hayes, much of the research focused on what were referred to as "listening devices," deployable from ships, sea planes, and dirigibles. The submarines *G-1* and *G-2* stationed at the newly created submarine base in Groton were also outfitted with these listening devices and conducted experiments with various surface craft, specifically submarine chasers (SC-class) and a variety of what were referred to as "converted yachts" classed as "SP" or patrol ships, including the 224-foot steam yacht USS *Narada* (SP-161). The destroyer USS *Jouett* (DD-41) arrived in January 1918 and spent the next six months supporting submarine detection experiments, including the first design of paired line-arrays of hydrophones that *Jouett* towed port and starboard far aft. Along with an assortment of newly developed "binaural" devices, the scientists demonstrated that *Jouett*, operating at speeds approaching 20 knots, was able to detect a submarine at a range of up to two thousand yards, or one nautical mile. A "listeners school" was established at NES, where sailors were instructed in the operation of these devices, which increased the effectiveness of destroyers deployed as convoy escorts, and significantly reduced merchant ship losses during the final years of the war.

A parallel effort by the Navy Consulting Board, also initiated by President Wilson, was under way at the coastal town of Nahant, Massachusetts, near Boston, by a group of inventors, including Thomas Edison and engineers from General Electric, AT&T, and the nearby Submarine Signal Company. The submarine *G-1* also participated in their experiments. Although initially unaffiliated with the Navy Experimental Station, their efforts included experiments with the Fessenden Oscillator and microphone-based listening devices. During 1918, much of the work at Nahant had shifted to New London, where the staff had increased to over thirty scientists and seven hundred military officers and enlisted men.

The American scientists and their allied counterparts in Britain, France, and Italy provided the first engineering approach to adapting the physics of underwater sound to submarine detection (figure 13). The second photo, taken along the Experimental Station waterfront, shows military representatives from these countries flanking a U.S. Navy commander. The individual on the far right is an Italian army lieutenant from the *Battaglione Specialisti del Genio* (Specialist Battalion of the Engineer Corps) which "specialized" in the use of airships. The others are naval officers and include (left to right) a French lieutenant, an Italian lieutenant, the U.S. commander, and a British lieutenant commander from the Royal Navy Reserves.

Figure 13. *Above:* The scientific staff, led by Harvey C. Hayes (front row far right), is shown with the commanding officer, CAPT J.R. Defrees, in front of the main Navy Experimental Station building ("**2**" on Figure 12). *Below:* Military observers from France, Italy, and England join an American Commander (center) on the NES waterfront. (*Photo archives of Dr. Harvey C. Hayes; Courtesy Bernie Cole*)

Figure 14. *Above:* The Curtis HS-2 airboat (left) was used extensively for testing submarine detection "listening devices." (*Fort Trumbull State Park*) *Below:* The HS-2 flight crew. Both photos were taken at the location marked "**1**" on Figure 12. (*Photo archives of Dr. Harvey C. Hayes; Courtesy Bernie Cole*)

At the beginning of the war there was little technology available to effectively detect and counter the U-boat threat. The British were depending on static defenses—moored mines and submarine nets—and dragging explosive devices behind surface vessels, hoping they would contact a very unlucky submarine. Aircraft, including a variety of airships, made sorties over coastal waters with hopes of spotting a submarine transiting just below the surface, but met with little success. The Navy Experimental Station pioneered the use of the "listening devices" by aircraft for submarine hunting (figure 14).

Charles Domville-Fife's book *Submarine Warfare of To-Day* (1920) emphasized the importance of the hydrophone during World War I: "Of all the weapons used in the anti-submarine war the two most important were the *hydrophone* and the *depth charge*." The British deployed "hydrophone flotillas" to patrol the waters surrounding their island nation, operated by members of the Royal Navy Reserves. The flotillas would meet convoys entering these dangerous zones, where U-boats were known to be operating. Destroyers carrying depth charges were deployed when flotilla vessels with this new hydrophone technology detected the distinct sounds of a submarine. Domville-Fife, who commanded one of these hydrophone flotillas, described the "games of 'hide-and-seek' played on and under the seas with the aid of this wonderful little instrument."[27] A similar game was played a half-century later by submarine commanders tailing Soviet nuclear subs during the Cold War.

THE SUBMARINE CAPITOL OF THE WORLD

A sign in the shape of a submarine profile just beyond the Gold Star Memorial Bridge proclaims Groton, Connecticut, as the "Submarine Capitol of the World," and rightly so. With the submarine base a few miles upriver, a company that builds submarines just south of the bridge, and what was once the Navy's principal submarine sonar research and development facility on the New London side, this area has been the center of submarine warfare development since the early years of World War I. Even the name of the bridge that connects New London with Groton is a testimony to the area's military presence, because it honors the gold star presented to families of those who have lost their lives during war.

Only two decades after the Armistice ended the fighting on November 11, 1918, war again accelerated throughout Europe and Asia, eventually drawing America into this second world wide conflict. The submarine capital of the world rushed to respond to a war in which the undersea battlespace became a decisive factor in both the Atlantic and Pacific theaters. Submarine construction at Electric Boat rose from a total of fourteen during the ten-year period, from 1930 through 1939, to nearly eighty during the war years.[28] As soon as these new boats slid down the ways, they moved upriver where the submarine school had expanded its capability to send qualified sailors out to sea; by the end of the war, two thousand officers and twenty-two thousand enlisted had qualified. The submarine base also contributed to the increasing need for divers, where the medical research department provided Second Class Diver training to sailors who would serve on submarine tenders, rescue and salvage vessels, and naval bases.[29]

The threat from German and Japanese submarines required immediate attention. The years between the wars had seen a reduced emphasis on developing an effective antisubmarine capability. This neglect was soon remedied. President Roosevelt, as Assistant Secretary of the Navy during World War I, had helped establish the Navy Experimental Station in New London. The work accomplished in New London, and similar efforts at several academic institutions in 1917 and 1918, yielded technologies with a high degree of potential, but had been shelved during the 1920s and 1930s for lack of a threat.

In June 1940, FDR tasked his military technology advisor, Vannevar Bush, to establish a similar but more comprehensive approach.[30] Bush, who was involved with the research in New London during World War I and had been the dean of MIT, School of Engineering, now took on the responsibility to tackle the German U-boat threat as chairman of the newly formed National Defense Research Committee (NDRC). Under this mandate, Bush brought several thousand scientists and engineers under the NDRC wing to rapidly tackle the many technological challenges in a global war. The people and the academic institutions involved during World War I were still around, and had never lost enthusiasm for the underlying science.

31

The first of three facilities dedicated to antisubmarine warfare was established on April 21, 1941, at Point Loma in San Diego, California, under a contract with the University of California, Division of War Research. Two months later, on the fifth of June, NDRC scientists began working at the Harvard Underwater Sound Laboratory in Cambridge. It was there, in 1942, where its director, Frederick V. Hunt, is considered to have created the acronym SONAR (for SOund Navigation And Ranging). Within a year the term *sonar* became accepted by the Navy, and sailors trained as sonar operators given an official rating as "sonarmen."

Vannevar Bush had a busy summer in 1941. On July 12, under a contract with Columbia University Division of War Research, Bush established the third antisubmarine warfare group at the same facilities where research was conducted during World War I, now officially designated the "U.S. Navy Sound Laboratory, Fort Trumbull, New London, Connecticut." The urgency for success over the deadly German and Japanese submarines demanded an aggressive approach to connecting the war machine with science and engineering.

OPERATIONS RESEARCH—A SLIDE RULE STRATEGY

The British had been expanding the effectiveness of their antisubmarine capability, and their successes inspired a similar mission on the part of the U.S. Navy, in a process initiated in Britain called "Operational Research."[31] Although applicable to any technology, OR takes operational data from an existing system and quantifies the data into mathematical models. These models enable scientists to study the effectiveness of a system, since they provide feedback for either enhancing a system's operation or modifying its design. The use of OR principals requires access to the most accurate data, often best obtained by scientists and engineers joining the warfighter in battle. When used in a military context, operations research is sometimes referred to as combat science.

With his mandate in hand, Vannevar Bush created the Antisubmarine Warfare Operations Research Group (ASWORG), responsible for analyzing current systems and operational tactics used to detect and destroy the U-boat. In an article titled "Operations Research: Slide Rule Strategy Begins," first published in the January 2000 issue of *Submarine Review*,

John Merrill states that "increased mastery in sinking U-boats starting in May 1943 is attributable . . . in part to operations research." Merrill stressed the importance of "solving problems based on careful analysis of data collected from direct experience in real time operations in a wartime environment."[32]

As you read the chapters that follow, collecting data "from direct experience in real time operations" is what this book is all about, and the legacy of scientists and engineers who accompanied the war fighter during World War II deserves mention. In *Fort Trumbull and the Submarine*, John Merrill describes the wartime contribution of three such engineers who were involved with the development of the "sonobuoy," a device instrumental in a successful antisubmarine campaign in both the Atlantic and Pacific.[33] The sonobuoy is deployed from an aircraft or surface ship, and left to float in the search area. It is designed to lower a hydrophone that "listens" for the sounds of submarines and relays the data through its radio antenna to a central location on board the ASW ship. With data coming from multiple sonobuoys, the ship can deduce the location of the threat. After decades of modifications and modernizations, the sonobuoy still plays a major role in what is termed a "distributed sensor network."

An early successful test by Columbia University's laboratory occurred off New London in 1942. During the test, the submerged submarine *S-20* was detected by a sonobuoy deployed from the blimp *K-5*. Russell I. Mason monitored the buoy's radio transmissions on board *K-5*, operating within a five-mile radius of the submarine. Mason continued his involvement with the sonobuoy throughout the war and was joined by two additional engineers, Russell Lewis and Walter Clearwaters, both of whom were active at USN/USL when I arrived in 1967, twenty-two years after the war. In 1943, Clearwaters headed to Iceland to install sonobuoy equipment on a squadron of patrol planes. From there he went to Wales, where he participated in flights in an area where the Luftwaffe was operating. Clearwaters returned to Iceland and was on a Royal Air Force flight when they detected and engaged in an air attack on a German submarine. But his association with sonobuoys was far from over. He trained flight crews on board the escort carrier *Bogue*, and eventually was reassigned to a shore-based squadron in Casablanca.

Russell Lewis was involved with sonobuoys during the war also. The summer of 1943 brought Lewis, along with Russell Mason, to Argentia, Newfoundland, where they joined a Navy squadron assigned to escort convoys into the North Atlantic. There they flew with many antisubmarine patrols, in front of the convoys, to the mid-Atlantic and back. Throughout the year, Lewis continued his sonobuoy work, supporting operations around Britain, Bermuda, and Hawaii.

The following summer, in 1944, during an encounter off the coast of West Africa between German U-boats and the escort carrier *Guadalcanal*, *U-505* was captured, and with it the Allies obtained the German code-breaking key. (After the submarine was brought to the United States, Sound Lab engineer Carl T. Milner rode *U-505* to evaluate its advanced sonar system.) One of the U-boats in the area torpedoed and sank *Guadalcanal*'s sister carrier, *Block Island*, where Russ Lewis had been assigned as a sonobuoy advisor (figure 15). Luck fortunately followed Lewis, who had only spent two hours in the water when he was rescued by a destroyer and brought to Casablanca.

Figure 15. *Above:* Escort carrier USS *Block Island* during ASW patrol, just prior to being torpedoed. (*National Archives; via Navsource.org*) *Below:* During this engagement a second submarine, *U-505*, was captured. (*US Navy Photo*)

SIX DEGREES OF SEPARATION

It has been said that there are only six relationships separating any two people on the planet. You know someone who knows someone who knows someone, etc. The impact you as an individual have on that last person may be infinitesimal, but when lives are at risk, even infinitesimal is too much. We, as engineers in the Department of Defense, all use the computer to produce tools that the warfighter will rely on in combat. The farther removed we are, the more "degrees of separation" there are between the cubicle and the conflict, the greater the risk to those who carry the spear.

The three men whose stories I have related—Walt Clearwaters, Russ Mason and Russ Lewis—were not satisfied with simply pondering the potential of underwater sound. They were operations research pioneers who personified the marriage between civilian engineers and the warfighter. Sitting within the cockpit of a plane over the North Atlantic hunting U-boats, or riding an escort carrier off North Africa, reduced the degrees of separation to one. They and all of their colleagues in New London were extraordinary people working during extraordinary times.

But we live in a digital world now, and there is a tendency to rely on "virtual reality" rather than the real reality. The computer is an essential tool in modern warfare. There is no question of the advantages of the digital revolution. Extremely complex ideas can be modeled and multiple parameters evaluated. But how "real" the assumptions and data are that eventually enter the virtual model will determine how close the virtual world represents the real one. There is a danger that the cubicle and the computer screen become reality to the designer, risking an ever-widening gap in the degrees of separation between the engineer and the warfighter. The computer enables the engineer to fill that separation with an incredibly vast amount of information, but only if that information is relevant and accurate—and that requires a continuous feedback loop.

What the warfighter, who lives in the real world, needs is confidence in his technological advantage in a real fight—hence confidence in the engineers who provide his high-tech systems. There is no easy path to the "real" reality other than to walk with the warfighter. In Navy terms, there has to be a connection to the deckplate, and the organization that sends its engineers to the base, to the shipyard, and to sea fills the credibility gap. In 1976, after returning from a series of sonar system sea trials on *Nautilus* (Chapter 4), I began to better understand the implications of a designer's creations and decisions. The project director, Alan Ellinthorpe, made these implications perfectly clear in a letter of appreciation to the engineers involved:

> The MACS [Mobile Acoustic Communication System] sea trial was an exceptional event in many respects; the complexity of the mechanical and hydrodynamic engineering, the magnitude of the mechanical forces, the method of monitoring the stresses, and, not least, the stakes that were at issue. [The engineering] was carried out under the burden of risking the safety of the ship in the event of an error.

It is absolutely understood that not everyone is willing or able to participate at sea. Their inspiration and contributions arise from intellectual tenacity, but not from walking the deckplate. It is essential, therefore, that every design team include a few individuals—the field engineers—who can live in both the real and virtual worlds, and serve as that direct connection between the warfare designer and the warfighter. An organization that recognizes this relationship will also incorporate current and former active duty officers and enlisted into its staff. These individuals can close gaps in the degrees of separation by providing a perspective that those of us who were career engineers but never served in an active duty role may not fully grasp. Good managers and responsible decision makers recognize the team concept and that there are opinions with merit other than their own.

WHEN LIVES ARE AT STAKE

Many engineers from New London teamed with submariners on countless experimental missions, where close calls were an expected part of the Cold War. There's a reason submarines practice an operation known as an "emergency blow." Although none were from the Sound Lab [please see note[34]], seventeen civilian engineers and technicians were on board USS *Thresher* when she sank in 1963—all of them aware that they, along with the 112 officers and enlisted crew, were involved in a risky operation. There was nothing "virtual" about their fate. Yet the *Thresher* disaster initiated the SUBSAFE concept, in which every critical system on board a submarine must be designed and built to meet strict safety standards.

The twenty-first century brought us a War on Terror. Any future global conflicts that emerge will present challenges with threats as real as Nazi Germany or the Soviets during the Cold War. It is essential, and I say this with total conviction, that when a design team is assigned a task that impacts a military system and where ultimately lives are at stake, every opportunity must be taken to minimize the degrees of separation between the engineer and the warfighter. We cannot depend on phone calls, emails, and a "virtual presence." Engineers need to bring ideas and action—in person—to the Navy on the waterfront and to the Navy in Washington. The message conveyed herein to *any* agency or industry responsible for designing military technology, and in particular to their staff, is this: *get your ass out of the cubicle and out to sea.*

Figure 16. *Above:* An underwater photographer might have carried as many as three Nikonos cameras to cover all aspects of an operation. (L-R): A Nikonos camera with an early 21mm wide angle lens; with a standard 28mm lens; with a 35mm lens and 1:3 close-up attachment; and a high intensity strobe light. *Below:* Dennie "Mac" McClenny photographs details of a submarine installation. (*Roy Manstan*)

CHAPTER 3
Calm, Cool and Collected

When I walked into Mac's office at the photo lab, I was unprepared for this first visit. He had retired from active duty in September 1966, and immediately signed on as an USN/USL civilian underwater photographer. But first and foremost, Mac was still a Navy Chief at heart—tough, opinionated, and willing to tackle any assignment under any conditions.

Dennie "Mac" McClenny had joined the Navy in August 1942; he was involved in D-Day at Omaha beach, and spent the war years in the European theater as a gunners mate on PT boats. After the war, Mac became a photographer's mate with the Navy Combat Camera Group, specializing in cinematography and the production of training films. He was stationed at Pearl Harbor and San Diego, with assignments in post-war Japan. While on the west coast, he tried his hand at the new sport of scuba diving, which was beginning to gain popularity after Jacques Cousteau had perfected, produced and marketed his Aqualung through the company U.S. Divers. It wouldn't be long before Mac's Command sent him off to Navy dive schools (scuba at Pearl Harbor in 1956, then to Key West, qualifying as a Second Class Diver in 1959), adding his name to a very small group of military underwater photographers.

Mac hadn't mellowed much when I first met him in 1970, and had little good to say when I showed him my first attempt at underwater photography. I had just taken a civilian scuba course at the local YMCA and immediately bought a Nikonos camera. Other than an array of very expensive housings for land cameras, the Nikonos remained the workhorse of underwater photography for many decades, and the USN/USL photo lab had several (figure 16). I think Mac's comment, "you might as well shitcan that camera," was his way of motivating me to try again. My composition sucked, the exposure was dreadful, most were out of focus, and: "Don't come back until you use some decent film." Then he tossed me a roll of Kodachrome. "Try this."

Over the next two years, I tried a lot of Kodachrome, bought a wide-angle lens and some accessories to shoot macro, and took an underwater photography course at Cabo San Lucas. Mac warmed a little to my persistence and to the quality of my photos. "It's easier to teach a photographer to be a diver, than a diver to become a photographer," he said one day, and asked if I would be interested in becoming a Navy diver. Hmmm—my ticket out of the cubicle?

I had arrived at the Sound Lab in 1967. Bad timing, I guess, as the era of manned submersibles was rapidly coming to an end. My old mentor Guy Williams was right. Westinghouse had moved on to kitchen appliances after funding for their *Deepstar 20000* project began to recede in the late 1960s. "Don't be discouraged," he told me. "There will always be something at the Lab that will strike your fancy. Plenty of great things here to work on. If you get bored, it's your own fault." But I was still young and stupid, and that fall I found myself at a justice of the peace getting married. The three-year marriage mercifully ended in 1970, and as a diversion after the divorce, I took a civilian scuba course. At the Lab, however, I was still disappointed in not being involved with submersibles. At Guy Williams' suggestion, I worked with several different groups, finally settling into a mechanical design department where I was surrounded by PhDs—a great bunch, but a bit out of my league. When Mac suggested becoming a Navy diver, I jumped at the chance.

"SHIT-FOR-BRAINS"

I spent a lot of time in Mac's office over the years, and many times he would shake his head and growl, "Shit-for-brains was on the pier today." I had no idea who he was referring to—it was the name he gave to a lot of engineers. I was pretty sure I wasn't included, but remaining off his shit list kept me on my toes. People either loved or hated Mac. What many saw was an obstinate and terse personality, but underneath his tough skin was a generous individual dedicated to the Navy, who simply wanted you to "pay attention, dammit!!!"

Mac never spoke about his service during the war, preferring to talk about past diving projects, which were much more relevant to the establishment of a Sound Lab dive team. Mac's first association with the

Sound Lab, albeit indirect, was during the Navy's Sealab program in 1964. The Lab had established an oceanographic research station in Bermuda at Tudor Hill, along with Argus Island, an offshore "Texas Tower" facility located on a sea mount known as Plantagenet Bank. Installed during the summer of 1960, Argus Island was used as a platform for conducting deep ocean acoustic propagation research where the sea mount drops precipitously into the Atlantic abyss. Water depth at the base of the tower legs, however, was slightly less than two-hundred feet, ideal for the Navy's early Man-In-The-Sea program.

Argus Island hosted Sealab I, the first of three similar habitats where Captain George F. Bond conducted experiments with saturation diving.[35] After the USS *Thresher* disaster in 1963, the Navy turned its attention to developing technology for deep-water rescue and salvage. Deep diving had always been a challenge, in part because of the serious physiological effects on a human body exposed to a pressurized environment for extended periods.

It was long understood that the body's tissues and blood absorb the nitrogen component of air at specific rates when breathed by divers, an effect first experienced by caisson workers in the nineteenth century, whose jobs took them into submerged enclosures. Many either died or were severely injured after long hours of working under pressure and returning too rapidly to sea level before their bodies could release the absorbed nitrogen. This potentially fatal condition was first known as caisson disease or diver's palsy; the term commonly used today is "the bends," but is more correctly referred to as "decompression sickness."

In general, the longer a diver remains submerged, the more he is at risk for increasingly dangerous levels of nitrogen absorption, which will require a proportionate amount of time to allow the gas to exit the body via the blood-stream, and then to the lungs, as the diver slowly returns to the surface, a process called "decompression." Based on many years of trial and error and extensive human testing, the Navy established a series of decompression tables to minimize the potential for experiencing a case of the bends. Replacing the nitrogen with helium in the breathing mixture improved the divers' ability to access deeper water, but the body still required extended periods of time to return to atmospheric conditions.

The time was right to investigate the physiology of deep-sea diving, and develop procedures for enabling a human to work at depths never before attempted. Captain Bond had been testing his saturation diving theories while assigned to the medical research department at the submarine base in Groton, Connecticut. His Genesis project set the stage for the Navy's Sealab experiments, which demonstrated that when diving for extended periods of time, gas absorption reached "saturation," a point at which decompression time would not increase with longer exposure. An elite group of Navy divers who conducted covert wire tapping of Soviet communication cables in deep water of the Sea of Okhotsk and the Barents Sea[36] owed their success to the human physiology research during Bond's decade-long participation in the Man-in-the-Sea program.

On July 19, 1964, the Sealab habitat rested on Plantagenet Bank at the base of Argus Island. Although only four aquanauts occupied the habitat between July 20 and 29, there were many project support personnel who worked under Captain Bond's direction. One was Chief Photographers Mate Dennie "Mac" McClenny. Mac was the Sealab cinematographer documenting the aquanauts' excursions from the habitat onto the sea floor. The support divers, in scuba, were typically limited to no-decompression dives. After a fast descent to join the aquanauts working outside the habitat, Mac had learned to aim and shoot his reel of film in three minutes before returning to the surface. "No time for sightseeing . . . no mistakes allowed . . . no retakes . . . do it right the first time." These words may seem obvious, but when a mentor tells you this, the words arrive with clarity and blunt credibility, borne with the force of experience. Of course, when Mac was talking, you quickly learned to "pay attention, dammit!"

During the summer of 1965, Mac followed Captain Bond to Sealab II off La Jolla, California. By this time, he had established a relationship with Sound Lab staff while in Bermuda, leading to other cooperative efforts between active duty Navy divers and the Sound Lab, which now included a small number of Navy-trained civilian divers. Mac's stories continued to amaze and motivate my interest in becoming a part of the dive team. He had accompanied USS *Skate* (SSN-578) in 1962, during her transit and surfacing at the North Pole. At one point during the deployment, *Skate* had damaged a propeller blade. When the captain realized that Mac was a Navy diver, a roll of sheet rubber and glue arrived, and the captain "asked" him to make a wet suit. Mac then devised a method (which included clamps, an I-beam, and a very large hammer) to perform a waterborne repair to the propeller's rolled edges.

My career would take me on two paths: one led to being a Navy diver, and the other as an engineer—both would eventually merge into one. Mac kept me on track for more than fifteen years. After he retired in 1989, his voice continued to echo in my ears. Maintaining one's passion throughout a long career can be a struggle when facing those inevitable hurdles, and it falls to our mentors to help us to "get over it, get on with it, dammit!" Outside of work, Mac's interests also caught my attention. He and his son Dennis and I spent six weeks during the summer of 1975 on a motorcycle ride that would encompass a ten-thousand-mile figure-eight path across the country. Mac's role in my life would be as a friend and mentor, and it is, of course, for this reason that I have dedicated this book to him.

CALM, COOL, AND COLLECTED

The demand for excellence, both physical and mental, in the training of Navy divers has a tradition that extends a century into the past. The selection of diver candidates has long been a contentious issue. There are, and should be, the obvious physiological restrictions associated with respiratory and circulatory function. The psychological and motivational criteria, however, are far less quantifiable and often left to the discretion of the selecting authority.

The 1905 *Handbook for Seaman Gunners, Manual for Divers* includes a list of "requirements for divers," which disqualified candidates with "palpitations of the heart . . . [and] fainting spells," and those "affected with cough, asthma, or catarrh [inflammation of the sinuses and throat]." The manual also suggests that "men who have long trunks with well developed chests and loins generally make good divers," and, in a bit of wishful thinking, recommends that they not "be hard drinkers, nor have suffered frequently from venereal disease." A candidate's personality, however, was only described as "cool-headed, calm, and of a phlegmatic temperament."[37]

Prior to World War I, divers were typically selected only from Gunner rates. The 1905 manual, and diver training in general, was sorely in need of improvement. In 1914, Gunner George D. Stillson, assigned to the Experimental Diving Station in Brooklyn, New York, worked with Navy surgeon George R. W. French.[38] Under the direction of the Bureau of Construction and Repair, Stillson and French conducted a series of tests with divers at sea aboard the torpedo boat destroyer *Walke* (DD-34), and with what Stillson described as a "high-pressure diving tank" at A. Schrader's Sons Inc., also in Brooklyn. *Walke* had been outfitted at the New York Navy Yard specifically for these tests, and on October 22 Gunner Stillson and divers Drellishak, Neilson, Crilley, and Anderson headed out to find suitable sites for their dives.

For the next two weeks, Stillson and his divers moved to locations around the eastern end of Long Island where they (including Stillson) could dive at increasing depths: first to 84 feet, then to 90 feet, next to 137 feet, and on to 171 feet. After searching for a deep area, *Walke* anchored near the Race, where the Atlantic Ocean pours in and out of Long Island Sound. The Race is a treacherous area with a very brief slack tide. At 11:28 on the morning of November 3, 1914, Chief Gunners Mate S. J. Drellishak began his descent to what would become a record depth of 274 feet. Drellishak's dive included a seven minute descent, five minutes on the bottom, and a slow one hour and twenty minute ascent, all accomplished while the Race raced along at two knots. These men certainly fit the Navy's need for "cool-headed, calm" divers.

Prior to 1914, however, little attention was given to establishing criteria for becoming a Navy diver, and the team Stillson selected for the deep diving tests included the best the Navy had to offer. Stillson canvassed the diving community for feedback on improvements to equipment, operational procedures, and candidate selection and training. The responses, many sent from ships on deployments, generally echoed the section relating to training in the 1905 manual.[39] Gunner Herbert Campbell, writing from Vera Cruz, Mexico, on the Cruiser USS *Montana*, emphasized that candidates be "cool and collected." Chief Gunner A. S. Pearson (on the Dreadnought USS *Texas*, Lobos Island, Mexico) noted that divers should be "physically strong, resourceful men; men recommended for showing extraordinary initiative."

The most insightful response came from Gunner Arthur D. Freshman stationed at the Boston Navy Yard. "The present practice is to make divers of all the men in the seaman gunner's school who are physically qualified, *regardless of other qualifications, such as temperament, degree of intelligence, and physical courage.* It is believed that these characteristics should be considered before men are sent to the service as qualified divers, and that *it is just as easy to turn out good divers as the other kind."* Gunner Frederick Evans (serving on the Battleship USS *Minnesota*, Tampico, Mexico) offered a suggestion as valid then as it is today, that if, during training, "he does not show the proper aptitude and indications of a thinking head, *it is folly ever to allow him to enter the water."* (Italics added for emphasis)

MEN OF HONOR

On March 25, 1915, the submarine *F-4* (SS-23) set out from Honolulu on a training mission and was lost at sea. The following day an oil slick and a stream of bubbles indicated the position of the lost sub—the depth was 305 feet. It had been less than five months since Gunner Stillson and his divers had completed their deep-diving tests, and *F-4* was thirty-one feet deeper than Drellishak's

record dive. Stillson and most of his team, including Navy surgeon George French, were dispatched to Hawaii, where they were joined by another experienced diver, Lieutenant W. F. Loughman. Frank Crilley made the first dive to 305 feet where he and the other divers eventually secured lifting cables. *F-4* was lifted slightly and was moved in stages into shallower water, each time requiring divers to prepare for the lift. As Lieutenant Loughman

Figure 17. *Above:* Medal of Honor recipient Frank Crilley (center) preparing for a dive in 1914. (*Stillson 1915*) *Below:* Fred Michels, second from left holding the diver's hardhat, twice received the Silver Star. (*Courtesy Michels' grandson, Mike Peirson*)

was returning from his dive, he became tangled around the lift lines at a depth of 220 feet. Crilley went in to attempt to free Loughman. After working for four hours, Crilley was able to extricate Loughman from his trap and brought him to the surface, unconscious but alive; for his lifesaving effort, Chief Gunners Mate Frank Crilley received the Medal of Honor.[40] (Figure 17)

Similar disasters continued, sadly in most cases with the loss of all on board. Divers were called to recover these lost submarines . . . but most importantly, to bring home their crew—all men of honor. Chief Gunners Mate Fred Michels was involved with two of these. The first occurred late at night on September 25, 1925, when *S-51* (SS-162), transiting south of Block Island on the surface, was struck by the steamship *City of Rome*. Three members of the crew survived by escaping through the conning tower, but within a minute, *S-51* was "on the bottom," the title of Commander Edward Ellsberg's book, which relates the more than nine-month effort to recover the sub and the remains of her crew.[41] Another submarine was lost only two years later, on December 17, 1927. *S-4* (SS-109) was in the process of surfacing off Provincetown, Cape Cod, when she was hit amidships by the Coast Guard cruiser *Paulding*. The distress call brought several vessels to the site where divers found *S-4* at a depth of 102 feet. The divers, including Michels, heard survivors tapping against the hull, adding to the urgency. Severe weather set in, however, and there could be no attempts at a rescue. It was ten days before a recovery could begin. In recognition of his various actions during the three-month *S-4* recovery, Chief Gunners Mate Michels was twice awarded the Navy Cross.[42]

There is a personal reason for including the stories of Frank Crilley and Fred Michels. I have known and worked on the waterfront with their grandsons, the late Chris Crilley and Michael Peirson, both of whom have had distinguished careers as Navy divers. Chris Crilley was attached to the Naval Facilities Engineering Service Center (NFESC) East Coast Detachment at the Washington Navy Yard and was also a Navy trained civilian engineer/diver. Mike Peirson is a long time member of the NUWC Engineering and Diving Support Unit in Newport. His outstanding contributions to NUWC and the Navy will be described later.

UNDERWATER SWIMMER SCHOOL

As the Allied powers began their offensive moves in both the Atlantic and Pacific theaters during World War II with massive amphibious assaults, the need for beach recon and obstacle clearance escalated. This task had previously been assigned to Naval Combat Demolition Units, but these teams were not equipped or trained as swimmers or divers.

In 1943, explosive ordnance disposal units merged with Navy Seabees to create underwater demolition teams (UDT). Their missions would require that they deploy offshore, swim to the beach to gather intelligence, and set explosive charges on obstructions. There were other operational combat swimmers who had been supplied with various closed-circuit oxygen underwater breathing apparatus, but UDT swimmers were essentially limited to the use of the basic mask, snorkel, and swim fins.

The open-circuit "self-contained underwater breathing apparatus" that we know today by its acronym "scuba" originated in France early in 1943. Jacques Cousteau, Emile Gagnon and several others had experimented with this underwater breathing system with which a diver could carry a supply of compressed air in high-pressure cylinders. As the diver inhaled, a valve reduced this high pressure air to that of the ambient water, enabling the diver to comfortably and safely breathe from the cylinders carried on his back. Scuba provided mobility, but the air supply was limited, and left a telltale stream of bubbles on the surface not conducive to stealth.

Cousteau's scuba equipment improved as he continued his experiments in the Mediterranean. He was a member of the French resistance during World War II, but his scuba saw little if any use. Shortly after the war, however, he had been able to produce a marketable version that he called the "Aqualung" initially through Spirotechnique, a French company. By 1947, almost as soon as these units became available, underwater demolition teams began experimenting with the Aqualung at the submarine base in Groton. A deep sea diving and underwater welding school, under the direction of the medical research laboratory, at Groton was begun in 1942 at the submarine escape facility and which lasted throughout the war. This facility was an ideal location for these early Aqualung trials.

The 1959 U.S. Navy Diving manual noted: "In 1947, the first submersible operations platoon was organized in Underwater Demolition Team Two for the purpose of applying scuba to UDT operations. Men assigned to the platoon were trained in many skills such as underwater reconnaissance, underwater long distance swimming, and the application of these and other techniques to offensive and defensive operations." In 1948, the Navy had only a dozen of these new Aqualung diving systems, but within a year forty additional units had been acquired for operational and training use.

A 1952 issue of *Diving Notes, U.S. Naval School, Deep Sea Divers* contains a brief article titled "'Aqua Lung' or Costeau[*sic*]-Gagnon Shallow Water Swimming Outfit," which describes the device as "a self contained, open-circuit . . . diving outfit of French Design," and which also mentions its use "by underwater demolition teams for shallow water swimming." But the Navy was slow to accept the system for general use. Closed-circuit oxygen rebreathers were still the equipment of choice for combat swimmers, who relied on stealth, which open-circuit systems could not provide.[43]

During the 1950s, after the experimental work with the Aqualung was complete, the submarine base in Groton no longer trained deep sea divers but continued to provide scuba qualification to underwater demolition teams. Occasionally, their pool training would occur at the Sound Lab's testing facility (figure 18). The majority of the training, however, soon shifted to a new location according to an entry in the 1959 Diving Manual: "In 1954,

Figure 18. *Above:* An underwater demolition team trains in the USN/USL pool, c. 1954. (*Fort Trumbull State Park*) *Left:* UDT combat swimmer using the Aqualung; early scuba systems often included three high pressure air tanks rather than the single or twin tanks in common use today. (*US Navy photo; Best 1962*)

the U.S. Naval School, Underwater Swimmers, was established in Key West, Fla., specifically for the training of SCUBA divers." It was apparent that by the mid-fifties, scuba had become an accepted diving system. So, what did the Navy Underwater Sound Lab and Navy Underwater Demolition Teams have in common?

SUMNER "JOE" GORDON

The first mention of a member of the Sound Lab staff becoming a Navy qualified diver appeared in the Lab's weekly newsletter, ECHO, on April 3, 1959. The article described the training and subsequent underwater activities of Sumner "Joe" Gordon, a wiry, energetic engineer with a passion for the emerging science of underwater photography and the application of high-tech electronic devices to solving issues associated with tactical missions. The piece provides insight into Gordon's early exploits, including underwater demolition teams:

> Realizing that he would be concerned with the design and evaluation of underwater photographic equipment and other underwater vehicles, [Gordon] volunteered to take the underwater swimmer course given by the Navy, at the Submarine Base Diving Tower . . . As a result of [his training] he has been able to acquire first-hand information on the performance of underwater equipments by operating them himself and has been called upon to assist other Laboratory programs requiring underwater swimming ability. During sea tests last fall [1958] Gordon undertook the most difficult UDT underwater swimmer assignments in rough seas and deep water in order to assure adequate underwater photographic coverage of a submerged submarine under test.

I didn't know much about him when I first considered becoming a diver, but Mac explained that Joe Gordon was planning to transfer to the NUSC facilities at West Palm Beach, Florida. With this new assignment, Joe had relinquished his role as diving supervisor and Mac was next in line for the job. I met Joe briefly before he headed south, but we only talked about the projects he and Mac had worked on together. It was only after I began researching the origins of diving at the Lab that I discovered some of the unique technology which passed through the early dive team.

Harold E. Nash, who had been part of Harvard's World War II surface ship sonar program, came to New London in 1945 and headed the Sound Lab's Sonar Development Division. During the late 1950s and early 1960s, this division contained a Special Applications Branch, where creative minds were given unique tasks. A few of these individuals were assigned to the Special Devices Section where certain "special devices" of interest to particular military units were designed, built, and tested.

When Joe Gordon received his scuba qualification at the submarine base in 1958, all of his classmates were members of UDT platoons and were receiving their combat swimmer training. As an engineer with at least an equal level of security clearance, he would have discussed UDT mission profile and equipment issues that needed an engineering solution. One item being investigated by UDT was the "human torpedo," used so effectively by Italian combat swimmers of the Tenth Light Flotilla (TLF). Their two-man submersibles, also known as "Pigboats," had much success during World War II. The British had also successfully deployed divers in their "chariots," sinking the German battleship *Tirpitz*. Joe and his combat swimmer classmates would have discussed this unique technology as an ideal "special device" for the Sound Lab's Special Devices Section to consider.

Interest in these early swimmer delivery vehicles by UDT was described in 1962 by Herbert Best: "The UDT base at Little Creek has experimented with all the standard designs of swimmer propulsion . . . These are submersible canoes of various types . . . They also differ from true mini-subs . . . in requiring the crew to carry its own breathing apparatus, and are much simpler to get in and out of. In the future some may carry detachable war heads, but at present they are only suited to convey two swimmers." Best was referring to a wet-sub called the "Aquabat," where the crew of two, outfitted with scuba, was completely immersed in water. His caption to a photo of the Aquabat (figure 19) describes the vessel as "an intermediate form between a true miniature submarine and the Italian 'Pig[boat]' which was something like a torpedo ridden by two [Tenth Light Flotilla] men perched on top."[44]

The Aquabat had been designed, built, and tested by a team at USN/ USL in 1959, undoubtedly as a result of the relationship between Joe Gordon and his UDT classmates and two more Sound Lab engineers, who received their scuba qualifications specifically to develop the Aquabat. The UDT likely considered the Aquabat as a concept evaluation vehicle and for training, its Plexiglas construction being ill-suited for a combat mission. These wet-subs were, however, precursors of today's rugged, combat-ready

Figure 19. *Above:* The two-man submarine Aquabat, built and tested in the USN/USL pool, shown here being used by UDT divers. (*US Navy Photo; Best 1962*) *Below left:* Joe Gordon wears a USN/USL patented underwater communications system. (*USN/USL; ECHO August 12, 1966*) *Below right:* UDT diver outfitted with this system. (*US Navy Photo; Best 1962*)

SDV—originally an acronym for "swimmer delivery vehicle," now redesignated "SEAL delivery vehicle." A brief article regarding the vessel appears in the June 5, 1959, issue of ECHO titled: "USL 'Aquabat' two-man submersible."

> The two-man submersible was developed by the Laboratory's Special Devices Section, with James Catlow, Jr., serving as Project Engineer, George F. Carey as the mechanical design engineer, and Basil Deligeorges, electronic design engineer. It was in connection with this that Catlow and Carey completed the three-week SCUBA course at the U.S. Submarine Base in Groton. The Special Devices Section at USL is in the Special Applications Branch headed by Hugh P. McGee and the Sonar Development Division under Harold E. Nash.

Nash would eventually become the Technical Director and continue in that position when the Sound Lab merged with the Naval Underwater Weapons Research and Engineering Station in Rhode Island to form the Naval Underwater Systems Center in 1970. The USN/USL Special Devices Section continued to support diver technology during the early 1960s, including obtaining patents related to wireless acoustic underwater communications. Joe Gordon tested a system that became an early tool for the recently established UDT scuba teams. Herbert Best described the variety of underwater operations training under way when his book was published in 1962: "[Trainees] are required to swim, completely submerged, for a distance of a mile and a half and to surface within 100 feet of a mark on the shore line." According to Best, UDT also received instruction in "casting and recovery by a submerged submarine; [and] a new walkie-talkie which allows communication under water."[45]

This underwater "walkie-talkie" (U.S. patent number 3,337,841) packaged vacuum-tube circuitry in a canister carried on the diver's belt. Headphones incorporated a bone conduction device, while the microphone was mounted in a full-face mask.[46] This system (figure 19), which Best indicated was "still under development," relied on the relationship between acoustic energy and electrical signals known as piezoelectric transduction, the same technology used on the massive surface ship SQS-26 sonar array. A miniature hand held version of the huge sonar transducer was designed to be carried by a diver. When in the transmit/receive communications mode, the diver would point the transducer toward members of his team who were outfitted with the system. This same miniature transducer was also used as a homing device, enabling the UDT divers to return to (and possibly communicate with) the "casting and recovery" submarine.

An article in the March 9, 1962, edition of the ECHO described an award Joe Gordon received for his contributions to the Navy and "in recognition of unique and hazardous duty beyond the normal requirements of his position." Among the long list of accomplishments were "underwater electromagnetic measurements exterior to the hull of several submerged submarines"—a set of scientific data we would repeat on the next generation of submarines nearly twenty years later.

During the 1960s, USN/USL did not have a specific policy for maintaining a civilian dive team for the long haul. The Navy had established an abbreviated "scientific diving" course at the Washington Navy Yard, and a few of the Sound Lab staff opted to attend this course. But that option was short lived, and soon all civilians were required to complete the full military scuba school. A Lab project that needed divers might provide the funding to support an individual's training, but once the project was over, there was no commitment for that individual to continue as a diver. USN/USL's policy regarding its dive team changed after McClenny arrived in 1966, and by 1970 a systematic approach to establishing and retaining a team of divers with scientific and engineering backgrounds began to emerge. The scuba training that USN/USL and NUSC would expect of its staff had its origins at the Groton submarine base, where the diving school was responding to a growing need for scuba qualified divers on board the nuclear submarine fleet.

SUBMARINE DIVERS

As early as 1915, providing "qualification as divers of all members of the crew of submarines" was one of many dozens of recommendations made by Gunner George D. Stillson to the U.S. Navy Bureau of Construction and Repair in his *Report on Deep Diving Tests*. Stillson also discussed the use of "diving apparatus on destroyers and submarines," and pointed out that "by adopting the compressed-air method of diving . . . all the necessary apparatus for one diver can be contained in a single sea chest." Although Stillson's recommendation was not implemented, the idea was at least feasible, considering that by the beginning of World War I, the crew of a U.S. submarine consisted of only about two-dozen enlisted men.

The role divers could play in submarine warfare proposed by Stillson was far ahead of its time, as evidenced by his recommendation to provide the ability for divers to lockout from submerged submarines, a capability that would become a reality forty years later with the use of open- and closed-circuit diving systems by the Navy's special operations forces:

> It is recommended that, whenever practicable, a suitable diving compartment be required in the construction of new submarine vessels, for the reason that it appears that the ability of a submarine . . . to send out divers would be especially valuable in the placing or removal of submarine obstructions, cables, mines, countermines, etc. It would also be an advantage to the commander of a submarine when . . . running into an obstruction to submarine navigation to be able to send out divers to investigate and report the nature of the obstruction and the means of avoiding it without the necessity of rising to the surface and being forced to show his periscope above water or to disclose his identity at an inopportune moment. The possibilities and military value of such service are apparent.[47]

Before the days of scuba, however, there was little excess room aboard a submarine for the bulky equipment needed to support a diver. The early submarines Stillson was familiar with rarely ventured far afield, and there was typically a Navy base or a submarine tender near enough to accommodate minor repairs, or they could radio for a tow back to port. Besides, a routine inspection could be done by a swimmer, eyes open and peering into the blurry water—even before combat swimmers first had access to a mask and snorkel during World War II.

With the introduction of nuclear propulsion, a submarine, which could now remain submerged at sea for months, might find itself far from the availability of diving support. Even a minor problem could cause a disruption in a mission. With the development of scuba after World War

II, there was now a viable option for a submarine to carry scuba trained divers, who could make emergency repairs or provide an accurate damage assessment.

As submarines began requesting that their enlisted staff be provided an opportunity to train as scuba divers, the Navy turned to its existing diving schools. The Groton medical research laboratory had been qualifying underwater demolition teams in scuba at the submarine escape facility since the late 1940s, making the submarine base an ideal location for supplying the increasing need for divers. When SEAL teams were created in the early 1960s, the Navy consolidated its combat swimmer training at Key West, Florida. In 1964, the medical research lab was placed under the Navy Submarine Medical Center, but continued to oversee the scuba training until 1968, when the Navy established the Groton Submarine School as a separate command, and scuba training was transferred to the Submarine Escape Training Department. A scuba locker, the classroom, and the department recompression chamber were in a building connected to the escape tower.[48]

A minimum manning requirement of four scuba qualified divers had been established, but with the difficulties trainees experienced completing scuba school (my class, for example, graduated only fourteen of the thirty-two who began the course), submarines were authorized to conduct a dive with three qualified enlisted divers, plus a designated diving officer, who was not required to be scuba qualified. In February 1970, the Bureau of Personnel (BUPERS) established the Navy Enlisted Classification (NEC) code 5344 specifically for submarine scuba divers. Because every Navy dive is recorded and submitted to the Naval Safety Center, the creation of this NEC enabled the Navy to track diving operations conducted by submarine divers.

SELECTION

Becoming a member of a Navy dive team is a process, and a privilege. There is nothing about the selection of candidates, military or civilian, that Gunner Stillson and his contemporaries recommended in 1915 that is not appropriate in the selection process today. An individual volunteers for this qualification and serves in this capacity as a collateral duty. The Navy has recently created a diving rate that provides a career path for divers, but for the Navy's civilian engineers, as well as for submarine divers, qualification remains a collateral function.

By the 1960s, there was a growing need to improve sonar performance and more fully understand sound propagation, as was the need for scientists and engineers who could devise and run experiments that defined complex acoustic paths. Early sound propagation studies in the deep ocean laid the groundwork for the Sound Surveillance System (SOSUS) arrays, which listened for the distinctive radiated noise of approaching Soviet submarines throughout the Cold War. Shallow-water propagation was being studied at the Block Island-Fishers Island (BIFI) range, at facilities on Seneca Lake, New York, and at Dodge Pond and Millstone Quarry in Connecticut. Deep-ocean measurements were expanded at the Atlantic Undersea Test and Evaluation Center (AUTEC) in the Bahamas and at the Azores Fixed Acoustic Range (AFAR) in conjunction with the Mobile Acoustic Communication System (MACS) antenna carried on USS *Nautilus*. Facilities at Tudor Hill, Bermuda, contributed to ocean studies that defined the deep scattering layer. Other technologies were also being investigated, including the use of lasers underwater and measuring electromagnetic fields within the ocean.

Several members of the USN/USL staff who had become divers to support these early research initiatives were able to remain involved for only a limited time because of the increasing responsibilities of their primary jobs. As divers in the late 1950s, George F. Carey and James Catlow had built and tested the two-man Aquabat submarine for use by underwater demolition teams. By the early 1960s Carey and Catlow, project engineers with the Special Developments Branch, were assigned to the design and installation team for the SNAP-7E nuclear-powered deep-ocean acoustic beacon deployed off Bermuda.[49]

In 1968 another diver, Tom Cannan, became involved with a surface ship passive towed array system known initially as the Interim Towed Array Surveillance System (ITASS). Cannan participated in multiple ITASS sea tests, the results of which lead to the development of the SQR-14/15 tactical towed array. As the careers of these and several other engineer/divers moved in new directions, their association with Navy diving was unavoidably brief. Management at USN/USL, and later NUSC/ NL, initiated a move toward establishing a team from the technical staff that would be able to consistently support the Laboratory's, and the Navy's, underwater technologies. In the 1960s, there were also a few members of the NUWRES civilian staff in Newport who had qualified, including Kim Crocker and Frank Wyatt, and occasionally assisted the Sound Lab divers. They maintained their Navy qualifications through an association with the active duty divers who supported the torpedo range in Newport, and were not incorporated into the team being established in New London.

Scientists and engineers whose hobby was diving and had taken a recreational scuba course would often ask if they could join us in the water and help with their project. Navy regulations, however, are very specific about who can and who cannot use scuba equipment on a Navy project. SECNAV (Secretary of the Navy) Instruction 12000.20, "Civilian Diving in the Navy," issued in 1969, clearly stated that a civilian employee was required to complete, as a minimum, scuba training "at an authorized U.S. Navy Diving School," which included the scuba school at the Groton submarine base.[50]

There would be no exceptions, despite the fact that many on the staff at NUSC were experienced sport divers. Over the three decades I was a diver, I was approached at least once every month or two about joining the team. Most understood the requirements, yet there was the occasional NAUI or PADI diver who simply couldn't accept that their sport diving ability alone was insufficient to qualify them to be a NUSC diver—a few becoming a touch belligerent.

The sub base was willing to provide billets at their scuba school, partly because the instructors knew Mac and his reputation as a former active duty Navy diver. There would, however, be no favoritism, no slack given to a civilian candidate regardless of how technically competent he might be, nor how important his role as a diver would be at NUSC. The school's expectation was that after graduation, a Navy civilian would be equally qualified as his active duty counterpart, and that they may need to dive side by side. This expectation would soon become the rule rather than the exception, as our divers began working with military dive teams worldwide, including divers from foreign navies.

I had experienced firsthand the results of being unprepared for the school. I considered myself mentally motivated and had already completed a civilian course. Being in my twenties back in 1973, I thought I was physically strong enough—but strong enough for what? Mac had given me a few simple words like "run your ass off" and "do pushups until you pass out" and "do sit-ups until your tail bone bleeds." I had taken the YMCA course in 1970 with another Sound Lab employee, Ken Beatrice, who had been preparing for the Navy's scuba school, finally qualifying in 1971. Ken had given me some hints as to what the school was like, but with little personal experience, I found it hard to believe Ken's description, and I thought Mac was simply exaggerating. They had warned me, but I just couldn't accept that the school could be as bad as they claimed. That was my biggest mistake, and led me to the morning when I faced the Master Diver and checked out. Now a true believer in their warning that "the only easy day was yesterday," I was fully prepared for my second try and graduated honor man on May 31, 1974. I swore that I would never let any future candidate attempt the school as physically unprepared as I had been the year before.

By the mid-1970s, there was a general call within NUSC for volunteers to augment the small cadre of divers. When someone approached Mac about dive school, he asked Ken and me for our opinion as to whether or not the individual would be an appropriate candidate. Mac was an "old school" ex-Navy chief and had little interest in trying to convert a "shit-for-brains engineer" into a Navy diver. Before dive school, none of us knew how to tie a bowline, a clove hitch, or a stopper, and it would be hopeless if we needed to tie a knot in the dark. Mac spent many hours mentoring his fledgling divers on the waterfront. All he asked was that his divers have some degree of common sense and possess a few practical and mechanical instincts, traits that he considered lacking in an assortment of NUSC engineers, many of whom he considered "useless as tits on a boar hog." Bottom line: his hope, not always fulfilled, was that any future engineer/diver would just learn to "pay attention, dammit!!!"

After the interview, the candidate would be asked to accompany the team to the waterfront for a daily dose of "physical training" or PT. We instituted the lesson I learned about the essential need for physical conditioning, and required that all future candidates spend at least six months to a year training with the current team before we even requested a dive school billet. The PT requirement not only prepares a candidate for the physical demands at dive school, but demonstrates his ability to remain motivated over a long period of time and develops a feeling of membership with the team. We began this requirement in the mid-70s and it continues to this day. I will say at this point that we did try to encourage women to join the team, and although a few seemed interested, we were never able to get one to stay the course. So I use the pronoun "he" when referring to members of the dive team with a sincere wish that at some time in the future a female at NUWC will join the team.

Every NUSC diver was expected to retain a high level of physical conditioning. Although a few of us satisfied this requirement with twelve-ounce curls, some ran marathons, and some swam at the NUSC pool. But most of us participated in the "circle-of-fun," a noon gathering just outside the dive locker where we all enjoyed a series of exercises drawn from our scuba training—sometimes moving to the Bank Street Café for a round of those twelve-ounce curls.

Although I looked at diving as a career path, it was not a requirement—diving at NUSC was considered a collateral duty, secondary to a candidate's primary engineering career. For many who completed the training, the dive team provided occasional physical and mental challenges that may have been lacking in their behind-the-desk day job.

I recently spoke with former diver and NUWC retiree Vic Marolda about what attracted him to diving. One afternoon over a cup of coffee on Vic's back porch, he described the Cold War as "a challenge that included an entire class of problems with the urgency of an imminent threat." Vic explained that for him, "diving at NUSC offered a technological arena with opportunities for adventure that included inevitable hardships, but where success was essential and failure not an option." As Vic succinctly put it, "When our divers were sent out on the road to tackle a problem, we came back either a hero or a zero." The coffee had gotten cold so we dumped that out, rinsed the cups, and filled them with wine.

Vic reminded me that several of our divers had prior military service. Ken Beatrice had been an Air Force missile tech; Mike Paruszewski had served on USS *Seawolf* (SSN-575) in the 1970s; Pete Scheifele, Mike Rutkowski, and Bob Schmidt had all become scuba qualified while serving on their submarines. Over the years, we would continue to draw individuals who had been divers while in the Navy, and viewed our dive team as a means to retain a connection to their active duty past. In the mid 1970s, Bob La Bonte, a submariner on active duty assigned to NUSC, brought his diving qualifications with him, supporting acoustic ranges in the Azores, Bermuda, and locally at the Block Island – Fishers Island range. For the rest of us, civilians within the vast military machine, but with no military experience, facing dive school would be a daunting challenge, where, as Vic said, "failure is not an option."

Figure 20. *Above:* Launching Jacques Cousteau's *Diving Saucer* from *Burch Tide*, March 1965. *Below:* Cousteau discusses the operation with *Saucer* pilot Robert Kientzy. The *Diving Saucer* was among many deep submersibles used to collect data to feed the ever-increasing need for advancements in underwater ASW systems. (*USN/USL; Courtesy Jonathan Finkle*)

CHAPTER 4
Seventy-five Percent of the Earth's Surface

The emergence of the Soviet Union as a global power after World War II was dominated by their reliance on a nuclear capable military, but the reality of their threat patrolled silently beneath the vast oceans. During the Cuban missile crisis in 1962, four Foxtrot-class submarines were deployed to the area and although they were conventional diesel-electric powered, their armament included nuclear-tipped torpedoes. Communication between Moscow and their submarines was intermittent at best, and the decision to begin a nuclear war could have rested in the hands of a single captain. In his book *Red November*, W. Craig Reed (2010) portrays the nervous tension on board these Soviet submarines and how close the Cold War came to becoming a very hot one.[51]

The Soviet threat was real, and justified strong ties among the allies manifest within the North Atlantic Treaty Organization (NATO). As the dominant NATO power, the United States looked to its Navy as key to assuring the European members an uninterrupted supply route across the Atlantic as they struggled with post-war reconstruction. Although NATO countries were provided with ample U.S. air and ground forces, a Soviet thrust into Europe would require a constant stream of additional troops and supplies, which could only be accomplished by transport over the Atlantic sea lanes.

The great circle route from the east coast of America would have to be protected with an escorting fleet of destroyers and cruisers capable of intercepting and neutralizing (i.e. sinking) the ever-increasing number of Soviet submarines. Oceanographic environments varied across the entire route, from shallow coastal waters to the deeper continental shelf and out into the ocean abyss. Each region presented different acoustic conditions in which an enemy submarine could operate, and under certain circumstances, hide until rising to move in for the attack. The hunters on the surface would require efficient detection and swift prosecution of the threat—all dependent on the ability to search in any of these environments (figure 20).

Sonar designers had been limited to relatively short ranges over which they could effectively detect a submerged submarine.[52] Within a relatively shallow layer just below the ocean surface, also known as the "surface duct," sound would effectively transmit horizontally along a "direct path" to a target. This propagation path was limited to a depth of about 300 feet, corresponding to the isothermal boundary. Although this depth and the acoustic properties within the surface duct varied with seasonal temperatures and wind-affected surface conditions, the isothermal boundary was characterized by a sharp decrease in temperature, sufficient to cause sound waves to reflect upwards. With its horizontally directed sonar, a surface ship could only search within this limited depth enabling a submarine to hide below the isothermal layer. By the 1950s the most efficient sonar was capable of detecting a submarine in this direct path surface duct out to a range of approximately 10,000 yards. Detection ranges are typically measured in yards, or in some cases kiloyards. A nautical mile is 6080 feet, essentially 2000 yards. Thus, this 1950s sonar's range was limited to about five nautical miles, which was unacceptable, since Soviet submarines had become faster and more lethal, especially when the threat that slipped below the isothermal layer and into the ocean depths became nuclear powered.

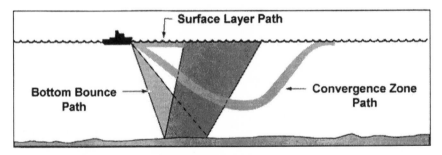

Figure 21. Sound propagation paths available to antisubmarine warfare sonar systems. *(Bell 2011).*

Some had theorized that if a ship's sonar could be directed at a sufficient angle, the sound waves would refract downward, hit the bottom, reflect upwards, contact a submarine hiding below the surface layer, and the echo would return along the same path. This potentially important propagation path was termed *Bottom Bounce* or the *BB* path. Another theory was proposed in which sound, again transmitted at a particular angle, would refract, or bend, downward as it passed through the isothermal layer, but as the sound waves continued downward, they would encounter water of increasing density and bend upward. The total path could take the sound pulse a distance of thirty to thirty-five nautical miles, to reach what was called the *convergence zone* or *CZ*. Great theories, but convincing conservative naval planners that money should be allocated to producing a new-generation sonar would require real-world data.

Thus it fell to the Underwater Sound Lab and other research facilities within the Navy research and development world to acquire a detailed understanding of the acoustic environment, in which this most likely naval battle would occur. In 1949, USN/USL partnered with the Naval Hydrographic Office, embarking on a five-year program known as AMOS (Atmospheric, Meteorological, Oceanographic Survey).[53] During a series of cruises, Sound Lab scientists measured specific parameters related to the transmission of sound in a variety of ocean environments. Prior to that, sonar designers had to rely on anecdotal data obtained from the operational systems used during the war. AMOS provided the first world-wide measurement program specifically targeting the development of active and passive sonar. The goal was an effective antisubmarine warfare (ASW) capability for both surface ships and submarines. A convoy escort system would eventually combine the resources of surface combatants with those of submarines, all carrying long-range sonar and powerful antisubmarine weapons.

The success of AMOS and other research initiatives resulted in the rapid development of ASW capabilities that could keep the Soviets at bay—at least for a time. By the late 1960s, a destroyer deployed as an escort within a carrier battle group could use its SQS-26 bow array to search for Soviet submarines operating more than thirty miles from the carrier. Detecting the presence of a potential threat well beyond its ability to prosecute an attack was essential to maintaining open sea lanes. No one believed, however, that a determined enemy would sit by and let their opposition maintain the upper hand. Any new sonar might soon not be good enough—there was always room for improvement, and the Sound Lab was ideally suited to the task. The 1960s became the decade of acoustic/oceanographic measurements, setting the stage for a search for the ultimate sonar.

"MORE DATA! . . . WE NEED MORE DATA!!!"

A true scientist, however, is never satisfied with the amount of data available to prove or disprove a hypothesis. As the AMOS data was being evaluated, the cry went out for "more data!!!" A few aging fleet submarines were being converted to sonar research vessels to help define the acoustic environment of the oceans.[54] But the appetite of scientists and engineers could not be easily satisfied. The Navy, fully behind the strategic and tactical value of their sonar, rushed to feed this growing appetite and the Underwater Sound Lab was first in line.

Two new approaches were initiated: the use of manned deep-submergence vessels and the establishment of the "acoustic range." Much of the data collected during the AMOS project came from sensors and measurement technology lowered from surface ships deployed on extended cruises. Oceanographic research was expanding at this time, in part due to an increasing public interest and concern about the ocean environment, popularized by French underwater explorer Jacques Cousteau. Private industry was responding by developing mini subs that enabled scientists and adventurers to explore the deep sea. The Navy had some limited experience with the bathyscaphe *Trieste* during a series of deep dives in the 1950s, including a three-month Office of Naval Research (ONR) program in 1957 when USN/USL's Russell Lewis joined Jacques Piccard, son of *Trieste* inventor Auguste Piccard, on four dives—the deepest to 9,200 feet.

JACQUES COUSTEAU

"The Underwater Sound Laboratory has announced its participation in a joint laboratory operation involving the famous Cousteau Diving Saucer." With this headline in the November 13, 1964, edition of the ECHO, the Sound Lab was about to embark on three years of oceanographic research using several state-of-the-art manned submersibles. Jacques Cousteau's *Diving Saucer* (see figure 20) was a perfect fit with the public's fascination with science fiction stories of flying saucers from Mars by supplying a real "saucer" that could explore an environment on Earth as inaccessible to the public as was the surface of Mars. Cousteau fed this appetite through television and in books, and many young engineers at the Sound Lab stood in line for an opportunity to become an aquanaut in his *Diving Saucer*.

Encapsulated in a pressure-proof high-strength steel bubble, there was no requirement to be a trained Navy diver, yet individuals who participated in the deep-submersible projects had to have the same ability to accept the calculated risk associated with any activity that takes a human into the undersea world. Divers would accompany these projects for support during launch and recovery of the submersible, and for underwater photography before the vessel descended.

The future aquanauts from the Sound Lab arrived at the Naval Electronics Lab (NEL) in San Diego on February 18, 1965, followed three days later by Cousteau's *Diving Saucer* on board its support ship, *Burch Tide*. The *Saucer*, recently transported from Marseille, France, was ellipsoidal in cross-section, with a six-foot-six-inch major diameter and five-foot minor diameter, and was capable of operating to depths of one thousand feet. It carried a pilot and an observer who had to lie prone, side-by-side; each with access to a six-inch diameter observation port.

The *Saucer* was available for several months, and the Sound Lab would be the first of five organizations lined up to conduct multiple scientific activities related to biological, geological, and physical oceanography. The host agency NEL, the Naval Ordnance Lab from China Lake, the Naval Missile Center from Point Magoo, and the nearby University of California's Scripps Institution of Oceanography were all involved.

During the first three weeks of March, the Sound Lab made sixteen dives in an area off the southern California coast. More than a dozen scientists and engineers came from New London to participate in the operation, providing opportunities for eight of them to ride the *Saucer*. Led by Ralph Austin, the Sound Lab team planned to measure various acoustic parameters at mid-water depths and at the one-thousand-foot maximum depth of the *Saucer*. A second, equally important goal was to measure electromagnetic properties within the ocean at two-hundred-foot increments from the ocean surface to the bottom.

The acoustics team leader was Gerald "Gerry" Assard, who made four dives, with Robert Dullea and Howard Scott each making two dives. Manuel "Manny" Finkle led the electromagnetics team and participated in two dives; followed by James Orr (two dives); RCA representative David Schwendinger (two dives); and USN/USL's John Flynn and Emil Soderberg, each making a single descent.

The project is described in the April 2, 1965, edition of the ECHO. The article includes an account of a near disaster as told by Gerry Assard, who noticed a leak in a hydraulic line when at a depth of one thousand feet. "I tapped him [Cousteau's *Saucer* pilot, Raymond "Canoe" Kientzy] to get his attention and told him about the leak. The first thing he did was try the hydraulic pumps, but they didn't work. Next he said 'We go up!'" Kientzy released a fifty-pound ballast weight and the four-hundred-pound emergency weight, which enabled the *Saucer* to ascend the one thousand foot distance in twelve minutes, rather than the normal thirty-minute ascent. "Before we reached the surface we had collected a 5-gallon mix of hydraulic oil and sea water inside the saucer." Gerry related this same story to me recently when I was researching this book, and I must say that after more than forty-five years, his story (unlike what you might hear from a Navy diver) was unembellished and reflected the same sense of the impending emergency that he related to the ECHO reporter in 1965.

THE DEEP OCEAN

Cousteau's *Diving Saucer* was limited to a depth of one thousand feet. Yet the ability to detect a Soviet submarine lurking over the horizon and below the isothermal layer depended on acoustic propagation through the deeper depths of the ocean, whether through a bottom bounce path or into the distant convergence zone. Acousticians and sonar designers were determined to obtain optimum detection range and targeting accuracy across these very long two-way propagation paths. They had a basic understanding of how the chemical composition of sea water affected sound absorption, and a general knowledge of the many physical and biological components within the water column that scatter sound waves. These effects were poorly documented relative to the vastness of the ocean environment and required, of course, "more data!" Exploration in the deep ocean required submersibles with a combination of mobility and depth capability, and the Navy research and development community, particularly USN/USL, moved beyond the limitations of Cousteau's *Saucer*.

The operational side of the Navy had also entered the deep submergence world after the loss of USS *Thresher* (SSN-593) in 1963, and *Scorpion* (SSN-589) in 1968. Multiple vessels were designed and built by several companies, including Electric Boat and Westinghouse, to meet both the operational and research needs of the Navy. Many had depth limitations, but were still appropriate for working along the continental shelf. Others, however, targeted the deep ocean well within the propagation paths that the new sonar systems would exploit.

A year after the completion of the *Diving Saucer* research off southern California, the following headline appeared in the June 24, 1966, issue of the ECHO: "USL to Start Year's Program of Research Using Deep Sea Vehicles for Ocean Studies." The program manager, Lou Maples, enlisted many of the same individuals who had worked with Cousteau's *Saucer* to participate in this next, more extensive research initiative, which would include scientists and engineers with backgrounds in acoustics and electromagnetics, as well as oceanography and marine biology. Two submersibles would be used to cover a broad range of deep-ocean environments.

In May, the submersible *Star III*, built across the river at Electric Boat, had been christened and launched at USN/USL. Throughout that summer, the vessel was used in research missions in the New London area and off Bermuda, where the Sound Lab had established a shore-based research station. *Star III* could operate at a depth of two thousand feet, twice that of the *Diving Saucer*.

Figure 22. *Above: Deepstar 4000* outfitted with a parabolic acoustic antenna on the deck of *Searchtide*, July 1967. (*USN/USL; Courtesy Jonathan Finkle*) *Below left:* Sound Lab divers prepare *Deepstar 4000* for its dive and, *below right*, with its electromagnetic sensor. (*USN/USL; "Mac" McClenny*)

To extend the depth capabilities even further, the project employed the Westinghouse submersible *Deepstar 4000* (figure 22), operating from its support ship *Searchtide*. Beginning in July 1967, *Deepstar* made over fifty dives at fourteen locations, from the Gulf of Mexico to the Grand Bahama Islands; then northward, east of the Gulf Stream, and finally to Newfoundland.[55] Divers assisted with the complex operation of launch and recovery, which required a reasonably calm sea state. By the mid-60s, USN/USL had assembled a small team of Navy qualified divers from its technical staff, led by Joe Gordon, which now included Ed April, who had been involved with Cousteau's *Diving Saucer*, Bert Fisch, who worked on the *Deepstar* project, plus Tom Cannan, Ed Hill, and "Mac" McClenny.

Sonar performance depends on the complexity and accuracy of the mathematical modeling of the acoustic propagation path. A ship's on-board computer-based signal processing system, however, must live by the cautionary rule of computer approximations: "garbage in, garbage out." Thus, computational algorithms must be developed using real-world oceanographic data from projects like AMOS and other data collection efforts.

There were several goals for *Deepstar*, but one of the most significant was its search for evidence of the "deep scattering layer," a troublesome phenomenon that significantly affects the propagation path of all sonar systems. Long suspected as being of biological origin, ships transmitting with their sonar experienced strong reflections from a massive "object" within the water column. This acoustic obstruction, an example of "volume reverberation," was known to rise into shallower depths around sunset, and descend into deeper water at sunrise.

Sound Lab scientists led by Charles "Charlie" Brown were instrumental in defining the composition of the deep scattering layer with information gained during the *Deepstar* cruise, and from a project known as Ocean Acre.[56] This oceanographic study measured the acoustic properties of the water column below a one-degree by one-degree area (i.e. one nautical mile square) of the ocean southeast of Bermuda. Biological sampling through this "acre" resulted in a sampling (100,000 individual specimens) of the marine life that comprised the deep scattering layer. Primarily composed of small fish within the Family Myctophidae, the scattering of sound was found to be caused by the vast assemblage of countless tiny gas-filled swim bladders, which these schooling fish use to control their buoyancy. Their movement en masse at sunrise and sunset is a phenomenon called "diurnal vertical migration." This phenomenon was observed by Dr. William "Bill" Von Winkle, Gerry Assard, and others during another Bermuda project called Fishbowl. For the sonar operator, this deep scattering layer meant struggling to peer into the distance through an acoustic fog.[57]

The cry for "more data!" was successfully accomplished, at least for now, as the deep-submersible research program wound down. An article in the December 8, 1967, edition of the ECHO summed up the project: "The advantage of actually putting the scientist down in the environment he is investigating [allows] him to establish 'eyeball' contact with his surroundings—nearly always an advantage over remote-controlled measurements . . . The program has contributed to [an understanding of] underwater acoustic reverberation and scattering, and ambient noise, both electromagnetic and acoustic. Now with the summer's work over, USN/USL scientists are involved in the mammoth job of further analyzing the vast amounts of data collected during the voyage." Even with these "vast amounts of data," the escalating Cold War and the ever-increasing threat from Soviet submarines meant that there would never be enough data.

ACOUSTIC RANGES

There are limitations on the measurement capabilities of manned submersibles and lengthy, expensive oceanographic cruises. Scientists thrive on collecting data that is repeatable and where parameters affecting the experiment are consistent and definable. As they continued to salivate over the possibilities for more data, Navy program managers authorized the establishment of acoustic ranges where propagation physics could be studied under relatively controlled conditions. The Underwater Sound Lab became a major benefactor in the creation and operation of multiple ranges in a variety of environments, both in the shallow waters around New London and at locations with access to the deep ocean.

The installation of these ranges and test facilities, their maintenance and upgrades, as well as the acoustic measurements, all depended on qualified divers. Qualified, in this sense: our divers had to be multi-disciplined, with the mechanical and intellectual dexterity necessary to accomplish an often complex underwater task. But our divers also had to be thoroughly versed in the Navy technology that we were supporting. These skills, both physical and technical, were what the people and their projects expected when they called for a dive team. It was simply not enough to claim that a person who had completed his training was automatically "qualified" to show up at the site and jump into the water; that qualification developed with time and experience.

It has always been a struggle to build and retain a team of divers long enough to acquire that physical and technological versatility. Some "short-timers" only lasted a few years before moving on to other careers, including almost all of those from the 1960s. Among those who trained in the early 1970s, John Fay soon left to complete his doctorate, but continued his career at NUSC and NUWC. Bill Fish and John were involved with the acoustic range diving at Dodge Pond and Block Island in the 1970s; Bill left NUSC to pursue another career path. Among the many short-timers was Nils Straatveit, who also left NUSC after a very brief association with the dive team. Several divers, however, did remain active for ten to fifteen years; the goal was fifteen to twenty; but those of us who passed twenty-five years as a Navy diver just wonder how our bodies lasted that long.

Over the years USN/USL, NUSC, and NUWC scientists and project managers depended on us—their own, dedicated dive team—to serve as their hands and eyes underwater, in projects that took us to Bermuda and the Bahamas, to the Arctic and the Azores, and as far away as Kwajalein. Closer to home, we spent a big chunk of our lives at facilities on Seneca Lake (New York), at Dodge Pond (Connecticut), and Block Island (Rhode Island), to name just a few. As will become obvious from the stories that follow, the variety of projects and technologies we tackled over more than a half century is exceeded only by the variety of personalities that composed our team. To those who were among the short-timers I thank you for adding a splash or two of color to our long history. As for the rest of us, thank God we're still around to tell the tale.

BERMUDA

We jump right in, so to speak, during the summer of 1960, when the Chief of Naval Operations (CNO) established an acoustic research facility in Bermuda, located on the Tudor Hill and High Point bluffs overlooking the Atlantic. Much of the oceanographic work carried on there was sponsored by the Office of Naval Research (ONR). Technical management of the operations fell to USN/USL, where, during its initial four years, the Tudor Hill laboratory staff grew from five individuals to more than sixty scientists, engineers, technicians and naval personnel. The detachment drew interesting members of the Sound Lab staff, including Francis G. "Fran" Weigle, an engineer who had participated in several acoustic research cruises for the AMOS project.[58] Weigle had also been a member of the scientific team aboard USS *Skate* (SSN-578) during its Arctic transit, passing under the North Pole ice on August 11, 1958, just eight days after *Nautilus* made its historic North Pole transit.[59] The Tudor Hill Laboratory continued to operate as a base for acoustic research for thirty years until its disestablishment in September, 1990.

Bermuda was discovered by Spanish explorer Juan de Bermudez in 1505. This island oasis in the mid-North Atlantic played a significant role throughout the maritime history of North America, and continued in that capacity during the Cold War. Bermuda's strategic location provided access to acoustic environments characteristic of the sea lanes crucial to maintaining our edge over the Soviet submarine threat. Sonar system designers and the mathematicians who modeled acoustic propagation saw the Tudor Hill laboratory as an infinite source of real-world data.

The nearly 140 islands that comprise Bermuda sit atop an extinct volcano, which rises from the ocean floor three miles deep. With hilly terrain as much as 250 feet above sea level, the long narrow island chain runs along the southern boundary of a nearly 400-square-mile shallow plateau fringed with a treacherous barrier reef. To the southwest are two additional sea mounts, the tops of which reach within 200 feet of the surface. One of these, Plantagenet Bank, became the home of the Tudor Hill companion facility known as Argus Island.

Soon after Tudor Hill and Argus Island were established, project engineers began installing acoustic arrays from shore into shallow water and out to the nearby deep ocean. Initially, the small team of civilian divers at USN/USL was unavailable to support the installations, so the engineers depended on active duty divers. In 1960, one of the first installations brought a team from the salvage tug USS *Atakapa* (ATF-149) to set the near-shore cables and junction boxes, which connected to the data transmission cables and arrays placed nearly four miles from shore.[60] The thirty-year life span of the Tudor Hill laboratory would be a book in itself (there are many book-worthy stories with origins at the Underwater Sound Lab)—there is only room in this one for a few highlights.

As the complexity and variety of research and experimentation intensified, the technical staff detached from New London to Bermuda grew in response. The Tudor Hill lab was run by an USN/USL (later NUSC) chief scientist and a naval officer-in-charge (OIC), with their corresponding technical and military staff. All laboratory activities were supported by local Bermudians. The nearby ocean proved irresistible to Sound Lab engineers. Many had opportunities to ride aboard a variety of submersibles, exploring the Argus Island plateau in the Perry *Cubmarine*, or descending the steep walls of the sea mount in *Alvin* to its maximum depth of six thousand feet. Even the Navy's nuclear-powered research submarine *NR-1* enjoyed an operational visit. For three decades the Tudor Hill lab provided opportunities for scientists and engineers to test their theories with a physical piece of hardware that could be deployed under real-world conditions.

ENTER THE DIVER

By 1970, when USN/USL had merged with NUWRES to form the Naval Underwater Systems Center (NUSC), there was a growing need to expand the number of qualified divers among the NUSC technical staff. One of the first to respond was Ken Beatrice, at that time an electronics technician, but more important, he was a "make-it-happen" person. Ken's dad was Portuguese and his mom a descendant of the local Native American Narragansett tribe and he had inherited a professional tenacity that carried him through a long and varied career, including a well-earned degree in mechanical engineering from Roger Williams College and completing several graduate level courses from the University of Rhode Island. Engineers knew that when Ken signed on to a project, there was little that could stand in the way.

In the mid-1970s two of these engineers, Gerry Mayer and Michael Ricciuti, had been developing lightweight, portable linear arrays that could be rapidly deployed and retrieved at sea. An array called Tripline, linked to a response team via a sonobuoy, was designed to detect high speed surface craft attempting to infiltrate an operations area. Installed and anchored in shallow water, its horizontal line of small hydrophones was held well off the bottom by subsurface buoys at each end. During installation, Tripline was laid out on the surface between two small-craft. Weights and anchoring riser cables at both ends were released, pulling the array beneath the surface. As the weights dropped to the bottom, they tended to swing beneath the buoys until they hit the bottom. Now firmly anchored, the engineers had to determine the final depth and orientation of the array, the angle of the riser cables, and how close the final installation matched the desired trapezoidal configuration. Led by Ken Beatrice, a dive team from NUSC was sent to Bermuda

Figure 23. *Top:* Gerry Mayer (L) and Mike Ricciuti (R) hang on while *Erline*'s crew secures gear at the stern. *Center:* One of *Erline*'s small-craft on a typical Bermuda day, while Ken Beatrice (*below*) collects Tripline data on the bottom at 80 feet. (*Roy Manstan*)

to assist with the Tripline deployment and answer these questions (figure 23).

Much of the water on the Bermuda plateau is less than one hundred feet deep, ideally suited for experimentation with shallow-water acoustics. Nearly all of the off-shore operations depended on the R/V *Erline*, a converted oil field personnel transport vessel. While its 105-foot length provided plenty of open deck for conducting operations, and its spacious deckhouse accommodated all of the needed electronics, the vessel was long, narrow, and rock-'n'-rolled with every wave. The days we worked with Tripline were no exception, and we often experienced four-foot seas.

The small inflatable boat we used for the diving was certainly capable of safely operating in these sea states. Navigating back to *Erline* only required that we catch a glimpse of her as we crested each wave before descending into the trough. The difficulties arose, however, when coming alongside *Erline*—and getting us, our equipment, and our boat back on board. As *Erline* rolled thirty degrees to port (the side we typically approached) it was easy to just hand items to the crew before she rolled thirty degrees to starboard, giving us a good view of the barnacles that were growing below her waterline. Getting our bodies back on board, however, required good timing. We waited until she rolled again to port. With the railing now in our face we could grab hold as a starboard roll lifted us from the dive boat. A firm "death grip" on the railing was an occupational necessity, when the crew grabbed our backsides and hauled us over the rail. The crew then timed another port roll in order to haul the inflatable boat up and onto the deck, while we secured our dive gear. We finally staggered into the deckhouse, thinking to ourselves, "The only easy day was yesterday," knowing full well that this was a typical day working offshore around Bermuda. The fact that after many similar operations I can relate stories, which have a "happy ending," is entirely attributable to *Erline*'s all Bermudian crew and, in particular, her captain, Richie Lambert.

BACK ON SHORE . . . AT LAST!

From our table we could see the kitchen where Sarah, a large, pear-shaped woman, moved with efficiency, developed from years satisfying the local Bermudian appetite. Maybe it was a steel drum band or a favorite singer that occupied her thoughts, but while her body swayed to an island rhythm, her hands required little direction as they danced from grill to pot. Ken and I often enjoyed a meal at Woody's, a local restaurant where we might be the only white customers, and where we could depend on Sarah to prepare her kitchen magic.

Ken had been working with Gerry Mayer, Mike Ricciuti, and several others in New London building Tripline and other experimental arrays, and was a frequent traveler to Tudor Hill. Although I occasionally joined Ken when additional help was needed with an experiment on board *Erline*, my trips to Bermuda were typically limited to diving operations. Ken had befriended many of the Bermudian staff at Tudor Hill, and had become a "regular" at nearby eating and drinking establishments far from the tourists. When on assignment from New London, he would rent an apartment from a Bermudian family.

It was a short motorbike ride from our apartment to Woody's, just past the causeway that connects Somerset to the next of Bermudas many small islands. Knowing that we wouldn't be returning home for Thanksgiving, Woody had promised us an appropriate meal—at least one that was suited to Bermudian standards. We were confident that whatever Woody and his wife Sarah put on our table would be prepared with local flair, and that it would not be one of the frozen turkeys flown to Bermuda to satisfy hotel guests—Woody had sent his brother, a fisherman, out to dip into the ocean grocery.

Woody's delight with the meal Sarah had prepared was as big as the smile that attended the delivery to our table of the largest lobster either of us had ever seen—a ten-pounder, at least. Woody motioned toward the kitchen, where Sarah cooked with a look of complete satisfaction while moving to the rhythm of that unseen musician, and proclaimed with a satisfied sigh, "A woman eez like de lobster . . . all de meat eez in de tail."

A typically peaceful crown colony, racial tension lurked in the shadows during the 1970s. Protests led to riots on December 2, 1977, in response to the execution of two Bermudians who had been convicted of several murders four years earlier, including the governor, Sir Richard Sharples. Martial law was declared and a curfew imposed. We were at sea on board

Erline when this all started. As soon as we returned late that afternoon, Tudor Hill chief scientist A. Donn Cobb met us at the pier and rushed us off to our apartment. That night, through our window, we watched the orange glow from fires in the distance, a tear coming to my eye as I learned that one of the fires was the Gosling's distillery—oh, how I loved (and still do) their Black Seal rum.

Lobster is certainly one of Bermuda's favorite ocean treasures, but not the only one. The many reefs in the surrounding shallow waters took a huge toll on the thousands of vessels that approached Bermuda's harbors, leaving a five-hundred-year legacy of tragedy and treasure strewn among the abundant reefs. Local history entrepreneur Teddy Tucker knew these stories (and their treasure) well. We contracted Tucker one summer, in

1982, when we had been tasked to locate a fault in an array data transmit cable (the cover photo was taken during this operation). His dive boat was tied to a dock at the foot of a hill just below his home. On our way out from the dock, Tucker slowed to give us a chance to view a row of cannons lying neatly side by side on the shallow bottom, where he stored them in hopes they might find a home in some museum. He soon brought us to the location where NUSC had laid its array cables, an area where Tucker had also found the remains of eighteenth-century warships. Probably on purpose, Tucker dropped us into the water where our first sight was, yes, another cannon. (Figure 24) We were

Figure 24. *Above:* For centuries, the treacherous reefs surrounding Bermuda have taken a toll on hundreds of ships. Cannons are often the only remnant of the tragedy that befell the ship and her crew. *Below:* NUSC diver Kurt Hansen inspects an acoustic sensor cable. (*Roy Manstan*)

impressed with his jovial nature, and learned his secret to a happy life on our way back to the pier. Tucker opened a mason jar containing his favorite recipe—pickled prunes—which kept both his smile and his digestion working at top speed. This may sound like an unusual snack, but by "pickled," Tucker was also referring to the eater, as he handed us the jar filled with prunes soaked for months in Gosling's 151-proof rum.

ARGUS ISLAND

Built along the lines of a Texas Tower, Argus Island sat fifty feet above the ocean surface, firmly secured to the sea floor by four thirty-four-inch diameter pipe legs imbedded seventy feet into the sediment.[61] In the two-story building were laboratory facilities, a small machine shop, recreation room, galley, and sleeping quarters. The roof was designed to facilitate the helicopter link with Bermuda nearly thirty-five miles away. Although created primarily for oceanographic and acoustic research, Bermudian fishermen enjoyed the bounty of shark, barracuda, and tuna that congregated near the tower legs.

During its fifteen years as a research facility, Argus Island hosted many world-class scientists sponsored by the Office of Naval Research. The Navy, however, also saw this location as ideal for the first in a series of three "Sealab" experiments, designed to measure the physiological effects on humans living for extended periods in a deep-water underwater habitat. The Sealab team occupied Argus Island during the summer of 1964, and is where Dennie "Mac" McClenny, the Navy underwater cinematographer assigned to Sealab, first encountered the Sound Lab staff on Argus Island and Tudor Hill (see chapter 3).

Mac and I returned to Argus Island in 1977, but under much different circumstances than when he was there in 1964. By the mid 1970s, Argus Island's life as a research facility was over and had been decommissioned. A Navy underwater demolition team was tasked to sever the tower legs at the sea floor and at their junction just beneath the two-story building. After detonation, the tower tilted to its side and settled horizontally on the bottom. The building, severed from its support structure during the initial blast, floated briefly before sinking alongside the tower legs. The now-submerged Argus Island became an artificial reef—a magnet that drew both a vast and diverse biological community and a fleet of island fisherman. Because of local interest, NUSC sent a dive team out to film the fast-developing artificial reef and produce a short documentary for Bermuda television.

We arrived in August, 1977, fifteen months after its demolition. The weather Gods were on our side that week—flat-ass calm, even thirty-five miles out in the open ocean, where *Erline* easily stationed itself right above the site. Because of the depths involved, Mac and I could only make two

dives a day (figure 25). The first took us to the top of the building, at a depth that allowed only minutes to film various details before returning to the surface. The water was so transparent that standing along *Erline*'s rail, we could look down at the surface of the water and see the tower legs ninety feet below, where, after a lengthy surface interval, we made our second dive. Mac filmed with a 16-mm movie camera while I shot stills, some of which were incorporated in the film documentary. An underwater photographer's paradise, the site was filled with an incredible abundance of sea life, all drawn to the food chain that collects around any reef, natural or man-made.

Figure 25. *Above:* Argus Island in the 1960s. (*US Navy photo; Courtesy Ray Ingram*) *Bottom left:* "Mac" McClenny with Bolex underwater movie camera, filming around the Argus Island legs in 1976, after it had been decommissioned and laid onto the bottom. *Bottom right,* looking up through the radio antenna tower from a depth of 130 feet. (*Roy Manstan*)

Argus Island had been Mac's home during Sealab, and was filled with memories of a very important and successful mission. Although the interior of the flooded building beckoned, we managed to resist the temptation, and limited our tour to the roof where we filmed around

the crane, the small-boat cradle, and the radio tower, where I climbed inside and shot a photo looking up through the depths to catch an image of the sun—visibility was infinite that day. Because of the time needed to cover the photographic requirements, we planned to make decompression stops at twenty and ten feet. While there, we spotted a shark circling in the distance. As its curiosity increased, the diameter of its circle decreased. Fortunately, *Erline*'s observant crew also saw the shark, and David Simmons, Richie's first mate, brought the inflatable boat between us and the shark while Mac and I completed our decompression before climbing aboard with David.

Whether it was sharks, unpredictable seas, lobster feasts, or Teddy Tucker's pickled prunes, we could always depend on an interesting experience working in Bermuda. On our days off we might play darts with *Erline*'s crew at the Charing Cross, tip a few with *NR-1*'s captain and exec, or head to the beach on rental scooters to snorkel in the shallows. Bermudians always surprised us with their courteous nature—even the local Hell's Angels. With limits on the size of motorcycle engines, these dudes, wearing the obligatory leather vests and German helmets, rode 120 cc bikes bored out to gain a few extra horsepower. The approaching whine of a dozen two-cycle Yamahas modified with extended forks, ape-hangers, and cut-down mufflers certainly got our attention as we putted along on pedal-assisted motorbikes.

All of the New London staff silently mourned the closing of the NUSC Tudor Hill Laboratory in 1990, as Center management, headquartered in Newport, consolidated its operations in Rhode Island. In 1992, NUSC was renamed the Naval Undersea Warfare Center and the New London Laboratory became the New London Detachment, an ominous sign of the physical changes that would occur four years later under the Base Realignment and Closure Commission (BRAC).

DODGE POND

Bermuda offered researchers access to an ocean environment representative of where Soviet submarines operated. Acoustic research, however, could be carried out at more modest facilities, and in water much closer to home. To feed that unending appetite for "more data," a test facility was established in a fresh water pond in Niantic, Connecticut, a mere five miles from the

Sound Lab. Dodge Pond was selected because of the extremely low level of ambient noise in the water.

The test facility has been in operation for over fifty years. Because power boating is not allowed, that typical human-generated source of noise is absent. Mother Nature is also kind—the tree-lined shore minimizes wind-generated surface noise, and the creaks and groans from shifting winter ice simply add a bit of background music. When the water is quiet, it is very quiet, and scientists revel in the quality of their data.

Formed as a thirty-three-acre "kettle pond" after the last glacier receded from southern New England thousands of years ago, the shallow basin, with its soft bottom sediments, is ideal for testing and calibrating individual sonar elements, which find their way into the massive arrays the Navy depends on to carry out its antisubmarine warfare mission. The task of evaluating an entire sonar system fell to another fresh water facility, where a two-hundred-ton-capacity crane located in the middle of New York's Seneca Lake could handle a complete bow module for the latest submarine. But that story will wait as we dive into Dodge Pond.

A modular 36-foot by 103-foot floating barge was launched onto the pond in April, 1959.[62] Supported by foam-filled steel cubes, a twenty-two-foot high building contained a bridge crane used to lower sonar components into a well nearly sixty feet long and six feet wide. Over the years, two additional barges were added, and the site became a dependable source of quick-in quick-out dives to retrieve the inevitable piece of equipment dropped into the well. Dodge Pond also gave us a unique opportunity to provide our newly "qualified" divers with their first right-out-of-dive-school initiation dive. New divers, sent to the bottom on "good housekeeping" missions, brought back a signal amplifier, coils of wire rope, a desk, several chairs, and a shopping cart.

Within the Navy diving community, successfully completing dive school only punched your ticket. Gaining experience necessary to create a productive member of the team became the responsibility of the Command to which the new diver was assigned. The ol' timers on the NUSC dive team carried on this tradition, and looked forward to sending each new diver to the bottom of Dodge Pond, which has been collecting organic material over several millennia. The experience separated those who acclimated to the vagaries of diving from those who may have had second thoughts about their choice.

In the absence of any current, a heavy piece of equipment dropped beneath the Dodge Pond barge will head straight down and sink deep into the sediment. A weighted descent line was lowered as near as possible to where the object was dropped. Under the barge, however, light only penetrated a few feet below the surface, whereupon the diver was enveloped in total darkness. As he slowly moved down the descent line, a hand held light warned him of his approach to the bottom, its presence only distinguished by a grey blanket of silt. A telltale depression was the only clue where to probe into the slime and feel for the object.

The upper layer of this "bottom" is more of a detritus suspension than sediment, and the diver might find himself reaching down to his shoulder before feeling anything resembling a "solid" bottom. The diver had to descend head first, hovering above the sediment. A misplaced kick would raise a grey cloud that remained suspended above the same spot, rendering his light useless. Any further searching was done by touch.

It took less than a minute for the divers to descend. Topside, we watched their progress by the exhaled air hitting the surface. We knew that they had begun to search and probe the bottom when small clouds of bubbles surfaced nearby, carrying the obnoxious odor of rotten eggs. Disturbing the byproduct of bacteria munching on (anaerobic decomposition of) organic matter, released hydrogen sulfide trapped in the sediment, which then mixed with the divers' exhaled air and rushed to the surface. Molly the mud monster has very bad breath.

Pitch black water; a colony of eels living beneath the barge; a thermocline ten feet below the surface, where summer water temperatures drop from seventy degrees to forty degrees; a bottomless bottom; and the aroma of rotten eggs—this was simply the name of the game when diving at Dodge Pond. Maybe Karma or fate, a need for our services always occurred just after our latest trainee graduated.

Time took its toll on the steel flotation modules, and one by one, they leaked. As their foam interiors slowly absorbed water, the effect of the diminishing buoyancy on the floating barges became evident. Closed cell foam blocks known as "billets" used by marinas proved to be an ideal solution. We strapped each billet to a cradle, where a total of about three hundred pounds of weight was suspended at each end to make the whole assembly neutrally buoyant. Two divers guided the cradle under the barge and into position. The weights were also tethered to the overhead crane, and on the count of three, the divers released pelican hooks holding the weights, which dropped down and under the crane. With its six-hundred-pound pound buoyancy, the billet was now firmly in place, and the divers could remove the cradle and return for another. As each billet was installed, one by one, the barge rose ever so slightly. We repeated this process several times over the years until the underside of the barge was covered with three layers of foam billets. A smart decision was made to replace the barge with a new facility, which was completed and operational in 1993.

Dodge Pond continues to support the Navy's acoustic research, although its sixty-five-mile distance from NUWC has made it inconvenient for our initiation dives. The facilities have recently provided a location where the Naval Submarine Medical Research Laboratory (NSMRL) has conducted various experiments with their own team of divers, occasionally joined by our divers when additional test subjects were needed.

BIFI

Although Bermuda is only a two hour flight, there was a distinct need for access to a shallow sea-water test range. If convenience was the only criterion, then the waters off New London were ideal. Acousticians required specific acoustical/environmental conditions to ensure scientific precision and relevance—the Block Island-Fishers Island (BIFI) Range provided it all.

Block Island (Rhode Island) and Fishers Island (New York) are two of a series of small islands that run east of Long Island, all created from a glacial terminal moraine. This is important from an acoustics sense in that the coastal waters, which formed after the mile-thick glacier receded, are ideally suited to measurements of shallow water sound propagation. The region between these two islands, where the BIFI range was established, is known as Block Island Sound. Water depth along the nearly nineteen nautical mile range is less than two hundred feet, while the shallow near-shore water is readily accessible by divers (yup . . . that would be us) for the installation and maintenance of source and receive sonar equipment.

With convenient ferry service from New London, we brought vehicles, personnel, and equipment in order to install and operate the Fishers Island side of the BIFI range, located at the Navy's facilities on the site of Fort Wright, along the island's south facing coast. Although we could dive from shore, some of the systems required access from the *NUSC-1*, a small-craft with ample deck space and an enclosed cabin—a necessity for winter operations.

The importance of Long Island Sound and its access to New York City increased in the minds of nineteenth-century military strategists, who watched with interest, the rapidly evolving post-Civil War battleships and their massive firepower. In the 1880s, with Fishers Island facing directly toward the primary entrance to the Sound from the Atlantic Ocean, a small parcel of land was leased for military training exercises. Over the next decade, there was increasing interest in Fishers Island. America declared war on Spain in April 1898, after the loss of the battleship *Maine* in Havana Harbor, and there was an immediate push to move forward with the purchase of 215 acres at the western end of the island. The construction of gun emplacements at Fort H.G. Wright in December was the beginning of a half-century-long military presence, encompassing two world wars.

The Spanish-American war also saw the construction of additional long-range gun batteries on nearby Little Gull Island (Fort Michie) and Plum Island (Fort Terry). Although battleships and dreadnaughts dominated the oceans during World War I, the likelihood of attack from a foreign fleet diminished in the minds of a peaceful post-war America. While the role of all coastal defenses, including Fort Wright, also diminished, the coastal artillery batteries on Fishers Island remained ready to defend the country.[63]

The submarine, however, was beginning to take on a greater role in naval strategy. Submarines based at Groton all passed Fishers Island en route to and from their operating areas, and if an enemy submarine entered Long Island Sound, it would also have to pass the island. This possibility no doubt occurred to military minds, and the concept of setting seafloor-mounted passive listening sonar was first attempted at Fort Michie in 1927. Built by the Submarine Signal Company for the War Department, the experimental system consisted of thirty-two microphone-based elements, which were able to detect the sounds of a submerged submarine and provide an indication of the direction it was travelling.[64]

A military presence on Fishers Island continued through World War II when, once again, the thought of an attack by a fleet of German battleships generated a buildup of defenses at Fort Wright, including a massive bunker, Battery III, capable of mounting long range 16-inch guns. The Harbor Entrance Control Post (HECP), a building disguised as a farm house, was constructed on Mount Prospect, the highest point on the island, and served as headquarters for operations associated with protecting Long Island Sound. On and around HECP were an assemblage of radar systems (one built to resemble a water tower) and antiaircraft searchlights.

Nonetheless, the threat of a U-boat entering Long Island Sound was real. *U-853* had been patrolling off the Rhode Island coast, sinking the collier SS *Black Point* on May 5. 1945. The following day, sonar searches by several U.S. warships located *U-853*, which was attacked with a barrage of depth charges. The attack was joined by two K-class dirigibles from Lakehurst, New Jersey, and by the end of the day, on May 6, 1945, *U-853* and its entire crew were permanently consigned to the ocean bottom (a scene I visited in 1971). The presence of U-boats near the entrance to Long Island Sound must have inspired the installation of prototype sonar equipment at the eastern-most end of Fishers Island.[65]

In 1949, the military left Fort Wright. The facilities at HECP, Battery III, and the Wilderness Point shoreline adjacent to Mount Prospect were all transferred to the Sound Lab for research in acoustics and electromagnetics. In addition to the BIFI range, the proximity of transiting submarines made this an ideal location for sonar accuracy testing at the Fishers Island Fleet Operational Readiness Accuracy Check Site (FORACS).

Block Island is a bit further off shore, and we would either fly from one of the local airports and charter a small-craft from an island fisherman or run out there on the NUSC LCU-1647. Although we wanted to call this the U-boat, the old timers preferred to simply refer to it as the "LCU" (the Navy acronym for Landing Craft Utility). It was an ideal platform for conducting diving operations—with its forward ramp lowered we could simply walk into the water. The LCU was later assigned to NUWC's Atlantic Undersea Test and Evaluation Center (AUTEC) at Andros Island, Bahamas, but has since been decommissioned (figure 26).

Figure 26. *Above and Below left:* The LCU-1647 supported many Sound Lab projects. These photos are from the BIFI acoustic range installation at Block Island. *Below right:* The MIC-6, a smaller landing craft also used during the BIFI installation, with Fishers Island's Mt. Prospect in the background. (*USN/USL*)

In the late 1960s, USN/USL decided to install a submerged stationary platform at the Block Island side of the BIFI range. A barge was towed to the island and set on

the bottom just outside the entrance to the Great Salt Pond, also known as New Harbor. A central mast extended above the surface, with a beacon to mark its location. A variety of test equipment could now be installed on the submerged platform and mast. Acousticians used the BIFI range for collecting data on a variety of parameters affecting shallow water sound propagation—among the most important were bottom and surface reverberation. The sea floor conditions were fairly consistent across the range, but the sea surface could change from flat calm to a Sea State Three in minutes, at the approach of a weather front.

The shore stations on both islands were located well above storm surge levels, where the data links, which enabled the range to be remotely controlled and monitored from New London, were expected to be operational throughout the year. During late summer and fall, when frequent nor'easters blow through New England, bottom-mounted equipment was often damaged. For our dive team, this meant a lengthy trip on the LCU. With multiple tasks, water depths around ninety feet, and tides a factor, we often brought the LCU into New Harbor for the night—not an easy task to squeeze the landing craft's wide beam through the narrow channel, but a necessity when seeking refuge at the approach of a storm.

Often, after a long day on site, we made one last dive. The barge was our own, personal fish market. Mussels hung off the mast guy wires in huge clusters, and we could fill a sea bag in minutes. Fed by mid-water tidal currents, they were fat and healthy, without the sand found in bottom feeding shell fish. We could expect a very long trip back to New London, and a relaxing meal on board the LCU made the time pass. Ken Beatrice brought his recipe for steamed mussels:

1. Collect bag of mussels from the mast
2. Place mussels in large stew pot
3. Add suitable liquid
4. Place stew pot on propane grill
5. Pour unused liquid into plastic cups
6. Melt butter
7. When shells open, remove pot and serve with butter
8. Feast

By the time the Base Realignment and Closure Commission (BRAC) did its dirty deed in the mid-1990s, moving the New London Laboratory to Newport, acoustic testing at the BIFI range had been fully realized, and the equipment was removed. The barge was left in place and has become an underwater site of interest to sport divers, in part due to its role in the history of Cold War technology.

Although BIFI, FORACS, and other acoustics testing no longer occurs at Fishers Island, this area is still used by USN/USL's and NUSC's successor, the Naval Undersea Warfare Center, for submarine communications development. The ability to simulate at-sea conditions is available at the over-water radio frequency (RF) range, between the "mile site" and the lovingly named "dungeon" near Wilderness Point.

OPERATION ZODIAC

We called it "Operation Zodiac" because we spent two weeks in May 1982, offshore on a fourteen-foot inflatable, while our support boat, R/V *Schock* (contracted from the University of Rhode Island), and the project vessel, USNS *Lynch* (T-AGOR-7), stood by (figure 27). A vessel referred to as a

Figure 27. USNS *Lynch* anchored several miles south of Block Island, as divers report the condition of the acoustic source. (*Richard Thibeault*)

United States Naval Ship (USNS) is operated by the Military Sealift Command (established in August 1970, formerly the Military Sea Transportation Service). Ships designed specifically for oceanographic research, such as *Lynch*, are under the control of the Oceanographer of the Navy, and are unarmed and painted white.

Officially known as Project WEAP (Weapons Environmental Acoustics Program), NUSC researchers Bill Roderick and Jim Syck directed the acoustic range operations from *Lynch*. Our first task was to place the sound source and its support tower on the bottom, and vertical arrays of hydrophones and ocean current sensors nearby. The goal was to measure the scattering of high frequency acoustic energy striking the bottom at shallow grazing angles. We were operating at water depths of 115 feet, and dove in strict accordance with no-decompression dives. Because multiple dives were required over several days, and we faced depth and time restrictions, we teamed with the active duty explosives ordnance disposal (EOD) detachment from Newport. We also brought in an EOD team from Earl, New Jersey.

From the start of our operation, we could see a large vessel anchored a few miles from our site. A little investigation revealed that it was a Soviet "trawler." By the 1980s, these vessels had become a common sight in international waters, and often appeared when the Navy was conducting tests. We were surprised that our little acoustic range had garnered enough attention to draw a vessel from the Soviet "fishing" fleet, but soon realized that another event was underway—USS *Ohio* (SSBN-726), commissioned the previous year, was about to pass Block Island en route to operations in the Atlantic. The fishing would be good for the Soviets that day.

In his book *Stealth Boat*, Gannon McHale (2008) related his experience with Soviet spy ships, while a sailor on board USS *Sturgeon* (SSN-637) during the 1960s. Returning to Groton, *Sturgeon* surfaced in what was known as the Narragansett Bay Operating Area, and McHale took his position as a lookout in the sail: "We arrived at the spot where we usually made the turn to head up into the Race, and there we encountered a new Soviet ploy to disturb American submarine activity. Stretched out before us were five fishing trawlers, right in a row. Although they looked like fishing boats, they weren't really trawlers. Obviously spy ships, they all had dozens of antennas to gather electronic intelligence. One was larger than the other four and was obviously the mother ship. The ships sat right on the three-mile limit and waited for American submarines."[66]

On May 15, 1982, Kurt Hansen and I made our first dive for the installation of the parametric source tower. The sight of this operation must have caught the attention of the Soviet trawler, which later approached near enough to get a fix on our position, and then moved off to the horizon. We thought they were just curious about what a white-ship was up to, but soon found that they were probably enjoying a bit of a diversion while in the area, checking out the passage of *Ohio*. When we returned to the site the following morning, the first team in the water discovered that the tower was lying on its side, apparently dragged over during the night by *Lynch*, having moored too close. When the divers surfaced to pass along the bad news, we all expected to hear an R-rated response like: "Aw Shit!" or "Jesus F-ing Christ!" But Jim Syck was a calm and well-mannered scientist, and the exclamation we heard onboard was simply "Holy cow!" By the end of the day, *Lynch* had lifted the tower, enabling us to reestablish the range and resume testing.

Our plan was to spend each night on Block Island in the small maritime community at Old Harbor, returning to the range early in the morning. There were no sleeping accommodations on board *Schock*, so the divers found rooms in local hotels (normally the Gables Inn), while the researchers stayed on board *Lynch*, now anchored on site in a stable four-point moor. The presence of so many Navy divers from New London, Newport, and New Jersey certainly roused local curiosity. Although beer was readily available at Ballards along the Old Harbor waterfront, our first stop was always the bar at the National Hotel, where everyone knew that *Ohio* had passed their island, and a Soviet spy ship was patrolling off their coast. It only took a couple rounds of beer to stimulate diver imaginations, and a "story" soon emerged about why the U.S. Navy (and the Soviets) had converged off Block Island. Many of the active duty divers working with us had served on board submarines, and the local patrons at the bar were used to hearing our sea stories. We knew the conversation would inevitably get their attention. "Those poor bastards . . . what a way to go! I've been to sea a dozen times. I think about it every time they close the hatch." We were there—at least as far as the story went—because a Soviet submarine had been lost south of Block Island. Marie, the bar tender who became our unofficial team mascot, knew that it was just another bull shit story (she loved us anyway), and stopped the rumor before it made the papers.

THE SALAD BOWL

It was always late in the day when our diving operations were done, and R/V *Schock* returned to Old Harbor. By the time we reached the pier, we were all tired and ready to quench our thirst. There were few amenities aboard *Schock*, and the bar at the National Hotel beckoned. Old Harbor was accustomed to visits from all sorts of vessels, but most often provided overnight anchorage to spacious yachts and their well-heeled owners and guests.

When we tied up to the pier, we anticipated enjoying some peace and quiet and a few beers with dinner at the National. One evening, however, it was not peace and quiet that greeted us. Nearby, there was a loud gathering on board a very large yacht, hosted by a skinny Bostonian (from his accent), wearing Bermuda shorts, a white polo shirt, and that pretentious lime-green

Figure 28. *Above:* After each day's dive, R/V *Schock* returned to Old Harbor at Block Island. *Below:* The author relaxes while using *Schock*'s "salad bowl." (*Richard Thibeault*)

sweater draped over his shoulders: "AHOY, *Schock*! . . . Might you have a cook on board? . . . We are entertaining and in need of a salad bowl."

It was obvious that we were not being invited to share the champagne, but we were pleased to accommodate his request. We passed them a shiny white 5-gallon bucket and asked if they would kindly return it, as it was what we also used on board *Schock*—failing, however, to mention that it was not for salad, its real use recorded for posterity by Rick Thibeault (figure 28).

ON THE BOTTOM

Most of my mornings at the dive locker started with the question, "What's on the schedule today?" The answer would typically include equipment maintenance, and if I was really unlucky that day, I would have to get caught up on paperwork. It was late in the morning, June 3, 1993, when the pier master came into my office. There was a sound of urgency in his voice, "How fast can you get a team out to Block Island? The *Salmon* took on water and sank."

It sounds a lot worse than it was. No one was on board. The submarine was being towed out to the edge of the continental shelf near Hudson Canyon. Commissioned in 1956, USS *Salmon* (SS-573) was among the last of the conventional-powered fleet boats built in the wake of *Nautilus* and *Seawolf.* After a twenty-one-year career, the ex-*Salmon* was given one last mission—now resting at a depth of 360 feet, it serves as a target for sonar testing in the Narragansett Bay Operating Area.

While en route and under tow behind *Ensco Trojan*, the test plan included a stop off Block Island, where the procedures for submerging the submarine could be tested in relatively shallow water. Once on the bottom, air would be pumped into the hull, bringing *Salmon* back to the surface. *Trojan* would then continue to tow the old submarine out to its final resting place on the continental shelf. During the submerging operation, the air line from *Trojan* parted, and the submarine settled onto the bottom.

The message that our pier master received over the radio was short on details, but couldn't have happened at a better time. Several of our divers were at the locker preparing for the noon PT session, and there was no hesitation pulling a team together, when the job included recovering an antique submarine from the bottom. Besides, I had been cursed with the procrastination gene and was dreading an afternoon filled with paperwork.

The pier master tossed me the keys to the Boston Whaler; dive gear and scuba bottles were secured on board; and the twin 100 HP Johnsons quickly put the Whaler out past Fishers Island and into Block Island Sound. Couldn't have been a better day—flat-ass calm was a term we weren't often able to use to describe the seas, where the New England coast looks out over the Atlantic Ocean. It was a fast run out to where we could see the tow ship on the horizon. We were in radio contact with *Trojan* and with Sandy Traggis, who had followed *Salmon* in another small-craft. Sandy used his fathometer to locate the submarine, and was then able to mark the hull with a grappling hook and a surface buoy. We approached and set our anchor near Sandy's buoy (figure 29).

The fathometer read 110 feet to the sand, so my instructions were simple, "Make it quick! . . . I want you on the surface in twenty minutes." The first team in was Paul Gianquinto and Bob Schmidt. Their task was to follow the line from the marker buoy to the grappling hook, secure the descent line to the conning tower, survey the situation, and report back with the condition of the parted air line. When they reached the end of the descent line, the hook had slipped free of *Salmon* and was sitting in the sand. Because this was always a possibility, they carried a fifty-foot-long circling line as a contingency. With Smitty holding station at the hook, Paul moved out to the end of the line and began a long swim, with hopes that *Salmon* would be somewhere along the more than three-hundred-foot search circumference. By the time Paul came up on *Salmon*'s hull, almost ten minutes had passed. He and Smitty pulled the grappling hook over to the conning tower, secured the line, and made a quick run to locate and determine the condition of the air line fitting. They were back on the surface in nineteen minutes.

We contacted *Trojan*, where preparations were underway to connect into the air line. Vic Marolda and Ross Byrne were set to make the second descent. Weather was still on our side, and the Whaler was now securely tied with the buoy line to *Salmon*.

Figure 29. *Above:* The ex-*Salmon* on the surface. *Below:* Anchored above the submarine, NUSC/NL divers prepare for the recovery operation; (L-R), Ross Byrne, Vic Marolda, Paul Gianquinto, Roy Manstan, and Bob Schmidt. (*NUSC/NL*)

Even under the best of conditions, diving in New England at this depth includes two guarantees: the water is cold (we had all brought dry-suits that day) and the water is dark. Not too bad when you enter and begin the descent, but as the bright sunlight is absorbed within those first twenty to thirty feet, the colors darken to a pea-soup-green, and your dive buddy becomes only a shadow. By sixty feet, you are enveloped in a cold, dark cloud—not pitch black, but nearly so. The sunlight, what remains of it, still penetrates the water and reflects off any object in its path, including a submarine. "As we passed about fifty feet," Vic recalled, "we turned on our dive lights and continued down the descent line. The dark outline of *Salmon*'s conning tower emerged, and our lights caught every detail. Maybe I had seen too many reruns of *Victory at Sea* on TV, but I felt like I was being sucked into a World War II movie. I took a few deep breaths to calm my imagination . . . we had a job to do, no time for sightseeing."

It was 17:40 when Vic and Ross were back on the Whaler. As we slipped out of our mooring and anchored nearby, *Trojan* moved into position and spliced a new hose into the free end of the air line, now afloat on the surface, then moved off while pumping air into *Salmon*'s hull. The submarine slowly rose up through the surface as we watched what looked like a ghost ship emerging from the depths—just like in the movies.

The events that day rapidly spread to sport divers anxious to find any new site to explore (euphemism for pick clean). An article appeared in a local publication, *The Fisherman*:

> A diver . . . wrote asking about the whereabouts of the U.S.S. Salmon, the sub the Navy scuttled off Block Island, the event getting into the local press and causing a stir among the diving community since it was reported the vessel was dropped within the limits of scuba gear. A source on the Cape has told The Fisherman that the sub was raised and then towed to a position in 70-plus fathoms of water on the east side of Hudson Canyon, and scuttled again. It's been said the Navy will use it as a sonar target.[67]

As we pulled anchor, Smitty turned to me and asked, "So what's on the schedule for tomorrow?" Maybe I will be lucky, I thought, pondering all that paperwork, and I can procrastinate again. It doesn't take much (including raising a sunken submarine) to distract me.

BIGGER IS BETTER

During the mid-1960s everyone understood that within the current geopolitical environment, we had to anticipate a global battlespace—not just a regional conflict, which could be squashed with an equally regional response. As the Soviet submarine fleet grew in size and distribution, the need to concentrate on continually developing effective ASW sonar grew as well. Good science would lead to better engineering, which would lead to the best system. But good science meant gathering data appropriate to solving the problem.

Deep submersibles were measuring continental shelf and oceanic acoustics at specific locations; scientists at the Tudor Hill Lab were experimenting on the Bermuda Plateau and the surrounding deep ocean; acousticians at the Sound Lab in New London were studying shallow water propagation in Block Island Sound. From Bermuda to Block Island, sonar designers reveled in the variety of data they were able to collect. But no matter how interesting were the results, no matter how many theories were proved or disproved, no matter how advanced a ship's sonar had become, there was just no satisfying their thirst for more data.

This time it would come from a range, which encompassed the entire Atlantic Ocean.

Now fully engaged in the Cold War, USN/USL and its sponsors couldn't resist the concept of an acoustic range of this scope—and to make the pot sweeter, eight NATO countries would participate. But the temptation was even greater when the plan called for the participation of the first nuclear submarine to enter the Cold War fifteen years earlier.

The Sound Lab nurtured many visionary scientists, yet the magnitude of this particular vision required a leader with a personality to match. This type of leadership is rare, but without it science stands still, and a vision will be relegated to a long list of "woulda-coulda-shoulda" ideas. The Soviets weren't going to stand still, and neither would the Sound Lab.

In July 1968, a memorandum of understanding (MOU) was approved by NATO that would put this next idea into motion. USN/USL sent Jim Syck, a former Navy oceanographer, and Lenny Cormier out on USNS

James M. Gilliss (AGOR-4) to search the deep ocean terrain along the Mid-Atlantic Ridge. They struggled for a month in serious sea states, but eventually found the perfect location for the Navy's most ambitious acoustic range, which had ever been—or more likely will ever be—attempted.

AFAR

It was USN/USL's Alan Ellinthorpe, along with co-investigator Paul Radics, who had sent Jim Syck and Lenny Cormier across the Atlantic Ocean. All the players on Ellinthorpe's team were of that same breed of intellectual and physical risk takers, who were willing and eager to take on each challenge which crossed their desk. If that was not your forte, there was no need to sign up for the AFAR project—Alan Ellinthorpe and the Azores Fixed Acoustic Range were not for the faint of heart.

Jim and Lenny had located three seamounts nearly a quarter mile deep off the island of Santa Maria in the Azores, an archipelago of volcanic origin. Designated Echo, November, and Sierra, each location became the site of a 124-foot-tall tower, spaced in a triangular arrangement approximately eighteen miles apart. The upper portion of each tower held a massive structure, consisting of three parabolic acoustic reflectors—each designed to collect sound waves within different frequency bands and concentrate the energy at a focal point. The largest reflector, designed for frequencies of 50 to 1000 Hertz (Hz), was twenty feet in diameter. The two smaller reflectors operated in frequency bands of 1000 to 2000 Hz and 2000 to 5000 Hz. The assembly of all three reflectors created an acoustic antenna, which could be rotated in azimuth and elevation. Only one of the towers, Echo, could transmit as well as receive. From their research station on Santa Maria the test team could transmit sound toward the surface at various angles, or toward specific topographic features of the ocean bottom, and then receive and record the corresponding echoes.

This was the concept—monumental in scope, yet each of the infinite number of details necessary to convert the idea into reality required its own monumental effort. As a fairly new Sound Lab employee, I was working under my engineering mentor, Mike Tucchio. We were involved with the stress analysis of various components of the tower and the parabolic reflectors, and routinely briefed the project director, Alan Ellinthorpe, who looked to Mike for structural engineering issues, which might affect the progress of AFAR. Ellinthorpe wanted to know about potential bumps in the road well in advance; AFAR was moving ahead, and he was in the driver's seat—I was in the back seat watching the world go by. It was a good place to observe, however, and I learned how a project manager's knowledge, energy, and personality will keep the ball rolling . . . even uphill. When the phone rang during one of our meetings, Ellinthorpe picked up and, in one breath, switched from English to a technical discussion in French. After a brief but lively conversation, the ball kept rolling. Also conversant in German, Italian, Portuguese, and Spanish, he was the right person to control the activities of an international project.

I was impressed, but Mike and I returned to the office, and AFAR sped ahead. The construction of the towers was underway in France, and several ships from various NATO countries were preparing for the installation. Each tower would be connected to the shore station with a heavily armored, four-inch-diameter cable, which carried the acoustic data links and the power needed to operate the azimuth and elevation controls. Each cable, attached near the base of the tower, was coiled in the hold of a ship, and would be run to shore after each of the towers had been lowered to the Sierra, Echo, and November sites.

The seamount plateaus and surrounding bottom topography had been surveyed by the submersible *Alvin* and its support ship, USNS *Mizar* (T-AGOR-11). *Mizar*, outfitted as an oceanographic research ship, had an interesting history, having been involved with the search for *Thresher*, *Scorpion*, and the French submarine *Eurydice*. *Mizar* and *Alvin* had also been sent to locate the H-bomb lost off Spain in January 1966—*Alvin* located the bomb on March 15, with the final recovery accomplished by CURV, the Cable-controlled Underwater Recovery Vehicle.

For the deployment of the AFAR towers, however, the project needed a more impressive submersible. A successful relationship between a project director and his technical staff was evident in a story recently related to me by Lenny Cormier: "I was walking the Sound Lab waterfront and noticed *NR-1* heading upriver to its home at the sub base. Back in the office, I confronted Ellinthorpe. 'If you had any stones, you would call Rickover and tell him you need *NR-1* for AFAR.'" When Lenny made his "suggestion,"

Ellinthorpe's eyes lit up, the gears began to turn, and leadership stepped forward to confront (and run around) obstacles. When he realized that obtaining authorization to use the nuclear-powered deep submergence submarine *NR-1* by struggling up the normal chain-of-command was not an option, Ellinthorpe simply dialed the phone and spoke directly to Admiral Rickover—after all, *NR-1* was his baby. There is an old saying among make-it-happen people who use a tactical approach to solving problems: "Do it now, and beg for forgiveness later." Throughout the entire AFAR program, Ellinthorpe modified this make-it-happen philosophy into a more strategic approach: "Do it now, don't beg for anything—who the Hell needs forgiveness."

By the summer of 1970, the towers had been transported to the Azores (figure 30). They were set afloat horizontally under large pontoons and towed to the site in July, where a flotilla of a dozen ships had assembled. The installation required two ships with heavy-duty rigging to carry the weight of each tower, the base of which would be lowered to swing the tower into a vertical orientation. A third ship would pay out the multi-conductor instrumentation cable, as the tower was slowly lowered to the seamount. Once the tower was on the bottom, the ship would continue to feed the instrumentation cable to shore.

As can be seen in the following photographs, the towers were massive, dwarfing the individuals standing alongside the parabolic acoustic antennas. The rigging and handling procedures had to be executed with precision, regardless of the fact that it would all be accomplished in the open ocean. The NATO vessels involved, however, had plenty of experience working in the Atlantic, and much time had been spent preparing for what was hoped would be a straightforward operation.

Figure 30. *Above:* In preparation for transport to the offshore site, one of the three AFAR towers rests in its lifting bridle next to the French cable ship *Marcel Bayard. Below:* The individuals standing near the parabolic antennas provide a measure of the size of the AFAR installation. (*NUSC/NL*)

The plan was simple—the execution, not so simple. During one installation, a team of French divers was in the water preparing the tower for its deployment. A problem occurred with the lowering cable, and the tower began to free fall, trapping one of the divers when his scuba tanks became caught in the antenna structure. After a brief struggle, he realized that he could not push himself out from under the antenna. The diver no doubt imagined himself being dragged to his death. The tower accelerated through the water, submerging until the slack in the armored shore cable was pulled taught. Although military training can't prepare a diver for every emergency, it does build a level of confidence in the ability to quickly assess and respond to a situation. By the time the tower had stopped its free fall, it had carried the diver to a depth of more than three hundred feet. Finally able to pull himself free, his training kicked into gear and he made a controlled rise to the surface, being careful to exhale throughout the ascent. He did survive the ordeal.

Figure 31. *Above:* The AFAR tower antenna suspended near the surface, as divers check details before the tower is lowered to the seamount a quarter-mile below. *Below:* Divers from several countries worked together on this NATO project. (*NUSC/NL; "Mac" McClenny*)

Divers working on Navy projects are always alert to potentially life-threatening situations and are never sightseeing—the massive AFAR project was a prime example (figure 31). There was a reason I titled chapter 3: "Calm, Cool, and Collected," and emphasized the need for strict diver selection and training.

VIN ET FROMAGE

Within days, the cables to all three towers failed. It was the following summer, in 1971, before they were retrieved and repaired. I was on board the French cable ship *Marcel Bayard* during one of these repair operations, when I fully appreciated the advantages that field engineering had over the cubicle. The French have a very distinct palate and satisfy their taste buds with unique meals, accompanied by carafes of wine. During one memorable meal, we dined on lamb brains, served to us whole on a platter. The next evening, the steward brought us lamb tongues, also stacked neatly on a platter. We later enjoyed meals of tripe and liver. Any parts of the poor animal that couldn't be served whole were diced and stuffed into a sausage, and served with a selection of cheese. I was given a tour of the galley where, over one of the sinks, the hot and cold water faucets now dispensed red and white wine, the steward suggesting that I could take a glass (or a carafe) from a shelf above the sink, and satisfy my thirst whenever the mood struck.

Sober heads and skilled hands must prevail in any major project, however, and by 1971, the three towers were in position and operational. The repaired instrumentation/power cables were laid out from the seamounts, draped across the abyss, and up along the steep sloping sides of Santa Maria. Divers were sent in to secure the shore end with split pipe, fastened permanently to the bottom. When there were underwater tasks, divers from France, Italy, and the U.S. dove right into the project. At various times during the AFAR installation, NUSC sent its own divers, including "Mac" McClenny, Joe Gordon, Ed April, Ken Beatrice, and Bob La Bonte. There were also Seabees and an underwater demolition team on site. Although not from the NUSC team, a diver was sadly lost due to an embolism that occurred while surfacing. He died soon after he was brought to the on-site recompression chamber.

By May 1972, after several months where every phase of the operation depended on hundreds of experienced personnel from multiple countries, the Azores Fixed Acoustic Range was formally inaugurated. In a message specifically directed to NUSC New London, Admiral Elmo R. Zumwalt, Jr., Chief of Naval Operations (CNO) praised AFAR as "a unique accomplishment . . . watched step by step at the highest levels of the Navy Department. This operation reflects excellent planning, extensive coordination and superb execution. All participants are commended for the successful completion of this task."

USS *NAUTILUS* (SSN-571)

While AFAR was being designed, built, and installed, a parallel effort was underway to produce the Mobile Acoustic Communication System (MACS). Mobile was the operative word here, and *Nautilus* had been selected to provide that mobility. An acoustic antenna, identical to that used on the ECHO tower, was installed on the port side of the deck, just aft of the sail, and Mike Tucchio and I were involved from the start.[68] (Figure 32.)

Figure 32. *Above:* USS *Nautilus* underway, heading downriver past NUSC/NL. (*US Navy Photo, Courtesy Roy Manstan*) *Left and Below:* Views of the MACS antenna during installation at Electric Boat. (*NUSC/NL*)

Stepping aboard *Nautilus* in the mid-1970s gave me an appreciation for the impact that a one-of-a-kind installation has, not only on the ship's structure, but on the crew. No one was certain how the massive antenna would affect the operation of the submarine when underway, and no one could guarantee that the stresses in this huge, complex appendage, generated during extreme maneuvers, would remain below the breaking strength of the structure. There was a definite sense of nervousness among everyone involved with MACS, as *Nautilus* was being prepared for the initial sea trials—that two of the engineers, who had helped design this strange structure, were going to be on board did not relieve the tension. Although nothing of this magnitude would ever have been allowed on *Nautilus* without an incredible amount of scrutiny within the Navy, there was still a level of uncertainty among the crew.

All sea trials are designed to put a vessel through a series of maneuvers that represent worst case scenarios, and that would be the case with MACS. For *Nautilus*, a submarine that lives in a three dimensional world, the most important dimension—up and down—took us to its operational depth limit. This was a fairly graceful movement, which had little effect on the MACS antenna, other than compression of its components. Based in part on NUSC recommendations, Electric Boat had installed many (emphasis on many) strain gauges to record the stress in all of the critical components. Mike Tucchio and I alternated twelve-hour shifts, monitoring these measurements, and watching the panel of go/no-go lights from each gauge. After graceful, however, came the not-so-graceful maneuvers referred to as "blow-and-go" (emergency ascent to the surface) and "angles-and-dangles" (rapid high-speed up-angle and down-angle maneuvers), where you hung on to anything within reach. The first set of maneuvers was with the MACS antenna vertical, as in the photo. The sea trial maneuvers were then repeated with the face of the antenna angled upward and downward.

During our return to New London at the end of May 1976, *Nautilus* surfaced, and I had an opportunity to climb up into the sail and look back at the antenna. But to an engineer's eye, there was a beauty in simply watching the symmetry and curve of the bow wave as the boat moved through the water—of all the memories I have of *Nautilus*, the most vivid are those few minutes watching the sea roll by.

The entire AFAR and MACS team at NUSC was relieved (though not as much as we and the crew) that *Nautilus* had safely returned, the sea trials were a success, and the research could begin. Mike and I left and moved on to other projects. NUSC then sent its acoustics team out to sea with confidence in the operation of their antenna. Acoustic propagation through the surface duct, bottom bounce, and convergence zone paths was what AFAR and MACS were all about. ASW sonar for surface ships and submarines is dependent on what are referred to as the boundary conditions—for sonar these "boundaries" are the ocean surface, the base of the isothermal layer, and the ocean bottom.

As AFAR continued to measure the acoustic environment far into the rugged terrain around the Azores, *Nautilus* was off to other areas along the Mid-Atlantic Ridge. When operating along the Blake Plateau, the NUSC team could rotate the MACS antenna in a downward facing angle, toward where the ocean bottom is very flat; then transit north of Bermuda and into the Sargasso Sea, for example, where the antenna could be angled upward toward an ocean surface, which at times can also be very flat. Every project, however, has both a beginning and an end. In early 1977, *Nautilus* operated with MACS in the Gulf of Mexico, and after a year and a half, the experimental work with NUSC was complete.[69] *Nautilus* was decommissioned in 1980—soon to become a museum.

THE ULTIMATE SONAR

Figure 33. Shown here is a single echolocation pulse, repeated in a sequence simulating a portion of a dolphin echolocation pulse train. During an actual echolocation event, each individual pulse is slightly different. (*Roy Manstan*)

The above "quote" was derived from recordings made of our gracious co-investigator Mimi, who contributed her vast experience with echolocation during a series of experiments to document and characterize the ultimate sonar.[70] Mimi, an Atlantic Bottlenose Dolphin (*Tursiops truncatus*) was a resident at the Mystic Marinelife Aquarium during the 1980s, where we had an opportunity to study the uncanny ability of these marine mammals to detect and acquire items within their aquatic environment.

Intense ultrasonic echolocation pulses and frequency modulated (FM) whistles characterize the vocalizations of the world's cetaceans, including this most studied and observed species. For these marine mammals, survival depends on their ability to find a source of food within a vast ocean. Sight alone is insufficient for any creature living in this dark and hazy world. All aquatic species have evolved sensory systems, which enable them to detect the presence of potential prey far afield (or to avoid becoming prey); some species of fish, for example, can follow chemical and electromagnetic gradients directly to their next meal.

As land mammals evolved over eons to an aquatic life, embodied in today's cetaceans, they adapted the unique properties of sound propagation in the sea to provide a means of communication and prey location. Dolphins navigate through their world using their innate ability to transmit a series of extraordinarily high frequency acoustic pulses, which strike obstacles or, hopefully, a school of fish in the distance. Through some biological magic, which continues to baffle scientists, the animal is able to convert the echoes to a mental "image" that enables it to home in and acquire its next meal.

There is, however, no magic behind sonar we produce. Navy sonar, whether "active" (echolocation) or "passive" (listening), is limited by the sophistication of the electronics, which process sounds reaching the sonar sensors—the transducers and hydrophones. The mathematical algorithms that comprise the signal processing are designed to separate extraneous signals from those defining a potential threat, a process known as target acquisition and discrimination.

Target acquisition information hidden in a dolphin's vocalizations may be rooted in "cerebral signal processing." The multiple, precise, "clean" pulses, known as a pulse train, produced by the

Figure 34. *Top:* Former Mystic Aquarium executive director Stephen Spotte (left foreground) discusses the echolocation project with the research team. *Above:* Ken Beatrice (left) and Ross Byrne adjust the data acquisition system as Peter Scheifele works with the bottlenose dolphin, Mimi. (*Bruce Greenhalgh*)

animal propagate through the water, striking the target. The returning signal, or "echo," altered by the object's shape and material properties, now contains subtle variations, which trigger the brain to convert target information into what may be a mental picture. It is tempting to postulate that a dolphin's "imaging" capability is analogous to that of ultrasound technology, where an image is based on the processing of the information in a returning echo.

The experiments we performed, beginning in 1987 at the Mystic Marinelife Aquarium, were designed to record and analyze these echolocation pulse trains, and to define the characteristics of each pulse. Peter Scheifele, then a Navy lieutenant assigned as staff oceanographer at NUSC, was the principal investigator for the project.[71] Pete's scuba background during his early years as a submariner made him ideally suited for his dolphin behavior studies. Our dive team videographer Bruce Greenhalgh joined Pete in the pool to record these behaviors, while data acquisition fell to team members Ken Beatrice and Ross Byrne.

I had known the Aquarium and Sea Research Foundation executive director Steve Spotte for several years, and we had all agreed about the scientific value of the proposed experiment. Prior to this, I had brought the dive team with NUSC acoustician John Cooke to photograph and record the vocalizations of a Commerson's Dolphin (*Cephalorhynchus commersonii*) that had been brought to the Aquarium for rehabilitation. Having already delved into the world of bioacoustics, the Aquarium welcomed Pete and the NUSC dive team, confident in our ability to conduct a safe scientific experiment with their captive dolphins (figure 34). Over the next two years, Pete directed multiple data gathering visits, where the vocalizations of four "test subjects" were recorded while performing various trainer-directed tasks and in different pool environments. Our primary and very cooperative test subject, however, was Mimi.

During one series of tests, Mimi was "asked" through specific signals from her trainer to locate a thin-walled hollow polypropylene ring suspended vertically about eighteen inches below the surface. To ensure that she relied solely on her sonar, she was "blindfolded" using opaque rubber eye-cups, a procedure that the animals readily adapted to. Each measurement "trial" began as soon as Mimi submerged and turned to begin her sonar search, and ended with each successful "acquisition" when she swam her rostrum through the center of the ring.

A high-speed analog tape recorder, connected to a hydrophone hung several feet behind the target, captured all of Mimi's vocalizations—one hundred successful trials were completed. The echolocation recordings showed Mimi's rapid fire series of pulses or "clicks" emitted during her searches. Each click, which may have lasted only 0.05 millisecond (msec), was separated from the next by about 30 msec; thus transmitting 33 clicks per second. Played back at the recorded speed, the pulse trains had the same "static" sound that the divers could hear during the trials. When the replay was slowed by a factor of 32, each distinct click was audible. The individual pulse shown repeated in the "quote" at the beginning of this section (figure 33) is characteristic of the many hundreds that were analyzed from the initial two-second intervals of Mimi's one hundred successful echolocation searches.[72]

We had been offered an opportunity to peer into a window on nature's sonar, its performance evolving to perfection over millennia. With their "ultimate sonar," the acronym for "sound navigation and ranging" is just as applicable to Mimi and her entire species as it is to a Navy sonarman. Yet among Navy acousticians, whose mission is optimizing the ability to locate a potential threat, these marine mammals have instilled a high degree of "sonar envy."

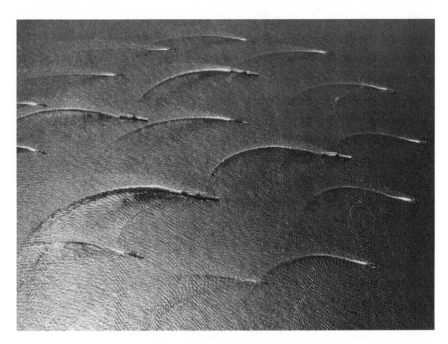

Figure 35. *Above:* Carrier Task Force 77 maneuvering in the South China Sea in 1965. The Cold War strategy of deterrence depended on global maritime superiority, and the aircraft carrier was its messenger. Four carriers shown are (clockwise from the bottom) USS *Ranger, Yorktown, Coral Sea,* and *Hancock.* (*Naval History and Heritage Command*) *Below:* In 1982, Task Group 70 brought the carriers USS *Ranger* (left) and *Midway* into the Philippine Sea. At all times the aircraft carriers were surrounded by a fleet of anti-air and anti-submarine assets, including frigates, destroyers, and guided missile cruisers. (*Department of Defense Photo*)

CHAPTER 5
Antisubmarine Warfare:
A Surface Ship Mission

Antisubmarine warfare (ASW) implies two roles for the hunter—search for the threat, and send it to the bottom. Whether the ASW ship is assigned to a merchant convoy, a carrier battle group (figure 35), a resupply/refueling group, or an amphibious landing operation, its mission is always the same: protect the high value assets.

During their first half century, submarines were diesel-electric powered, requiring lengthy periods on the surface recharging batteries, a process typically done at night. As they hunted submerged during the day, the tools available to ASW ships to accomplish the "search" phase were initially limited to passive "listening" devices called hydrophones. The "destroy" phase was, you guessed it, assigned to "destroyers" armed with depth charges. The implication: before a destroyer could accomplish its task, there had to have been a successful search.

The sinking of *Titanic* in 1911 inspired the development of a system capable of detecting the presence of icebergs at a distance sufficient for the massive vessels to maneuver out of danger. In 1913, a patent application was submitted by Reginald Fessenden for a device that could produce a pulse of high intensity vibration into the water. This energy pulse from the Fessenden Oscillator was designed to propagate through the water, hit an object (hopefully the subsurface mass of an iceberg), and return as an echo to the listening equipment on board the vessel. Fessenden's experiments were successful and his patent was awarded in 1916. But when engineers found that the sound also bounced off the ocean bottom, giving the vessel an indication of water depth, the fathometer was born. Fessenden's invention was the genesis of all echo-ranging devices, eventually leading to its application in submarine detection.

Although the idea of also bouncing a signal off a submarine hull to detect its presence occurred to engineers, echo-ranging was not available during World War I. As early as 1918, the British and French, working together under the Allied Submarine Detection Investigation Committee (ASDIC), had been experimenting with an active system designed by physicist Paul Langevin, but the first hull mounted system was not installed until 1919.

Moderate efforts continued on both sides of the Atlantic, but a peacetime Navy, and a weary public who believed this had been the "War to End All Wars," spent few resources on antisubmarine technology. Besides, it was generally thought that passive listening devices deployed from hydrophone flotillas and destroyers carrying depth charges generally worked well enough to meet any potential submarine issues—another world war was just not on anyone's horizon.

This complacency was shattered with the rise of Nazi Germany during the 1930s. America was deeply engaged in a world-wide depression, and preferred to remain isolated and neutral as war spread across Europe. Germany had been busy creating an efficient war machine and its submarine fleet would once again play a major role, as Adolph Hitler developed a maritime strategy for his Third Reich. But the lessons learned during World War I regarding the effectiveness of an escorted convoy were forgotten, and the U-boat again became a silent menace, causing appalling losses to merchant shipping.

With access to refueling by submarines designed specifically as tankers carrying diesel fuel, a U-boat could now patrol along the Atlantic coast, Caribbean, and Gulf of Mexico. It was May 1942, five months after entering the war, before America once again embraced the convoy. The role of naval warships evolved with the submarine—reluctantly at first—but as the true cost of unrestricted submarine warfare became evident, the convoy and its ASW-capable escorts returned. By 1943, with an average production of 140 Liberty Ships per month, and antisubmarine warfare technology taking hold, the advantage was back into the Allies' court.

"PROBING THE OCEANS FOR SUBMARINES"

As with all "modern" technology, the ideas are rooted in history. So it was with the origin of active sonar after that tragic encounter between an iceberg and *Titanic*. With the growing Nazi threat, adaptations of the Fessenden Oscillator and Langevin's ASDIC sonar were installed on destroyers, as allied navies embraced both passive and active sonar technology. In the United States, the Naval Research Laboratory had developed its QA series sonar that, between 1927 and 1933, was installed on eight destroyers, leading to an improved QC system, which became the operational echo-ranging system at the beginning of World War II.[73]

After President Franklin Delano Roosevelt created the National Defense Research Committee under Vannevar Bush in 1940, sonar development shifted to academic institutions. Columbia University focused on passive sonar at its laboratory in New London, Connecticut, while active sonar development was centered at Harvard's ASW research facilities in Cambridge, Massachusetts. By the end of the war, the sonobuoy and the "Q" series active sonar had all but put the potential submarine threat to rest. Yet the awareness of a strengthening Soviet presence kept ASW on the front burner, and research switched from academic to Navy laboratories. Most notable was the consolidation of the Harvard and Columbia efforts into the Navy's Underwater Sound Laboratory in New London.

The Sound Lab took on both active and passive sonar development for both surface ships and submarines, and was also tasked with radio communications and other electromagnetic issues. Among the many technology pioneers who staffed the Sound Lab during the early years of the Cold War, was Thaddeus "Thad" Bell.[74] In his book, aptly titled *Probing the Oceans for Submarines*, Thad Bell described the decades-long focus of USN/USL and NUSC scientists and engineers . . . a focus that, by the 1970s, would fully engage the efforts of the NUSC divers.

Bell defined in detail, the long process that took an idea from a concept to the eventual implementation of an operational system into the fleet, a 15-year journey. In 1955, William "Bill" Downes, Surface Ship Sonar Department head, assigned Thad Bell the task to develop a conceptual next-generation sonar system that could exploit the surface duct, bottom bounce (BB), and convergence zone (CZ) propagation paths, which had been studied over the previous several years. USN/USL's AMOS project had concentrated on the bottom bounce and surface duct paths, while the Naval Electronics Lab (NEL), San Diego, had focused on convergence zone testing.

Until this time, Navy sonar relied on high frequency, small-sized systems. The higher the frequency, the more that scattering and absorption affected propagation—hence shorter ranges to detection. What Bell and his Sound Lab colleagues understood, was that a lower frequency, higher powered sonar would be required in order to take advantage of the much longer BB and CZ detection paths. The downside of low frequency systems, however, was the requirement for a much larger diameter array.

During World War II, the British ASDIC and U.S. Q-series sonar operated at 20 KHz, and were mechanically rotated in order to direct the sonar toward the sector being searched. As the war drew to a close, the Harvard researchers developed the first "scanning sonar," i.e. one where the array is fixed and the sound is electronically trained in the direction of search. By 1948, this "QHB" sonar was introduced into the fleet. Yet while providing the Navy with a scanning sonar, it operated at 28 KHz, and still provided only limited range. Within two years, the QHB system was replaced with the SQS-10, operating at 20 KHz. In 1954, a series of SQS-4 systems, ranging from 8 to 14 KHz, provided improved detection ranges—thirteen of these would be installed on DE-1006-class ships, the first post-war escort.

In its continuing search for lower frequency systems, the Navy began replacing its SQS-4 with the SQS-23 that operated from 4.5 to 5.5 KHz. This became the sonar of choice for DDG- and DLG-class destroyers, the "G" signifying a guided missile capability. These ships carried the ASROC (antisubmarine rocket), with a range of approximately five nautical miles. Thus, the sonar would need to have a detection range at least that far (10,000 yards), and the SQS-23 fit the bill—just barely, however—squeezing a detection range of 12,000 yards on a good day.

All of these systems were limited to searching within the surface duct, enabling a submarine to hide beneath the thermal layer. The Soviets were racing to create a massive naval fleet, and by 1957, had built 236 Whiskey-class submarines. Concern within the Navy increased in proportion, and the large bow-mounted low-frequency sonar proposed by USN/USL, and spearheaded by Thad Bell, took on a high priority. CNO and BUSHIPS had been considering the design of a "scout ship," but the sonar that USN/USL argued would enable detection of submarines operating beneath the thermal layer, and potentially out to the convergent zone, was too large for the proposed ship. Nonetheless, the Navy decided to move forward with the sonar, designated SQS-26, and in 1958, contracts were awarded for two experimental systems that could be back-fit onto much larger destroyers. Three years later, in 1961, the SQS-26 (XN-1) was installed on USS *Willis A. Lee* (DL-4) and the XN-2 on USS *Wilkinson* (DL-5) the following year.[75]

The next step in the development of a Cold War search and destroy sonar, and one that eventually brought the NUSC dive team on its worldwide mission, was the sonar dome—the physical enclosure within which the transducer array was placed. The SQS-26 array was a 16-foot-diameter, 5.5-foot-tall cylinder mounted at the bow, thus presenting a challenge to ship hull designers and marine architects, who must consider ship speed and propulsion requirements. The SQS-26 was too large to be back-fitted onto existing ships carrying the SQS-23, so entirely new classes of ASW ships had to be designed. This requirement eventually led to the *Knox*-class (FF-1052) frigate and the *Spruance*-class (DD-963) destroyer.

The initial bow-mounted SQS-26 sonar dome was steel, its inner surface supported by a truss-like framework, and early trials were disappointing. The painted surface eroded and exposed the steel to corrosion and marine fouling. An alternative dome was proposed by B.F. Goodrich to replace the steel enclosure with a wire-reinforced rubber acoustic window, produced with a similar concept used for steel belted radial tires.[76] This construction allowed tires to be pressurized and retain their shape—also required for the sonar dome—while being resistant to mechanical damage and puncture. Remember the word "resistant" . . . not impervious.

The SQS-26 dome retained a steel supporting structure above and below the cylindrical array, but was modified to hold the wire-reinforced rubber window, creating a more acoustically transparent aperture. The window was initially referred to as the rubber dome window (RDW).

Because, however, the sonar dome was not entirely rubber, the portion that wrapped around the array was later, and more aptly, renamed the Sonar Dome Rubber Window, or SDRW.

The first B.F. Goodrich SDRW was installed on *Willis A. Lee* in 1965 (figure 36). Promising results were obtained during initial tests

in August 1966, but additional evidence was needed before the Navy would agree to this very expensive modification. Ship "self-noise," i.e. sources of noise from machinery and the propeller, was also a limiting factor. In March 1972, USS *Bradley* (DE-1041) sported a brand new SDRW. *Bradley* also carried a self-noise mitigation system known as the "Prairie Masker," where the ship could produce a bubble screen in the vicinity of the propeller and across the surface of the hull, where noise-producing machinery was located.

Figure 36, *Top and Bottom:* USS *Willis A. Lee* (DL-4) in dry-dock after installation of first Sonar Dome Rubber Window (SDRW) in 1965. *Center left:* Removal of original steel sonar dome. *Center right:* The new SDRW in its shipping frame positioned for installation around the SQS-26 sonar array. (*USN/ USL; Courtesy Fort Trumbull State Park*)

The improvement in sonar performance brought by the SDRW and the Prairie Masker, during testing on *Bradley* in the summer of 1972, was extraordinary. In 1973, a side by side comparison was made between USS *Knox* (DE-1052) outfitted with an SDRW, and USS *Kirk* (DE-1087) with its steel dome. The two ships were told to hunt within the CZ for USS *Guitarro* (SSN-665), operating north of the Hawaiian Islands. Both sonar domes were groomed to remove any imperfections and marine fouling, giving both equal initial conditions.

The ability to detect an echo was dependent on the level of ship self-noise around the dome. After several days of testing, the noise levels for *Kirk* were found to be significantly greater than *Knox*. The testing also demonstrated that *Knox*, with its rubber window, successfully conducted sonar searches at speeds up to 22 knots, while *Kirk* only reached 12 to 15 knots before self-noise masked target echoes. This meant that an SDRW-equipped ASW ship could search the CZ at high speed, an essential ingredient for an effective escort.[77]

The significance of this capability was captured in a comment by John Merrill: "ASW surface ships, typically employed in search and destroy, carrier group escort, and convoy protection operations, must travel at speeds of 15 knots or more."[78] Escort protection placed a defensive bubble around the high value asset—a picket ship and aerial searches may operate as far as 200 miles from the center, while close-in ASW protection could run along as much as a 25 nautical mile radius. A third level of protection was also provided, primarily for anti-aircraft and missile defense. The entire group, and in particular the ASW ships, had to operate at an optimum speed. A conventional 1950s Soviet Whiskey-class submarine was capable of 15 to 20 knots, while their nuclear powered attack subs were able to run at 25 to 30 knots, although the November-class that came on line around 1960, could reach 33 knots.[79] Being able to search the CZ well above 20 knots led to the final decision to specify the SQS-26 (and its SQS-53 successor) with an SDRW for all *Knox*- and *Spruance*-class ships. Acoustics, not just distance, could now determine the best route across the Atlantic Ocean.

A SYSTEM OF SYSTEMS

System Engineering—by its very nature, the word "system" unavoidably occurs multiple times in any sentence related to this engineering field . . . so *please bear with me*. The phrase "system of systems" is used to indicate that a complex system, no matter what the technology, is often comprised of multiple components, each of which is a system in itself and each of these built from a set of interactive subsystems. A naval vessel, for example, carries multiple systems, each critical to its mission—there are the ship's propulsion system, its communication systems, its weapons systems, its sonar systems, to name a few—each system, and its subsystems, kept at peak operational readiness by the ship's crew.

Occasionally, however, the ship would report that a critical system (sonar, for example) was OOC—out of commission—and beyond the capability of the crew to correct. Sonar, one of those "system of systems," consists of multiple subsystems: the signal processing, the array transducers (there are 572 of them on the SQS-53 sonar), the sonar dome pressurization and airlock, and the Sonar Dome Rubber Window. The Navy has always maintained teams of experts from its civilian workforce and from the private industries that build each subsystem—for the SDRW, this role fell primarily to NUSC and B.F. Goodrich.

The SDRW was designed to provide an acoustically transparent surface (the "window") that allowed sound to pass through this interface between the sonar and the ocean environment. If there were scratches on your window at home, visibility into your backyard would be degraded; if there were imperfections on the surface of the acoustic window, the ability of the ship's sonar to detect a target would likewise be degraded. The significance of the SDRW as a sonar subsystem was proven during the *Knox* testing in 1973, when it was shown that sonar performance was severely affected by the condition of the sonar dome surface and by the ship's speed—critical to an ASW ship hunting for a fast-moving submarine. The acoustic "transparency" of the SDRW would become a critical mission for our dive team.

Flow noise over the dome surface, however, was only one factor associated with sonar performance. There were also sources of a ship's self-noise from onboard machinery and the propeller, and ambient noise related to wind-generated sea states. Many sea trials were conducted to measure these noise sources. The Prairie Masker system and sound-mitigating baffles within the dome were designed to minimize their effect. Much of the data collected while a ship was underway, however, was a mixture of sound from all sources at once. An experiment was designed to isolate the effects by simulating individual noise sources with a calibrated transducer suspended at various locations under the hull with the ship at anchor. So off we went—to the warm tropical waters of Puerto Rico.

A YELLOW BIKINI—(#)

It was a scenic drive from San Juan to the Roosevelt ("Rosey") Roads Naval Station, and we beat the Hell out of our rental car getting there. With plenty of time to spare, we had driven the coast route along dirt roads, across a river on a rope ferry, and over the switchbacks up and down Puerto Rico's highlands. It was 1976, and we had a beautiful August day to enjoy the countryside. Our travel orders called for us to rendezvous with a team of NUSC engineers at the naval station, and ride USS *Trippe* (FF-1075) to an off shore anchorage. There, we would spend three days conducting acoustic measurements with the ship's sonar.

To our surprise, when we arrived at the gate, security personnel were unaware of the ship, and as far as they knew there were no vessels at the pier. Nonetheless, they gave us directions with our vehicle pass, and we were off to the waterfront. Rosey Roads was a sprawling naval facility (now closed), and we took our time to scout the two most important locations on any base—the exchange and the chief's club. We finally turned onto the waterfront and could see the long pier in the distance . . . but no ship. In fact, the waterfront was ominously void of any activity—no ships, no vehicles, no groups of sailors milling about—the place just seemed to be abandoned.

"Over there!!!" Ken pointed to a lone figure off in the distance.

We didn't think that the uniform-of-the-day was a bright yellow bikini, but sure enough, we were approaching an absolutely delightful young lady. She turned with a smile, as we pulled alongside (some things you never forget). We were concerned that the ship had been there, but may have left without us, so we asked if she had seen any activity at the pier.

"Sorry, boys, the pier's been empty for some time . . . park over there. Some of the guys might know."

She pointed to a massive, concrete cube-shaped building that was probably a relic from World War II. Okay, it was time to go to work, so we parked and followed our curvy guide through a small door at the side of the building. It took a few seconds for our eyes to adapt to the dim light as she led us to an interesting structure at the far corner, oddly built in the form of an outside bar you might find at a Caribbean resort.

"Hey, Lenny," she greeted the sailor behind the bar. "These guys are looking for a ship."

"Won't find one in here . . . just booze. My name's Lenny, how 'bout a beer." We shook hands and took a few swallows from the Heinekens he passed us. Had we died and gone to Heaven? Here we were, at a Navy base, in a dimly lit concrete bunker, sitting on bar stools in a Tiki hut next to a beautiful young lady wearing more skin than clothes.

Lenny was medium height, round face, crew cut, stocky but tough. He poured himself some gin (no beer for Lenny) and we talked. He was friendly, but cautiously inquisitive until we explained that we were divers from New London and were going to be operating off shore—if, that is, the ship ever showed up. Once he learned that we were divers, the information (and beer) flowed freely. Although my memory is about as dim as the light in the Tiki hut, I seem to recall that Lenny was from SEAL Team 2 and was on the island with UDT 21 where they were all on training missions (underwater demolition teams were phased out in 1983, when all Navy Special Operations Forces were consolidated within the SEALs). There were a lot of divers on the island that summer, including a group from the Experimental Diving Unit (EDU) evaluating the new MK 15 rebreather.

Lenny explained that the building was an abandoned helicopter hanger, and they had taken it over for the duration of their stay on the island. The bar was simply their home away from home, and we were welcome to stay with them . . . there were plenty of bunks in the back room. We immediately called the hotel, cancelled our reservations, and moved in. After all, the pier was right across the road.

The Tiki hut occupied about one-quarter of the hanger, and was a substantial wide-open post and beam structure, with waist-high walls and a roof made from palm leaves. The first of two rooms offered a visitor the choice of lounging on a couch set to the left of the entrance, or settling onto one of several bar stools and catching up on the day's diving activities with Lenny. In the right-hand corner behind the bar was a makeshift waterfall. At the top, a hose slowly fed water into a pivoting trashcan lid held in position by a spring. When full, the lid would tip, dumping the water downhill over a moss and rock covered trough and into a drain, while the spring pulled the trashcan lid back for a refill. Next to the waterfall was a stainless refrigerator—access was on the honor system. You wrote your name on the sign-up sheet, put a check mark when you took a beer, and paid your tab whenever you had the dollars in your pocket. The adjacent room contained another couch, a pair of easy-chairs, and a card table. We adapted quickly. Grabbed a beer, put a mark next to our name, settled into comfort, and from time to time checked the pier for activity.

That evening after finding a spicy meal in the nearby town of Ceiba, we headed back to the Tiki hut for a nightcap. It was a quiet evening and we got a good night's sleep, as most of the divers were off on a training operation. We awoke to find our ship approaching the pier. So we hung out, watching *Trippe* tie up, and waited to introduce ourselves and beg for breakfast.

TIME TO GO TO WORK

It was late morning when we heard a familiar voice, "We weren't sure if you guys had made it!" It was Jim Senkow, one of the project engineers from NUSC. He hadn't seen us at the hotel and was worried that his divers were lost somewhere on the island. Not wanting to expose the Tiki hut, my response was simple. "We got a room on base," and that was that. It was time to go to work. We helped load the electronics into the sonar spaces, and while they hooked everything up, we made preparations for diving— tagged out the propeller, fathometer, suctions, and the sonar. We hung a Jacob's ladder over the side and suited up, a simple matter in the warm tropical water, where a "wetsuit" consisted of a T-shirt and the standard issue UDT trunks all Navy divers wore—topside or in the water.

Our job that day was to "dry run" the system. We hung the rigging over the side and moved the transducer into its initial position, then came to the surface while the test team fired up the sound source and checked the electronics on board. If the data acquisition system was operating as expected, we moved the transducer to the next of several locations. The process was going to take a couple hours, and the spicy dinner, lengthy nightcap, and greasy breakfast began to take a toll on my interior.

The current Navy Dive Manual was supposed to prepare divers for any emergency, but intestinal panic had not been covered since the 1905 edition provided the following warning: "He should empty his bladder and, if the diving is to continue for any length of time, relieve his bowels before going down, as the increased pressure will not only cause great inconvenience, but probably disagreeable consequences if this precaution is neglected." The suggestion, of course, was for hard hat divers wearing a full diving dress, in which there *would* be very "disagreeable consequences" if the diver found it necessary to "relieve his bowels." My situation, however, was an easy one to resolve.

"Ken . . . stay put . . ." was my warning as I swam under the pier, and at a comfortable distance, lowered my UDT trunks. What a relief! I no longer had to pinch my cheeks together each time we returned to move the transducer to its next position. I now understand why a baby smiles when he poops in the bath tub.

Later that afternoon, while the test team continued to play with their electronics, we charged our scuba bottles, brought our gear on board, and then "checked out" of our room at the Tiki hut. We told Lenny we'd be back in three days, parked our rental car next to the building, and walked down the pier.

The weather was on our side this trip. Once at anchor, Ken and I immediately set to our task. The sun was high in the sky, and the sea was rather calm, considering we were far off shore and in the open ocean. We couldn't wait to cool off. It's a long drop from the ship's fantail, but nothing could delay us making the jump. Being accustomed to diving in New England, where water visibility is often measured in inches, we were unprepared for the sensation of being suspended—neutrally buoyant—in a fluid medium with an infinite horizon. No wonder astronauts trained under similar conditions, where neutral buoyancy simulated the weightlessness of space.

Soon, the J-13 transducer, a high-powered acoustic source designed to transmit at specific frequency ranges, was lowered to us. The ability of a ship to track a legitimate target was affected by machinery and propeller noise radiating into the water, and propagating forward across the array. The test plan called for the J-13 to be placed in the vicinity of these sources (figure 37), enabling the test team to correlate the simulated noises with

Figure 37. NUSC diver Ken Beatrice aligns the J-13 acoustic source beneath USS *Trippe* (FF-1075) anchored off Puerto Rico. (*Roy Manstan*)

the output from the sonar array. It was our responsibility to understand the critical nature of the installation, and to give the test director confidence in the accuracy of the setup underwater.

Our participation in the experiment, however, was not limited to the water. Once we climbed the Jacob's ladder and dried off, we put on our engineer hat and set to the task of collecting data. The data acquisition electronics had been installed as far forward in the bow as possible, just above the sonar dome—as the anchored ship slowly pitched and rolled, Ken and I, only mildly susceptible to sea sickness, were frequently asked to take a shift in the small, confined compartment.

On the third day at sea, and with all test objectives completed, we were able to return to the pier by early afternoon. Ken and I stood along the rail waiting for the ship to set the brow, while the NUSC engineers carefully dismantled and packed the electronics. Our feet were the first to touch the pier, and they took us running to our friends at the Tiki hut. After a three day dry spell, we sucked down three beers in record time. Lenny smiled, leaned forward and whispered, "Toga party . . . tonight . . ."

Now energized with a soft buzz and a party in the wind, we returned to the ship, ready to help off-load the gear. When Jim Senkow and his crew began moving their equipment onto the pier and into our rental car, a quizzical expression gave away his curiosity at these lightly toasted divers. As I drove him to the head of the pier where his vehicle was parked, he looked around at the desolate waterfront and finally asked: "Okay, how'd you do it . . . it's only been a half hour since we pulled in!"

"When a diver gets thirsty, there's always a way." There was nothing about the old concrete building, or my reply, that shed light on where we had been. Maybe Jim figured we had dashed off to the chief's club, but a little mystery is a good thing, and even to this day, the existence of the Tiki hut has remained a secret. We stood and waved as they drove off, waiting until the car was out of sight before checking in with Lenny, back from a training mission and already making plans for a busy weekend. The divers had been gathering aquatic cumshaw, which was about to be traded for steaks on the ship. With Lenny dressed as Julius Caesar, the toga party lasted thirty-six hours, ending with an Olympic-sized surf and turf cookout. We did manage to make it back to New London, in spite of the fact that we missed our flight by two days.

SIX-HUNDRED SHIP NAVY

Two hundred years after David Bushnell launched the world's first combat submarine, America claimed superiority in the world of submarine warfare—a claim based on continually improving and maintaining an effective antisubmarine capability in the midst of the Cold War. By the mid 1970s, with the SQS-26 installed on multiple ships, the U.S. Navy was able to remain one step ahead of the Soviet submarine, and the NUSC dive team stood front and center. As the decade came to a close, and anxiety over the Cold War increased, the Republican Party began to flex its international muscle, when announcing a strategy of national security through maritime superiority—a plank in the Republican platform included the goal of creating a six-hundred-ship Navy.

With Ronald Reagan's election in 1980, implementation of this policy of maritime superiority fell to his newly appointed Secretary of the Navy, John F. Lehman, Jr. In his book *Command of the Seas*, Lehman quotes a December, 1982 speech by President Reagan where he stressed how the Soviet Union, with its borders along Europe and Asia, had "created a powerful blue ocean navy that cannot be justified by any legitimate defense need. It is a navy built for offensive action, to cut the free world supply lines and render impossible the support by sea of free world allies." Reagan pointed out that "our navy is designed to keep the sea lanes open worldwide . . . Maritime superiority for us is a necessity."[80] To accomplish this, he announced that the U.S. would be "building a six-hundred-ship fleet, including fifteen carrier battle groups." The role of many of Reagan's 600 ships would be providing escort protection to these carrier groups, keeping the sea lanes viable for commerce during peacetime, and maintaining support to free-world allies when engaged in regional or global conflicts.

Deterrence rather than engagement, however, was the ultimate goal, and the Soviets our overt antagonist. As Secretary of the Navy, Lehman encouraged maximizing the incorporation of high-tech systems for maintaining this superiority over an ever-increasing Soviet naval capability—emphasizing that a threat by the United States to retaliate in the face of a nuclear attack must be believable. For scientists and engineers within the Navy's research and development community, this was an invitation to move ahead as fast as possible. Although we were part of a Cold War Navy, the spirit of teamwork and appetite for innovation during a cold war had all of the elements that surface when engaged in a hot one. The SQS-26 sonar was one of many ASW systems created with that combination of teamwork and innovation, filling the halls of all the buildings on the New London Laboratory campus.

Thad Bell related an observation from long-time USN/USL sonar engineer, Frank White: "This solid piece of mechanical engineering—the sonar rubber dome—was far more effective in increasing sonar performance than all the other electronic improvements taken together."[81] But as with any "solid piece of engineering," the rubber window came with a price. The excellent high speed performance was predicated on the low self-noise that a hydrodynamically smooth exterior surface provides. The quiet boundary layer could be disrupted by minor imperfections at critical locations, on and adjacent to the SDRW surface—the faster the ship went, the greater was the impact on performance. A thumbnail sized cut into the surface would not be noticeable below 15 knots, but as speed increased, water flow over the surface could lift the edges of a cut, creating a localized noise-producing effect characterized by a cluster of tiny bubbles called cavitation. The extent of the cavitation increased with increasing speed, to a point where the sonar became "blind" across a wide sector. Referred to as a "noise spoke," a ship's ASW capability, hence its escort function, became significantly impaired.

The SDRW provided an acoustically transparent aperture in both azimuth and elevation over the bearings that the sonar was designed to cover. The window, as much as eight feet high, wrapped around the sixteen-foot-diameter array, and extended about thirty-seven feet aft. When an inch-long imperfection created a blind spot, two questions were immediately passed to the divers: "Can you find it and can you fix it?" A sonarman could determine the general area, but when the ship is at rest, the cut would lay flat, only creating the cavitation effect when underway at high speed. With no way to pinpoint the location of the source of cavitation, a diver would be asked to search an area on the port or starboard side, which could be as much as one hundred square feet—that meant searching 14,400 square inches for a 1-inch cut (figure 38). Although some damage was obvious, finding that tiny cut could be an impossible job.

Figure 38. NUSC divers Ken Beatrice (foreground) and Kurt Hansen search for damage to a Sonar Dome Rubber Window in clear Caribbean water. Most inspections, however, occur under conditions where visibility is measured in inches rather than feet. (*Roy Manstan*)

NUSC acousticians theorized that a "spoke localization" procedure could be devised, where a ship's sonar could triangulate on the cavitation while the ship was underway at the speed at which the cavitation initiated. These scientists and engineers were certain that the location of a noise source could be precisely determined using the signal processing system, by isolating cavitation noise received by individual transducers in the array. For a dive team consisting of engineers and technicians whose daily lives revolved around the concept of sonar, and the implications of even the slightest degradation in performance, we jumped at the chance to prove this theory, when proposed to us during the summer of 1978. Besides, we were going to work with Jim Senkow and Henry D'Amelia, whose company we enjoyed at Rosey Roads a couple years earlier.

Our job was to provide a method to simulate cavitation at multiple locations on the surface of a sonar dome. One of our divers, Ken Beatrice, designed a fixture to hold a small noise-generating hydrophone at a precise one-half-inch standoff from the dome surface. We had also devised a system for mapping the surface in order to mark locations where the acousticians wanted the cavitation source placed. With the ship pierside, the same signal processing system would be used to locate the simulated cavitation, as would be used by a ship troubleshooting cavitation while underway.

USS *Comte de Grasse* (DD-974) was selected as the test ship. Its six-day availability in October 1978, at Port Everglades in Fort Lauderdale, Florida, provided an ideal location to conduct the experimental procedure. With Mac topside running the show, Jim Clark, Ray Munn and Ken and I logged over 40 hours in the water, while Jim Senkow, Henry D'Amelia, and the rest of the acoustics team were on board collecting enough data to keep them busy (and happy) all winter. The Navy now had a tool that could provide a diver with the location of a minor imperfection within a 10-inch diameter circle.

A less frequent issue, though more serious, was the occasional structural failure of the SDRW. Once a rupture occurred, the window, like a flat tire, could no longer hold pressure. The ship would have to reduce its speed to a crawl, or risk expanding the rupture and tearing back the rubber that protects a multi-million-dollar sonar array. The next step was to assess the damage, and then find a friendly port with a dry-dock capable of handling an SDRW replacement—or devise a field repair that would allow the ship to return to its mission.

Whether it was an acoustic blind spot or a structural failure, the battle group had lost one piece of its protective bubble, exposing a serious vulnerability. Over the next several years, our divers worked with active duty dive teams and with NAVSEA, SURFLANT, SURFPAC, and with the builder, B.F. Goodrich developing materials and procedures for what became known as "acoustic grooming" of the SDRW. In the world of antisubmarine warfare, a ship's sonar was the tip of the spear, and it needed to be sharpened. Sometimes this meant "act now, beg for forgiveness later," and the risk takers stepped forward.

STAN SILVERSTEIN

On February 19, 1981, NUSC divers made the first visit to a ship with a damaged SDRW—USS *David R. Ray* (DD-971), at the Navy base in San Diego. We had no idea that the name "Stan Silverstein" would open doors and get people's attention, no matter where in the world this new assignment would take us over the next half-decade. A week earlier in Washington, we met Stan at NAVSEA Code 63J to discuss SDRW issues. Every phone call—every CASREP (casualty report)—related to sonar dome issues was addressed to SEA 63J. The growing concern over recent structural failures and the persistent acoustic blind spots had sparked the creation of the Failure Analysis Team (FAT). Most of us, who considered ourselves "lean and mean," were uneasy about being referred to as the FAT team, and were pleased when the name changed to the Corrective Action Team (CAT). I would, however, have been happy with using both—a FAT/CAT.

Team members were drawn from Navy labs, industry, academia, and the military—all focused on evaluating the cause of these failures, and finding solutions. Was it the basic design and construction of the window itself, were the procedures for its shipyard installation responsible, or were SDRW failures caused by excess stresses generated during at-sea operations? Whether the SDRW had experienced a minor performance degradation or catastrophic failure, the problem often occurred during a deployment far from its home port. The ship would issue a CASREP that arrived on Stan Silverstein's desk.

Under Stan's direction the CAT was expected to pounce on the problem—no delays, no excuses. The Navy, and all branches of the military for that matter, always expected a level of readiness from the active duty warfighter, as well as their civilian technologists. When an emergent issue arose that degraded the ability to conduct a mission, whether in a Cold War or a hot one, a fast response was simply expected. All of the organizations participating in Stan's CAT had individuals on staff with their bags packed, in anticipation of the next CASREP, and the NUSC dive team was high on the list. Our role, as it was for the other responders, had two goals. First, we were to immediately assess the damage, phone Stan with our observations, and issue a situation report (SITREP) from the ship. Second, we were expected to complete a field repair that would enable the ship to return to its carrier escort role, or any mission for which the ship had been deployed. Once a ship was back on line, a casualty correction (CASCOR) message was issued—all heading for Stan's desk.

Certainly, our first priority was recovering a ship's sonar capability, but the long term goal was collecting physical data, and acquiring a photographic record of the damage as soon after it occurred as possible. The CAT engineers, scientists, and acousticians who were responsible for the development of the sonar and the SDRW, all depended on an accurate and timely failure analysis. The results would impact the system design, and provide a basis for recommending changes in its operational use.

As a Navy dive team, we considered the need for fast response to be a personal responsibility. Our Command, the Naval Underwater Systems Center/New London Laboratory, also considered the task to be a first priority. Every system, be it for surface ships or submarines, which NUSC was responsible for, had groups like ours—divers and non-divers— who were ready and on call. Because of this attitude, individual and organizational, nothing stood in the way of enabling fast response teams to perform any and all mission commitments—there's a reason the Navy uses the term "Tiger Team."

JULIE—WITH THANKS

The SOP (standard operating procedure) for members of a NUSC Tiger Team would start with being handed a classified CASREP, describing the issue, the location of the ship, and a list of our points-of-contact. Turn-around response could be less than 24 hours. After a brief visit with Julie Horr at the travel office . . . "Okay, Roy, where to this time?" . . . our itinerary was established and we were issued plane tickets. Julie could find creative ways to fly us to unusual destinations anywhere in the world. Among the more memorable were the Philippines, Liberia, Oman, Bahrain, Singapore, and Scotland. Just prior to our scheduled return from the Orkney Islands, where we had been diving on USS *Comte de Grasse* (DD-974), we learned that another ship had issued a CASREP. A call to Julie from Scapa Flow, and in a few minutes, she cancelled our return to Groton, and we (Jim Clark and I) were diverted to the Azores, where we would join other members of Stan Silverstein's CAT, and a dive team from Norfolk, on board USS *Moinester* (FF-1097).

But Julie was only one of the many support personnel at NUSC who were true enablers—who knew how to make the impossible possible. They took the administrative stress out of our hands, and allowed us to concentrate on the next mission. This was true of the procurement folks, the shipping department, the transportation and rigging department, and the machine shop. You can imagine how complicated our travel claims became—I was never sure how to explain to the gals in disbursing, the bribes we had to use to get in or out of countries. And thank God for the department secretaries, who ran interference when we might stray from the straight and narrow. The list of people in New London who were on our side was endless. But these folks never receive the recognition they deserve when histories are written. So—to Julie, and every one of you—thanks!

BANK STREET CAFÉ

Creativity was the name of the game, and there were times when operations planning had to shift to a more creative setting. We had established a long relationship with Lucky, the owner of the Bank Street Café, just around the corner from NUSC. His grandfather was a diver during World War II, and often joined us at the table Lucky reserved for these "briefings" in the far corner of the Café. To give our gatherings a modicum of credibility, we would encourage our branch head, Sarandos "Sandy" Traggis, to join us. Sandy loved blues music, and for that, the Bank Street Café was the local go-to bar—it took little inducement to assemble an "official meeting."

Being "on call" to respond to a CASREP required that we be available at a moment's notice. In an age without cell phones, that meant giving the Café phone number to a few trusted souls, who looked out for our interests (watch your back, as it is sometimes called). Jo Ann Bollinger, one of our buddies who would have a pretty good idea how to find us, reminded me recently how she often had to "call the Bank Street Café to interrupt your 'meetings' just to tell you that some Captain was trying to reach you." So, I add Jo Ann and Sandy and Lucky and his grandfather to the list of "enablers" who kept our dive team front and center.

THE AYATOLLAH—(#)

In 1981, our first few months as members of Stan Silverstein's Corrective Action Team were spent becoming familiar with all the players. We were called twice to San Diego, where we met with SURFPAC and began troubleshooting three ships that had reported cavitation noise. The ships had used the localization procedures NUSC developed in 1978, and we were able to quickly find and correct the problems. A run to Norfolk that spring gave us our first view of a ruptured SDRW. Repair procedures were still being developed at B.F. Goodrich, so this trip was simply an opportunity to meet with SURFLANT and to see the damage, while the ship waited for a dry-dock availability. It became evident that being able to provide a waterborne structural repair, even if just a temporary fix, could save the Navy the hundreds of thousands of dollars it would cost for an unscheduled docking.

So far, our involvement had been relatively routine, bringing us to naval bases on both coasts, and we were anxious for something more challenging. It would be a short wait. Word of our first overseas assignment arrived at the end of June and brought us to a small country just outside the Straits of Hormuz. Oman remains a friend to the U.S. in the Arab world, but we were still strangers in a culture very unfamiliar to us. Across the Straits, Ayatollah Khomeini rose to power in 1979, after the Shah of Iran was deposed during the Islamic Revolution. When we arrived in Muscat on July 1, 1981, it had been less than six months since Iran released a group of American hostages, just after President Reagan's inauguration. But the political atmosphere had calmed, and there was no issue with bringing a U.S. ship, or us for that matter, to Oman. Jim Clark and I had obtained visas from the Omani embassy in Washington, where we were received with the courtesy afforded visitors by the embassy staff.

For this repair, we wouldn't have access to the resources of the largest naval bases in the U.S.—we were about to understand the "make it happen" approach. We were joined on this trip by Stan Silverstein and B.F. Goodrich representative Jon Golden, as this would be our first attempt at a field repair of a ruptured SDRW. We caught a taxi from the airport in Muscat, the capitol of Oman, to the port of Mina Qaboos (named for the country's leader, Sultan Qaboos bin Said al Said) down the coast, where USS *Fanning* (FF-1056) waited for us. The July heat was a shock to a pair of New Englanders, and we wondered how Portuguese military units survived back in the seventeenth century, living in the small stone forts that lined the barren rock cliffs—bleak outposts from a time when European countries vied for control of maritime trade routes along the southern coast of the Arabian Peninsula.

But we were only going to be there for ten days—not ten months or ten years—so the sooner we could start, the better. Besides, with air temperature approaching 120 °F, the thought of a refreshing jump into the harbor was on our minds. Jim and I had brought scuba bottles, but a compressor was coming with a Navy dive team still en route from Diego Garcia. We were, as usual, in a hurry to start, so Jim went to a military base used by a British mercenary corps to check if they had a compressor, while I had the ship tagged for diving . . . or snorkeling, if Jim was unsuccessful.

The heat was excruciating and we were anxious to make the first jump—but there was to be no relief with that initial splash. While we waited for the dive team from USS *Samuel Gompers* (AD-37) to arrive, Jim and I made our inspection dive. None of us had any idea that the harbor water temperature in July was going to be 100 °F. Over a three decade diving career, this would be the one and only dive operation where we would be concerned about <u>hyp</u>erthermia. <u>Hyp</u>othermia, on the other hand, was easy to avoid. A good wetsuit or drysuit provided plenty of protection, but when water temperature rose above your body temperature, there was no convenient protection. We tried to minimize exposure, and then headed to an air conditioned space on board.

Our inspection revealed that the rupture may have grown during transit, and was nearly four feet long. There was nothing we could do until the rest of the dive team arrived, but it gave Jim and me a chance to discuss repair options with Stan Silverstein and Jon Golden. The dive team arrived on the 4th of July, and after making the joint decision to proceed in spite of the magnitude of the damage, we began the following day (figure 39).

The Sonar Dome Rubber Window was constructed of multiple layers of wire reinforced rubber plies. When pressurized, these strength plies maintained the window's hydrodynamic shape. The entire SDRW was then covered with a single ply that contained an imbedded antifouling compound. This first experimental repair was

Figure 39. *Above:* Divers from NUSC and USS *Samuel Gompers* on the Oman waterfront prepare to repair the SDRW on USS *Fanning.* (*US Navy Photo; Stanley Silverstein*) *Below:* Jim Clark measures a blister on the dome surface, an indication of an imminent rupture. (*Roy Manstan*)

designed to bond two layers of individual strength ply patches over the rupture, adding a final cover ply with the antifouling properties. The whole bonding operation required a continuous twenty-four-hour operation. Working with the *Gompers* divers, Jim and I alternated four-hour shifts, cooling off in one of the air conditioned spaces during the time we had between shifts. Under Master Chief Gary Decker's efficient direction, all of the underwater operations went without a hitch. We then waited another twenty-four hours, while the underwater epoxy cured sufficiently for a pressure test.

Jim was in the water during the dome pressurization, looking for signs of leaks or delamination of the repair plies. The dome was pressurized in increments, and all was proceeding as hoped, until Jim surfaced and signaled for the pressure test to be stopped. The repair was holding, but a blister had appeared at another location on the dome surface (figure 39). We surmised that there must have been a second break in the SDRW that hadn't ruptured through the outer ply. I went in briefly and took a few photos of the blister, while Jim stayed as they resumed the pressure test. Our patch held just fine, but the blister grew until it finally broke through.

Some of the broken wires had tell-tale corrosion, while the majority appeared clean, and likely had only recently parted. Our conclusions were that the initial rupture was small, as indicated by the small section with corroded wires, but the transit to Oman had extended the size of the split, and weakened the adjacent area. Later recommendations included requiring that any ship that experienced a dome pressure alarm transit more slowly to port, and as soon after the rupture occurred as possible. This precaution ensured any subsequent damage would be minimal and more readily repaired, and we could provide a better evaluation of the cause of the rupture.

The extent of the second rupture on the *Fanning* dome precluded any expectation of making a field repair, and it was time to pack and head home—but this would not be an easy task. Just before we planned to leave, political turmoil in Iran briefly escalated, and all communications (and travel) in and out of the Arab world came to a halt. News reports back in Connecticut detailed the unrest brought on by events in Iran, and the hostage memory was still fresh. We were stranded, with no opportunity to contact families at home. The uncertainties associated with a commitment to provide a fast response team was a tough road for families. The *Fanning* experience may have been unusual, but it was indicative of never knowing the "when, where, or how long" for each of these missions.

NEVER AGAIN

Like a hangover, our first thought after *Fanning* was "never again." But as with any hangover, it wears off and the thirst returns. After a bit of rehabilitation and a debriefing at the Bank Street Café, we were ready— naturally drawn to the challenges, and fed by a spirit of adventure, 1981 became a busy year for us. We were soon heading off to the first of several trips to the naval base in the Philippines—then that trip to *Comte de Grasse* in the Orkney Islands and *Moinester* in the Azores, and a run to Pascagoula to check out USS *Spruance* (DD-963). That took us through August and September, when we found ourselves on our way to another spot on the Globe—Liberia for USS *Conyngham* (DDG-17). From there, we occupied the fall with two ships at the naval base in Charleston, South Carolina; then off to the West Indies for two more ships in St. Croix, another in St. Barthélemey—finally rounding out 1981 with a run to Guantanamo, Cuba, where we once again worked on *Spruance*. For most of the operations that year, we were supported by a dive team from the Readiness Support Group (RSG), Norfolk, led by Master Diver Ralph Hernandez.

WHEN LIVES ARE AT RISK

For sonar to operate at a high enough power to transmit a pulse out to the CZ, the water immediately in contact with the array must be at a higher pressure than the ambient water surrounding the dome. For this reason, and to maintain its hydrodynamic shape, the interior of the sonar dome is pressurized. While the operational consequences of a ruptured dome are obvious, as was the case with *Fanning*, concerns about these structural failures extend beyond the loss of sonar capability.

The sixteen-foot-diameter cylindrical array is composed of 72 vertical "staves," each carrying eight individual transducer elements. Occasionally, one or more of these 576 transducers fails, requiring replacement. Provisions had been incorporated in the original SQS-26 design to accomplish this and other routine maintenance issues, with the ship pierside. The procedure requires removing the water from the dome, but in order to keep the flexible rubber window from collapsing, the process also requires pressurizing the interior with air to a value above external ambient pressure. An access trunk with upper and lower airlock hatches allows personnel to enter and work in the pressurized dome. The SQS-26 is set back from the bow by several feet but there is little space around the sides of the array for a person to slip past.

Put simply, the lives of everyone working inside the sonar dome depend on maintaining the internal pressure, making two issues of primary concern. First, if the SDRW ruptures, air will escape through the opening, and the interior will flood. Survival of anyone inside the dome would be very unlikely. Second, if the pressurization system or the seals around the access trunk airlock hatch fail, air pressure will quickly drop, and the flexible rubber window will be pressed inward against the array, trapping anyone who might be inside the dome.

Two of our divers, Ken Beatrice and Kurt Hansen, had a close call in the airlock on USS *Stump* (DD-978). The ship had recently completed an overhaul and was pierside at the Brooklyn Navy Yard. After completing an inspection of the interior of the dome, the divers and a ship's sonarman were preparing to return through the access trunk. They closed the airlock hatch that isolates the trunk from the dome, but as they were attempting to release the airlock pressure and open the upper hatch, they noticed that the dome was also losing pressure. It took several hours and a large hammer in order to obtain a sufficient seal, before they could open the airlock. Because of the extended time under pressure, the shipyard Master Diver was called in to ensure that the airlock pressure was reduced according to the Navy's decompression tables. Had these hatch seals failed while they were inside the dome, the consequences could have been fatal. Because of this incident, hatch seals are now routinely replaced, and anyone entering the dome carries a spare seal—and a bigger hammer.

The blister that formed on *Fanning*'s SDRW surface in Oman during pressurization gave us an opportunity to see the signs of an imminent rupture. NAVSEA responded by requiring a visual inspection of an SDRW exterior surface, before anyone was allowed to enter the dome. But NAVSEA also looked at the need for a long-term approach to the issue, and it became a priority in their overall failure analysis and corrective action mission.

Our role expanded beyond the fast response damage assessment and field repairs. We began working with B.F. Goodrich and the Naval Research Laboratory (NRL), in an effort to apply industrial non-destructive testing

(NDT) X-ray procedures for determining the condition of the wire plies within the Goodrich-designed SDRW. If we could "see" internal damage or corrosion of the steel wires, particularly in the area where the two halves of an SDRW are spliced together at the Goodrich plant, we might be able to assess the potential for a failure. Being able to perform an X-ray inspection when a ship was dry-docked was not going to be a problem—doing the same with the ship pierside presented an altogether different situation. In New London, a former EOD officer, Lieutenant Commander Ludwig Sorrentino, had been assigned to the SDRW team and became involved with the effort to determine the source of these serious structural issues.

EXPLOSIVE ORDNANCE DISPOSAL, DETACHMENT NEWPORT

For help, we turned to the Explosive Ordnance Disposal (EOD) Detachment, located at the NUSC facilities in Newport. This team was responsible for the northeast region, but because they sat within the NUSC chain of command, they could support projects that didn't interfere with their primary EOD mission. EOD teams were trained to deal with explosives, both on land and underwater. One of the tools of their trade was the use of X-ray technology to view the interior of a suspect device; this equipment, however, is used in air, not water. Because a pierside radiographic inspection would be accomplished with the dome pressurized with air, the X-ray device could be set inside the dome. The film, however, would have to be placed on the exterior of the SDRW (figure 40).

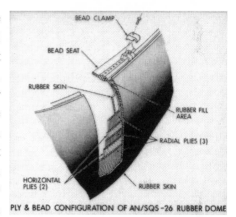

PLY & BEAD CONFIGURATION OF AN/SQS-26 RUBBER DOME

Figure 40. *Above:* Drawing of the wire ply construction of a sonar dome rubber window. (*Courtesy Fort Trumbull State Park*) *Below:* A diver adjusts the X-ray film retainer exterior to the dome. Broken wire plies hidden from view can be discovered with this technique. (*Roy Manstan*)

Throughout 1982, we worked with EOD on the radiographic inspection concept, with ships in dry-dock and pierside. Having proven the concept, NAVSEA asked us to begin transitioning the procedures to civilian NDT contractors, who could then make radiographic inspection part of a routine periodic preventive maintenance system for all SDRWs. The EOD team supported our divers on multiple operations—their role in the application of X-ray technology to pierside inspections, and their ability to mobilize and respond to the type of emergent issues we all faced, resulted in the Newport detachment receiving the Navy's Meritorious Unit Commendation.

By the end of 1983, the radiographic NDT procedures were in place, and we joined the contractor in San Diego for an initial test to see just how "routine" this would be. The challenge was to make the inspection a one-day evolution. On February 24, we all gathered at USS *Ingersoll* (DD-990), made the required visual inspection prior to entering the dome, and by the end of the day, the X-ray inspection of critical areas of the SDRW had been accomplished. No time to celebrate yet. On the 25th we completed the inspection of *Shields* (FF-1066), then *Callaghan* (DDG-994) on the 26th, *Young* (DD-973) on the 27th, and *Horne* (CG-30) on the 28th —we met our goal of one per day. Now we could celebrate, so off we went to Dirty Dan's with a handful of dollar bills.

During that same trip, we were told that USS *Oldendorf* (DD-972) had reported a significant level of flow noise, and SURFPAC asked us to make a visual inspection of the dome exterior. The noise-producing imperfections were quickly found, but when we checked the area where ruptures typically occurred, a blister was discovered on the SDRW surface, reminiscent of *Fanning*. We immediately informed SURFPAC, and suggested that the ship be dry-docked for a permanent repair, before proceeding with any further off shore operations. Had *Oldendorf* been among the ships scheduled for a pierside radiographic inspection, this visual check would have precluded any possibility of a dome entry. While structural failures were rare, they did occur, making pre-entry inspections an essential precaution.

DOLPHIN BITES

We had worked on ninety ships during the course of our involvement with NAVSEA's sonar dome failure analysis and corrective action team, and heard a lot of speculation as to how a dome had been damaged, creating a source of cavitation. One that stood out was blaming dolphins as the cause of lacerations to the dome—understandable, I suppose, in that dolphins were routinely observed riding a ship's bow wake. Our inspection, however, found evidence of a much more common cause of the cuts and abrasions often found on an SDRW—barnacle fragments (not dolphin teeth) ground into the surface. Occasionally, when a ship came alongside a pier, it approached a bit too close, and the dome became a fender, not surprising with its twenty-one-foot width.

There were, however, cases attributable to unsuspecting marine critters that simply got in the way of a patrolling ship. At speeds over twenty knots, a sonar dome would often blast through a school of fish. We have found their dorsal fin spines imbedded in the rubber window. What surprised us all was that a single spine, protruding from the dome surface at certain critical bearings, could cause a significant noise spoke. Removing the spine was all that the diver had to do, and the cavitation source was gone.

"DON'T MAKE A WAVE!"

We were sent to Bath Iron Works (BIW) in Maine—in February with plenty of ice in the Kennebec River—to check the SQS-56 keel mounted domes of three FFG-7-class ships that had recently been out to sea for their precommissioning trials (figure 41). One ship reported a problem with the pressurization of its sonar dome, and the SUPSHIPS representative at BIW was concerned with the condition of all three ships. Slack water on the Kennebec River was less than 45 minutes, making it necessary to take advantage of the tidal cycles over two days. The first ship was USS *Underwood*

Figure 41. After shoveling ice and snow off the platform, NUSC divers Vic Marolda, entering the water, and Rick Thibeault begin their inspections at the Bath Iron Works in Maine. (*Roy Manstan*)

(FFG-36), and Vic Marolda and I were the first in the water—but with visibility less than a foot, we had to depend on powerful lights as each of us checked different areas of the dome. Soon after we started, Vic tapped me on the shoulder and motioned to follow him. We went to the underside of the dome, where he pointed down toward the bottom. Just below us was an indentation in the sediment the exact shape of the dome. At low tide, when its keel was only inches from the bottom, the dome would be completely imbedded into the silt. It was high tide when we did our inspection, so we were happy there wasn't any wave action on the Kennebec that day, or there might have been an indentation on the bottom in the shape of a diver.

A BUSY TIME FOR US

Although it is tempting to tell all ninety stories that accompanied each ship we visited, I will spare you most of the dirty details and simply pass on the variety of places our divers were sent and then maybe toss out a couple more stories—remember the Preface, where I suggested that Navy divers "have a genetic need to tell sea stories."

During the five and a half years we dealt with SDRW issues, there were more than a half dozen trips each to Norfolk, San Diego, Fort Lauderdale, and Newport; several trips to Portland and Bath, Maine, and several more each to Brooklyn, Mayport, and Charleston; plus Pascagoula, Seattle, Philadelphia, Pearl Harbor, Long Beach, Port Canaveral, Key West, and Portland, Oregon. Overseas trips took us to Subic several times, and to Naples and Gaeta, Italy, to Scotland, the Azores, Liberia, Oman, Bahrain, Singapore, and to the Rodman Navy Base in Panama. The West Indies drew us to Andros (AUTEC), Puerto Rico, Guantanamo, Saint Barthélemey, and three visits to Saint Croix. Our bags were always packed, and we looked forward to the briefings and debriefings at the Bank Street Café with our branch head who, I will remind you, was a beer lover. Okay, so this was just a cheap way to lead into another sea story, and the Philippines was—well, you just had to go there once to appreciate the place.

"JUST A F—ING CIVILIAN"—(#)—(WARNING . . . R-RATED)

The relationship between the warfighter and the civilian world was often strained. The credibility gap widened, as active duty sailors on board a ship or submarine questioned whether civilians who traveled to their vessel truly had the best interest of the crew at heart. Their concern was that private industry was "bottom line" motivated, and would cut corners to make a profit at the sailors' expense. Likewise, they simply figured that Navy civilians like us were less concerned about the condition of the ship, and more about a paycheck. Closing this credibility gap had always been a part of our efforts while in the field. We represented NAVSEA, and were on their ship to maximize the vessel's capabilities—the welfare of the ship's company was our primary objective.

When on the road to any spot on the globe, where a naval vessel experienced an issue with one of its systems, accomplishing our mission required a team effort that combined our expertise with that of forward deployed units. Establishing that initial interaction, however, was sometimes less than smooth.

Ken and I had just arrived in the Philippines at the Naval Station, Subic, where our first priority would be to contact the local Navy dive team. In July 1985, USS *Fletcher* (DD-992) had reported a sonar dome pressure alarm, an indication that their acoustic window had ruptured. *Fletcher* was then immediately directed to leave the carrier group and proceed to Subic, where a team from NUSC would meet them, assess the damage, and attempt a field repair. The ship (*and* Ken and I) were assured that every asset needed to complete this mission would be made available. So, with that background, I made my phone call. I think I spoke no more than a dozen words before the chief interrupted . . .

"Wait one fucking minute . . . My divers are fucking tired!!! We've been on the fucking waterfront for the past three fucking days . . . There's no fucking way we can help a couple fucking civilians dive on some fucking ship today!!!" The chief's rather blunt assessment of our needs was not quite the greeting I had expected.

"Chief," I said, maintaining a matter-of-fact tone, "Forty-eight hours ago I was handed a CASREP. Three hours later we were on a plane out of New London. It took forty hours to fly out here, and a two hour bus from the airport to the base. We got two hours sleep at the 'Q' when the SURFPAC rep woke us, and now we're on board *Fletcher*."

"I don't know, man . . . nobody told us you were coming, dammit!!!" The chief had at least toned down and wasn't using the "f-word." They had been blind-sided by our arrival. No one had advised them to be ready to support us, and they had not been provided a copy of *Fletcher*'s damage report. These guys were deployed to a foreign port and in the water every day, dealing with operational problems. They just needed a heads-up that we were coming. I took a deep breath, realizing that he had been put in an impossible situation.

"There must have been some urgency for NAVSEA to have sent us out here." I tried to make my request short, "All I need right now is some support to assess the damage. Then we can all take a break, come up with a plan, and catch a few more hours sleep."

"I'll see what I can do . . ." a reluctant pause . . . "I'll have one of my dive sups come talk to you. Meet him on the pier." So, we waited. About a half hour later, a First Class diver and a couple young divers arrived with a pickup full of gear. One of them, on crutches, would be time-keeper. The other would dress out as standby diver. We showed the dive supervisor our travel orders and our Navy diver qualifications. He pointed to the truck—"Saddle up!"—the typical order to dress for diving. T-shirt and swim trunks were all that divers needed in these warm waters. After lifting a set of jugs onto our backs and taking a few breaths to check the regulator, we were in the water, facing a rather daunting repair.

The normal routine when responding to a CASREP was this initial damage assessment, followed (sometimes still dripping wet) by a briefing to the ship's commanding officer, the ASWO (antisubmarine warfare officer), and chief engineer in the ward room. Immediately after the briefing, we would use their phone to contact NAVSEA with our recommendations—with their blessing (and authority) we would put our plan in motion.

Fletcher's sonar dome had sustained serious damage, beyond what could be permanently repaired pierside. The dome would have to be replaced. The decision that NAVSEA would have to make was whether or not to dry-dock *Fletcher* in a foreign port, requiring the ship and crew to remain on an already long deployment, and wait for a replacement dome to be flown to Subic on a C-5A (the only plane capable of carrying the huge SDRW). The alternative was for Ken and I and the Subic dive team to install a "band-aid" temporary repair. The ship could then transit with the carrier group, already scheduled to return stateside, and find a home-port dry-dock.

This was the epitome of the "no brainer" decision, and once the dive team understood our mission and the implications to *Fletcher*, no longer "some fucking ship," the chief and all the diving assets under his control were brought to bear. Within a week, *Fletcher* was back at sea and heading home with her crew, most of them delighted to be returning to their families.

Not all of the crew, however, was eager to leave. Sailors considered Subic paradise during the decades following World War II, when the Navy maintained a major presence in the Far East. The Philippines were an island archipelago occupied by the Japanese throughout most of the war, and Americans represented a major post-war influence on the local economy. The Navy base at Subic (no longer used by the U.S.) was separated from the main island by a river. Sailors stayed on board their ships or in barracks, while personnel in transit were assigned to various enlisted and officer quarters (the "Q"), all isolated from town by a security gate on the river bridge. A sailor on leave, however, now authorized to conduct "a mission over Shit River," could make a speedy advance on the nearby town of Olongapo, where he would jump aboard one of dozens of local taxis. Known as "jeepneys," they were all surplus World War II jeeps, covered by their proud owners with extravagant decorations, to the point of surreal. For a peso each (about twelve cents), as many sailors as possible would squeeze behind and around the driver, who drove the over-loaded jeepney into town, where the sailors could enjoy cheap beer and the loving care of the ubiquitous LBFM, the acronym for . . . well, you'll have to ask a sailor who had been to this part of the world.

"ANOTHER FOSTERS PLEASE"—(#)

The Australian Navy had a wonderful policy that dated back two hundred years—a daily rum ration. It was very early in the morning, actually 2:00 am, on October 12, 1984, when Vic Marolda and I boarded HMAS *Canberra* (FFG-02), berthed at Sembawang Basin in Singapore; six hours later we would make our first dive. But the greeting and cooperation we received from *Canberra* couldn't have been more delightful. Whether we enjoyed a Courvoisier after dining with the Captain, or tossing down a Fosters on the fantail with the crew, this trip would take us to a "Navy" unlike anything we had experienced. The ship was spotless, and the crew's morale impeccable. *Canberra* carried a small team of divers, and Chief Peter Reynolds from Clearance Diving Team One, the Australian equivalent to a U.S. Navy Mobile Diving and Salvage Unit, joined us. The ship had

experienced a pressure alarm, signifying a failure in their sonar dome. This ship was the same as our FFG-7-class frigates, and carried the small SQS-56 keel mounted sonar with a dome constructed of the same wire-reinforced rubber used for a bow mounted SDRW (figure 42). The damage assessment and repair procedures

Figure 42. HMAS *Canberra* reported a pressure alarm in its keel-mounted SQS-56 sonar, an indication that the rubber dome had ruptured. The steel skirt is shown rigged to accommodate the tools and materials for a field repair in order to avoid dry-docking the ship. (*Roy Manstan*)

were the same, so when *Canberra* notified NAVSEA, we got the usual call from Stan Silverstein.

Our first dive told us two things: be careful of your neighbor, and find a better location to make a field repair. Although the two World War II-vintage Indian destroyer escorts berthed just forward of *Canberra* had been notified that we would be diving, something must have been lost in the translation. As soon as Vic and one of the *Canberra* divers hit the water, sirens went off on our neighbor's ships, their crew went to General Quarters, and the 50 cals mounted on the stern were pointed at us. Chief Reynolds made the 50-yard dash in 5 seconds, screaming obscenities. The Indian sailors stood down, and we proceeded with our initial dive.

We knew that the foul water in Sembawang Basin was not going to allow for a successful field repair. The epoxy B.F. Goodrich designed for underwater repairs had to be applied to a clean surface, just as any adhesive would need if used in air. We recommended that *Canberra* move to a cleaner harbor. The captain agreed. We left our not-so-friendly neighbors and headed to Pulau Tioman, a tropical island where the movie *South Pacific* had been filmed. No need to go into detail here—the repair process is boring. Suffice it to say that the water was warm, crystal clear, and our field repair was a success (figure 43). Anchored with a movie-quality backdrop, supplied by tropical rain-forest covered mountains, we celebrated on the helo deck, with an unlimited supply of Fosters and steaks on the "barbie." Ah yes, there's nothing like the Aussie Navy.

Figure 43. *Top:* NUSC diver Victor Marolda probes the rupture with his knife to determine the extent of the damage. *Middle:* The Aussie divers put the finishing touches on the patch. *Bottom:* After completing the repair, the sonar dome is pressurized, and the expansion across the patch measured. HMAS *Canberra* was able to meet its operational commitments. (*Roy Manstan*)

Over the previous four years, we had enjoyed the adventures and challenges of foreign travel, but our experiences were not always as convivial as that afforded by our Australian brothers in 1984. There were times when creativity trumped skill.

AROUND THE WORLD IN 18 DAYS—(#)

It had been three years—almost to the day—since the last time we had to respond to a ship in this part of the world, and we didn't expect any issues obtaining a visa. The staff at the Omani embassy had been exceptionally helpful back in 1981, and we were sure that this time would be no different. But now it was the end of Ramadan and we hadn't checked the Oman calendar. After staring at the locked gate to their embassy, we realized that this trip would squeeze our creative juices from start to finish.

There were four of us. Ken Beatrice, Vic Marolda, Kurt Hansen and I were the most experienced divers working with surface ship sonar at the time, and we were tasked to participate in the repair of an SQS-23 dome on the guided missile destroyer USS *Preble* (DDG-46), currently operating with its carrier battle group in the Indian Ocean. Ken and I went to Washington for a briefing at NAVSEA and to take care of our visas. Vic and Kurt headed out to B.F. Goodrich to pick up the repair materials. We were all scheduled to meet in DC. At our travel office, Julie had provided us with a twelve-day itinerary and tickets: Groton to Washington to London to Oman and return—seemed simple.

Departure on Monday, July 2, 1984, would have brought us to Oman on the 5th, and to the ship the following day. Four days to complete the repair and a three-day return would get us to New London by July 13. Besides, we had an important event back home, which we couldn't miss. Ken and my sister Bonnie were getting married on the 21st. Bonnie was familiar with the uncertainties associated with NUSC and the dive team, having dated Ken for a couple years by then. But according to our plane tickets we'd be back with a week to spare, so while the bride-to-be continued with the wedding planning, the four of us, including the groom, the brother-of-the-bride, and the best man, boarded a twin Otter for the first leg of what would turn into a longer than twelve day trip.

After our morning meeting at NAVSEA with Stan Silverstein and his staff, the next stop was the embassy. "Closed For Holiday" was the greeting we found hanging on the locked gate. After taking a deep breath, "Okay . . . now what?" was the only thing we could say. There would be no Oman visa, so in less than six hours from the time we started our twelve day adventure, it was time to make an adjustment. The folks in Stan's office were a bit surprised to see us, but like all military agencies, adapting to Murphy's Law was a way of life, and the network of Navy contacts world-wide were geared to facilitate contingencies. By this time it was evening in London, and our only contact was the person on phone duty at CINCUSNAVEUR—the lengthy acronym for Commander in Chief, United States Naval Forces Europe. We spoke to a petty officer who had his long list of contact points throughout Europe and the Near East. His suggestion: fly to London as scheduled—don't worry about the visas, he would have a solution waiting for us. Great! We're back on schedule.

Vic and Kurt arrived in DC on the 3rd, and we all caught the flight to London. There is an old saying among divers: "two is one, one is none." Always carry a spare, particularly when involved in a mission where any one item was critical to its success. We had two sets of equipment, one set became carry-on luggage, the other set we checked through—but checked through to where? It wasn't at the baggage claim area when we arrived in London. So while Ken and Vic tried to locate the gear, Kurt and I called CINCUSNAVEUR. There was a new petty officer on duty, but he knew our situation, and told us that he had already contacted the Navy's liaison office in Bahrain. But it was the middle of the night there, so we would have to call the next day to work out the details.

When we finally spoke to the liaison office, they expressed confidence that they could take care of getting us connected with *Preble*, although there would likely be a bit of a delay. A local "expediter," we were told, would be waiting for us at the airport in Manama. He would put us up in a hotel and also take care of visa issues. The expediter, we were also warned, would need some dollars to help with the expediting.

After spending several hours at Heathrow, Ken and Vic returned with bad news and good news. The spare set of equipment had flown to Germany, but the good news was it would be sent to London the following day, the 5th of July. We had no problem switching our London to Oman plane tickets, but couldn't get seats until the morning of the 6th. We passed the updated schedule to our Bahrain contact, and to NAVSEA, and just waited in London. Everything had slipped a couple days, but if all went well, we would still easily be back for the wedding.

We arrived in Bahrain on the 6th, where our expediter was very efficient—even more so after we handed him the recommended "expediting fee." He brought us to the liaison office for a briefing. Then, as instructed, we handed him our passports, and he drove us to our hotel. "Don't leave. There is everything here you need. There is good food, a bar, and plenty of British Airways stewardesses! I will return the passports to you when you fly from the island," were his parting words. The good news—we were getting closer. The bad news—it would take another three days before there was any chance of getting out to the ship. The bump in the road was that a plane would have to be sent from the carrier to Bahrain. Obtaining authorization to fly through the air space of several countries was going to take time. Ken was getting a bit worried. We were going to be at least three days late, and we already knew that the return trip was no longer going to match Julie's itinerary.

"You're leaving . . . here are your passports . . . good luck." I don't recall what time our expeditor came for us, but it was in the middle of a very dark (fortunately not stormy) night, when we were escorted quietly from the hotel, to a black limo parked behind the building. We had sent Ken back home the day before, having decided that if the wedding party was going to be stuck on an island in the middle of the Persian Gulf, the groom had to get back for the party at the wedding. The three of us could take care of the sonar. A team from USS *Proteus* (AS-19) was on tap to provide support, so there would be plenty of divers. A NAVSEA representative from Norfolk, Roy Johnson, had joined us in Bahrain. He was familiar with the SQS-23 pressurization system, and was there to address the post repair operational use of the sonar.

Dark night, dark roads, dark airport; we were driven right out onto the airstrip where a C-2A cargo plane was waiting. A quick look at our passports and it became clear why we were asked not to stray outside of the hotel—according to the various entry and exit stamps, we had been in and out of another country and were just passing through Bahrain, where we had been provided a 24-hour visitor's visa. We landed at a military airbase on the Omani island of Masirah. Our instructions were simple: "Wait here!" No problem. There was nowhere to go—a hanger off in the distance, asphalt in front of us, dozens of pallets loaded with boxes next to us, and desert everywhere else. The C-2A took off and returned to the carrier, so we sat on a pile of equipment . . . and waited.

It could have been a scene from Armageddon—tiny dots in the sky grew into a swarm of helicopters Hell-bent on attacking our pallet fortress. Then, off to our right, a truck loaded with helmeted troops blasted out of the hanger and raced toward us. There was nowhere to run, nowhere to hide! . . . Sorry, my imagination just got in the way of relating this one-pound story (okay, so this one might turn into a two-pound story).

The boring truth . . . the troops were there to help load supplies, stacked on the pallets, into helos for transport out to the carrier group. We were just another load. It was, however, turning into a bright but stormy day. Winds and seas were up. No problem for the helo, but there was no chance of landing on *Preble*. As we hovered, the ship rose and fell with the sea, green water rolling across the aft deck. After some brief instructions, a horse collar was placed under our arms, and one by one, we were winched with a very small diameter cable down to the ship. The Navy liked simple instructions—better listen, you would only hear this once: "Wait until the ship comes up, lift your arms and drop." A sailor with a tag line was waiting to grab hold when we dropped free, and drag us through the water-covered deck, past the missile launcher, and into the ship's deck house. It was the 9th of June and had been a long commute, but we finally made it to work.

Weather predictions were not good. As the ship pitched and rolled in the near-monsoon conditions, it was decided to move north to a better anchorage off Ra's al Hadd. It was better, but still not the best for a diving operation. The *Proteus* team, led by Ensign Kern, was confident that we could proceed. For the next four days, *Preble* rose and fell nearly four feet, and so did we. The rigging we brought was designed specifically for the SQS-23 dome, giving the divers the ability to hang on with one hand and work with the other. Bottom line: we patched the ruptured rubber window; Roy Johnson ran the pressurization system and gave the ship its operational restrictions; *Preble* made a successful high speed test, and we all shook hands. But then we asked how we might get back home . . . there was a wedding to get to. "Not sure . . ." was the answer. It was July 14, and we only had seven days to find our way back for a wedding on the other side of the world.

Preble was now operating with its carrier, and they (and we) were underway. A carrier battle group moved at its own pace, and some divers from New London were just sucked into the milieu . . . no complaints here, that's just the name of the game. Certainly, *Preble* was grateful for what we all had done, but could only help if it didn't impact the operations. The prevailing thought: we might spend a long time accompanying the deployment. From here on, creativity became the master, and that included finding a few of the more creative members of the crew.

HEADING HOME

A ray of hope hit when word was passed to us that a resupply operation was being scheduled: arrangements might be possible for a helo to bring us to USS *San Jose* (AFS-7), and we might be able to catch a ride with them. We had a chance to watch an underway resupply operation—lines were draped across what seemed like a much-too-close distance between two very large ships, moving much too fast, while soda, seafood, and sailors transferred back and forth on cables and pulleys. This was an impressive operation, and our entertainment, as we waited for the next leg of our commute home. The *Proteus* divers were also anxious to get back, and they pulled a few more strings. Okay! Let's go! The return trip had started with a helo that brought us to the deck of *San Jose.*

We rode *San Jose* for two days, until the ship was able to provide an opportunity to get us one step closer to home—another helo that brought all of us back to the airfield on Masirah—a short stay, thanks to a few of those strings pulled by *Proteus.* On Tuesday, July 17, we all left Masirah on a C-141 transport, heading to Diego Garcia, an isolated island in the Indian Ocean far from everything—except the Navy, and it was *Proteus*'s home. There were also occasional MAC (Military Airlift Command) flights from the U.S, and we were told that one was on its way from New Jersey—we could stay overnight on the island and sign up in the morning. New Jersey!!! We could even hitchhike back to Connecticut if we had to! We finally had an opportunity to phone home with our status, and the conversation immediately switched to the booze that Ken and Bonnie had planned for the wedding. We were *very* thirsty! But right after I hung up the phone, our thirst quenching bubble popped when we heard that the MAC flight had a problem, forcing it to land in Africa. The replacement part would have to be sent from Germany . . . no idea when! Okay, back to the phone booth.

The *Proteus* divers told us that it was simply our fate to stay on board with them. There was plenty of good food, and the diving around the island was great. It was a tempting thought, but there was a wedding to get to. In the morning we returned to the terminal—maybe there had been a change in the status of that MAC flight. No such luck, so we just sat back and thought about options. That's when the Wedding Gods touched us with their magic wand.

Every three months, ships from the Military Sealift Command deployed to Diego Garcia have a crew change, and today was the day. While we sat there, a chartered DC-10 from San Francisco was dropping off the new crew, and the old crew was standing in line, waiting to board. They were scruffy, bearded, and wore old blue jeans. There we sat—scruffy, bearded, wearing old blue jeans. There was no hesitation, no time to ask questions, no time for a phone call. We stood up, got in line, and boarded the plane. No one asked for a ticket or boarding pass—who the Hell would be leaving Diego Garcia, except a bunch of civilian sailors. Nobody cared. We were stowaways who just blended in, and were now heading east rather than west. It was Wednesday the 18th, when we lifted off the airstrip at Diego Garcia. After a lengthy refueling stop in Yokosuka, Japan, we were on our way to good ol' USA, passing through Customs in Alaska, en route to San Francisco.

But the clock was also on our side. We had crossed the International Date Line, and got to enjoy Wednesday the 18th twice. We actually began to believe it would be possible to make the wedding—but we were in California, and Connecticut was three thousand miles away. It was late in the evening and too late to contact our travel office at NUSC, so we went to the agent and handed her tickets that were supposed to bring us from Oman to London and back to New York on the 13th (it was now the 18th). We simply asked if any of this old stuff would work, but that was during a time when airlines loved customers. "No problem," she informed us, but there were no seats available until late the following day. "Oh, wait," she said, and we stood there while she checked the computer. "You might be able to catch a red-eye from Oakland. You better run for it—grab a taxi!" And that we did. Back in New York, we strolled over to the Pilgrim Airlines counter. "We're late for our flight. Any seats back to Groton today?" The agent checked our tickets, and then looked up at us, "Yup, you missed the flight . . . it left six days ago." But our tickets were still good, and we caught the afternoon cattle car. It was Thursday, July 19, when we drove home from the airport. We had travelled around the world in eighteen days.

Ken and Bonnie had a great wedding, and after ten years with the closure of the New London Lab on the horizon (chapter 8), Ken retired in order to pursue his bucket list with Bonnie. While Navy divers have a bad record of maintaining long-lasting relationships (including marriages), my sister knew all about Navy divers—her brother was one. For years she had joined us at the Bank Street Café, so there were no surprises, no misconceptions of what to expect. It's been thirty years, so Happy Anniversary!!! (Figure 44)

Figure 44. *Above:* After circling the globe, the dive team arrived just in time for Ken and Bonnie's wedding. (*Courtesy Ken and Bonnie Beatrice*) *Below:* It's the thought that counts! A layer of slime on the ruptured sonar dome that brought Ken to the Naval Station Subic provided an opportunity to express this sentiment on their first anniversary (divers are not known for their spelling ability). (*Roy Manstan*)

THE CURTAIN BEGINS TO CLOSE

The procedures for inspecting and patching a sonar dome were beginning to move past the experimental stage, and NAVSEA was expecting that

all of this would transition from a NUSC-based operation to one that could be a routine repair capability for active duty dive teams. Diving was among the many Navy activities that NAVSEA controls, specifically through the Supervisor of Salvage and Diving, Code 00C. There were groups within

SEA 00C responsible for different diving functions, including underwater ship husbandry. During the summer of 1984, we were assigned an officer, Lieutenant Karin Lynn, from this group to observe and participate in our SDRW operations, with the goal of transitioning the repair procedures to fleet diving units responsible for all waterborne repairs.

In August 1984, while operating in the Indian Ocean, USS *Brumby* (FF-1044) experienced a sonar dome pressure alarm. After an unsuccessful attempt to inspect the dome by divers from USS *America* (CV-66) due to high seas in the area, the ship anchored off Ra's al Hadd, where divers from USS *Proteus* (AS-19) and *Suribachi* (AE-21) confirmed the rupture. Because of the difficulties we experienced with the *Preble* repair off the coast of Oman, the decision was made to wait for *Brumby* to transit the Suez Canal, allowing us to attempt the repair in Naples. On September 7, Lieutenant Lynn joined three of us from NUSC, including Kurt Hansen and Rick Thibeault, on board *Brumby*, along with a dive team led by Master Diver Don Draper from USS *Puget Sound* (AD-38), to set up a dive plan for the following day.

The rupture in the SDRW was only six inches long, as first reported. We did, however, notice that the dome was indented just below the split, indicating that the rupture may have been more extensive, but had not penetrated the surface. The new flexible patches supplied by B.F. Goodrich were ideally suited for the damage, covering both the obvious rupture and the adjacent weakened wire plies. We completed the repairs that day, and waited thirty-six hours to ensure a full cure of the bonding material. On September 10, we successfully pressurized the dome and *Brumby* was able to return to its operational commitments in the Mediterranean. The last we heard was that after a year and a half, *Brumby* was still operating with its repaired dome. The repair team all received a letter from Rear Admiral Robert Fountain, NAVSEA Assistant Deputy Commander for ASW and Undersea Warfare Systems, expressing the Navy's appreciation for a job well done.

By 1986, NUSC and NAVSEA decided it was time for us to transition out of the SDRW work. This was a tough pill to swallow, as we felt that it was essential to keep in touch with fleet issues, and to do that meant physically being on the waterfront. That summer, Ken Beatrice and Bruce

Greenhalgh completed a rupture repair on USS *DeWert* (FFG-45) at Fort Lauderdale. Vic Marolda and I worked on USS *Kinkaid* (DD-965) with the Consolidated Divers Unit at San Diego, where we accomplished the most extensive repair ever attempted. But we all realized there was nothing magic about what we were doing. Our five years of experience enabled us to develop training materials, which we used during a transition period when we trained teams from SURFLANT and SURFPAC to be the core groups on each coast that could tackle emergent issues. The course materials were passed to SEA 00C for future training.

We were done, and it was time to look elsewhere for another underwater challenge. But after more than five years of intense involvement, it was hard to let go. Over the next several months we heard that the teams we just trained had been called to Alexandria, Egypt, and Buenos Aires, Brazil. But a tear came to my eye when I received a phone call from Chief Reynolds, letting me know that his divers were going to work on another ship in Australia. No need for me to go there, he said. He just had a few questions I could answer over the phone . . .

Figure 45. *Above:* USS *Flying Fish* (SS-229), a war-weary submarine that survived twelve war patrols in the Pacific. In 1951, *Flying Fish* was assigned a new role (and a new designation, AGSS-229) as a sonar research vessel, carrying an experimental array in the elliptical structure surrounding the vessel's conning tower. (*US Navy Photo*) *Below:* USS *Tigrone* (SS-419) returned to New London in October 1945, after two war patrols in the Pacific. Redesignated AGSS-419 in 1963, *Tigrone* continued to serve the Navy as a sonar research submarine, carrying the BRASS II sonar in the sail and BRASS III in the massive dome at the bow. (*Navsource.org; Carlos Estrella*)

CHAPTER 6
Submarine against Submarine:
Hunter vs. Hunter

Antisubmarine warfare implies two roles for the hunter—search for the threat and send it to the bottom. If this sentence sounds familiar, it should. It was the first sentence of Chapter 5, introducing the role of the destroyer and other surface vessels as ASW hunters. Now we look at the submarine as both the hunter and the hunted.

The inherent underwater stealth of a submarine allows it to prey, uninhibited, upon any unlucky vessel transiting the ocean surface. From the first successful attacks against British warships during the early months of World War I, engineering minds had wrestled with this problem. They understood that submarines, essentially invisible, had one exploitable vulnerability—they were very noisy.

Soon after the turn of the century, the Submarine Signal Company began installing underwater bells on ocean buoys and lightships as a navigation tool along the East Coast of the United States. Because sound travels much faster underwater and with less attenuation than in air, ships outfitted with what were referred to as "telephone receivers" could detect the sounds from as far away as ten miles.[82] In order to avoid the hazard, the navigator needed an indication of the direction from which these signals were coming. To provide some directionality, albeit limited, Submarine Signal Company arranged three of their telephone receivers 120-degrees apart, and mounted four such sets in a vertical column.[83]

Before the advent of efficient radio communication, bells were installed in surface ships as a way to send basic signals to vessels equipped with telephone receivers. The rudimentary receiving equipment, however, could also hear sounds coming from other sources, including the mechanical noise of a vessel's machinery and rotating propellers. The applications for this system in undersea warfare were obvious—the operator on board a destroyer could turn his attention to the sounds generated by a nearby submarine. Yet the same detection capability was also available to "listeners" on a submarine. In a 1904 patent, this transmit/receive concept had been proposed for exactly that application: "The invention is particularly applicable for communication between a submerged submarine vessel and a station on shore or on board another ship or between two such submerged vessels."[84]

In his book *Submarine Warfare of Today*, published in 1920, Charles Domville-Fife described both the progress and the frustrations dealing with the rapidly evolving submarine threat. Having commanded a British hydrophone flotilla during World War I, Domville-Fife had first-hand knowledge of how the hydrophone became a device widely used by both sides: "A game of hide-and-seek [was] played between a hunting vessel and a hunted submarine. Nearly all U-boats were fitted with a number of hydrophones and therefore were as well able to receive timely warning of the presence of an approaching surface ship as the surface ship was of the presence of the submarine."[85]

There was no expectation by either side that a submerged submarine could effectively search for and attack a submerged enemy submarine. The technology simply did not allow it. The very covert nature of a submerged vessel, however, supplied one tactical method that did have some limited ASW use. The British employed a decoy ship that, when viewed through a U-boat's periscope, would appear as a merchant or fishing trawler. Rather than using one of its limited numbers of torpedoes, the U-boat would surface and attack the "unarmed" vessel with its deck gun. The decoy, however, was towing a submerged submarine that was immediately set free, and while submerged, approached the unsuspecting enemy submarine. Domville-Fife described the scene after the British sub fired its torpedo: "The water around the U-boat rose up in a vast upheaval of white. The plan had succeeded, and when the air cleared . . . there was nothing afloat on the surface of the sea around—except an ever-widening patch of oil and bubbles."[86]

Between 1914 and 1918, 178 U-boats were lost from a variety of reasons, including 21 that were rammed by warships and merchant ships, 26 that were destroyed by depth charges, and 34 from mines. Many were caught on the surface where submarine launched torpedoes resulted in the loss of 18, only ten percent of the total; many more were sunk by gunfire. There were also 37 losses from "unknown" causes, although most were likely from contact with the many mine fields laid around Britain. Domville-Fife was confident that in spite of the relatively ineffective antisubmarine campaigns during the war, technology would eventually find a solution:

> With the experience gained and the brains of almost every nation focused on the problem of providing an effective counterblast to the under-water warship, there can be little doubt that in the next great naval conflict new and more scientific means of attacking these pests of the sea will have been perfected, though what degree of success they will attain in the stern trial of war the future alone can tell.[87]

As Domville-Fife predicted, U-boat losses were much higher during World War II, based primarily on the development of an effective ASW capability. Surface vessels and supporting aircraft sank 297 out of a total of 821. Another 388 were sunk by aircraft operating alone. Percentage-wise, submarine torpedoes were even less effective against the U-boat during World War II, with only 25 (approximately three percent) recorded.[88] But in a post-War to End All Wars environment, there was only limited interest in antisubmarine warfare technology.

BETWEEN THE WARS

By early 1919, submarine detection research carried on at the Navy Experimental Station in New London (chapter 2) came to an end. During the 1920s, the Submarine Signal Company continued to pursue its interest in the underwater sound technologies it had been developing. The Navy also began to consider its own scientific interests in submarine detection. The first Q-series echo-ranging devices were developed at the newly formed Naval Research Laboratory (NRL) in Washington, DC. In 1927, the QA system was tested at Key West, Florida. Although detection range was limited to one mile, the QA was installed on destroyers, while a similar system, the QB, was produced for submarines. By 1934, engineers introduced a new technology called magnetostriction, which provided substantially greater echo-ranging capability. With a range of 10,000 yards, this new QC system, produced by Submarine Signal Company, became the Navy's echo-ranging system on surface ships and submarines at the beginning of World War II.[89]

In a two-part article that began in the April 17, 1959 issue of the ECHO, USN/USL Technical Director Dr. John M. Ide summarized the development of passive sonar, specifically for submarine use.[90] He described that during the late 1920s, German submarines were using multi-element arrays mounted in "streamlined enclosures located below the bow," and "bulbous appendages known as a 'balkan' [balcony] welded below the keel [where] hydrophones mounted in its surface formed an array shaped like a horseshoe." These were conformal arrays (arrays that "conform" to the shape of the hull) that operated in a low frequency range of 1-2 KHz, and provided not only excellent detection ranges, but directionality as well. Ide noted that these German systems were significantly more advanced than the American counterpart, introduced by Columbia University's research laboratory in New London (the future USN/USL) early in the war. Even though passive sonar on submarines was improving, it was still primarily used as a listening system for targeting, or avoiding, surface ships.

THERE ARE TWO TYPES OF VESSELS

Ask a submariner, and he will tell you that the Navy operates two types of vessels—submarines and targets. By the end of World War II, the fleet submarine had proven itself as a deadly predator; yet it had also become more vulnerable. Private industry and research labs established at the beginning of the war had been tasked to do exactly what Domville-Fife had predicted in 1920: finding "new and more scientific means of attacking these pests of the sea." Radar was improving; aircraft could now patrol far from shore; the new magnetic anomaly detector could "see" the effect of a submarine passing through the Earth's magnetic field; but by far the improvements in sonar made life on a submarine tenuous at best. In reality, the submarine was as much of a target as any other naval combatant, and new and more powerful weapons were on the drawing board.

Early in the war, the Bureau of Ordnance (BUORD) had tasked the Harvard Underwater Sound Laboratory with the development of underwater weapons. Improvements in hydrophone technology led to the development of the MK 24 air-dropped self-propelled acoustic homing weapon—known as both a mine and a torpedo. These MK 24s demonstrated their effectiveness on May 14, 1943, when two U-boats were sunk—one by a B-245 "Liberator," the other by a Navy PBY "Catalina." The next step was to include the acoustic homing capability in a submarine launched torpedo. A successful test occurred in October 1945, too late to be a factor in the war.[91]

When a U-boat was unlucky enough to have been sunk by an Allied submarine torpedo, it was invariably on the surface. Richard Compton-Hall (1988) described the only recorded instance when both submarines were running submerged. *U-864* was operating off the coast of Norway in February 1945, when the British submarine HMS *Venturer*'s ASDIC sonar recorded the distinctive sounds from the machinery of the U-boat's electric-powered propulsion. While following *U-864*'s course, *Venturer*'s captain was able to confirm the position of its target when the U-boat's periscope was sighted. Shortly after noon on February 9, a torpedo sent *U-864* to the bottom.[92]

From its creation at the beginning of the war, Columbia University's New London laboratory had focused on surface ship sonar and sonobuoys. By 1943, the emphasis began to shift from antisubmarine to "prosubmarine" warfare, and in particular, to support the growing need to increase the Navy's effectiveness in the Pacific theater.[93] There had been some improvement in the ability of a fleet submarine to find and sink its Japanese counterpart, but there was little success when both were submerged—throughout the war, submarines remained more vulnerable to attack by surface ships and from the air. It was the advent of the nuclear powered submarine and the challenges of the Cold War that created the true antisubmarine submarine.

SEARCH AND DESTROY—SUBMARINE AGAINST SUBMARINE

The target of World War II fleet submarines was the surface ship. With slow submerged operating speeds and relatively low self noise, submarines could use their passive sonar to detect the very loud sounds of surface ship machinery. But the role of the submarine was about to change. The technology that could enable a submerged submarine to locate and target another submerged submarine would not evolve until a decade after World

War II. Although the Soviet fleet contained hundreds of conventional diesel-electric submarines during the 1950s and 1960s, their vulnerability while on the surface, or snorkeling just below the surface, made them a target for surface and air ASW assets. During the Cold War, the Soviets played the numbers game—to control the oceans, simply produce more submarines. Sink as many as you can—the assumption was that enough would survive to accomplish their strategic goal.

When the November-class attack submarines joined the Soviet fleet in the early 1960s, the element of speed, stealth, and extended submergence at deeper depths made them a difficult target. A nuclear powered Soviet submarine could now operate at speeds between 25 and 30 knots, and as high as 33 knots for their November-class boats, pushing the limits of surface ASW assets.[94] As Soviet intentions escalated during the early days of the Cold War, American naval planners began looking seriously at providing its submarines with the ability to strike a submerged submarine, and accelerated the development of accurate fire control capability and an acoustic homing torpedo.

Submarines had always participated in convoy support, but with the increasing use of a carrier battle group strategy, nuclear-powered attack boats became an important element in the defensive bubble around the battle group. For U.S. submarines, the "search" once again depended on the best sonar possible; the "destroy" assumed the best weapons and most sophisticated sonar-directed fire control system.

In their book *Meeting the Submarine Challenge*, John Merrill and Lionel Wyld quote sonar pioneer Walter Clearwaters, who noted the impact sonar would have on future submarine design: "The size, pressure hull geometry, and internal space requirements were designed to allow sonar equipment and systems first choice of ship's space."[95] The first nuclear submarines, *Nautilus* and *Seawolf*, were experimental models, which in many aspects of hull design followed in the footsteps of their fleet boat predecessors. When I first stepped on board *Nautilus* as it was being outfitted with the MACS acoustic antenna system in the mid-1970s (chapter 4), I was taken aback by the flat, teak-covered deck. I had spent time aboard USS *Pargo* (SSN-650) in 1970, where I first saw the streamlined 637-class hull, designed, as Clearwaters put it, "to allow sonar equipment and systems first choice."

Walter Clearwaters began his Sound Lab career on the staff of the Columbia University Division of War Research in New London in 1943, later becoming head of the USN/USL Submarine Sonar Department, and finally NUSC Technical Director in the early 1970s. Under his direction, U.S. attack submarines, embodied in the SSN-594-class, and its 637- and 688-class successors, entered the Cold War as potentially lethal combatants. The principal tools of their trade were sonar, and the battle could now be taken beneath the sea—submarine against submarine.

Following the same development path as the SQS-26 system for surface ships, work began in the mid-1950s on what USN/USL proposed to BUSHIPS as an "Integrated Submarine Sonar System." As Thad Bell (2011) pointed out, the surface ship sonar and submarine sonar divisions were both pursuing the concept of using active echo-ranging to detect a target below the isothermal layer. In 1955, the Sound Lab's Russell Lewis (the same Russell Lewis who was a sonobuoy advisor on *Block Island* when it was sunk by a German U-boat) proposed mounting an experimental Bottom-Reflected Active Sonar System (BRASS) to the deck of USS *Blenny* (AGSS-324). The promising results obtained in 1956 led to a more comprehensive experiment (BRASS II) in 1959, where both the transmitting submarine and its target were operating below the isothermal layer.[96] USS *Tigrone* (AGSS-419) became the primary BRASS test platform in the 1960s (see figure 45).

The BRASS results confirmed the notion that long-range active sonar was feasible for both surface ships and submarines. But the underlying motivation was to provide the hunter with the ability to find its target. According to Thad Bell, the experimentation with a system that exploited this bottom-reflected path served "as a basis for planning convoy routes upon which long-range detection performance would be expected."[97] Bottom line—selecting a route across the Atlantic based on knowledge of the oceanographic environment, including favorable bottom bounce conditions, would give the convoy escorts an advantage over any threat.

The SQS-26 sonar included a sixteen-foot diameter cylindrical array mounted at the bow of cruisers, frigates, and destroyers, and housed within an efficient, hydrodynamically-shaped sonar dome. By 1957, a specification for the new submarine sonar system included a bow-mounted fifteen-foot diameter spherical array, likewise housed in a hydrodynamically-shaped dome. But incorporating a spherical array at the bow required approval by the Ship's Characteristics Board, and a persuasive argument had to be made—and quickly. The Navy was about to approve significant changes to the hull form, and as John Merrill and Lionel Wyld put it: "turned the entire forward area of the submarine to the sonar system."[98] The spherical array would not only define the dimensions and shape of the submarine's nose, but its location required moving the torpedo tubes from their prominent location in the bow.

Designated the AN/BQQ-2, the first system was installed on USS *Tullibee* (SSN-597) in 1960. *Tullibee*'s sonar suite consisted of the BQS-6 active bow sphere and BQR-7 passive conformal array, located along the sides of the forward portion of the hull. This boat also carried an experimental BQG-4 Passive Underwater Fire Control Feasibility System (PUFFS). By the mid 1960s, while the destroyers *Wilkinson* and *Willis A. Lee* were running technical evaluations of the SQS-26, *Tullibee* was completing its evaluation of the BQQ-2. As the decade came to a close, and digital computers overtook analog technology, sonar systems became more sophisticated, with additional signal processing capability included in what was being referred to as an "integrated submarine sonar system." Just as the surface ASW SQS-26 became the SQS-53, the digital world saw the submarine BQQ-2 system evolve into the BQQ-5, and later the BQQ-6.[99] These three-letter designations can be confusing, so I include the following—first letter: S=surface ship, B=submarine; second letter: Q=sonar; third letter: S=active (echo-ranging) sonar, R=passive (listening) sonar, G=fire control, Q=multi-purpose system.[100]

The hull mounted BQQ-2 had limitations, so additional passive sensors were being considered and "integrated" into the overall sonar suite. None of this was going to happen without a significant amount of experimental work, which the post-war Sound Lab was known for and fully capable of continuing. As a program manager for the next generation BQQ-5, George F. Carey drew on his career-long experience with risk takers, and became an enthusiastic supporter of any and all in-house and at-sea experimental efforts. Carey (chapter 3) qualified as a Navy diver in 1959, and during his short diving career was one of the USN/USL engineers who designed and tested a two-man submarine for the Navy's underwater demolition teams.

By the mid to late 1970s, the 688-class submarine was going to be the platform of choice to carry tactical systems that evolved over decades to improve detection and targeting, if and when that "submarine versus submarine" encounter occurred. Off-hull passive towed arrays, a technology that had a long history at USN/USL, plus a revolutionary concept in hull-mounted conformal arrays were about to provide a new capability for the U.S. attack submarine.

Our divers had been fully engaged in the SQS-26 and other surface ASW systems in the 1970s and 1980s, but with submarine sonar rapidly evolving during the same timeframe, we would also be drawn deeply into the underwater testing and evaluation of these developing systems.

SUBMARINE ANTISUBMARINE SONAR

Antisubmarine warfare, whether conducted by a surface ship or a submarine, relies on a five-step sonar-dependent sequence. Regardless of the sophistication of the technology, success is always in the hands of the operator: 1. Detection ("Captain, I hear something") 2. Classification ("What the Hell is it . . . Ohhh Shit.") 3. Localization ("There it is . . . I know where you are, you SOB!") 4. Tracking ("We're gonna run right up your fat ass!!") 5. Torpedo firing ("Take that, Mutha!!!") Okay, maybe I'm being a bit dramatic here, but every step, from detecting a potential target to pulling the trigger *before* the bad guy knew you were on his tail, required a fully operational sonar system, in the hands of well trained, experienced sonar techs.

Surface ASW employed a combination of hull mounted active sonar and passive variable depth sonar (VDS) towed aft. The assumption was that a Soviet submarine would likely know when a noisy surface ship was tracking it, and there would be no surprise when the ship began transmitting from its SQS-26 or SQS-23 sonar. A passive VDS (i.e. the SQR-19 and its predecessors), however, became an exceptionally effective ASW tool, making the active systems on surface ships nearly obsolete, as long as the targets remained noisy enough to be detectable with a passive sonar.

A submarine on the other hand, whether hunting or being hunted, depended on stealth. Passive sonar operated by listening only, and this very design meant that the target would have no indication it is being stalked. The relatively low frequencies associated with radiated noise from a Soviet submarine, propagating long distances through the water, offered the possibility of early detection (step 1). Because each Soviet Class submarine produced distinct and definable sounds from their machinery and propellers, classification (step 2) became feasible.

Being able to localize and track the position of its target (steps 3 and 4) before engaging step 5, however, required more sophisticated technology than available with the BQQ-2 system used on 594- and 637-class submarines. The small BQR-7 conformal array located along the forward hull was insufficient to obtain the needed precision. Its "aperture" (the length of an array needed to determine in a three-dimensional ocean, the origin of the target's radiated noise) was insufficient for the low frequency, long wavelength sounds.

This requirement was no mystery, however, and a great deal of post-war research had been underway at USN/USL and other Navy laboratories. The Passive Underwater Fire Control Feasibility Study (PUFFS) mentioned earlier, for example, was developed by the Naval Ordnance Laboratory as an experiment in improving targeting accuracy, by gathering acoustic data from multiple sensors spaced along the hull. Beginning in the late 1950s, PUFFS systems were being mounted on several submarines. But among the several Navy research laboratories, the Sound Lab continued to lead the overall development of sonar for all five steps—from detection to launch.

GRUPPEN HORCH GERÄT (GROUP LISTENING APPARATUS)

During World War II, the German navy was convinced that passive sonar was the most efficient method of detecting and locating a noisy target. The Germans referred to passive "listening" sonar as Gruppen Horch Gerät, or GHG, which was produced in many styles for application to a variety of vessels. The sophistication of their sonar began to be realized when the British captured *U-570* in 1941, but a true appreciation of GHG came after the war, when the Sound Lab began to take a critical review of its capabilities. In 1947, Lee E. Holt published a review of the GHG in an article, "The German Use of Sonic Listening" in the Journal of the Acoustical Society of America. Holt included information about their sonar technology, obtained by fellow Sound Lab engineer Carl T. Milner (see chapter 2) who rode another captured submarine, *U-505*:

One marvels at the evidence of close cooperation between ship designers and scientific experts. The Germans do not seem to have thought of listening devices as accessory equipment to be added to already completely designed ships; on the contrary, they redesigned hull shapes and entire ship structures in accordance with the demands of their acoustic engineers.

The GHG was used on cruisers and battleships, on submarines, destroyers, mine sweepers, submarine chasers . . . the equipment aboard the Prinz Eugen, for example, is reported to have picked up a British cruiser at a range of 30 kilometers while the Prinz Eugen itself was travelling at a speed of 30 knots.[101]

Holt was probably sending a message to the U.S. Navy that sonar will define the future of naval warfare and that "acoustic engineers" (specifically those residing at the Sound Lab) will have the answer. The Navy must have been listening, as the Sound Lab quickly began to take on the critical experimental evaluation of the GHG, and similar U.S. design concepts. A Quonset hut located along the Sound Lab waterfront contained, along with Carl Milner, the remains of various German sonar systems, including the GHG from *Prinz Eugen*, an American war prize acquired in January 1946 (this ship—a vessel our divers visited in 2002—has an interesting post-war story. See chapter 8). Around 1948, Milner installed a GHG array on USS *Cochino* (SS-345) with spectacular results, demonstrating its ability to track a submerged target. Coincidently, a young naval reserve officer was on board and observed its performance—that officer was Thaddeus Bell, who would soon become a sonar pioneer at the Sound Lab.

John Ide's article in the April 17 and 24 issues of the ECHO emphasized the decade-long experimental work carried out by USN/USL to better define the potential capability of hull mounted passive sonar. USS *Quillback* (SS-424) was outfitted with a small 6-foot-diameter circular array, followed by a larger 11-foot-diameter cylindrical array on USS *Threadfin* (SS-410) mounted just forward of the conning tower. These post-war experimental arrays were constructed in the 1940s, specifically for gathering acoustic data. In 1951, a 48-foot-long by 24-foot-wide and 10-foot-tall elliptical array was installed on the deck and surrounding the sail of USS *Flying Fish* (SS-229, re-designated AGSS-229 as a research submarine—see figure

45), along with a linear array totaling 200 feet mounted on the side of the hull. The operational data obtained from these experimental arrays, tested during the post-war decade, convinced Navy planners that passive listening technology held promise, setting the stage for new and ambitious ideas for a nuclear Navy that would dominate the Cold War.

But in order to take advantage of the long-range detection afforded by low frequency long wavelength sounds, the passive device would need to provide the large aperture needed for bearing accuracy and tracking. There were two approaches available to a submarine. One was to tow a line of hydrophones mounted along a cable, and extending far behind the boat. The second was to mount along nearly the entire length of the submarine, multiple arrays that conform (i.e. "conformal arrays") to the curvature of the hull. The spacing of the hydrophones along the towed array and the location of hull-mounted conformal arrays would provide the needed aperture for determining range and bearing of the sound producing target. Both technologies are now integral components of the modern submarine fleet, and the NUSC divers have been involved from the beginning.

WIDE APERTURE ARRAY—RAPID PASSIVE LOCALIZATION

In 1975, a year after the successful demonstration of passive ranging capabilities of a prototype BQG-2B system on USS *Barb* (SSN-596), CNO (Chief of Naval Operations) specified that a hull mounted conformal array be included on SSN-688-class submarines. The experimental BQG-2B sensors had been installed within the mid and forward ballast tanks on earlier-class submarines, but because the 688-class boats no longer included a mid-hull tank, this next generation submarine would require the conformal arrays to be mounted external to the hull.

Originally designated the Wide Aperture Array for Rapid Passive Localization (WAA/RAPLOC), the RAPLOC acronym was eventually dropped, in favor of the simplified use of WAA for the system. The necessity of placing the arrays outboard created design challenges associated with operating within the flow stream. In 1975, immediately after CNO proclaimed WAA for future attack submarines, a lengthy multi-faceted development program jumped into full gear at NUSC. The first few years were dedicated to experimenting with prototype system components, but by the end of the decade, the system was becoming better defined.[102]

Although the NUSC dive team was heavily committed to surface ship ASW sonar issues, we knew there would soon be a need for a similar commitment to this new technology. One of our divers, Tim Sullivan, was already in the submarine sonar department. Another engineer, Roger Maple, had recently attempted to complete scuba training, but faced the same disappointment that I had experienced during my first attempt. Unfortunately, Roger was not going to have an opportunity for a second try. Vic Marolda, who qualified in 1979, would eventually transfer into that department. It was these three individuals who would draw the NUSC dive team into various aspects of WAA development. By 1985, ten years after the program was turned on, a full scale advanced development model (ADM) was installed on the newly commissioned USS *Augusta* (SSN-710).

SUBMARINE SELF-NOISE

A conformal array consists of multiple hydrophones arranged over a particular segment of a vessel's hull. Each hydrophone sends a signal to the electronic processor, which then attempts to determine if the signal is from a target or from all of the other noise sources arriving at the array, including the vessel's "self-noise." Because the performance of a conformal array is highly dependent on the ability to discriminate between the target signal and this self-noise, acoustic baffles can be placed behind the sensors to isolate the array from noise radiating through the hull. In 1980, under Dr. Wayne Strawderman's direction, Roger Maple and Tim Sullivan

Figure 46. *Above:* NUSC diver Rick Thibeault briefs Tim Sullivan (L) and Roger Maple on the installation of the WAA test panel. *Below:* A model of the test panel in position near the bow. (*NUSC/NL; "Mac" McClenny*)

developed an experiment to measure noise from various mechanical systems, the results of which would feed into the design of the acoustic baffles (figure 46).

The plan included measuring this hull-borne self-noise at the Carr Inlet Acoustic Rage (CIAR) at Fox Island near the southern end of Puget Sound.[103] The range had the capability to suspend a submarine from a pair of massive destroyer buoys, each equipped with a winch that, after the submarine was ballasted to be slightly negatively buoyant, could lower the vessel to a prescribed depth. But the precise placement of the measurement array was critical to acquiring meaningful data. A prototype test panel was built to train the NUSC divers in the installation procedures, and demonstrate our ability to position the array at precise locations on a submarine hull. With the CNO mandate to proceed with WAA development, we wouldn't have to look far for a platform to try our test panel—the Groton Submarine Base was only a few miles away with an ample supply.

On December 20, 1980, we arrived at the pier in Groton where USS *Richard B. Russell* (SSN-687) was waiting. The air was well below freezing that day, and we had to be careful lowering the now stiff and frozen polyurethane array into the water, where it could thaw enough to conform to the curvature of the hull. In those days before we owned drysuits, our bodies were also frozen and the 40 °F water offered little relief. Over the next six hours, we cycled three teams in and out of the cold New England water—no need to try this system in warm water, Puget Sound was no better. This dive, and a second test on USS *Gato* (SSN-615) the following May, were enough to enable NUSC to request a submarine for Carr Inlet.

USS *POLLACK* (SSN-603)—NO DIVING VACATION

When it comes to acquiring access to an operational submarine, however, there is no room for slippage or alterations in the schedule. When your window of opportunity opens for two days, you had better be there—rain or shine (figure 47). *Pollack* arrived at the Carr Inlet range on January 15, 1982. We finally had access to the boat at midnight, when we located and marked the five positions along the hull where measurements would be made. With only a 48-hour window, we split the team into day (McClenny, Marolda, Clark, Aiksnoras, and Paruszewski) and night shifts (Manstan,

Thibeault, and Jolie). We were also able to depend on support from Puget Sound Naval Shipyard (PSNS) dive team—the same divers who had joined

Figure 47. NUSC divers arrive at the Carr Inlet Acoustic Range for the morning shift. (*Richard Thibeault*)

us during a previous measurement program in 1979 (chapter 7). After nearly a decade as a NUSC diver, Tim Sullivan, who had been instrumental in the design of the Carr Inlet test, left NUSC in January to pursue his doctorate, and would soon move on to a new career.

The following morning, on the 16th, the boat ballasted and was lowered into position; by mid-afternoon data was being collected. This was, however, not going to be a warm sunny day at work. High winds and rain made life (and diving) miserable at Carr Inlet. At 0100 on the 17th, we shifted the array to its next location—then again at 0930, again at 1630, and to the final position at 2300. At 0400 on the 18th, we removed the array. Excessive ambient noise associated with the bad weather had been a problem for the acoustic measurements. When we noticed that January 18 was about to become a beautiful quiet day, no amount of begging could induce *Pollack* to remain on station. Later that morning, she surfaced and bid us farewell (figure 48).

Figure 48. *Top:* USS *Pollack* (SSN-603) is suspended beneath the white destroyer buoys. *Middle and Bottom:* After deballasting, the submarine slowly surfaces. (*Richard Thibeault*)

In spite of the occasional bad weather, Carr Inlet was an ideal location, in fact at that time the only location, where field engineering could be accomplished on a fully submerged yet stationery submarine. As field engineers, we all understood how valuable the Carr Inlet facility was for evaluating concepts in a real but controlled environment. The submarine suspension capability has moved to Ketchikan, Alaska.

USS *CAVALLA* (SSN-684)—FINALLY, THAT HAWAIIAN VACATION

As the development of WAA moved ahead, questions arose about the service life-cycle of the components that were being designed for the final array. There were multiple materials involved with the baffles, the hydrophone modules, the hydrodynamic fairings, and various mechanical fasteners. A scaled down version of WAA called the "Patch Test" contained representative components of those used on the full scale array, and was installed on USS *Cavalla*. The Patch Test and its location on the hull ensured that the components would be subjected to the same environmental and operational conditions that the final WAA array would experience. At last, however, we would find ourselves working in warm water—at the submarine base in Pearl Harbor.

It may have been the plane tickets sticking out of my shirt pocket, but I had to field comments from colleagues as I walked down the hall in Building 80, all undoubtedly said in jest—at least I think so.

"So . . . what boondoggle are you heading for this time . . . another Hawaiian vacation? . . . I hear Kauai is beautiful this time of year."

My standard response: "Yup . . . goin' on vacation. I'll send you a post card from Waikiki."

Those who weren't frequent travelers, but worked closely with those of us who were, certainly understood the mission, but nonetheless, couldn't resist making a comment. Many of us wished we could make that side trip to Kauai, but a schedule is a schedule, and we never knew if another set of plane tickets were waiting for us back in New London. During a particularly busy time in 1983, the first eight months brought us to Pearl Harbor four times. That in itself wasn't so unusual, but during those same eight months we also went to Bath, Maine; Mayport and Fort Lauderdale, Florida; and San Diego.

WORK HARD—PLAY HARD . . . PEARL HARBOR—BOZO'S BAR

Being divers, we spent the one day we had off (having worked very hard) during those four trips to Hawaii—you guessed it—sport diving in Hanauma Bay. That doesn't mean we couldn't take time to enjoy the local establishments. We simply made sure that we accomplished the "work hard" part before switching to the "play hard" part. We had been travelling to Pearl Harbor on so many occasions in the 1980s, that the Hotel Ilima staff recognized us by name. We also had become after-hours regulars at Bozo's, a neighborhood bar just a few steps down the road from the hotel. Having spent the day diving alongside *Cavalla*, it was a place where formality was unknown, and we could settle into the comfort of a bar stool and gab with the gorgeous bartender. The scene was always the same, but never seemed to get old.

A huge picture window separated the bar from the sidewalk, and we could enjoy the sight of each curvy, colorful Wahine walking to and from Waikiki Beach. It was a busy street where cars patrolled, looking for parking, and we watched as several cars tried to squeeze into an obviously too-small space. We would raise our glass to acknowledge their futile attempt. Then, at last, a lovely young lady in her VW bug approached and made yet another attempt at parallel parking. Being the fine gentlemen that we were, Vic and I sped out of the bar to assist this damsel in distress. She had backed into the space, but just couldn't see how to steer the front of her bug into position. Vic held up his hand, motioning her to stop trying. He and I then grabbed the bumper, lifted the front of her car, and swung it over to the curb. Although there was a look of panic on her face, it all ended well. To the sound of applause from the bar, she thanked us and hurried down the sidewalk, probably grateful that she had escaped.

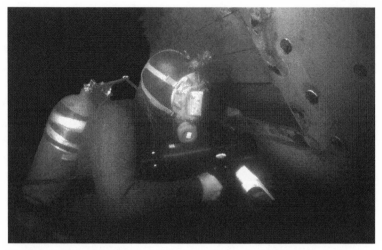

Figure 49. "Mac" McClenny uses an underwater video system to record the condition of a test panel on USS *Cavalla* (SSN-684). The full face mask provides a communication link between the diver and the surface. (*Roy Manstan*)

After several visits to *Cavalla*, the Patch Test provided significant insight into the materials that were being incorporated into WAA (figure 49). We would eventually help with acoustic tests at the NUSC Seneca Lake facility, and with the WAA installation on *Augusta*. But we still had just one last trip to Pearl Harbor, and as that wrapped up, one final memorable visit to Bozo's Bar:

THE RED SOCK INCIDENT—(#)

"Tap . . . . Tap . . . . Tap . . . Tap . . . . TAP-TAP-TAP!"

"Jim . . . . JIIIMMM . . . . Open the dooorrrrr . . ."

It was 2:00 a.m., and a miracle that Jim Clark, infamous for his snoring, woke to the sound. Groping his way through the dark hotel room, Jim looked through the peep hole and all he could see was an eyeball peering back, and then in a whisper . . . "Jim . . . PLEASE OPEN the DOOR!"

There he stood—stark naked—well, almost. The urgent need to pee had awakened Mac from a deep sleep. He stumbled around in the dark in search of the bathroom, opened the door, and made a dash for the toilet—only to discover that he was standing in the hallway, as the door to his room, not the bathroom, closed and locked behind him.

It was a stroke of luck that Jim's room was on the same floor. Now wide awake and aware of his dilemma, Mac attempted to raise him . . . without drawing the attention of other hotel guests. There's no telling how long Mac discretely tapped on the door, before Jim finally woke up. There's also no way to describe what Jim saw when he opened the door, but there was Mac, naked except for a single red sock—the only piece of clothing he hadn't removed when we all staggered to our rooms and crashed, after returning from Bozo's.

Jim kindly went to the front desk and retrieved a spare key, promising never to relate the red sock incident to the rest of us. Jim's promise had a short life, however, and soon the story was out. At Mac's retirement, all of the divers wore our team blue-and-gold T-shirts, UDT trunks—and one red sock.

USS *AUGUSTA* (SSN-710)

The path from concept to reality is long and understandably difficult. When CNO established the requirement for a passive Wide Aperture Array in 1975, all mechanisms within the military machine surged forward, and NUSC would keep the machine turning. Much of the system design and testing occurred in parallel—while the patch test was underway on *Cavalla* in Hawaii, there were quarter-scale flow noise measurements at the "pop-up" facility in Lake Pend-Oreille, Idaho, and full-scale hull-segment prototype acoustic measurements at the NUSC Seneca Lake, New York, facility. With the installation of the WAA advanced development model (ADM) on *Augusta* in 1985, the Navy could now send an attack submarine into the Cold War with a new capability, which would continue to keep the Soviet submarine threat at and beyond arm's length.

Every phase of WAA development required individuals who brought different perspectives to solving a problem. While multiple opinions sometimes created confusion and tension among conflicting strong personalities, the path to the prize was only successful when multiple perspectives were respected. Note the comment by the Navy's Chief Engineer, Rear Admiral Melville in 1902: "The advances made in making the submarine boat more efficient have been almost altogether along engineering lines. It is because the capabilities of the engineer are progressively increasing that still further advance will be made."[104]

Melville also encouraged "competition among designers" and warned against the belief "that in this mechanical age the solution of any technical problem can only be solved by a few persons." He would certainly have approved of the engineering team concept fostered by Howard Schloemer, PhD, the Submarine Hull Arrays branch head. When I spoke to Vic Marolda about WAA development, he described a typical design meeting:

> Howie called it 'management by walking around.' He would come by a meeting, sit and chat about everything . . . including job, home life, just about anything on his or your mind. He'd leave pretty well informed about the overall project, offered feedback on the spot, and never asked you to provide him with status reports—he simply left, well informed about how the group was functioning as a team. He never felt the need to micromanage his group, preferring to hand-pick his people and get rid of malcontents. Howie crafted a small but strong engineering team. We have remained friends, and kept in touch for nearly a quarter century.

It's no wonder WAA was a success, or for that matter, any project Howie Schloemer undertook. Vic and his hull arrays colleagues were thoroughly entrenched in WAA, undertaking multiple field engineering missions—some, but not all, requiring Vic's skills as a diver. This ability to multi-task was characteristic of everyone on the NUSC dive team, where our qualification as a Navy diver was just one, albeit unique, of many field engineering skills. Just as was the case with Howie's design team, we skillfully avoided micro-managers and thrived on individuals who functioned best in a team setting.

OPERATIONS RESEASRCH—A COLD WAR EXAMPLE

I have nothing to base this assumption on, but I have to imagine that while assigned to a shore-based ASW squadron in North Africa during World War II, Walt Clearwaters (chapter 2) may have tipped a few with his military comrades at some back street pub in Casablanca. With the same spirit that sent Clearwaters, Russ Lewis and other civilians in search of German submarines with a new technology called the sonobuoy, NUSC engineers boarded *Augusta* on February 9, 1986, and embarked into the Atlantic Ocean with a crew of anxious submariners.

But now the threat was from Soviet nuclear submarines, not German U-boats. The Cold War called on the next generation of engineers from the New London Laboratory, who would need to gain the trust of the next generation of submariners. The team from NUSC heading out for the WAA sea trials on *Augusta* was there because they were intimately familiar with the mechanical, electrical, and signal processing systems. But their technical expertise would not be enough. They would also have to blend in with the crew, share the risks and discomforts of sea duty, and finally enjoy the satisfaction of a successful mission—maybe not in Casablanca, but certainly in a suitable port.

When *Augusta* proceeded down the Thames River that winter in 1986, Cold War operations research was alive and well, and heading out to sea. As Vic Marolda recalled, "The captain let me look through the periscope and I could see my wife and kids standing near New London Light waving to their old man." Vic turned away from the eye-piece, and he and the other NUSC riders shifted gears. It was time to integrate with the crew—to let them know that these civilians were there to learn as well as instruct, and that NUSC was on board to give this boat the best tools available for finding their Soviet adversary. *Augusta* and the Cold Warriors on board— active duty and civilian—would pioneer this new technology, and the crew understood the significance of their next three months at sea. But the operations research underway on *Augusta* would only be successful if the relationship between the engineers and the crew was built on a spirit of trust and cooperation. Everyone on board knew the stakes were high.

Back in New London, Howie Schloemer, Wayne Strawderman, Emilio Recine, and all the rest who collectively conceived the idea and spearheaded the WAA program for the past ten years, waited anxiously for feedback from the boat. Vic had been selected to join the first leg of the WAA trials, in part because of his knowledge of the many pieces of hardware he helped develop. But Vic was also on board as a NUSC diver. Vic and our dive team had been involved with WAA from concept to installation. We had experimented with procedures for waterborne grooming of the array surface, using the same approach we took with maintaining the acoustic performance of surface ship sonar domes. We had followed the prototype installation from Electric Boat to Port Canaveral, Florida, and back to Groton and the Sub Base.

But now Vic was on board *Augusta*, and we all had confidence in his ability to tackle any waterborne issues that might arise with WAA. Vic had brought a large collection of spare parts plus repair tools and materials. He could also rely on diving support from the boat's scuba team—a senior chief and three petty officers. Sleeping accommodations for riders were located on empty torpedo skids (I remember my trip on *Pargo* in 1970, sleeping next to a SUBROC missile)—anyone climbing into the much-too-soft inflatable mattress was referred to as a hotdog-in-a-bun. After one night of this, Vic switched to hot-bunking with the crew.

The first stop for *Augusta* was St. Croix on February 13. Each morning over the next several days, *Augusta* left its mooring off Frederiksted and conducted a series of acoustic trials, returning in the late afternoon when Vic could inspect the array (figure 50). He and Senior Chief Brinkman were able to accomplish several repairs that ensured optimal performance of WAA—this sea trial being of the utmost importance to the evaluation of the system. The port call at St. Croix also gave the crew time for "liberty," the term used to describe when the crew could take a breather from the tensions of long periods submerged . . . also a time when Vic could solidify his acceptance as a participant and not just a civilian taking up space and getting in their way.

Figure 50. *Above:* Model of USS *Augusta* (SSN-710) showing the arrangement of WAA along the hull.

Below: A boat diver inspects one of the WAA arrays in St. Croix during its sea trials. (*Victor Marolda*)

With *Augusta* moored off Frederiksted, Vic went ashore to rent a van and find a dive shop in Christiansted where he could fill the scuba bottles. It had been six years since Vic had been to St. Croix on a previous project, and he had some familiarity with the island. With a van at his disposal, however, the crew saw him as their liberty chauffeur, and of course, he accommodated their needs. The "party van" made multiple excursions to bars, anxiously waiting for an influx of thirsty submariners. Each group expressed their thanks by offering Vic a drink or two, and of course, he accommodated this as well. "After many hours of this," Vic recalled, "I had consumed about all the Planter's Punch I could hold. I found a small restaurant with a second floor balcony where I could hide and settle my stomach with a little food. Ken [NUSC diver Ken Beatrice, an experienced beer consumer] had recommended a glass of chocolate milk as a preventive self-medication for the inevitable hangover."

As Vic related the story, he had integrated into the crew with as much gusto as he could hold that day and all he wanted was a little quiet time. From his balcony table, Vic could look out over the road below and watch for sailors trying to find him for just one more ride to just one more bar. It was late in the afternoon when Brinkman spotted him. "When he saw me,"

Vic recalled, "he had that 'Gotcha' expression as he pointed his finger at me and hollered 'just one more Planter's Punch, Vic' and, of course, I had to accommodate him; after all, he's a Senior Chief!"

During this initial leg of the WAA sea trials, not only had Vic been accepted as part of the crew, it is likely that decades later these same sailors will tell their grandchildren about the crazy civilian from New London. On February 19, Vic flew home as *Augusta* headed out to continue its acoustic trials. Over the next several months, *Augusta* had a busy schedule. She returned briefly to Groton, soon heading out to AUTEC . . . then out for open-ocean operations . . . then to Port Canaveral, Florida . . . back to sea . . . back to Groton . . . back to the open ocean. During each return stateside, Vic brought a team of our divers to continue the pierside grooming of *Augusta*'s prototype array.

The spectacular success of the WAA advanced development model (ADM) precipitated the eventual development and production of a final engineering development model (EDM). In 1993, the original ADM was removed and replaced on *Augusta* by the updated EDM, which was also installed on USS *Cheyenne* (SSN-773). The concept of a hull-mounted wide aperture array has continued, and new developments, including a light-weight version, are planned for the next generation fast attack submarine.

BUILDING 21

Launched in 1995, USS *Seawolf* (SSN-21)—the third U.S. submarine to carry this name—began construction in 1989. *Seawolf* was the first of what was intended to be twenty-nine Cold War submarines that would replace the *Los Angeles*-class. As the Cold War came to a close, however, only two more, USS *Connecticut* (SSN-22) and *Jimmy Carter* (SSN-23), were authorized. Submarine construction would eventually switch to the less expensive fast-attack USS *Virginia* (SSN-774), the first of its class launched in 2003. When the newly commissioned *Seawolf* moved up the Thames River, the boat arrived at the Groton submarine base to become a fixture along the waterfront. With the typical issues associated with a new class boat, the extended time spent pierside resulted in it being dubbed "Building 21."

Seawolf was carrying the latest sonar, including a NUSC-designed bow-mounted spherical array, which brought us to the Seneca Lake test facility frequently in the early 1990s. Diving at Seneca presented its own challenges. In the summer you could dive in your skivvies where water temperatures near the surface approached 70 °F, but as you descended through an agonizingly cold thermocline the temperature dropped to 40 °F. In the winter the thermocline disappeared and the temperature was 40 °F from the surface to the bottom. The lake never froze, but a persistent wind that often approached 20 knots, pushed up high "sea" states and drove a spray of water that froze on contact with the barge, creating icicles hanging at a 45-degree angle.

We travelled to Seneca Lake many times over the years, but the most impressive sight was an entire *Seawolf*-class bow module, suspended from the 200-ton-capacity crane on the Systems Measurement Platform (SMP) moored out in the middle of the lake (figure 51). The bow sphere

Figure 51. The Systems Measurement Platform (SMP) at Seneca Lake includes a 200-ton-capacity crane that could readily handle the weight of the SSN-21 bow sphere. (*NUSC/NL*)

incorporated a new array design, and would change the concept of submarine bow mounted active/passive sonar. Because of the significance of the acoustic tests, and the need to evaluate multiple parameters, our divers were on call to make "quick" adjustments to the array. A typical trip might put us on the road at 0400, arriving at the NUSC Seneca Lake shore facility at noon, on the barge and in the water by 1300, back on shore at 1500, an order of beer and Buffalo Wings at a local watering hole at 1600, arriving back in New London by midnight—then, with dive gear packed and ready, we'd wait for the next phone call.

For fifteen years we had focused on hull mounted sonar systems— both surface ships and submarines. We had successfully followed ASW ships operating around the world during the Cold War, and helped the NUSC-designed wide aperture array become a successful addition to the sonar capabilities of submarines. The dive team would move on to another passive submarine sonar that had been evolving for more than two decades—its importance to detection, tracking, and fire control required operational reliability, but its mechanical complexity presented many challenges. Meeting these challenges would become a career changing experience for many of our divers.

SUBMARINE TOWED ARRAYS

In March 1970, I was presented with a Letter of Appreciation that began: "The performance of Underwater Sound Laboratory personnel on board PARGO during the Near Term Sonar Improvement Program was outstanding to a man." The Commanding Officer of USS *Pargo* (SSN-650), Commander David R. Hinkle, could not have been happier with the results of this very successful system evaluation, and his letter made particular note of the contributions of test director Bob Garber and senior advisor Harry Weaver.

By the beginning of 1968, the Soviets had introduced their Charlie, Victor, and Yankee-class submarines, and there was a pressing need to increase the ability to detect and track these new, quieter submarines. The Near Term Sonar Improvement Program (NTSIP) that Commander Hinkle referred to was created in November 1969, through the Naval Ship Systems Command (NAVSHIPS) and the Chief of Naval Operations (CNO), to provide passive towed array sonar to 594- and 637-class attack submarines.

I didn't realize it at the time, but I had been given an opportunity to join a test team that would be taking the first at-sea data of a prototype towed array. During two sea tests in February and March, 1970, *Pargo* roamed the Atlantic with USN/USL's advanced onboard signal processing electronics and its array trailing far behind. I still remember the quiet that spread through *Pargo* when one of the Sound Lab engineers whispered, "It's Charlie . . . I think we have a Charlie!" I never found out if we had actually tracked and recorded this new Soviet submarine, but as Bob Garber recently mentioned to me, interest in towed arrays quickly gained momentum throughout the submarine fleet as word of *Pargo*'s tests spread among boat captains.

Their wish would soon come true. By September, only six months after the *Pargo* tests, the Navy had established the Submarine Tactical Array Sonar System (STASS) Program that within another six months would begin to move the prototype we took out on *Pargo* to a fleet-wide system.[105] Bob Garber would continue on as the STASS program manager at what was now the Naval Underwater Systems Center—the Sound Lab was a thing of the past—USN/USL had now become NUSC.

The hydrophone arrays, which could be around three hundred feet long, had to stream far astern for the sonar to discriminate between the sub's own noise and sounds coming from a target. These early STASS arrays were carried on a support craft, often a tugboat, and brought out to an offshore buoy, where a submarine waited. After making the connection to the STASS tow-cable, the sub would move out, while the tug un-reeled the cable and array. When returning from a deployment, the tug would then meet the sub and retrieve the STASS. This was an awkward operation, but served the purpose while future arrays were being developed. Several years would pass, before an on-board handling system was designed where the array could be deployed and retrieved from within the submarine.

The connect-at-sea STASS continued to serve the Navy for more than a decade. Then in the late 1970s, the TB-16 array began its introduction into the fleet. Known as "Fat Line" because the array itself was about three-and-a-half inches in diameter, the TB-16 was stowed in a housing mounted along the hull to accommodate its 240-foot length, while the half-mile-long tow-cable stowage drum was located within the pressure hull.[106]

As hydrophones became smaller, array diameters could be reduced to that of its tow cable, and by the mid 1980s, the first of what are now referred to as Thin Line Towed Arrays began to appear.

With an array of multiple hydrophones, the time delay between when the sound arrived at each successive hydrophone determined whether the target was in front or behind you. Thus, if the first hydrophone detected the sound before the second one, the target was forward of the array; if the aft-most hydrophone detected the sound first, then the target was behind you. But more information was required to localize the target in a three-dimensional ocean.

A single linear array had one inherent problem—each hydrophone in the array "hears" sound arriving from all directions with equal sensitivity. Thus, if the array detected the sounds of a distant target moving in a direction that, for example, might have been forty-five degrees to the path of your submarine, the hydrophone sensors could not determine if those sounds were coming from above, below, or to port or starboard. This directionality issue could be improved by towing a pair of arrays— for example, if the starboard array detected the sounds before the port array, then the target was transiting along a starboard track. The logical conclusion? If towing two arrays improved performance, then three . . . or four . . . or maybe even more arrays could resolve the target localization and tracking problem.

MLTA—MULTILINE TOWED ARRAY

It was 12:28 on October 5, 1992, when the watch informed the captain of USNS *Bold* (T-AGOS-12) that the divers had entered the water, his observation through binoculars confirmed by radio from the dive supervisor on the small inflatable "Zodiac." As his ship drew closer, the captain knew that within sixty seconds, *Bold* would have to pass as close as possible to a marker buoy, while the Zodiac hovered nearby. The large red buoy, visible from a significant distance, provided the ship with a navigation target, but the divers were out of sight.

In tow behind *Bold*, one of a small fleet of MSC vessels designed specifically for Navy acoustic research and ocean surveillance, was a state-of-the-art multiline towed array (MLTA), designed and built at the towed array facility, which had recently transitioned (see chapter 8) from NUSC to the Naval Undersea Warfare Center, New London (NUWC/ NL). A wing-shaped depressor caused the arrays to tow below the surface, simulating their position if towed behind a submarine. The test plan called for the divers to descend to a depth well below the draft of *Bold* and wait— with visibility in excess of one hundred feet, they could readily watch for the approaching ship. But the captain was being asked to drive his ship right over them, and trust that they would not get hit by his propeller, or snagged by the array and dragged across the ocean.

Earlier that morning, the test team assembled for a final operations briefing. In his previous career, the civilian captain of *Bold* had been the commanding officer of an aircraft carrier. He was accustomed to risky operations, but this one had raised the cautious captain's pucker factor to a new level. "This operation goes against all of my instincts," he proclaimed in an apprehensive tone. "I want the divers—just the divers—in the wardroom." After the detailed technical briefing with the entire test team, the no-nonsense captain expected a no-nonsense conversation with the four divers from New London—in private. Led by Vic Marolda, the team included Bob Schmidt, Paul Gianquinto, and Bruce Greenhalgh; all were experienced divers and had been involved with MLTA from the beginning. Their knowledge of the system and matter-of-fact description of the upcoming dive provided the captain with a level of trust in their capability. As the divers rose to leave the wardroom, one more comment from the captain: "At the end of the run I want a head count and status as soon as the divers are on the surface. Thank you, gentlemen . . . let's make this happen."

Bold approached within feet of the buoy on its starboard quarter, and in a matter of seconds, this 224-foot vessel would cross directly above a team of divers who, it had to be presumed, were well below the ship's two propellers. Within minutes, the tow cable passed by and the divers intercepted the multiline array, swam into prescribed positions, and recorded the motion and relative track of each line array on video.

At 12:37, only nine minutes after they hit the water, the dive sup on the Zodiac reported: "Three divers on the surface . . . three divers okay!" *Bold* and MLTA had transited beyond the buoy and began to change course for the second run. Throughout the day, *Bold* repeated the towing operation, but at increasing speeds. The divers' observations and their video documentation verified the towing characteristics of MLTA, allowing *Bold* and the NUWC/NL engineers to proceed with the acoustics testing. Paul Gianquinto remained on *Bold* as a member of the test team, while the other divers were transported to Port Everglades, and then returned to New London.

By the end of October, after operating in a variety of locations off the Florida coast and eventually in the Gulf of Mexico, the experimental verification of MLTA came to an end. The NUWC/NL team on *Bold* had demonstrated the ability to tow several line arrays in multiple configurations that could increase target detection, localization, tracking, and fire control. These successful tests convinced acousticians and system developers that "the future of submarine towed arrays seems to center on the multiline volumetric array program."[107] Yet this 2004 assessment by longtime sonar designer Stanley G. Lemon, published in the IEEE Journal of Ocean Engineering, recognized that ideas and technology never stand still, and that fiber optics and other acoustic sensors will continue to open new possibilities.[108]

The multiline program had been initiated as a scientific endeavor in the same vein as the research conducted by acousticians during the very early days of the Cold War—encourage risk takers to propose advanced concepts, assemble a team to create the hardware, and take these ideas to sea. NUWC expected the potential improvement in passive sonar, demonstrated during the MLTA tests, would result in a major effort to solve the complex design issues associated with the deployment, retrieval, and on-board stowage of a multiline array. Commercial ships working in the oil exploration industry routinely used multiple arrays to pinpoint drilling locations, but these large surface ships have plenty of room on deck. Space, however, was a luxury not found on a submarine. The Navy opted to depend on its hull-mounted sonar sensors, used in conjunction with the TB-16 "Fat Line" array and the TB-23 and TB-29 "Thin Line" arrays, which had been evolving over the past decade. Besides, the Navy considered that the Cold War had been "won," and funding to carry MLTA beyond the prototype stage was gone.

TLTA—THIN LINE TOWED ARRAY

The STASS arrays, which were attached at sea when the submarine left port and removed prior to entering port, were long gone, and the design of onboard deployment and retrieval systems eliminated this awkward procedure. By the mid-1980s, the capabilities of the TB-16 "Fat Line" array used by the Navy's fast attack submarines were being supplemented by the TB-23 "Thin Line" array.

The TB-23 array and its lengthy tow-cable were stowed on a ten-foot-diameter reel, mounted in an aft ballast tank. The array was deployed and retrieved with a capstan and hydraulic motor, also located in the ballast tank—all of this referred to as the OA-9070 towed array handling system. The array had to pass through a series of guide tubes that enabled the array to move along a curved path within the starboard horizontal stabilizer, before exiting through a bell-mouth and an outboard sensor assembly. But the mechanical systems that comprised the OA-9070 were complex, and several problems emerged as submarines operated their TB-23 array during deployments.

By 1994, in response to increasing feedback from the fleet regarding the OA-9070 handler, the NUWC/NL towed array division established a Blue Ribbon Panel at their Crystal Avenue facility to discuss the technical issues. At the same time, NAVSEA Code 92K created a Towed Array Project Team (TAPT) to coordinate efforts for resolving the problems and expediting necessary engineering changes. The approach would be the same as what we had experienced when NAVSEA Code 63J established the surface ship sonar dome Corrective Action Team (chapter 5)—define the problem and advance to a solution as fast as possible. This meant pulling together specialists from the Navy and private industry, who fully understood the mechanics of the handling systems, could evaluate the deficiencies, design engineering changes, and most importantly, produce a rapid response within the fleet.

THE 1990s—FROM SURFACE SHIPS TO SUBMARINES

Our six-year commitment in the 1980s to surface ship ASW issues world-wide fits the expression "pales in comparison to," when looking back on the commitment NUWC and the dive team made to the wide aperture array, the multiline towed array, and most significantly, submarine passive ASW system known as the Thin Line Towed Array. It is safe to say that our surface ship tiger teams were simply a training ground—a prelude to meeting a challenge that once again brought our divers around the world.

As we phased out of the SQS-53 surface ship sonar work, several of our divers moved on with their careers. We initiated another call for dive school candidates to begin the training process. The response was immediate, but we retained the high standards of selection and preparation for dive school that we had learned from experience were essential for establishing a dedicated team—in particular, our policy to require a candidate to train with us for at least a year prior to school.

The person most instrumental in transitioning our dive team to submarine sonar issues was Victor "Vic" Marolda, a pragmatic, focused engineer who knew how to shovel through the bull shit as fast as possible and get right to the problem. An artist at heart, his eye for detail and sense of perspective merged. He could visualize the problem . . . visualize detail . . . visualize the solution, all while working on a snow covered pier, coping with 20-knot winds, then jumping into 36-degree water. Few people could perform, both mentally and physically, under conditions that would send most running for the exit.

Vic's commitment to the modern warfighter, however, was understandable, considering the role models in his family. Two of Vic's uncles served in the Pacific theater during World War II—in 1942, his Uncle Ed, a member of the National Guard 43rd Infantry Division, deployed to the South Pacific where his 102nd Regiment was involved with Operation Bobcat, building the strategic defenses of Bora Bora in the French Solomon Islands. His Uncle Ted survived Guadalcanal as a member of the 1st Marine Division and participated in the Marine landing at Cape Gloucester on the island of New Britain. Vic's father, also Victor, was a Naval Air Corps First Class Aviation Machinist Mate, who was involved with the research and development of radio-controlled "flying bombs," and worked with then Chief (later Lieutenant) Wilford J. Willy. The drone concept was initially tested using aircraft made of plywood. These first generation drones were replaced with old and tired military aircraft that would be given one last mission.

Designed to be flown in formation with several supporting aircraft, the drone pilot and a radio-control expert would parachute into friendly territory, after turning control over to the mother-ship. On August 12, 1944, during a top secret mission codenamed Project Anvil, U.S. Navy pilot Lt. Joseph P. Kennedy attempted to fly his drone, a converted PB4Y-1 Liberator carrying over 21,000 pounds of explosives, over occupied France. Within minutes of passing control to the mother-ship, Kennedy's aircraft exploded, before he and the other airman, Lt. Wilford Willy, could parachute free of their drone.

Anyone who worked in and around the water with Vic knew that it would be a non-stop, make-it-happen experience. In the December 2005 issue of NUWSCOPE, Vic summarized the spirit of the NUWC dive team, during an interview with editor Jane Tracy: "The common denominator through us all is that we love diving, love that type of work, and the challenge of being in the hot seat to get it done . . . You're on your day job and then you get the call. You've got to be ready to go."

Jane Tracy described the dive team as "an elite group [that] for over 40 years has supported the fleet worldwide [and] doesn't have to go through a lot of channels to make decisions." Vic told her the basic tenant of all Navy divers: "We cut right through the bureaucracy [NUWSCOPE printable version of 'bull shit'] and red tape." As was the case for many of us on the dive team, Vic's work ethic and his success on the waterfront were influenced by his lifelong friend and mentor, "Mac" McClenny.

But we were all descended from a long line of Navy divers, who simply knew how to shoot from the hip and hit the bull's eye. Moving forward to a solution when you're in the field required creative action. Captain George F. Bond, Navy diver and the guiding light behind the Sealab saturation diving experiments, once commented: "We weren't given priority for material or equipment; we took what we needed from any place that had it. It was rumored that base personnel locked their doors when they saw us coming."[109] I suspect some fathers also locked up their daughters when they heard that a Navy diver was in the area.

TIGER TEAMS

The several issues discovered with the thin line towed array program, their urgency, and their solution embodied what the Navy expects when it establishes a Tiger Team. Our divers would attack towed array problems with the same commitment we enjoyed as members of surface ship sonar Tiger Teams in the 1980s. There would be a few new players now, and in anticipation of a heavy workload, we obtained temporary transfers of Ross Byrne, Mike Rutkowski and Mike Peirson from other codes to the Submarine Towed Array Division. Under Vic's leadership, our towed array divers followed the Navy diving community's tradition of hard work—whenever and wherever there was a need.

During the summer of 1994, the Blue Ribbon Panel and NAVSEA's TAPT had fairly well defined the problem, and assigned system evaluation and design tasks to the Tiger Team players. The handling system, located in ballast tank MBT 5-alpha (starboard side), was readily accessible when a boat is in dry-dock, but not so when pierside. NAVSEA was determined that the NUWC/NL towed array divers should have access to the ballast tanks. In the past, one hundred percent of our diving only required that we be qualified in scuba. A ballast tank was considered an enclosed space, and Navy divers were required to be trained in the use of the MK-20 Enclosed Space Diving System (ESDS). Although the MK-20 used the standard scuba full-face mask we had been using for ten years, the Navy had adapted it for their shallow-water surface supplied diving system. It didn't matter to us, whether the air came from bottles on our backs or from an umbilical hose to the surface, but it mattered to the Navy.

Vic and I discussed this with two of our new towed array divers, Lou Sansone and Paul Gianquinto, and we knew that it would take some horsepower to provide the needed qualification training. We hoped that a mobile training team from the Naval Diving and Salvage Training Center (NDSTC) would be sent to the Sub Base in Groton, as suggested by Master Diver Donlon at the Submarine School Escape Training Facility. But the path of least resistance was not always the path the Navy took. Early that fall, in 1994, we travelled to NASVSEA and discussed the issue with our sponsor. They agreed to endorse any solution and generate copious quantities of paperwork that would facilitate pierside access by our divers—just make it happen! Even as late as the end of October, we expected a mobile training team from NDSTC, but that would not be the case.

Our dive team chain of command included the Officer in Charge (OIC) of the NUWC New London Laboratory, at that time Commander Barry Holland. Commander Holland was a Navy qualified diver who had served as commanding officer of USS *Sunbird* (ASR-15) during the space shuttle Challenger disaster and recovery. He was well respected within the diving community, and helped expedite the process that would eventually lead to our divers receiving MK-20 ESDS qualification. Because providing this training would set a precedent, and a waiver had to be established showing that civilian specialist divers could receive the training, the Navy decided that NUWC would have to send its divers to NDSTC in Panama City, Florida, rather than send three instructors to Groton. Because it would simply be too expensive to fund the entire team, we had to pick a group from our team who would most likely participate in ballast tank operations. On January 28, 1995, nine of our divers returned from Panama City to New London—MK-20 ESDS qualification letters in hand.

"BOAT BAG"—FROM THE DRY-DOCK TO THE WATERFRONT

By the mid 1990s, there were fifty-five OA-9070 handling systems in the fleet, and with each commissioning, a new fast attack submarine would head to sea with its TB-23 thin line towed array. When a system-wide problem was being reported and the same piece of equipment had to be replaced or modified on every system, the process was called a "block upgrade." The Navy planned to have sixty-two 688-class fast attack boats built and commissioned by the end of the decade—the block upgrade to this class-wide engineering change would eventually address fifty-eight, with the remaining four under construction.

The Navy generated an engineering change instruction (ECI) that defined the problem with the handling system, and specified the required upgrade. Within months, the components that the Tiger Teams would carry to the waterfront were being assembled, and NAVSEA planned to schedule the block upgrade to commence in August 1995. The teams arrived at each boat, with bags of tools in hand—hence the name "Boat Bag."

Six teams were established; four led by NUWC/NL towed array divers Vic Marolda, Lou Sansone, Ross Byrne, and Mike Rutkowski. The dry-dock Tiger Team leaders were Frank Rubin and a Navy sonar tech assigned to NUWC/NL, STCS Bruce Getman. Each upgrade was expected to take about fourteen days. Thus, scheduling a pierside Boat Bag operation only required an in-port availability of two to three weeks. Because fleet divers were required to be available for any emergent situations, they could not guarantee an uninterrupted commitment to the upgrade. The Navy, through NAVSEA Code 00C, established contracts with commercial divers who could provide the dedicated support that a Navy project such as Boat Bag required.

The first installation began August 15, on USS *Phoenix* (SSN-702). All of the teams were on site in Norfolk for this dry-dock Boat Bag—after that "learning" experience, it would be a sprint to the finish. Each team included at least two representatives from NUWC/NL, the installation work supported by shipyard personnel or contractors. On September 12, Vic Marolda was assigned the first pierside upgrade in San Diego for USS *La Jolla* (SSN-701). On September 26, while Vic was wrapping up the *La Jolla* upgrade, Mike Rutkowski was in Pearl Harbor on USS *Los Angeles* (SSN-688). On October 11, Vic headed to Groton for USS *Minneapolis-St. Paul* (SSN-708), and six days later Ross Byrne was also in Groton on USS *Providence* (SSN-719). In November, Lou Sansone was in Norfolk on USS *Boise* (SSN-764), and Mike was off to San Diego for the USS *Cheyenne* (SSN-713) upgrade. Mixed in among the pierside operations were four Boat Bag dry-dock upgrades. Ten boats completed in four months, but the pace would increase.

By the end of 1996, the block upgrade was complete—fifty-eight systems (every commissioned 688 submarine) in less than eighteen months. Thirty-five had been accomplished pierside with no impact on ship schedules. A submarine could make a port call, and the divers would be on site when she arrived. Working in the aft ballast tanks had minimal impact on other pierside operations, so multiple activities could be accomplished, enabling the boat to leave port on schedule and with its upgrade completed.

Without the capability to accomplish the Boat Bag waterborne, each of these submarines would have been forced to make a very costly, unscheduled dry-docking. There was no question that by being enablers, the New London management, and certainly the Officer in Charge, CDR Holland, made it possible for these risk takers to aggressively pursue the notion that engineering solutions to fleet problems could be accomplished by well trained divers. For the Boat Bag block upgrade, our divers, along with many others from the New London staff, dedicated a year and a half of their lives to save the Navy millions of dollars, and avert a diminished operational capability. This same aggressive approach to supporting emergent fleet sonar issues has continued to characterize our team's collective spirit.

WE SUPPORT THE FLEET THE WORLD OVER

The EDSU logo proudly printed on our Blue-and-Gold T-shirts contains the phrase, "We Support the Fleet the World Over"—a promise that rose from our worldwide commitment to surface ship sonar during the Cold War. There were still global tensions in the 1990s, and the U.S. submarine fleet continued to be sent on multiple deployments around the world. The success of Boat Bag had demonstrated that solving towed array system issues were no longer restricted to dry-dock operations, and our divers soon found themselves in demand. When a boat returned to port with a towed array problem, they were sent in to inspect the handling system, or help replace a damaged array, and then could return to the drawing board with first-hand knowledge of the situation. Troubleshooting a problem often required our divers to install an underwater video camera in the ballast tank, and remotely record the handling system operating during an underway array deployment and retrieval.

A solution to a difficult problem would evolve from the cumulative insights of all the players—divers and non-divers, Navy and industry. But equally significant was that our management in New London—and NAVSEA—recognized that computer modeling alone can't solve every problem; they understood how important it was to maintain a connection between the laboratory and the waterfront.

Political forces within the Department of Defense that had been fermenting within the Base Realignment and Closure Commission (see chapter 8) would soon boil over and turn the New London Laboratory upside down. In 1992, NUSC had become the Naval Undersea Warfare Center (NUWC), with the Division headquartered in Newport, and soon what was the NUWC New London Laboratory was designated a Detachment. By the end of 1996, this Detachment was closed forever, and all of the New London facilities were quickly packed into 18-wheelers and transported to Newport, where buildings were being renovated to accommodate more than a thousand from New London—the dive team included. Our name was changed to the Engineering and Diving Support Unit (EDSU), and we shifted from a Command support role to a component of the Test & Evaluation Department.

It would only take a few months to settle into our new home on the Newport waterfront, but towed arrays remained a significant focus of NUWC. The Navy still depended on the EDSU divers to mobilize and respond to issues anywhere at any time. Ross Byrne left NUWC and brought his towed array and diving expertise to the Fleet Technical Support Center at the sub base. As far as the Navy was concerned, it didn't matter if their civilian scientists and engineers were in New London or Newport—we simply had to suck up to the fact that we had to commute to NUWC—it was the submariner and his

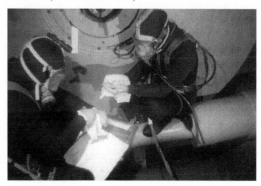

Figure 52. *Above:* As the setting sun casts shadows across USS *Hampton* (SSN-767), divers working alongside remained through the night. *Below:* The MK 20 Enclosed Space Diving System (ESDS) is the Navy-approved system for pierside ballast tank operations. When air quality inside the tank has been tested, divers are allowed to remove their MK 20 full-face masks. (*Victor Marolda*)

boat that depended on a ready supply of field engineers on the waterfront (figure 52).

TROMSØ SJØFORSVARSDISTRIKT DYKKERGRUPPE

If you can pronounce this, I will buy you a beer! Unlike a surface ship that will anchor just about anywhere, a submarine operating overseas will of necessity pull into a friendly naval base when experiencing a system problem. In August 2000, Bob Schmidt was sent to tackle an emergent towed array issue on one of our 688-class boats operating off Norway. To our divers, the term "emergent" means "address the issue ASAP and let us know when the problem has been resolved!" So with those verbal orders and plane tickets in hand, Bob arrived at the Tromsø Sjøforsvarsdistrikt Dykkergruppe—loosely translated, the Tromso Naval Defense District Diving Team. A few days later, the submarine was underway—problem resolved.

Because of the critical missions associated with submarine operations, our divers would typically address towed array handling systems prior to deployment, when there was even a hint of a potential issue. Countless trips were made to the sub bases in Groton and Norfolk, as well as to Electric Boat and Portsmouth Naval Shipyard. In nearly every case, our divers would depend on support from local active duty or civilian Navy diving assets. On the west coast, the EDSU would arrive (also on countless numbers of times) at San Diego, Pearl Harbor, and occasionally, the Puget Sound Naval Shipyard where our divers were joined by the same team (now a bunch of old timers) who worked with us during the WAA testing in 1982.

Nonetheless, there were still a few calls to meet a boat in some foreign port, making a passport an essential document to have at the ready. Faslane, Scotland, was just a quick hop across the Atlantic, and there would be another visit to the Tromsø Sjøforsvarsdistrikt Dykkergruppe. Just a bit farther away—actually, on the other side of the world—our divers would find themselves in Yokosuka and Sasebo, Japan, and in Bahrain, Singapore and Guam. In most cases, our divers were supported by a team of active duty Navy divers.

In the decade and a half after the OA-9070 block upgrade, EDSU divers were sent out on nearly three hundred of these visits. As with the support we provided to surface ship ASW in the 1980s, we occasionally received a written appreciation from a very happy captain. Our mission as members of a fast response team was just that—fast response, return home, keep your bags packed—that was our job, and although we invariably received verbal thanks from ship's forces on the spot, a letter to our Command was always a good thing. The following are excerpts from one particularly appreciative submarine captain:

> Commanding Officer, USS *Connecticut* (SSN 22) takes pleasure in commending Mr. Michael Peirson for services set forth in the following citation:

> For professional achievement in the superior performance of his duties while supporting USS *Connecticut*'s (SSN 22) inaugural deployment in August 2002. When *Connecticut* suffered severe technical problems with her towed array system, Mr. Peirson provided exceptional diving support in the troubleshooting and restoration of *Connecticut*'s sonar sensors thereby allowing *Connecticut* to continue her deployment . . . . Mr. Peirson worked under physically demanding conditions, diving through the night to provide round the clock support throughout the week.

Mike Peirson arrived at NUSC as an active duty member of the EOD Detachment in 1985, having recently completed his scuba training, and then qualifying as an EOD Assistant Technician. After leaving active duty in 1989, Mike remained at NUSC, serving as a hazardous waste and environmental specialist. Mike soon became an engineering technician and towed array diver in the Submarine Sonar Department. He remained associated with the military, joining the Navy reserves, first as a member of Reserve SEAL Team Two DET 201, where he completed jump school, then transferring to Reserve Mobile Diving and Salvage Unit (MDSU) Two DET 101. In 1999, Mike joined Reserve EOD Mobile Unit 10. During his time with the Navy reserves, he participated in overseas operations in Panama and Costa Rica, and deployed to Italy in 2003. But after Mike retired from his years with the Navy Reserves, he continued his civilian career at NUWC with the submarine towed arrays branch. Mike was one of the NUWC divers to qualify in the MK-20 Enclosed Space Diving System in 1995, and his letter from the commanding officer of *Connecticut* was just one example of his dedication to the Navy diving tradition of "excellence under pressure."

JOHN WIEDENHEFT

John Wiedenheft, a mechanical engineering technician with an irrefutable eye for detail, arrived at NUSC in 1982. His career has revolved around the oversight of thousands of design details essential for the development, and eventual installation, of systems heading for the Navy warfighter. John worked with Vic Marolda for several years before deciding to take on the "challenge," and in December 1999, he returned from Panama City, the first EDSU diver to qualify in scuba and MK-20, after the team received its training for the "Boat Bag" in 1995. At Vic's retirement in 2012, John recalled how teamwork at the office guaranteed success on the waterfront—and with towed arrays in particular.

> Over the years I have been involved in many brainstorming sessions with Vic, working to find a solution to a problem. These sessions usually go like this: Vic and I with one or two others meet in a conference room where we all put forth ideas. Invariably, Vic comes up with some unique way of framing the problem . . . my job in these brainstorming sessions often evolves into pointing out flaws in Vic's proposed solution. After discussing my critique, Vic will then suggest a brand new solution, coming from a completely different direction. I have rarely met anybody so unconstrained by presumptions.

"Engineering and Diving" were the cornerstones of the EDSU mission, and John's description of a typical meeting was a true assessment of the dive team's technical versatility. It was through these meetings that the EDSU could offer credible cost saving options to the Navy.

SAVING THE TAXPAYER MILLIONS

Just the act of putting a submarine in dry-dock could be measured in hundreds of thousands of dollars. Soon, hordes of riggers, machinists, welders, inspectors, planners-and-estimators, safety engineers, and of course, plenty of supervisors, arrived on site. Every submarine pulling in to the base in Groton had a mission to complete—a problem that occurred in MBT-5 had to be resolved and the boat might sit along pier 8N waiting for a solution. A meeting would be called where a crescendo of voices from the local shipyard screamed "DRY-DOCK!!!" A collective groan arose in a room filled with Navy representatives from among the waterfront commands—SUPSHIPS, NSSF, STSC, DEVRON 12, SUBGRU 2, and the boat's commanding officer. Let's take a hypothetical look at what might have transpired during similar meetings at many naval bases and shipyards; the questions were always the same.

Navy: "Will the submarine still be able to meet its mission objectives?" "Is a dry-dock available?" "How long will this take?" "What's this going to cost?"

Shipyard: "We will take care of the submarine ASAP." "We will delay another job to provide access to the dock." "We've never confronted an issue like this before, but we're certain that once our engineers look at it, we will find a solution to your problem." "We can provide an accurate cost estimate once the boat is in dry-dock."

The Navy cringed—each of these assessments meant lots, and lots, and lots of dollars. As the discussion progressed, a hand rose from the far corner of the room, followed by a familiar voice. "We can do this pierside." The Navy: "Vic . . . Do you really think it's possible?" The shipyard: "This problem is too difficult for divers to tackle." [Translation: shut up, Vic!] Everyone at those meetings knew that NUWC had individuals with the knowledge required to provide critical recommendations—with realistic solutions—to the decision makers.

Our divers had been involved with towed arrays from the first day they donned the MK-20 Enclosed Space Diving System, and entered a ballast tank in 1995. By the late 1990s, the Navy's towed array handling system experts resided in Newport, and a few of them had spent a lot of time in MBT-5, with submarines tied pierside. We never really kept count, but whenever a towed array problem occurred, or a design improvement was being considered, the Navy turned to Vic and an experienced team of EDSU divers. Every decision to attempt a problem resolution would cross Vic's desk with the questions: "Can this be done pierside? Can we save the

Navy and the taxpayers millions of dollars?" Many times the answer has been "Yes."

TO CUT OR NOT TO CUT [A HOLE IN A SUBMARINE]

During its construction, a submarine received many of its systems prior to the addition of its superstructure. When, for example, the OA-9070 handling system for the TB-23 towed array was installed in MBT-5; the aft portion of the 688-class submarine was fully exposed, facilitating installation of the large handling system components. Once the hull sections that enclose the aft ballast tanks were welded in place, the capstan drive wheel and stowage drum were far too large to be removed through the ballast tank opening. From the start, if a problem occurred, the assumption had been to dry-dock the vessel, and then make a hull cut in the superstructure sufficient to handle these components.

In 1996, soon after 688 boats began deployments with their TB-23, there had been reports of array damage. The small diameter array and its tow cable nest in the hydraulic-motor-driven capstan drive wheel during the deployment and retrieval. The diameter of the drive wheel groove and its alignment with the guide tube were critical to a smooth passage out through the starboard horizontal stabilizer. Our divers had successfully contended with alignment issues, but when it had been determined that array damage was caused by an out-of-spec drive wheel groove, the cry went out, "Dry-dock the boat, cut a hole, and pull out the capstan."

It was when this "only option" landed in Vic Marolda's lap, that Vic and John Wiedenheft brainstormed a solution that became known as the machine-in-place (MIP) procedure. Whether the submarine was already in dry-dock or pierside, the MIP system could be easily brought into MBT-5 through the open ballast tank grate. The drive wheel groove was then "machined" to the correct diameter, eliminating the need to make that very expensive hull cut. The MIP success on 688-class boats was repeated on *Seawolf* in 1999, and has since been passed on to submarine repair facilities as a standard procedure.

As our divers developed engineering solutions to issues that submarines encountered with their towed arrays, it became on operational necessity that fleet divers receive formal training in the Standard Operating Procedure

200

(SOP) of OA-9070 handling systems and the associated routine pierside troubleshooting, maintenance, and repair. Over the years, our divers would continue to be called to address towed array issues on the waterfront. But their experience also called them to the classroom, serving as instructors for active duty dive teams deployed to support submarines operating throughout the world's oceans.

AN UNEASY PEACE

The Cold War had "officially" come to an end in December 1991, but in spite of the euphoria and celebration at the end of forty-six years of tension, it remained an uneasy peace. The Soviet Union had not been the only nuclear capable country, and it would fall to the United States to remind the world of the consequences of any nuclear confrontation.

Although submarines that sail hidden beneath the blue-water oceans are no longer "Soviet," Russia will always present itself as a global power. The pursuit of maritime superiority embodied in the submarine continues to dominate their naval strategy. The massive 505-foot-long Russian Oscar II-class SSGN attack submarines were conceived in the last years of the Cold War, and with twenty-four P-700 Granit anti-ship cruise missiles, they were designed as a major maritime threat (figure 53). Travelling at thirty-

Figure 53. One of many Russian Oscar-class guided missile submarines that patrol the world's oceans represents the capability of potential adversaries to contend with US maritime superiority. (*Department of Defense Photo*)

two knots submerged, they were quiet, and the low magnetism of their outer hull made them difficult to find with magnetic anomaly detection systems. The most notable Oscar II was *Kursk* (K-141), lost in the Barents Sea on August 12, 2000, due to an explosion in its forward torpedo room.

Many Russian submarines, including the Oscar IIs, patrol the Atlantic sea lanes and could pose a significant threat to carrier battle groups. In order to deter global adversaries, an American submarine presence is thus still on the strategic agenda. Sonar will continue to dominate the technology that enables our submarines to retain their hidden presence in the world's oceans, where they remain capable of launching a variety of weapons, or deploying Special Forces teams whenever and wherever needed. The balance of power still resides beneath the sea.

Over the two decades that followed the Cold War, passive "listening" sonar systems remained center stage in both submarine and antisubmarine warfare. These systems had their origins nearly a century ago with concepts developed by scientists, engineers, and a dedicated military contingent at the Navy Experimental Station in New London during World War I. Twenty-first century conformal hull-mounted arrays, along with an assortment of increasingly efficient towed arrays, continue to be developed, tested, and deployed on submarines and surface ships. But sonar isn't the only submarine technology that our divers have tackled.

Figure 54. *Above:* Electronic warfare began with Guglielmo Marconi's wireless telegraphy during World War I. Surface navies quickly adapted the technology by erecting "cage masts" that served as observation posts and to install Marconi's antennas far above the water, as on USS *Missouri*. (*Naval History and Heritage Command*) *Below:* Submarines, such as USS *K-1* underway c. 1916, were restricted to wireless communications while on the surface, but antenna heights limited range to around fifty miles. (*Naval History and Heritage Command; O.W. Waterman*)

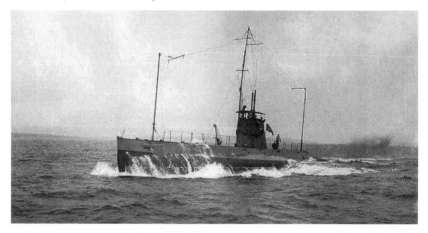

CHAPTER 7
Not Just an "Underwater Sound" Laboratory

When the *Titanic* struck an iceberg at 11:20 on the night of April 14, 1912, radio operators on board sent a distress message in Morse code. The operators, however, were not Cunard Line employees; they worked for the Marconi International Marine Communications Company. Guglielmo Marconi was one of several scientists, including Nikola Tesla and Heinrich Hertz, who pioneered the development of wireless communication technology that, during the early years of the twentieth century, had become a common system on board commercial as well as naval vessels. Another scientist who had a major impact on wireless technology was Reginald Fessenden, who also patented an early acoustic communication and echo-ranging system, the "Fessenden Oscillator," used on post World War I destroyers.

This well-regarded wireless technology appealed to military strategists who understood the advantages of an ability to instantly transmit information across long distances, the essence of what is termed today as C3—Command, Control, and Communication. This capability was as eagerly sought after at the end of the nineteenth century, as it is now at the beginning of the twenty-first.

The path over which these "Hertzian waves" travel depended on many factors not fully understood at that time. But what the designers of wireless systems did understand was that the distance between sender and receiver was directly related to transmit power and the design of the antennas— most significant to maritime applications, however, being the height of the antenna above water. Neither of these was an issue for surface ships, where there was ample room on board to carry the then massive transmitters. During World War I, many naval vessels were equipped with "cage masts," which on Battleships, enabled large antennas to be mounted more than 150 feet above the waterline (figure 54).

For a World War I British or American submarine, however, nearly every inch of interior space was dedicated to propulsion and torpedoes— there was little room left to support the equipment required for powering the wireless transmitter. But there were also limits on the ability to mount the antenna at any significant height, restricting the range over which reliable communications could be expected to about fifty miles. Germany, on the other hand, understood the importance of wireless telegraphy and designed telescoping antennas that increased the ability of U-boats to communicate, often through a network of relay stations, over hundreds of miles.[110]

Most submarines at that time were poorly equipped to operate far out in the open ocean, preferring to remain closer to shore where more targets of opportunity would be encountered. Because transmitting radio waves was not possible while submerged, a submarine had to be on the surface in order to communicate. A surfaced submarine was vulnerable to detection during daylight hours by shore-based aircraft including dirigibles, thus relying on its periscope when searching submerged for targets. During World War I, before the advent of radar, submarine captains often risked surfacing during the day to approach and attack a vulnerable unarmed vessel. Nonetheless, radio communications remained problematic.

Antennas, if permanently mounted exterior to the hull, were vulnerable to damage; hence, most were stowed on board. It then became a time consuming affair to surface, open the hatch, and install the antenna—then transmit, wait for a reply, remove the antenna, and submerge. For a vessel that depended on operating submerged for its very survival, any excess time on the surface was an invitation for detection, restricting use of the wireless until after dark when the submarine's batteries were being charged.[111]

With radio communication limited to as little as fifty miles, there was only one alternative for a submarine captain operating off a distant coastline. Lieutenant Commander Kenneth Edwards, an officer in the Royal navy during World War I, described the use of an ancient technology that dates to the Egyptians and Persians three thousand years ago— carrier pigeons. At the beginning of the war, naval vessels carried many of these birds and depended on their innate ability to navigate to their terrestrial home. According to Edwards, when telegraphy was not an option, "communicating and reporting had to be done by carrier pigeon . . . A flying speed of 30 miles an hour was allowed for the pigeons." This technology, while it proved effective on many missions, did have a serious flaw. Edwards: "Unfortunately the seaman in charge of the pigeons had made pets of them and fed them too well . . . a 'C' class submarine tried to report by carrier-pigeon, to find that they had been so over-fed by their keeper that they could not fly. They fell into the sea, and were rescued with considerable trouble and risk."[112] Certainly, there must be a better solution. As with so many emerging technologies, there is a transition from a less efficient system that works, to a new system that has yet to reach its potential.

NO MORE BIRD SEED ON SUBMARINES

During World War II, submarine and antisubmarine technologies that evolved at the Columbia University Division of War Research in New London were focused on sonar and underwater acoustics. Submarine communication development primarily fell to the Naval Research Laboratory (NRL) and the Bureau of Ships (BUSHIPS) in Washington, and to the Massachusetts Institute of Technology (MIT). But as the war came to a close, the proximity of the submarine base in Groton to the technological initiatives underway in New London inspired a shift in communications research to the newly formed U.S. Navy Underwater Sound Lab.[113]

In October 1945, Cletus Dunn, an engineer who had been part of the Columbia University activities in New London, was handed this new mission. His initial tasking included operating from a small building within the grounds of Fort Wright on Fishers Island. The building had been used by MIT for similar submarine communications research during the war. Located on Mount Prospect, the highest point on the island, the building provided ready access to submarines transiting to and from the submarine base. This location was ideal for testing new concepts in the electronics associated with transmitting and receiving radio signals and for evaluating new submarine antenna designs. The submarine communications research that began with MIT in 1943, and transitioned to the Sound Lab two years later, has continued uninterrupted at this unique facility for seven decades.

The Sound Lab created the Submarine Electromagnetic Systems Department in 1948, in part due to the rapidly increasing role (and staffing) that submarine communications and radio frequency (RF) research played within the Lab's mission. Over the next twenty years, the range of radio frequencies being considered expanded from the initial very low frequency (VLF) systems, to now consider extremely low frequency (ELF) and very high frequency (VHF) for submarines. By the mid-1960s, experiments with satellite communications brought USN/USL into the ultra high frequency range (UHF). But this book is about a team of Navy engineer/divers. What role would we have in the Submarine Electromagnetic Systems Department where radio waves operate above—not below—water? Again, it brought us to the scientists who were investigating the physics of their piece of the electromagnetic spectrum, and a few of these pieces occurred underwater.

NON-ACOUSTIC SUBMARINE DETECTION—USING THE EARTH'S MAGNETIC FIELD

The Submarine Electromagnetic Systems Department had also taken ownership of technologies that were unrelated to RF communications, but still fit within the USN/USL, and later NUSC, mission to explore possibilities that encompassed the entire electromagnetic spectrum—from the Earth's magnetic field to radar and infra-red, and to optical systems (including periscopes) operating in the visible light band. Richard Compton-Hall (1988) described a phenomenon he referred to as "magnetohydrodynamics," a long word that relates to how the Earth's magnetic field "is disturbed when a ferrous metal object passes through it." He was referring, of course, to a submarine.[114] During World War II, equipment with the sensitivity needed to detect this disturbance—thus a submarine—had been designed to be operated from aircraft, a technology that found application in the hunt for Cold War Soviet submarines

Thad Bell (2011) described an operation in the summer of 1969, where the destroyer escort USS *McCloy* (DE-1038, reclassified FF-1038 in 1975), operating from Naples, Italy, and equipped with an SQS-26 sonar, was searching for Soviet submarines operating within the convergence zone in the Ionian Sea. The first contact occurred at 41 kiloyards (just over twenty nautical miles). The ship then vectored an ASW patrol aircraft to the location where sonobuoys confirmed that a submarine had been detected. The aircraft then continued to maintain contact via its magnetic anomaly detection (MAD) system. When the submarine sensed it was being tracked, it made an evasive maneuver and contact was lost. After about seventeen hours, the aircraft sighted and identified the contact as a Soviet Foxtrot-class submarine on the surface, causing it to immediately submerge. *McCloy* continued to search within the convergence zone and after six hours the submarine was located—the aircraft was again sent to the location with its MAD system. The submarine was tracked for another fourteen hours before losing contact. For more than two-and-a-half days, *McCloy*, working with the vectored aircraft, played the cat and mouse game that characterized much of the Cold War interplay with Soviet submarines.[115]

Although acoustics dominated antisubmarine systems, the potential of adding electromagnetic sensors to the ASW toolbox sent scientists out for "more data." Whether a system used acoustics or electromagnetics, the ability to detect a submarine depended on a thorough understanding of the ambient background levels. The extensive acoustic measurements using submersibles, which dominated the 1960s (chapter 4), provided opportunities for Sound Lab scientists to join the deep-sea acousticians and collect electromagnetic background data within the ocean.

In addition to magnetic anomaly detection, a transiting submarine, being a massive metallic object, is itself affected by the Earth's magnetic field. The hull will become "magnetized" with time, and will occasionally be required to go through a degaussing process. There are also electric fields generated by galvanic currents between zincs and paint holidays, which contribute to accelerated erosion of a submarine's cathodic protection. The concept of detecting a submarine's electromagnetic field is not new, as evidenced in a report by the Navy Experimental Station's Harvey Hayes at the end of World War I: "The steel shell of the submarine must be surrounded by a magnetic field, due to the polarization induced by the earth's magnetic field."[116] A detection technology, which the report suggests was "applicable to the case of a moving submarine," was simply not available when first proposed. That would change during World War II and the Cold War, and access to scientific data. Recalling an early USN/USL effort by Joe Gordon, who received an award in 1962 for "underwater electromagnetic noise measurements exterior to the hull of several submerged submarines,"[117] NUSC divers would become involved with a similar series of measurements in November 1979, and January 1980.

EMIL SODERBERG—A TRUE GENTLEMAN SCHOLAR

Emil Soderberg was among the Sound Lab scientists who joined Jacques Cousteau and his *Diving Saucer* for a series of dives off San Diego in February 1965. Emil descended to a depth of 1000 feet during one of the eight dives dedicated specifically to electromagnetic measurements—the first time such measurements had been made along the ocean floor. In the 1970s, the NUSC Electromagnetic Systems Department, including Emil and co-investigator Bud Middleton, became involved with Project Linear Chair. A 1977 NAVFAC (Naval Facilities Engineering Command) Report described Linear Chair as a program "for measuring the near field and far field magnetic, electric, and electro-magnetic signatures of various underwater platforms." [118] In Navy language, a submarine is considered an "underwater platform."

Our engineer/divers spent several months working with Emil, designing and testing a device for measuring these same electromagnetic fields "exterior to the hull of submerged submarines," which Joe Gordon had supported two decades earlier. Emil had promised that we would be diving in the Caribbean, but a trip to a tropical climate would be preceded by a series of measurements much farther north—and in November. To access a submerged submarine, NUSC turned to the Navy's submarine suspension facility at the Carr Inlet Acoustic Range (CIAR), located along the southern-most end of Puget Sound (this facility has moved to Ketchikan, Alaska).[119] There, the submarine was connected fore and aft to cables running from a pair of massive "destroyer buoys." The boat then added ballast until only slightly negatively buoyant, and was slowly lowered and suspended at a prescribed depth beneath the buoys (see chapter 6, figures 47 and 48, for photos associated with another trip to CIAR).

It's time to dive! Puget Sound in November was a mighty cold body of water, but nothing out of the ordinary for our team, used to New England diving. Our divers included Mac McClenny, Jim Clark, Ray Munn, Rick Thibeault and me. We were joined by a team from the Puget Sound Naval Shipyard, kindred souls when it came to working in cold water, and there was no hesitation when it was time to make the scientific measurements that Emil was expecting. The advantage of having a dive team consisting of engineers and technicians comes from our ability to multi-task. Those not in the water, or who have reached their maximum time at depth and are now waiting through their surface interval, can take on a data acquisition role, thus providing some of that "value added" feature that MBAs and bean-counters love.

We spent several days on USS *Theodore Roosevelt* (SSBN-600), hanging below the Carr Inlet buoys. During our off-hours, we did manage to enjoy the buffalo stew, carrot cake, pool table, and a round or two at nearby Tides Tavern, as we contemplated that a successful test was going to be a ticket to the West Indies—at least that was what Emil had promised!

PROJECT ANIMAL—(#)

Back in New London, we waited anxiously for word from Emil about the data we had collected, and if the procedures and test equipment needed any modification. We were, however, most interested in whether Emil would keep his promise. It may have been a need to squeeze a bit of additional angst from the divers, but it took several weeks before we were given the word to pack for St. Croix. Packing, however, would now be for diving in water thirty degrees warmer than Carr Inlet where you drank lots of coffee—first to warm the inside of your body before making the jump, then to provide

Figure 55. *Above:* Working in 45 °F water at the Carr Inlet Acoustic Range, NUSC diver Jim Clark calibrates the data acquisition carriage in the first of a two-part Linear Chair project. *Below:* Now in water thirty degrees warmer at St. Croix, Jim Clark calibrates the carriage for part two. (*Roy Manstan*)

ample ability to warm the inside of your wetsuit. Now we would be in water where, if it weren't for the fact that the Navy doesn't approve of on-the-job skinny dipping, minimal thermal protection was recommended but not a necessity (figure 55).

The slight delay in getting the word out about St. Croix was the time needed to obtain access to a submarine—they're not just a phone call away. Once it had been determined that our Carr Inlet trip was a success, there was no hesitation expediting access to a boat, but we would be required to work on a not-to-interfere basis. We were given an early Christmas present when we were informed that USS *Sam Rayburn* (SSBN-635) would be making a January port call at Frederiksted, a marginally popular tourist location in St. Croix (most visitors preferred Christiansted, the more civilized and tourist-friendly part of the island). We would be provided access to the boat, but were told to plan for the possibility of night diving, as she might be running daily operations off shore.

The team heading for St. Croix consisted of the same NUSC divers who had supported the Carr Inlet tests, but now included Vic Marolda. Vic had qualified in scuba the previous September and helped design and test the underwater carriage used for collecting data. In November, when the Carr Inlet team was being assembled, Vic approached his branch head, who responded by denying him permission to participate, and telling Vic that joining the dive team was not going to be a good career choice. Vic then realized his mistake and made another career choice. He cleared off the desk in his cubicle, said "sayonara" to his branch head, and by December, transferred to the applied mechanics group where Jim Clark, Ray Munn and I worked.[120]

As with the Carr Inlet tests, there would be a significant amount of diving, and we enlisted help from the Navy's Combat Camera Group. Prior to joining the Sound Lab staff in 1966, Mac had been a member of Combat Camera, and was able to arrange for a team of their divers to join us. They were on an assignment at Naval Station Roosevelt Roads, not far from St. Croix, and were delighted to support a Navy scientific mission, unique to their typical underwater photographic operations.

Field work always required that all involved be as flexible as possible; this facilitated a great working relationship between everyone (including the officers and crew of our submarine host), and provided realistic expectations at all levels. Diving for Emil's project would occur during the day or at night—we could accommodate any schedule; it was the data that counted.

Prior to running any diving operation on a naval vessel, specific systems (e.g. sonar, fathometer, suctions, cathodic protection, and propeller) were secured, or "tagged out." A red tag was attached to the controls for the operation of these systems, mandating that the equipment was not to be operated while divers were in the water. We did, however, run into one close call. When diving alongside the submarine, it was necessary to set belly-bands around the hull, marking the off-limits areas specified by RADCON diving requirements. Running these demarcation lines was a very simple task, and our divers swam the lines with just snorkels. We later discovered that one of the suctions had not been tagged and could have trapped the swimmer, had he come too close. Having avoided a potentially fatal experience, the lesson here was to check and double check the tag-out procedure, making sure every item was accounted for. Taking a deep breath, we moved ahead with the task at hand. We were

Figure 56. *Above:* USS *Sam Rayburn* (SSBN-635) pierside at St. Croix. The bubbles seen at the bow are from the divers working below. (*Richard Thibeault*) *Below:* (L-R) Vic Marolda, Jim Clark, and Roy Manstan operate the carriage. (*NUSC/NL; "Mac" McClenny*)

there to collect data, and this was going to be a long day (figure 56).

Because the sub was in operational mode, the status of its reactor required us to limit our diving to specific regions on the hull. This would not be a problem, as we could conduct our measurements well within the prescribed limits. We received the necessary RADCON (Radiological Controls) briefings from the boat, and were issued TLDs (thermoluminescent dosimeters). We were required to wear a TLD to quantify any radiation exposure that we might encounter during our dives. Our operations were tightly controlled, and after completing several days of testing there was no measurable exposure.

There were, however, diversions. The Seven Flags Virgin Bar and Grille sat near the head of the pier—way too convenient for those of us who had acquired a powerful thirst after several hours in the water. Because the boat would be underway the next day, we had time that first night to "debrief" at the Seven Flags. Knowing full well that we could sleep late, our debriefing continued on . . . and on . . . and on, as we proceeded to build team spirit with our brother divers from Rosey Roads. We were all very happy that the boat wouldn't be back until late in the day.

We took every opportunity to run our tests—night or day—according to the submarine's operational schedule. While setting up the test equipment for our second night operation, I swam out to place a component in the far field and noticed a single jelly fish float past the beam of my dive light. As I was returning to the rest of the divers working on the stern planes, illuminated by additional lights, I saw another jelly drift by. No big deal at the time, and we were able to complete a good amount of testing that night, before the boat got underway.

Our submarine returned pierside the next afternoon when we expected to be back for a third night of testing. When we arrived at the pier late that afternoon to run the tag-out, the boat had just suspended a swim call after two sailors experienced severe anaphylactic reactions to jelly fish stings. A quick look over the side, and there was a swarm of these bad-boys hovering around the hull—and just about everywhere around the pier. I recognized them as the same as I had seen the night before. But there were hundreds of them—not just two—and now visible in daylight, we could distinguish details of their translucent bodies and four thick yellow-tipped tentacles.

We had fortunately avoided contact with one of the highly venomous species of Box Jellyfish. No wonder those sailors ended up in the hospital.

We returned a few hours later, hoping these critters and their mean disposition had moved on. But that was not the case, and Mac ordered us all to a briefing. We saluted and marched off to our briefing room at the Seven Flags. I only have a vague recollection, but there must have been an extensive agenda, as the briefing continued long after the bar had closed. Having consumed all of their Heinekens, the bar tender had to wake up the owner of a neighboring bar, who soon brought over a case of some local beer—more like bottled bull piss (I don't recall the name, but the label included a picture of a bull). The sun was just about to creep above the horizon when the bartender finally kicked us out. We all stumbled to the hotel.

In spite of the scheduling uncertainties and occasional distractions, we completed the goals of this second series of measurements. As tradition required, a successful operation must be followed by an appropriate celebration—thinking back over several decades, there were a lot of successes. Not everyone, we felt, would enjoy dining at the Seven Flags Virgin Bar and Grill, in spite of its nearly endless supply of Heinekens, friendly bar tender, and resident tattoo artist, where one of the Rosey Roads divers got the MK 5 artwork on his leg.

A couple streets up from the waterfront, we found a great restaurant where we all assembled for the post-test celebration. After a bit of hootin' and hollerin', even the typically reserved Emil joined the revelry. Rick Thibeault, one of our more celebratory divers, stood and presented the toast:

"For bringing us to this island paradise, after two freezing miserable weeks in Puget Sound, we lift our glass to Emil . . . no . . . to 'An-E-mal' Soderberg!!!"

We all stood, beers raised, and responded . . . "To Animal!!! . . ." and downed another Heinekens.

I'm sure that Emil enjoyed the salute, but likely preferred to forget that a bunch of drunken Navy divers had dubbed this soft-spoken unassuming scientist, "Animal."

OPTICS AND PHOTONICS

Over several decades, the Submarine Electromagnetic Systems Department had evolved to include divisions and branches with specific scientific and engineering missions: there were communication systems and antennas, electromagnetic compatibility issues, periscopes, and the optics and photonics associated with imaging systems. It was this last one that brought the divers into the undersea world of lasers.

Light, as opposed to other components of the electromagnetic spectrum, is defined in terms of wave length, rather than frequency—visible light ranges from violet at about 390 nanometers (nm—one billionth of a meter), to the red end of the spectrum at 750 nm. As light penetrates deeper into water, wavelengths at either end are rapidly absorbed. Blue light, followed by green, penetrate the farthest, and it was the development of lasers in the 1960s, with the ability to generate light at wavelengths associated with the green portion of the visible spectrum, which stimulated interest in underwater applications.

PEERING INTO THE DARKNESS

Although miniaturization of laser systems was not yet available in the 1970s, the Navy saw its potential in submarine applications: object imaging, data transmission, and communications. The first of these, object imaging, led NUSC scientists and engineers to propose a series of experiments known as Projects "Deep Look" and "Look See." In 1971, Dr. William "Bill" Stachnik brought a team of NUSC divers to Lake Winnipesaukee in New Hampshire, where an underwater optical range had been built off Diamond Island. Supported on a truss-work designed to provide optical stability, a set of rails had been installed at a depth of thirty feet, well above the bottom to avoid disturbing the soft unstable sediments. A movable carriage carrying a large laser system was mounted on this track. Working at night and in extraordinarily clear water, the divers were responsible for alignment of the laser and placement of the optical target—a panel with a standardized arrangement of lines and bars to quantitatively measure image resolution.

After obtaining promising results from the Lake Winnipesaukee tests, the optics team shifted its efforts during the fall of 1972, to the Atlantic Undersea Test and Evaluation Center (AUTEC) on Andros Island in the

Bahamas. Although diving support was available at AUTEC, NUSC sent

Joe Gordon, Mac McClenny, and Ken Beatrice to conduct the underwater "Deep Look" experiments (figure 57). Bill Stachnik's above-water optics team included several young engineers whose experiences at AUTEC would encourage them to continue on with long field engineering careers at NUSC.

The electronic systems associated with laser imaging provided an ability to peer through moderate turbidity and "see" objects beyond the range available to standard white-light illumination. This was important to deep submersibles, searching through the pitch blackness along the ocean bottom.

Figure 57. NUSC diver Ken Beatrice hovers alongside the Project Deep Look laser system being tested at the AUTEC optics barge, 1972. (*NUSC/NL; "Mac" McClenny*)

While the AUTEC testing was limited to shallow water, the laser was operated at night, when the divers, swimming and operating a small Diver Propulsion Vehicle (DPV), were among the objects being imaged. The laser beam, however, attracted swarms of plankton and other members of the aquatic food chain, including a very large barracuda the divers named "Blackie."

A MISSING TORPEDO—THE MYSTERY SOLVED—(#)

The laser system was mounted in a high-strength titanium housing, the intent being to install laser imaging capability in the Navy's deep submergence submarine, *NR-1*. The AUTEC imaging tests included objects set on the bottom, the optics team hoping to simulate the locating and recovery of interesting Cold War items. Ken grabbed the keys to the truck and headed out to the base disposal area, where he found the scattered remains of an aircraft among a lot of rusting junk. Ken loaded parts and pieces onto the truck, and soon the laser team had plenty of Cold War realism sitting on the bottom.

One thirsty afternoon, while gaining inspiration one swallow after another, the NUSC engineers mused about how great it would be to have had a Soviet torpedo as an imaging target. Creative ideas were abundant, as they pondered ways to set a long, large-diameter cylinder on the bottom . . . maybe the divers could lay out a row of 50-gallon drums end to end. But the well-lubricated gears were turning in Ken's mind. "I need the keys to the truck . . ."

That night, there was one less torpedo on display along the roads that pass through the AUTEC base. Ken threw a coat of paint on what was a dingy old empty relic, and added the contrasting black letters **CCCP**. As the laser team gathered the following morning, they stared in disbelief at their "Soviet" torpedo now sitting on the optics barge. As they turned toward Ken with an obvious question on their minds . . . "Don't ask" was his reply.

The goals of this project would push the limits of 1970s state-of-the-art optical imaging, and NUSC brought along an underwater photography pioneer, Dr. Larry Mertens.[121] Andros Island was honeycombed by now-submerged caverns, created when sea levels were significantly lower during the ice ages. As sea levels rose over the millennia, roofs over many of these caverns collapsed, resulting in the creation of multiple Blue Holes scattered across the island. These incredibly clear bodies of water, with their deep blue color, were irresistible to divers. Ken and Dr. Mertens took an opportunity to descend the circular opening of one particularly enticing Blue Hole and peer into the cavern, where their lights illuminated stalactites formed many thousands of years in the past.

When I spoke to Ken about his experiences, his stories reminded me of a diving vacation I enjoyed decades ago, to Glover's Reef off the coast of what was then British Honduras. A side trip to Lighthouse Reef brought me into a huge Blue Hole where I saw the effects of tectonic motion. The stalactites that had formed vertically from the cavern ceiling by dripping mineral-saturated water, now hung at an angle, definite evidence that the entire cavern had tilted.

LASER TESTING—THE 1990s

It had been nearly twenty years since there was serious interest at NUSC/NL in using lasers underwater. Laser systems in the 1970s were expensive and their large size made their application for underwater systems difficult. It was the development of component miniaturization that again brought lasers into the underwater world. This time, however, the technology was being considered as a data link, rather than the imaging system we experimented with in the 1970s.

The potential of using laser light to pass information through the water led to a series of feasibility tests—first in pool environments, then follow-on testing in sea water. While light absorption through water was well understood as a critical factor governing the effective range of lasers, scattering by both organic and inorganic particles—certainly more significant in sea water than filtered pool water—also affected laser propagation. It was important, therefore, to obtain baseline data in controlled and relatively optimum pool conditions.

In September 1990, after the success of two small scale propagation tests, Dr. Judith Snow approached us about a more comprehensive experiment later that month for a project called Hydracoms. Judith had arranged access to a test pool used by the NUSC Newport launchers department. The length of the pool, approximately 160 feet, was ideal for investigating the feasibility of using lasers as an underwater data link.

By this time, the NUSC official underwater photographer Mac McClenny had retired. Several of us had learned the techniques from Mac, but by the early 1990s, we needed another contact within the photo lab. Bruce Greenhalgh took on that role, and was trained and designated as a NUSC (later, NUWC) photographer. We all continued to carry underwater still and video cameras, but Bruce provided the "official" designation, which provided access to lots of high-tech equipment.

Our divers and the technical team from the electro-optic systems branch, gathered at night at the Newport pool. The light source, a modulated, or "pulsed," argon (green) laser, was set above water on an optical bench at one end of the pool. The laser beam was directed from the surface and into the pool through a periscope-like system. The detector was installed and aligned at the opposite end of the pool. Throughout the installation and underwater video of the test, the divers took great care not to disturb the fine particulate that covered the bottom. Water clarity remained excellent during the test—the diameter of the laser beam at the target detector, where data rate was measured, remained small, indicating minimal scattering.

For a support team trying to provide scientists with as accurate an experiment as possible, the excitement garnered from that evening at the pool made us all look forward to the next phase—taking the Hydracoms experiment off shore. The most important people to satisfy—the project sponsors at ONT (Office of Naval Technology)—were also happy. The following year we would all be heading for the Bahamas. After two decades, NUSC returned with underwater lasers to the Atlantic Undersea Test and Evaluation Center on Andros Island. The results from the pool experiments and these AUTEC tests were published in an article, "Underwater propagation of high-data-rate laser communications pulses," in the Proceedings of SPIE (International Society for Optics and Photonics), 31 December, 1992.[122]

AUTEC JULY 27-AUGUST 7, 1991

We had selected AUTEC as a location with typically clear water and the convenience of a well-staffed logistical support organization. A temporary plywood structure had been assembled for us near the end of the harbor breakwater for our test equipment, and we were provided with a small rigid-hull inflatable boat (RIB) to allow ready access to and from the AUTEC facilities—a necessary capability, as we would discover a few days later.

After a day to install the optical range out from the breakwater, we were scheduled to spend the next ten days (and nights) completing an extensive list of objectives. Two pulsed green lasers were used, including the argon laser from the 1990 pool tests. The underwater range was designed to allow for varying the propagation distance, and to adjust the detector position within the beam of laser light (figure 58).

Figure 58. *Above:* The small inflatable boat used to support the AUTEC Hydracoms testing, with (L-R) Dr. Judith Snow, Paul Gianquinto, and Roy Manstan. (*NUSC/NL; Bruce Greenhalgh*) *Below:* Paul Mileski aligns the laser. Compare the size of this laser to the one used nearly two decades earlier, figure 57. (*NUSC/NL; Bruce Greenhalgh; from video frame*)

We were working in shallow water, where rain and a surface chop from the persistent breeze kept the bottom sediments stirred into the water. While particles suspended within the laser path were an issue, this was a quantifiable parameter and we monitored water clarity throughout the project. The test plan required that we compare propagation during the day, when sun light affected the receive sensor's ability to discriminate between ambient light and laser light, and at night, when there was little if any ambient light.

Operating at night, however, presented other issues. Although a pulsed laser was being used, the pulse rate was high enough that it would appear to the eye (both human and planktonic) as a continuous beam. Shortly after turning on the laser, in fact within seconds, the light along the path of the laser beam attracted swarms of plankton. This attraction was particularly evident around the transmitter, where the laser created a bright green glow as it passed through the optical glass port (plankton samples were taken and later identified as primarily crab larvae). As the density of these biological scatterers increased, there was a corresponding decrease in the light making it to the detector—eventually dropping out entirely.

On the second night, we encountered one of the hazards of tropical diving—the same hazard we had avoided at St. Croix in 1980—the venomous Box Jellyfish. It was nearly midnight when Paul Mileski surfaced in obvious pain from the thick translucent tentacles attached to his arm. If not treated promptly and with care, the countless stinging cells called nematocysts lining the surface of each tentacle will continue to sting long after being pulled from the animal. We knew that time was of the essence. Trying to remove the tentacles would only trigger more of the nematocysts to fire. We immediately raced back to shore in the RIB, while notifying the AUTEC emergency response team via radio. Paul was in pain, but had none of the anaphylactic response that had sent the swimmers to the hospital back in St. Croix. After a good night's sleep, and purchasing nylon body suits for the divers, we were ready to head "back to the office" along the AUTEC breakwater—now more watchful of what might swim with us.

A BRIEF DIVERSION—(#)

We had been on site for two days and two nights. It was our third afternoon; Paul had recovered from the jellyfish, but we were all tired and looking for a diversion. A small-craft with two sport divers on board had anchored less than a hundred yards off our test site. We could see them watching our divers enter and exit the water, no doubt curious why there was a diving operation underway along the breakwater. They eventually put on their scuba tanks and rolled off their boat and into the water.

We were relaxing after just having completed one more phase of the testing, when Bruce's imagination took hold. The underwater loudspeaker we used to broadcast instructions to our dive team was still in the water. Bruce grabbed the microphone:

"Divers! Divers! Divers! . . . Signal when the explosives are in place and ready for test?"

A brief pause . . . then Bruce again:

"Commencing test . . . Divers! Surface and exit the water immediately."

Another pause as we looked to see if the sport divers were returning to their boat. Then, four warning blasts on the underwater loudspeaker . . . and Bruce:

"Detonation will occur in 30 seconds . . . Mark! . . . 29! . . . 28! . . . 27! . . ."

Bruce had barely finished broadcasting "27!" when the water near the small-craft turned to froth as the two divers broached the surface. From where we sat, it looked as if they had found the secret to walking on water as they vaulted over the gunnels, hauled anchor, and sped off. Ah yes . . . we had our diversion. But it was back to business as usual—diving until midnight.

ANOTHER DIVERSION

At 16:00 on day seven we finished the afternoon's testing. The usual plan was to head back to the base for a quick dinner, and then return for yet more night operations. I could sense a bit of frustration on everyone's mind. The project had been progressing well, and I feared that our efficiency and attention to details was about to degrade unless we took a break—just one night off. I brought the RIB ashore with a few of the divers, ostensibly to wait for me to retrieve the rest of the test team and then head for dinner.

But their orders were: "Save us seats at the Beach Bar!" I returned to the site where Bruce and Judith and a couple others had been moving the equipment into the lab, preparing the site for a quick return after dinner. As Judith was boarding the RIB, I whispered to Bruce: "Padlock the building!" Bruce understood. When we arrived at the Beach Bar for "a snack before dinner," Happy Hour was in motion and remained so for several hours. We wouldn't be back to the site until the following day. I think Judith was happy to take a break, and understood that we would remain more focused after taking the night off. Remaining focused by incorporating diversions, and we were good at it, has been a lifelong goal.

PROJECT ISICLE—PART 1

The AUTEC tests had demonstrated limitations in laser propagation underwater, yet the desire to gather more data under a variety of conditions remained strong within the scientific community. This persistent interest and the experience we gained in 1990 and 1991 led NUSC to propose an investigation into the use of lasers for one particularly unique application, and several of our AUTEC team (Dr. Judith Snow, Jacob Longacre, Mark Landry and the NUSC divers) created Project ISICLE—the In-Situ Ice Characterization Laser Experiment.[123]

The Office of Naval Research (ONR) had established an Electromagnetic Properties of Sea Ice (EMPOSI) program, primarily to investigate the transmission of radio waves through the arctic ice sheet. Although the Cold War had wound down by this time, tensions were still in the air, and the need to send submarines into the arctic remained an important capability. Individuals from the NUSC electromagnetic systems department had participated in the Navy's series of ICEX projects during the 1980s and early 1990s, with the specific goal of optimizing RF capability in the arctic, and this remained a significant objective within the department.

While not directly related to radio communications, the optical properties of sea ice still fit within the realm of electromagnetic science. The ISICLE tests were going to be funded through a NUSC initiative to investigate additional applications of lasers and electro-optics. Because participation in an ICEX was a very expensive proposition, and space for researchers was limited to specific programs, it was very unlikely that

ISICLE would participate in a future ICEX. Yet from the very beginning, we all felt that an arctic ISICLE test, if not part of an ICEX, was feasible.

With that in mind, our ISICLE team gathered to discuss developing a proof-of-concept experiment that could be conducted locally—the assumption being an availability of ice. Winter temperatures in southern New England, however, rarely remain cold enough to freeze sea water sufficiently thick to carry out a meaningful test. The alternative was to head north and begin with lake ice. This would provide two important results. First, we would be able to use the same, or similar, test setup that could be brought to the arctic; and second, fresh water ice would establish a baseline for comparison to the much more complex structure of arctic sea ice.

ICECAMP-92

The more we looked into the feasibility of running experiments under the ice, the more likely it became that this same approach might appeal to other programs. At this point, I decided to make this a test case and put the word out that while we were creating a capability to support Project ISICLE, similar low-cost ice experimentation was available in what we began referring to as ICECAMP operations—the CAMP referring to the test site, and not the nearby Inn where we lived in comfort compared to the plywood ICEX accommodations in the arctic.

Although the optics team was responsible for the experimental design, it fell to us, the NUSC divers, to take responsibility for the operational logistics, for locating and outfitting a suitable site, and for conducting the under-ice experimental procedures. I contacted one of our past divers, Jim Clark, whose heart was in northern New England. Jim had left New London to become Branch Chief of the Naval Research Laboratory (NRL) Polar Oceanography Branch, the Navy's technical representatives at the Army's Cold Regions Research and Engineering Laboratory (CRREL) in Hanover, New Hampshire. Jim and I looked at potential sites in the area and selected Lake Morey in Fairlee, Vermont, only a half-hour from CRREL. Jim's staff had extensive arctic experience, and they were willing to provide assistance that would facilitate the logistics for our February 1992, field test now dubbed ICECAMP-92. Besides, we could "make camp" at the comfy Lake Morey Inn.

IF JESUS COULD DO IT, SO COULD WE . . .

. . . walk on water, that is. Navy divers, by nature, come with a fair amount of self confidence, but Project ISICLE required something for which few of us had any prior experience—diving under the ice. We had a lot of experience diving under a variety of difficult conditions, and in very cold

Figure 59. With ice nearly two-feet thick, we were able to park our vehicles next to the diving operations Quonset hut. The Vermont hills provided a beautiful backdrop for our project. (*Richard Thibeault*)

water, but this was entirely new. Deserved or not, our perpetual can-do personality gave people we worked with, the confidence necessary to move forward; it also helped us gain access to equipment at a moment's notice—essentially putting us at the head of the line. So it was with our friends at the motor pool who were pleased to allow us the use of their cargo van, a vehicle in constant demand, in spite of the fact that we would need it for ten days. After the project was over, I just couldn't wait to hand John Muschinsky, head of the transportation division in New London, a photo of the van parked in the middle of a lake (figure 59).

Navy diving regulations included a list of specific equipment authorized for ice diving, but the procedures for the most part were based on common sense. Nonetheless, I decided to make ICECAMP-92 an opportunity to train prior to beginning the ISICLE project. Our plan was to establish a core of ice-experienced divers, including Vic Marolda, Bob Schmidt, Paul

Gianquinto, Paul Mileski, Ross Byrne, and Bruce Greenhalgh. Bruce was also a certified emergency medical technician (EMT), and had been reviewing the procedures for treating hypothermia and other potential diving emergencies.

It had been a cold winter and the ice on Lake Morey was nearly two feet thick (no problem parking our van out there). Jim brought two of his most experienced staff to the site, and they quickly cut a three-foot by six-foot access opening with a chain saw. By the end of the day, we had assembled the twelve-by-twenty-foot arctic Quonset hut over the hole. Twenty feet away, we set up a second Quonset hut, which served as the optics tent. Late that afternoon—February 27, 1992—I sent in three of our divers for their first experience under the ice.

For a typical dive, we were trained to test breathe the regulator prior to submerging, but there was nothing typical about ice diving. When the air temperature dropped below 32 °F, taking this initial breath may result in the regulator freezing in the open position, causing the compressed air in the bottle to blast through the regulator. A major precaution when making an extreme cold water dive was to wait until the regulator submerged before taking that first breath, the water being warmer than the ambient air. The Navy thus limited the types of regulators used for ice diving, to only a few that have undergone considerable testing under extreme conditions. During our first two days we became familiar with the equipment by running simulations of the anticipated ISICLE measurements. This was also an opportunity to test our underwater wireless and hard-wired communication systems as well as the emergency diver-recall loud speaker.

The team was gaining confidence in running an ice diving operation, and phase two of our training plan was to document an ice diving emergency— the one we all feared—a lost diver. Safety precautions required that each diver be tethered to the surface via a tending line clipped to a D-ring on the divers harness. The lost diver scenario called for the tether to have pulled free of the D-ring, far from the access hole. The diver, his lifeline [hypothetically] gone, was instructed to remain in a fixed position. The standby diver was sent in and circled under the ice until he contacted the lost diver, and brought him back to the opening. Bruce, our EMT, then ran through the procedures for attending to a diver who may have lost consciousness, or was suffering from hypothermia. After two days running through various emergency drills, we felt confident in our ability to operate under the ice, and that our divers could now concentrate on the science.

The next day, Monday March 2, the ISICLE team arrived, and we set to the task of performing what was, as far as we knew, the first time a field experiment of this nature had ever been attempted. An optical bench was set in the second Quonset hut, and an opening in the plywood floor provided access to the ice. The divers then placed strips of two-inch-thick by four-inch-wide closed-cell foam directly beneath this opening, creating a two-foot by four-foot perimeter around the test area. This barrier ensured that the divers' exhaled air would remain outside the perimeter,

leaving an undisturbed surface where the laser beam would be directed. The divers then installed a track across this test area, where a carriage carrying the optical sensors could be positioned at specified locations (figure 60).

Working under the ice was certainly in that category of diving where sufficient precautions must be in place: proper tending lines, the buddy system, and a standby diver fully ready to assist in an emergency. On a bright sunny day there was little chance of a diver becoming lost or

Figure 60. *Above:* Diver under the ice at night makes adjustments to Project ISICLE apparatus. *Left:* Paul Gianquinto stands on the ice while recording the operation. (*NUSC/NL; Bruce Greenhalgh*)

disoriented—looking up at the ice, the access hole was readily visible, and tending lines ensured that divers won't stray too far. But a bright sunny day was not exactly what ISICLE was after. The sensors also detected ambient light and to get a more complete understanding of the optical properties of the ice based on the laser, it was necessary to also dive at night. While this part of the test plan certainly increased the pucker factor, the many hours we had been training over the previous days built confidence that our divers could submerge beneath the ice at night, into the pitch black water and simply—go to work. The test procedures were straight forward, and we had excellent communications with the divers. After each change in the test setup, the divers would move aside and hover up against the ice while the measurements were underway—a process that soon became routine, even at night. To help keep the divers occupied, we would broadcast music over the underwater loudspeaker.

Our training had truly paid off. The mystery and uncertainties associated with ice diving were removed, and we had established a team of experienced divers. I could now with confidence offer our services to any project interested in working under the ice here in New England. The first step was to describe the ISICLE tests in an article published in the July 31, 1992 issue of the Center newsletter now renamed NUWSCOPE, after the Naval Underwater Systems Center became the Naval Undersea Warfare Center in January.

A lot of changes were underway back in New London, but we maintained our focus on supporting Navy science, whenever and wherever there was a need. But my eye was still on the prize—our success at Lake Morey begged for an opportunity to bring ISICLE to the arctic. We were convinced that there was no need to ride along with a future ICEX—we could do this on our own. Persistence and confidence paid off, and that opportunity arrived in April, 1993.

YELLOW SNOW

Windblown granular snow drifted across the airfield, leaving only patches of the black runway visible. Canadian Airlines flight 404 made its approach and in minutes was taxiing to the terminal. Not a lot of travelers on that flight; most of the seats on the Boeing 737 had been replaced with cargo containers. It was Friday, April 30, 1993, and ICECAMP-93 was underway.

"Jim . . . we made it," I shouted!!! I couldn't help it . . .

Jim Clark and I had been working (euphemism for scheming, begging, cajoling, and expecting to ask for forgiveness later) for nearly a year and a half to make this trip happen. In one of those moments of sheer relief plus an equal amount of disbelief at having achieved a seemingly impossible goal, I wanted to kneel and kiss the ground. The ever-sensible Jim reminded me, however, that my lips would freeze to the tarmac. We later expressed our mutual relief at having arrived by writing our names in yellow snow—not a problem, considering both of our names only have three letters.

We had come to Cornwallis Island—one of the northernmost year-round communities (second only to Grise Fiord on Ellesmere Island) in

the vast frozen archipelago that comprises the Canadian arctic. The small town of Resolute (Qausuittuq: "place with no dawn" in the local Inuit dialect) included a community along the airstrip, where outfitters supplied modern travelers hunting for oil reserves or simply hunting for adventure, and a nearby Inuit village located at the north end of Resolute Bay.

Figure 61. *Above:* A twelve-inch auger was used to bore holes through the ice, creating a diver access opening. (*Roy Manstan, from video*) *Below:* By the end of the day, a local expedition outfitter had erected the Quonset hut, which would be our laboratory for the next ten days. (*Ross Byrne*)

Our purpose was to conduct a series of experiments that were part of the larger ONR Electromagnetic Properties of Sea Ice (EMPOSI) program. There were few commercial flights in and out of Resolute, two per week from Montreal and two from (as I recall) Yellowknife. Jim and I had arrived early to check the inventory of test and dive

equipment shipped previously. It would be a busy time for us, preparing the test site on the ice before the rest of the dive team arrived a few days later (figure 61).

For several months, as we assembled our logistical and material needs for the trip north, we had communicated with Buster and Mary Welch, a husband and wife team who had been in Resolute for several years studying the aquatic food chain for Canadian Fisheries. They would provide critical resources for our base of operations, accessible by snow machine nearly a mile offshore on the single-year ice that characterizes much of the Arctic Ocean.

ICECAMP-93

For the past eighteen months, all of our energies had focused on this goal—to show the feasibility of establishing a base of operations in an arctic environment with ready access to logistical support, and where sophisticated experiments could be accomplished at a relatively low cost. We had already demonstrated our capabilities, with the successful under-ice testing at Lake Morey in Vermont. This is not to say that working under the ice off Cornwallis Island was in any way a simple task. But when a scientist has an idea that requires data from the real arctic environment and not from a simulated one, Resolute could provide the best alternative to joining one of the Navy's ICEX operations. At 74° 42' North, the average daily temperature in May ranges from 5 °F to 15 °F, providing optimum conditions for studying fully matured single-year sea ice just prior to the melt season.

Planning for an operation as complex as this meant depending on the arctic experience of others. This was not a case of learning everything on the fly—too much was at stake here. There were several individuals working for Jim Clark, branch chief for NRL's polar oceanography group at CRREL, who offered many valuable suggestions. But we relied on the experience of our own arctic expert, Paul Mileski. Although not as a diver, Paul had participated in ICEX 86, 88, 89 and 91, as well as projects that took him to Thule, Greenland, the north cape of Norway, and the Antarctic research station at McMurdo. Back in New London, Paul's ICEX logistics had been in Colleen Schillinger's capable hands, and she jumped at the chance to help put us and all of our equipment on flights to Resolute.

Nonetheless, in order for us to acquire sufficient funding to support our arctic goals, Jim Clark and I had conspired to make this a joint operation. We offered our presence at Resolute with a dive team to other organizations interested in gathering scientific data, and evaluating prototype and proof-of-concept designs. Although our primary mission was to support NUWC measurements of the optical properties of sea ice, our tasking included an NRL project to test a contractor-designed air-dropped ice-penetrating buoy. Our team also provided assistance to Dr. Glen Cota from the University of Tennessee Knoxville, who was going to be at Resolute in May, studying the distribution of the algae layer on the underside of the ice.

To further reduce total costs, we planned to minimize the number of participants and the duration of their stay on the ice. Thus only two of us, Jim and I, would be the first to arrive, and could initiate the logistical requirements needed to establish our base of operations. We soon made contact with the Canadian Fisheries scientists, Buster and Mary Welch and a research assistant, who could not have been better hosts. They were diving in the area and had a fully operational and certified compressor for charging scuba bottles. They also had a twelve-inch diameter auger that we took out onto the ice and bored a group of nine holes in a three by three pattern, creating an access opening known as a "moon pool." Jim and I also hired a group of outfitters at Resolute to erect a Quonset hut over the site. The heated enclosure had an insulated wooden floor with an opening over the moon pool. A similar hut, where Glen Cota was setting up for his experiments, was located about a quarter mile from ours. We took the snow machine across the ice to visit Glen, and discuss how and when we could provide diving support.

On the 4th of May, with the logistics for our diving operations in place, the next flight from Montreal brought our divers and the initial test team with NRL's prototype buoy. Although designed to be air-dropped, the mechanism that triggered the heat generating chemical penetrator could also be activated by hand. Because this was an early prototype, and the interest was in the ability of the penetrator to melt through six feet of sea ice, it was not necessary to test the air dropped features.

There's always a nervousness associated with a "first." Here we were, in the arctic staring down at a three-foot by three-foot opening in the ice. Our core dive team included Vic Marolda, Bob Schmidt, Ross Byrne, and Paul Mileski. They had all spent several hours under the ice in Lake Morey, but we still felt that we were about to experience something new. No more delays—it was time to go to work. The NRL team was ready to trigger their ice-penetrating buoy, and we had to be in the water to record the chemical penetrator as it melted its way through the ice. On May 5, at 12:58, Paul Mileski and Ross Byrne made the jump. Sea water freezes at about 28 °F, and when we dove that day in early May, the water just below the ice hovered around 29 degrees.

A [SIMPLY] AWESOME EXPERIENCE—(#)

It was my turn. Paul and Ross had completed the first of several hours of underwater video, and now I was about to slip down and under the six-foot-thick ice sheet. My personal goal was not just to get us all there. I had to have the same experience Paul so succinctly described as he surfaced a few minutes earlier: "It's fucking awesome down there!!!" With that kind of endorsement, how could anyone resist the opportunity?

Okay, it was my turn, and I lowered myself down into the moon pool. The water compressed the dry-suit around my legs as I began to submerge. Even with a well insulated suit, the chill still got through as a reminder that this is nearly the coldest water on earth. As my head submerged, the ice-cream headache was excruciating and I quickly resurfaced to ask Paul what was so fucking awesome about this (figure 62). Jim was standing next to the opening, and in an instant, I had a flashback to a time

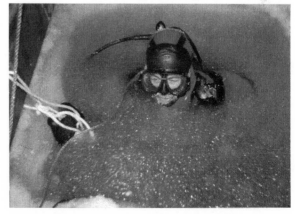

Figure 62. Roy Manstan surfaces through the ice slurry that quickly forms on the moon pool. Keeping the opening clear is a constant effort. (*Vic Marolda*)

twelve years earlier when Jim and I were diving alongside USS *Fanning* in the Gulf of Oman. The memory of water that was 100 °F provided a momentary distraction from my current situation. Down I went—and Paul was right!!!!!

Forget the job; I'll talk about that later. I was astounded at what I saw. The water was clear and the underside of the ice disappeared far off into a blue-grey horizon. The largest comb jellies I had ever seen meandered along the frozen roof, no doubt gorging (if one can say that about these translucent invertebrates) on the planktonic menagerie that thrives at the water/ice interface.[124] It is the transition out of twenty-four-hour darkness that stimulates the growth of algae within the granular, highly saline underside of the ice sheet. This annual phenomenon was followed by a bloom of animal plankton that thrives on the algae-rich layer and which, in turn feeds other aquatic life; it was to study this food chain that brought the Canadian fisheries scientists to Resolute. While we didn't encounter the top predator in this arctic feast, we did see one polar bear skin stretched out on a wooden frame alongside an Inuit home.

Ah, but this brief digression was a reminder of what had initiated this arctic experience. It was to study the transmission of light through single-year ice, when by May, sunlight dominates the arctic sky. Our experience with arctic marine life also began that day. While I was under the ice with the video camera recording NRL's chemical penetrator, and in spite of what I saw approaching from the distance, I had to finish my assignment. There were two more divers anxious for the opportunity to freeze their asses off. Vic and Bob would not be disappointed.

With each breath, our exhaled air rose up against the ice and collected in elongated flat pools. It was quite a shock when I turned to face the rather large form of a Ringed Seal, approaching within about ten yards of me. With her nose pressed up into the pool of air, this obviously well fed marine mammal investigated my also well fed torso, I presume to determine if I was a predator or fellow finned pinniped. From a distance, she had likely seen the sun light streaming through our access hole that, to this air breathing mammal, was typical of the natural breathing holes they depend on when on the prowl for fish. I must have created a dilemma, as she approached what was to be her next breath before continuing on in search of food, and then encountering such an unfamiliar creature. This first visit was short, only long enough to look me over before disappearing out of view. She returned to our test area every day and would approach closer each visit, always taking time to grab a fresh breath from the pools of our exhaled air. After about a week as a hesitant visitor, she finally surfaced into the moon pool and eyed with incredulous curiosity the colony of marine mammals clad in smooth black rubbery skin and standing upright supported by long finned feet (figure 63).

Figure 63. *Above:* Bob Schmidt prepares for his dive. In addition to the standard scuba cylinder, each diver carries an emergency air supply with a separate regulator. *Below:* After warily approaching the divers for four days, this Ringed Seal finally surfaces into the moon pool. (*Ross Byrne*)

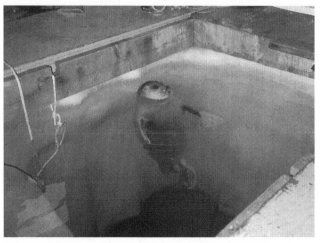

We called her "Gramma" in honor of Rick Thibeault, one of our divers back in New London, who had been given the same name as a result of the slow pace he moved when dressing for a dive. It was, however, the similar shape and appetite of these two "Grammas" that made the name of our arctic mascot so appropriate.

That first day we logged several hours under the ice. By the end of the day, the NRL team gained a great deal of information and was ready to head back to the drawing board. That afternoon, Glen Cota came by our site, where we put the details of our diving operations on the table and discussed how we could best support his project. Glen was quantifying the first link in the arctic food chain—the algal component that thrives along the underside of the ice. This same layer was of particular interest to the ice optics group who would soon arrive from New London. After we sent the NRL team on their way, we began planning the next day's diving.

Glen and his fellow researchers showed us the device they brought for sampling the algae. They augured a hole through the ice and lowered an articulated, mechanical arm that could reach under the ice and scrape a section of the algae-laden layer into a cup. Without a method to observe and document the sampling technique, there would be a level of uncertainty as to its effectiveness—and thus the accuracy of the data. It would be our job to record the sampling operation with video. Our second day of diving operations was dedicated to working with Glen, where we logged another four hours under the ice.

THE IN-SITU ICE CHARACTERIZATION LASER EXPERIMENT (ISICLE)—PART 2

Soon after we completed diving for Glen Cota, Jim and I went to the airport and welcomed the NUWC researchers to Resolute. We quickly moved their gear to the edge of the ice, where we boarded snow machines and hauled the loaded cargo sleds out to the site. It was time to prepare for the primary reason that ICECAMP-93 came about. Jacob Longacre and Mark Landry had designed a mechanical device similar to what we used at Lake Morey in 1992, and they were anxious to assemble the mechanism.

With access to an ice coring device, we removed 4.5-inch-diameter cores from the ice sheet adjacent to the test site. The cores provided a clear view of the algae layer, and gave Glen Cota additional samples for his biological studies. That base layer of algae will diffuse and scatter the laser light passing through the ice sheet, and was of particular interest to the optical measurements team. But there were other scattering factors, and these core samples provided a detailed view of a cross-section through the six-foot column of ice, showing features such as layers of bubbles and brine channels, which would disrupt the path of a laser beam.

Although it had been a difficult decision on my part, I soon returned to New London. My goal was to provide as many of our divers as possible, the unique opportunity to participate in an arctic project. Vic Marolda took my place supervising the diving operations, and Paul Gianquinto flew to Resolute to fill the dive team. Because Jim's association with the NRL portion of the project had also been completed, he and I returned on the afternoon flight to Montreal.

In May, at the high latitude of Resolute, the sun never set, only skimming the horizon at midnight. At the airport in Montreal, however, darkness had returned. But the night was not typical—we looked to a sky filled with the pulsing green veil of a spectacular display of the Northern Lights. Although Jim and I were heading home, I was confident that far to the north, our research team was well prepared to continue the experiments. They had all spent many hours the previous year working under frozen Lake Morey during ICECAMP-92, where each of the divers had gained the skills and confidence to operate beneath the arctic ice.

After having completed Project ISICLE-Part 1 in New Hampshire, we were determined that Part 2, the "In-Situ" portion, would include this final goal of measuring the optical properties of sea ice in the arctic, where it was most representative of what was important to the Navy. Over four days beginning on May 8, the divers logged nearly fourteen hours, completing the test objectives plus a few extras, all of which were recorded with underwater video. Project ISICLE was a success.

WINTER WAS ONLY SIX MONTHS AWAY

Back in New London that summer, we knew that our successful experiments would provide project engineers with so much data, that their creative appetite would be fed for months to come. The results of both the Lake Morey and Resolute ISICLE tests were described in a 1994 paper by Jacob Longacre and Mark Landry titled "In-situ measurements of optical scattering from the water-ice interface of sea ice," published in the Proceedings of SPIE (International Society for Optics and Photonics).[125]

We continued to look for technologies that we hoped would eventually return us to the arctic. Our next ICECAMP brought us back to Lake Morey in February 1994, for a two-part operation. While at Resolute, we had struggled to keep the test areas free of exhaled air. We decided to try the Navy's standard shallow water oxygen rebreather, the Draeger LAR-V, a system that does not discharge bubbles—the diver breathes pure oxygen where each exhale is recycled through a CO_2 scrubber. We teamed with an Army Special Forces group stationed at Fort Devens, Massachusetts. They were interested in using this as a training opportunity, and were willing to provide our divers with what turned out to be a highly successful experience diving with the LAR-V. Three of our arctic divers, Vic Marolda, Bob Schmidt and Paul Gianquinto, were there, along with Mike Rutkowski who came for the ice diving training.

Phase two of ICECAMP-94 was related to the continuing emphasis on submarines surfacing through arctic sea ice. Submarine sails had been hardened to make breaking through the ice less dangerous. Much testing of the mechanical properties of arctic ice had been accomplished, including tests that were underway at Resolute when we were there. We thought that we could demonstrate a proof-of-concept experiment at Lake Morey, measuring the effect of contact with ice on other submarine mounted equipment—a method that could be accomplished at Resolute without requiring a submarine. We devised a procedure to press up against the underside of the ice, a small fiberglass dome typical of what is used to house a hydrophone or other electronic system external to a submarine hull. The dome was instrumented to measure the stresses as we increased the contact forces against the ice. The phase-one test team had returned to New London, but Mike Rutkowski remained and joined Ken Beatrice, Bruce Greenhalgh, Paul Mileski and me for the mechanical testing.

In spite of the success of ICECAMP-94, we were unable to find sponsors for a return to Resolute. The ice optics measurements from the previous year were being analyzed and a simplified device that did not require divers had been designed for a series of experiments planned for Barrow, Alaska. In April 1995, Jim Clark and I accompanied Mark Landry during one of these operations, unofficially dubbed ICECAMP-95, where the data could help answer the remaining through-ice laser propagation questions. Mark presented the results of this experiment in a paper, "Optical propagation through sea ice," at the International Geoscience and Remote Sensing Symposium in July, 1995.[126]

It would be three years before we found another ice diving project. Submarines operating in the arctic have limited RF capability while submerged, and the NUWC electromagnetics department was interested in trying additional antenna designs. As with Project ISICLE, an initial baseline test would involve fresh water ice at Lake Morey, and on January 31, 1998, ICECAMP-98 was born. Jim Clark and his arctic branch at CRREL once again provided the on-ice logistics, while the dive team included Bud Vincent, Mike Rutkowski, Mike Peirson, Bruce Greenhalgh, Jack Hughes and me. After three days on the lake, we moved our operations to the Army's simulated sea ice freeze pond, where we collected data from the same antenna system transmitting through salt water ice. Opportunities to simply gather vast quantities of scientific data were what stimulated ideas among the intellectual and physical risk takers—over the next five days Paul Mileski, also there as a diver, and Brian Pease did just that. The data Paul and Brian collected in 1998 would eventually lead to our final ice diving operation during the week of February 26, 2001.

ICECAMP-01 brought us back north to work with Jim Clark at CRREL and their salt water freeze pond. We brought the same antenna we used in 1998, but this time we would test the system through nearly a foot of simulated sea ice. The experiment would now include other antennas designed for a wide range of frequencies, including those used for a standard Emergency Position Indicating Radio Beacon (EPIRB), now included on submarines—not surprisingly referred to as a SEPIRB. This time the divers included Mike Rutkowski, Jack Hughes, Bruce Greenhalgh and me, while Paul Mileski and Pat Gilles worked with the data acquisition. ICECAMP-01 also provided us an opportunity to share our experiment with a group of students via an internet video connection to the American School for the Deaf (ASD) in West Hartford, Connecticut (see details of our education outreach efforts at the end of chapter 8).

A TRAGIC CHANGE OF FOCUS

Six months later, on September 11, 2001, we would be facing a terrorist enemy that caught all of us off guard. Al Qaida had been exploring a variety of methods for carrying out a terrorist attack, and was providing scuba training to members of its organization. NUWC would soon enter the world of what became known as "swimmer defense." The EDSU, in a partnership with the Department of Homeland Security, the Coast Guard, and the Navy's Force Protection program, became actively involved with the technology to detect and interdict a terrorist diver—all described in chapter 9.

Returning to the arctic became a lost goal for us, although NUWC and the Navy continued to carry on with improving the ability of submarines to operate under the ice. Mike Rutkowski had found an interest in arctic research and, although not as a diver, he participated with the torpedo recovery team during ICEX-03. He then joined ICEX-07 and -09, developing a robust arctic-capable underwater digital acoustic communications system (ACOMMS), which provided the primary link between the submarines operating under the ice and the Applied Physics Laboratory Ice Station (APLIS) on the ice. For his time in the far north, Mike received the civilian Arctic Service Medal.

Our dive team had become well established on the NUWC waterfront. While swimmer defense was now a major focus, our divers continued to support submarine sonar issues, particularly towed arrays (chapter 6). NUWC's history in Newport, reaching back to its origins at the Naval Torpedo Station in 1869, had been primarily devoted to weapon systems, and we were always watching for opportunities to support this aspect of submarine warfare.

Figure 64. *Above:* Robert Fulton successfully destroyed the brig *Dorothea* during a demonstration of his "torpedo" in 1805. (*Pesce 1906*) *Below:* In 1869, Lieutenant Commander J.S. Barnes published this illustration of the sinking of *Housatonic* by *Hunley* using a spar torpedo. (*Barnes 1869*)

D VAN NOSTRAND, Publisher.

DESTRUCTION OF THE U.S. STEAM SLOOP OF WAR HOUSATONIC.

CHAPTER 8
The Infernal Machines of NUWC/Newport

"In twenty seconds, nothing was to be seen of her except floating fragments . . ." is how Robert Fulton described the destruction of the brig *Dorothea* after demonstrating the use of a "torpedo" in an attempt to sell the concept to the British in 1805 (figure 64). Described as "infernal machines," the torpedo, and for that matter, any form of submarine warfare, was considered by most nineteenth century naval brass as an immoral mode of warfare. During the first decade of the nineteenth century, Fulton had been in France, England, and finally America trying to sell his concept of "Torpedo War, and Submarine Explosions," the title of a pamphlet he published in 1810.[127] In March of that year, Congress approved $5,000 for Fulton to continue with his experiments; the hope, expressed by the Senate, being to "extricate a suffering world from that system of oppression, now exercised by the great maritime belligerents on the high seas." The War of 1812 was on the horizon, and Congress was interested in any new technology that might be used "for the better defense of the ports and harbors of the United States."[128]

Even with the expanding mechanical advances brought on with the industrial revolution, Fulton's ideas, and those of David Bushnell a generation earlier, were beyond the technology available to them. It would take another disastrous war a half-century later to inspire a new generation of engineering minds to renew the development of a viable torpedo and submarine warfare strategy. Only four years after the close of the Civil War, in 1869, Lieutenant Commander J. S. Barnes published *Submarine Warfare, Offensive and Defensive*, a review of torpedo technology that emerged during the war, primarily in the South. Torpedoes, according to Barnes, created "a revolution in naval warfare . . . borne of circumstances forced upon the world at a time when mechanical arts and sciences were in a condition to make experiments fruitful . . ." adding that torpedoes were so "extraordinary that it seems to have sprung with one bound into the foremost rank of the novel and tremendous engines of war which have so completely changed the aspect of modern battle-fields and scenes of naval conflicts." While Barnes included a prevailing sentiment that torpedoes were an "inhuman system . . . a merciless, barbarous idea" he also expressed the military point of view that the ends justify the means.[129]

That same year, in 1869, the Naval Torpedo Station was established in Newport, Rhode Island, where those "fruitful experiments" suggested by Barnes would evaluate the rapidly expanding use of torpedoes and the vessels designed to carry them; and where a school for their active use was created.[130] From the spar torpedoes of the 1860s, followed by the Whitehead "automobile torpedo" carried on USS *Holland* in 1900, to the 3,400-pound, 19-foot-long wire-guided MK 48 that is part of the weapons compliment carried by modern fast attack nuclear submarines, Newport has been the Navy's leading center for torpedo development. Many of the great engineering innovations in submarine weapons have caught the attention of the public, spawning articles in popular magazines.

> Quickly the sleek missile glides away under the water to seek its target, leaving scarcely a ripple behind it and paying out the wire cable from the stern as it advances. An operator manipulates a keyboard, steering the weapon to the right or left . . . until the enemy's vessel is reached; [then] a column of snow-white water, a dull jar, and a majestic ship . . . sinks beneath the waves.[131]

The writer, Ensign John M. Ellicott, is describing a modern torpedo that relies on a wire guidance system controlled by an operator working on a keyboard—yet the article is not referring to the twenty-first century wire-guided MK 48, rather something that was "modern" in 1891, the wire-guided Patrick Torpedo (figure 65), that Ensign Ellicott noted was soon "to be tried at Newport."

Figure 65. *Above:* Nineteenth-century wire-guided Patrick torpedoes were tested at the Navy Torpedo Station. (*The Illustrated American 1891*) *Below:* This 1928 photograph shows an air-dropped torpedo test in Narragansett Bay. These aircraft, flying at 90 knots at an altitude of 50 feet, operated from a Torpedo Station facility on Gould Island. (Courtesy *NUWC*)

Rapid advances in mechanical and electrical engineering during the Civil War had created an industrial capability that could translate wishful thinking into reality. Within a decade, naval warfare would never look back—the Age of Sail was over. Young naval officers at the Torpedo Station were soon serving as instructors in what was then the embodiment of the future. During the summer of 1876, as Lieutenant Francis Barber was lecturing on the Whitehead Torpedo and the potential of "submarine boats," brutal hand-to-hand ground warfare was underway on the Montana hills overlooking the Little Big Horn. A generation later, technology would send even more deadly "infernal machines" onto twentieth century battlefields on land, at sea, and soon in the air.

The Naval Torpedo Station played a significant role in the development of submarine warfare, evolving through two world wars and the early years of the Cold War to become the Naval Underwater Weapons Research and Engineering Station (NUWRES) in 1966. The emphasis in Newport had been submarine weapons and fire control systems engineering. Nearly sixty miles away, in New London, USN/USL was the Navy's lead laboratory developing submarine and antisubmarine sonar. These two organizations would eventually merge into a single center of submarine warfare research and development, but the transition was far from smooth.

1970 . . . USN/USL + NUWRES = NUSC/NLL + NUSC/NPT

1992 . . . NUSC/NLL + NUSC/NPT = NUWC(DET/NL) + NUWC(DIV/NPT)

1996 . . . NUWC(DET/NL) $\rightarrow$ NUWC(DIV/NPT)

As an engineer, it is easier to relegate several years of political turmoil and administrative in-fighting to simple equations, the details of which deserve a book in itself.[132] However, a few words to explain the above equations are appropriate here.

By the late 1960s, and with military budgets being sucked into the Viet Nam War, Congress was looking for ways to save money, and the Navy laboratory system came under scrutiny. In part driven by the potential duplication of effort among more than a dozen Navy labs, and a behind the scenes drive to place more research and development dollars into private industry, there was a push to consolidate the various laboratory missions. The relative proximity of USN/USL to NUWRES was a temptation too great to pass up, and after a quarter century the USN/USL we all knew was about to be handed a new mission.

On June 30, 1970, the U.S. Navy Underwater Sound Lab was renamed the Naval Underwater Systems Center, New London Laboratory, or NUSC/NLL (also referred to as NUSC/NL); and the Naval Underwater Weapons Research and Engineering Station, Newport, became NUSC/NPT. In New London, Harold Nash, who had been the Technical Director (TD) of USN/USL, continued in that role at the administratively merged NUSC. With offices at both locations, Nash struggled for five years to retain and carry the research and development role of USN/USL into the new NUSC establishment. During that time, he was diverted to an overseas assignment from September 1973 to July 1974, while the very capable Walt Clearwaters took on the TD leadership.

These two individuals, both having been involved with sonar research during World War II (Clearwaters at the Columbia University Division of War Research in New London, and Nash at the Harvard University Underwater Sound Laboratory), were now the leaders of the merger. In the mid-1970s, however, there was another push from Washington at the highest levels within the Navy Department to replace the old guard with new leadership and consolidate the Center's management in Newport. Harold Nash retired, and the choice for Technical Director was between Walt Clearwaters and Newport's Caesar Spero. Yet after a lengthy unsuccessful selection process, Washington settled the situation, and in July 1975, installed C. Nicholas Pryor, an outsider from the Naval Ordnance Laboratory White Oaks. The leadership of NUSC was now centered in Newport, leaving New London as a laboratory component of a Newport-based Underwater Systems Center.

In spite of assurances in local newspapers, rumors spread through the city of New London that the Lab would close and everything moved to Newport, with potentially devastating consequences to the local economy. Yet there was also hope that the opposite could happen—that NUSC Newport would move to New London. Management teams at both locations sought ways to strengthen the role of their respective technologies; sonar and antisubmarine warfare in New London, weapon systems in Newport.

At both laboratories, the 1980s were a time of consolidation of effort under what was referred to as "product lines" formed around a concept of undersea warfare systems integration. As digital technology raced to take over old analog systems, computer software revolutionized the capabilities of submarine and antisubmarine systems. Both labs retained their focus on their traditional missions, but the direction of these missions was evolving into a Newport centered management, where powerful influences by Caesar Spero and John Sirmalis were building and strengthening this systems integration policy. There were still many movers and shakers at both locations who were committed to their craft, and equally committed to maintaining the respective missions at their physical locations.

Yet as the 1980s moved ahead, the handwriting was on the wall—we didn't know whose handwriting it was, but the message was becoming clear. In 1982, NUSC Technical Director Nick Pryor was replaced by Newport's Earle Messere. As each year went by, we all saw the likelihood that these two locations would eventually consolidate at a single location. There were political forces that fully intended for this to happen, and New London seemed the most vulnerable. That was the impression held by many of us who worked in New London—far removed from the politics.

We saw these political currents strengthen, and from our viewpoint, threaten to drag the New London Lab from its strategic location on the Thames River within sight of the nation's major submarine construction facility and within reach of a thriving submarine base, to a new home on Narragansett Bay. Yet there was still enough influence in Washington by tough individuals in New London, Bill Von Winkle and Larry Freeman in particular, who managed to obtain authorization for construction of a new Surface ASW building, in what eventually became a futile attempt to anchor the New London Lab. If anchoring was a function of adding buildings, then Newport was ready to throw in its own anchors.

BRAC

By 1989, the Cold War was winding down as we witnessed the dissolution of the Soviet Union. Under congressional pressure to reduce the military footprint, and with it a reduction in the budget, a Base Realignment and Closure Commission (BRAC) was formed. There would only be one NUSC, and both locations had set their anchors. Consolidation was inevitable and New London was losing the battle—ultimately economics as well as politics drove the decision.

In New London, we read about the intentions in the April 26, 1991, edition of NUSCOPE—page 1 headline: "SECNAV approves consolidation and realignment proposal for NUSC." The article summarized the plans to close or realign multiple facilities on both the east and west coast under a new organization to be named the Naval Undersea Warfare Center (NUWC), headquartered in Washington, DC, and within the Naval Sea Systems Command (NAVSEA). NUWC would consist of two Divisions, one in Newport, Rhode Island, and the other in Keyport, Washington. We also read that the final realigned NUWC would retain facilities in New London, yet we all felt that the comment was simply added to pacify concerns over the economic impact that closing the New London Laboratory would have on local area businesses.

Our test would occur during BRAC hearings in Boston on May 28, 1991. Several bus loads of NUSC/NL staff took leave to attend the hearings, joined by a Connecticut congressional delegation, which included Senator Chris Dodd and Representative Sam Gejdenson. We all assembled in a large auditorium and waited for the commissioners to file in and take their seats behind a long table. I think we all realized our fate when only one elderly gentleman arrived and sat next to several empty chairs to receive any testimony offered by the Connecticut attendees who filled the auditorium. After many individuals provided their verbal testimony to this single commissioner, who most likely was only thinking about what restaurant in Boston would provide his next meal, we all simply returned to the busses and went home.

By early July, BRAC had passed on its recommendations to the president for his approval, and then on to congress, where the process would continue to grind slowly ahead. While the major provisions were irreversible, decisions about the fate of specific military bases were still being considered. Within this air of uncertainty, the New London Laboratory seemed safe, even when the Naval Underwater Systems Center became the Naval Undersea Warfare Center in January, 1992. But internally, we all felt that NUWC management was determined to consolidate all of the research and development facilities on Narragansett Bay. Meanwhile, as the politics associated with a major closure raged on, the final nail in New London's coffin came when its designation as a "Laboratory" was changed to a "Detachment." With this designation, a facility could be closed with a simple signature, while a Laboratory required congressional approval—at least that's what we were told—and that it was only a matter of time before we had to pack our suitcases and rent a U-Haul.

During ceremonies held on October 4, 1996, the New London Detachment of the Naval Undersea Warfare Center was decommissioned, with its official closure occurring on December 31. The ceremonies brought several speakers with long associations with the research and development of Navy systems at New London. One of these was Juergen Keil, formerly a department head and now the NUWC Executive Director. A November 1996 NUWSCOPE article about the closure described his comments, which reflected what many of us were thinking: "Juergen Keil spoke of the spirit of community that has always characterized the Detachment and its predecessors, and pointed out how the New London 'experts in the early 1940s helped turn the tide of war.' But most of all he reminisced about the people. 'The New London legacy is not in the empty halls . . . but in the people who walked them . . . We had a truly outstanding past.'" Over the next several years, Juergen Keil remained an active and important supporter of the dive team, as well as the many people from New London who would now be walking the halls in Newport.

For several months, eighteen-wheelers moved equipment and furniture to the many "anchors" at Newport, built specifically to accommodate the arrival of hundreds of New London scientists, engineers, technicians, and administrative staff. On March 31, 1997, the buildings and grounds that once housed a thriving research and development organization were turned over to the Naval Facilities Engineering Command (NAVFAC).

Most of the post-World War I, World War II, and Cold War buildings were removed, a notable exception being the building that was to be New London's anchor, but now houses the Coast Guard Research & Development Center. The Coast Guard has long had a presence at this location on the New London waterfront, beginning with its establishment in 1915 after the United States Lifesaving Service merged with the Revenue Cutter Service. The Revenue Cutter Service had already established an officer school at Fort Trumbull in 1910. The old granite block fort is included on the National Register of Historic Places and in 2000, along with several other eighteenth and nineteenth century structures, became the Fort Trumbull State Park.

WATERFRONT REAL ESTATE

We were all moving to Newport and the role of our dive team, no longer a command support asset, was changing. Recently designated the Engineering & Diving Support Unit, the EDSU was assigned to the Test and Evaluation Department. A positive aspect of our newly acquired space in the NUWC block diagram was our newly acquired space in an old building on the waterfront. Joe Murphy, NUWC's Facilities Development Division Head, and EDSU divers Jack Hughes (who worked for Joe) and Paul Gianquinto were actively establishing our new home. Joe was a former NUSC diver who had been a major player in the SSN-21 bow sphere development.

On April 1, 1997 (yup . . . April Fools' Day), the day after the decommissioned NUSC/NL was turned over to NAVFAC, I began the agonizing daily 150-mile round trip commute. Until then I had maintained an office at the now deserted remnants of the Sound Lab, but occasionally travelled to Newport while the building was being prepared to accommodate the EDSU. The majority of our divers also remained in New London, where they continued to support waterborne towed array issues at the Crystal Avenue Annex. The activities at the Annex would, of course, eventually move to a renovated building at NUWC.

While still in New London, I managed to designate a variety of old but still beautiful furniture from an office in an area known as Mahogany Row, to be shipped in one of those eighteen-wheelers heading to Newport. As the NUWC Diving Program Manager and EDSU diving officer, I could run the operations from behind a massive mahogany desk that had been the home of a NUSC/NL department head. When the weather turned sour, I could snooze overnight on an exceptionally comfy couch, which had been in a visitors lounge in New London. At least now, when the divers assembled for meetings, training, and operations planning, we could all enjoy the glass-topped mahogany conference table and the comfortable chairs. I also shipped multiple desks for any diver needing an occasional home away from the cubicle. Our second-floor view overlooking Narragansett Bay (figure 66) would slowly change over the years, as more people wanted to move down to the waterfront, and we were squeezed (along with our furniture) to the back of the building.

Figure 66. *Top and Above:* Aerial views of NUWC and the Gould Island torpedo test facility. An elevator and firing platform are located along the corner of the building at the end of the causeway. *Right:* A MK 48 test shot being readied for firing once the elevator platform is lowered below the surface. (*NUSC*)

In actuality, we were quite pleased with the accommodations that were established for us. We shared a building adjacent to the Stillwater Basin breakwater, with personnel from NUWC's Narragansett Bay Shallow Water Test Facility (NBSWTF) and the Explosive Ordnance Disposal (EOD)

Detachment. We had brought our twin-engine rigid-hull inflatable boat (RIB) from New London, and there would soon be a new boat launch ramp, reconditioned wooden pier, and a modular floating platform with berthing for all of the small-craft, including our RIB. The wooden pier was home to the NBSWTF torpedo weapons retriever TWR-841 and the range support craft YFRT-287, an old lighter outfitted with a torpedo launch tube. The 287 was used in a documentary film about the rescue of survivors from USS *Squalus* (SS-192), which sank in 240 feet of water on May 23, 1939. The 287 resembled the rescue vessel USS *Falcon* (ASR-2) that on the day after *Squalus* sank, sent divers to the distressed submarine. Using the McCann rescue chamber, *Falcon* brought thirty-three survivors to the surface during a thirteen-hour operation. Four Navy divers were awarded the Medal of Honor. YFRT-287 was eventually decommissioned, and sold at auction in 2000 to an individual in Massachusetts intending to convert it to a floating restaurant.

Figure 67. Above: MK 48 torpedo is offloaded from USS *Annapolis* (SSN 760) at the Groton submarine base. *(Department of Defense Photo; John Narewski) Below:* Torpedo retriever near Keyport, Washington. *(Department of Defense Photo)*

With a new home in Rhode Island, it was necessary to solidify our post-Cold War mission, and we struggled to find new applications for our talents. For more than a century, torpedo development had been at the forefront of all of NUWC's predecessors in Newport. After BRAC and the inclusion of the Center's Keyport, Washington, Division, the Navy could rely on submarine weapons development on both coasts, where the reliable MK 48 torpedo (figure 67) continues to serve our country's

undersea warfare capability. But now, as the staff from New London integrated into the Center's Newport Division, sonar shared the spotlight. For our divers, the Navy continued to expect that same fast response to issues with submarine towed arrays (chapter 6). Over the years, however, our team had little involvement with torpedoes, yet there were a few occasions when we were needed, and one of our old timers had plenty of experience.

TORPEDO LAUNCH

In the late 1950s, the Navy was asked to support the production of Universal Studio's *Operation Petticoat,* and Chief Photographers Mate "Mac" McClenny would be tasked to film the underwater scenes. Mac was very familiar with torpedoes, having been a Gunners Mate on PT-boats during World War II ("PT" is the designation for "Patrol Torpedo"). When the movie script called for a Navy nurse on board *Sea Tiger* to accidently fire a torpedo, Mac hovered with his camera just outside the forward tube to film the World War II torpedo speeding off with a trail of bubbles. Later in the movie, *Sea Tiger*, mistaken for a Japanese submarine, was being depth-charged by a U.S. Navy destroyer. After sending an oil slick and debris to the surface, and failing to convince the destroyer that the submarine had been sunk, *Sea Tiger* loaded the nurses' bras and panties and blasted them out of the torpedo tube as Mac caught the scene on film.

TWENTY-FIVE YEARS LATER

The MK 48, already loaded into the torpedo tube, greeted us as we walked out onto the elevator at the Gould Island torpedo test facility. The procedure for launching torpedoes was simple. The elevator would be lowered to a prescribed depth; the test director then activated the torpedo propulsion system, spinning the propeller. The weapon would then accelerate and launch itself [the Navy uses the term "swim"] from the tube, traveling at a high velocity far out into the range. The success of the test depended on the initial conditions that the weapon experienced at launch. Our task was to observe and record the motion of the torpedo at the instant it exited the launcher. The end of the launcher tube, however, extended beyond the elevator platform making it impossible to simply stand alongside the tube and point the camera. Mac sent Vic Marolda and me onto the elevator with orders to create a human tripod.

With the elevator submerged, we sat with our legs wrapped around the launcher tube. Vic held my tank manifold as I leaned 90° out to the side where I could aim the camera at the torpedo, extending just beyond the muzzle. We were using our Underwater Damage Assessment Television System (UDATS), which transmitted the video through a cable to a surface monitor, where Mac and the engineers watched and recorded the launch. Although they were most concerned with whether the tail of the torpedo kicked up or down as it launched, Vic could also view any sideways motion from his position, looking down on the muzzle. I had two-way comms with the surface and let topside know when we were in position. We were then told it would be a sixty-second countdown.

With a moderate current, it was difficult to hold station. About half-way through the count, we slipped and lost position. Our situation was obvious to those watching the monitor and the countdown was immediately stopped. We repositioned and were soon ready, leaning hard against the current. I screamed an obscenity or two when they restarted the count back at sixty seconds, but this time we held tight. I still remember when the countdown reached zero, and heard the sounds from the propeller as it engaged and began increasing its rpm, struggling to overcome the inertia of the massive

Figure 68. *Above:* Torpedo is loaded into the Gould Island elevator launcher tube. *Below:* Divers Roy Manstan (foreground) and Vic Marolda ride the elevator back to the surface after filming the launch. (*NUSC*)

torpedo and the friction within the tube. Topside, the engineers stared at the small TV monitor.

Vic and I could feel the launcher vibrate slightly, as the nose of the torpedo began to slowly move forward. I kept the camera lens focused along the side of the muzzle, while on the monitor the nineteen-foot-long, twenty-one-inch-diameter torpedo could be seen accelerating to its launch velocity under the thrust of its propeller. It was over in a matter of seconds. At the moment the tail cone and its propeller emerged from the tube, I panned forward following its path. I could hear the cheers over our comms, as the engineers watched the torpedo disappear into the distance. (Figure 68)

NAVY DIVING—A TRADITION DATING TO THE NAVAL TORPEDO STATION

With the establishment of the Naval Torpedo Station Newport in 1869, the future of torpedo development was solidified within Narragansett Bay. The facilities were housed on Goat Island just off the town of Newport, eventually adding Gould Island further up the Bay. The Torpedo Station was also a location for training naval officers and enlisted personnel in the use of torpedoes as a tactical weapon. Several officers were assigned as instructors, including Lieutenant Francis Barber who published a series of lectures on torpedoes and torpedo warfare. These pamphlets were printed at the Torpedo Station where a printer's school was also located.

In 1882, the Torpedo Station brought on board an instructor who was also a Navy diver, and created a diving school as an elective course for enlisted Gunners Mates, the rate responsible for operational handling and firing of torpedoes. A need for divers had accelerated during the Civil War and in particular during the post war years for the salvage of sunken warships. A formal Navy diving school was established at the Torpedo Station in 1915, just in time for the next major conflict that drew America into World War I.

There had always been a need for diving support over the years as the Torpedo Station and its Cold War successors continued to develop a wide range of underwater weapons. Test-fired torpedoes were designed to float to the surface at the end of a run. Working from a Zodiac, the active duty range support divers at what was then NUSC/NPT would attach a small cage and tow-cable to the nose of the floating weapon. Often, however, a torpedo would sink, requiring post-test recovery from the bottom of Narragansett Bay or one of the other torpedo ranges along the east coast. Because torpedo recovery operations often occurred in deep water, NUWC maintained a well equipped dive boat with an onboard recompression chamber.

Our divers would occasionally fill in when the Newport divers were on another assignment. During one of these events, and after attaching the tow-point cage to the nose of a MK 48, none of us could resist recreating that Doctor Strangelove moment. Vic was the first to climb onto the weapon, and while riding the torpedo as it was towed back to the test ship, he could be heard hollering Slim Pickens' famous line, "EEEE-Hahhhhh," as Pickens' character, Major T.J. "King" Kong, rode the atomic bomb to its target. The active duty range divers continued to support torpedo testing until the recovery of test shots began to be accomplished with a large cage lowered from a helicopter.

NUWC also hosts the explosive ordnance disposal detachment that services the EOD Northeast Region, and their strategic location at a torpedo development facility is a logical choice. They are occasionally called out to take care of a long-lost torpedo that commercial fishermen had dragged off the bottom in their nets, or as happened during underwater navigation training (chapter 9), when Frank McNeilly and José Arteiro discovered an old torpedo (unarmed, as it turned out) barely visible in the mud, less than fifty yards off our pier. The EOD detachment had worked with our divers during the Cold War (chapter 5), and remains on the NUWC waterfront, where they continue to provide assistance to the EDSU.

One of the pleasures of running a collateral duty dive team is access to an incredible variety of quality talent. Two things become evident: first—these individuals are involved in unique and challenging projects; and second—these individuals are committed to a successful operation. My philosophy has always been that we can dive anywhere and under any conditions, yet I considered sending Frank McNeilly out for a sanity check when he approached me about a scientific study, which would require diving in a fluid-like medium with a specific gravity of 1.5.

INTO THE PRIMORDIAL OOZE

Frank was involved with a group of NUWC scientists who were proposing an experiment to determine the potential of exploiting an energy source that could tap the infinite numbers of infinitesimal life, saturating the bottom sediments of the world's oceans—bacteria. What Frank described was a microbial fuel cell. Electrons are a byproduct of the bacterial decomposition of organic material that settles onto the seafloor. A diver would imbed an anode deep into the bacteria-laden sediment and place the cathode nearby, all wired to a data acquisition and monitoring system ashore. It would be a messy process, the diver wallowing in mud to set multiple anodes. All diving operations required the supervisor to brief the team regarding the procedures if, for example, an emergency ascent became necessary during the dive—even though some of the installations would be in water less than five feet deep. Not wanting to bypass the required pre-dive speech, the dive sup simply declared, "In the event of an emergency ascent—stand up!"

Beginning during the summer of 2004, and over the following twelve months, our divers installed fuel cells at a variety of sites in the vicinity of the NUWC waterfront. In some locations the anodes were set just beneath the upper sediment layer; in other locations the diver, armed with a small shovel, would find himself burrowing deep into that primordial ooze. The anode/cathode relationship produced what we referred to as a "mud battery," the output of which Frank and the scientists he worked with recorded day and night, summer and winter. The experiments were designed to determine the amount of energy that could be extracted from the electro-chemical process—as long as these microbes were well fed, the anodes would continue to accumulate electrons.

Although I had hoped to tap into these mud batteries and keep the dive locker refrigerator running, the goals of this experiment were to understand the science behind benthic microbial generation of electrical energy. As a demonstration, the output of one of the nearby fuel cells was used to power an incandescent light on the pier—not the frig. The results have been published in the conference proceedings of SPIE (the International Society for Optics and Photonics).[133] Testing continued through 2009, and as modifications improved fuel cell efficiency, a successful experiment included the operation of an underwater pinger and hydrophone.

With the natural curiosity of a scientist and the tenacity of a Navy diver, Frank's willingness to try unusual things became evident during the winter, in 2005, when another "never-been-done-before" opportunity arose.

TORPEDO TUBE—THE ULTIMATE ENCLOSED SPACE DIVING

When the outer shutter doors swing open, a fast attack submarine is preparing to fire a weapon with a lethal capacity, proven throughout a century of naval warfare. The weapon is loaded into its torpedo tube and the interior hatch secured. The torpedo tube is then flooded and the muzzle door swings open. When the MK 48 is fired, its nose passes out of the muzzle and enters a long, cylindrical torpedo tube extension that guides the weapon through the submarine superstructure and out past the open shutter door. There is less than a two-foot gap between the muzzle and the torpedo tube extension (also referred to as a "guide can"), which provides space for opening the muzzle door. In this space are cables and the muzzle door limit switch that guarantee a smooth and safe firing procedure.

Although this area within the bow superstructure is adjacent to forward ballast tanks, a bulkhead isolates the free-flooding space, which accommodates the torpedo tubes and the guide can extensions. When a submarine is afloat pierside, there is only one access to the muzzle door limit switch—when the shutter door is opened, a diver must maneuver his body through the 15-foot-long guide can, finally pulling himself into that small space. So . . . why would a diver ever venture down a long cylinder only slightly larger in diameter than his body? To save the cost of putting the submarine into dry-dock, and enable the boat to complete its operational requirements on schedule.

Engineers were interested in conducting an experiment that required the installation of sensors in the guide cans. The sensors, it was felt, could be adapted to use the limit switch cables, but the limit switches were located in a flooded area. The cables would have to be disconnected from the limit switch and reconnected to the new sensors, but these electrical connections had to be done in a dry environment. One option: dry-dock the submarine. Another option: send in the EDSU—"E" is for Engineering, "D" is for Diving. The EDSU engineers, including Frank, designed a cylindrical "bubble chamber," which the divers could slide down the guide tube and into that 22-inch gap; an opening at the underside of the bubble chamber enabled the diver's head and arms to fit inside. Air would then be pumped into the chamber to provide a dry "bubble" in which the diver could make the sensor connections.

The EDSU ran initial procedural tests on the bubble chamber in a pool at NUWC. The divers also paid a visit to a similar submarine in dry-dock, where they walked through the spaces and became familiar with what they would experience when the submarine selected for the testing arrived at the pier. A team from a Mobile Diving and Salvage Unit (MDSU-2) was tasked to support the installation and provide the surface supplied MK 20 Enclosed Space Diving System. The EDSU team led by Vic Marolda included Jack Hughes, Frank McNeilly, Mike Peirson, and John Wiedenheft.

There are reasons why Navy diver training tests an individual's comfort zone, and why the title of chapter 3 is "Calm, Cool, and Collected." This sensor installation, located in an extremely tight space with a very limited exit path, required just that kind of cool head. The divers squirmed down the guide cans and entered the area around the torpedo tube muzzle . . . then drilled ten mounting holes into the guide can's high-strength HY-80 steel . . . then the diver test-fit the sensor . . . then the bubble chamber was sent in . . . then the dry connections were made . . . then the chamber was removed and the sensors installed. Each procedure required two divers to enter through the shutter doors, move down the guide can, complete each task, and then exit for the next pair of divers. All of this was done in a pitch black enclosure, where the only illumination was provided by small lights brought into the tight spaces by the divers.

One sensor was installed in one of the port guide cans and another sensor in a starboard guide can, requiring a total of six diving days. Had this all occurred in the summer, the hours spent working within the free-flooded superstructure would have been a pleasure, but that was not the case. The installation occurred in the middle of January 2005, at the submarine base in Groton—plenty of ice on the Thames River in January—plenty of cold winter wind blowing across the pier. The MDSU team brought a water heating system that pumps hot water down hoses and into the divers' suits, but when the wind destroyed the enclosure set up on the pier, the hot-water system froze. The divers continued working in the near freezing Thames River, but the operation had to be suspended due to the real danger of hypothermia. The sub base divers soon pulled alongside the pier with their dive boat, but their hot-water system also froze. With the wind-break tent repaired, a third system was drawn out of storage and brought to the site, finally providing that one element of comfort absolutely essential for lengthy diving in extreme cold water.

But what goes in must come out, and at the end of February, the testing was complete and the submarine returned to Groton. By the beginning of March, the incessant winter winds had subsided and removal of the sensors was a quick three-day operation. In spite of the extreme cold, the project was a success. This operation was an example of how individuals were motivated to try new ideas in spite of the potential risks.

Another project high on the "uniqueness" list brought our divers to the Kwajalein missile range in the Marshall Islands, far out into the Pacific Ocean and far from the cold New England water. That opportunity arrived through the efforts of Richard "Rich" Kaiser. As with so many of our divers, Rich has unique personal interests that attest to his adaptability (and likewise that of our team in general) to mental and physical challenges within and beyond the Navy. It was his involvement at the missile range and a willingness to face physical challenges that motivated Rich to complete scuba training and join the dive team in 1995. In addition to participating in local lacrosse and hockey leagues, Rich earned his pilot's license in 2004, and began his flying years in a 1991 French-made, single-engine, four-seat Socata Tampico TB-9C.

KMISS—KWAJALEIN MISSILE IMPACT SCORING SYSTEM

Beginning at the onset of World War I, the Marshall Islands remained under Japanese control for three decades until February 1944, when the islands, including Kwajalein Atoll, were captured by American forces. As the Cold War turned hot during the Korean War, Kwajalein provided a strategic refueling and communications base, and by 1959 had become the site for the Nike-Zeus missile testing program. The Navy transferred its control of the Kwajalein missile testing facility to the Army in 1964, and in 1986 the facility became a part of the U.S. Army Strategic Defense Command (USASDC). In 1999, the facility was designated the Ronald Reagan Ballistic Missile Defense Test Site; it has also been used as a manned space flight tracking station.

In 1993, the Army became interested in creating a system that could accurately locate the point of impact on the ocean surface, of its Peacekeeper and Minuteman III missiles. The Army funded the NUWC Newport acoustic range department to integrate and install components of the in-water and shore-based subsystems for its Kwajalein Missile Impact Scoring System, or KMISS.[134] The KMISS program manager at NUWC was Barry Wall and the project engineer was Robert Connerney, but much to my delight, the in-water subsystem (IWS) manager was one of our divers, Rich Kaiser. Rich had travelled to Kwajalein numerous times during the planning phase, including the bathymetric survey of the ocean bottom in 1994, to determine where to locate the hydrophones that would "listen" for the missile impact.

During the mid-1990s, Rich had gained extensive experience with range installations, including the Australian Range Activity (AURA) located off Rockingham, Western Australia; then the East Coast Shallow Water Training Range (ECSWTR) off North Carolina, later moved to Florida; then the Bi-Directional Fiber Optic Telemetry (BIFOTEL) system at the Pacific Missile Range Facility (PMRF) offshore of Kauai, Hawaii, where in June 1996, Rich surveyed the sensor cable while diving with Underwater Construction Team Two (UCT-2). For much of this installation work, including the KMISS bathymetric survey, Rich was accompanied by Harold "Bud" Vincent, another Newport-based member of the NUSC dive team.

Beginning in July 1996, Rich spent eight weeks as the IWS manager, overseeing the installation of hydrophones at depths ranging from 5,000 to 14,500 feet. Located as much as twelve miles from the island, the cables lie along the bottom and then rise up the escarpment that characterizes the volcanic origins of Kwajalein Atoll, and finally onto the shallow water fringing reef shelf. Toward the end of the IWS installation, Paul Mileski flew to Kwajalein, joining Rich, Bud, and Michael Dick, an engineer/diver from Kauai's PMRF, to complete the shallow-water portion of the

IWS. Their job was to splice the hydrophone cables to the armored multi-conductor shore-side cables in a junction box, and secure everything onto the rough coralline bottom. The junction box was set at a depth of forty feet. The heavy-duty hydrophone cables ran out to what divers refer to as "the drop-off," where they hung down into the abyss. The armored shore-side cables were secured within steel pipes pinned to the bottom; then buried underground through the sea-to-shore interface, where seasonal storm waves beat against the Kwajalein shoreline.

The operations of the KMISS range continued uninterrupted for almost five years when, in 2001, one of the hydrophone cables failed. The system had been designed with enough redundancy to allow the KMISS range to function, but a repair was considered essential for its long-term operational viability. Rich and Bud, with fellow EDSU divers Vic Marolda, Mike Peirson, Jack Hughes, and John Wiedenheft, plus an electrical engineer, Jim Pazera, arrived in August 2002. Using a device called the time domain reflectometer (TDR), the team determined the cable break to be 950 feet down its length, putting the break at a depth of 450 feet and far beyond access by the divers. The team was, however, able to stabilize and provide additional protection to other cables at risk of being damaged where they crossed sharp coral formations.

After completing the range cable inspections, the divers had an opportunity to relax and explore the shallow water reefs within the atoll. Protected from ocean swells that roll up against the island, the calm water within the atoll provides great opportunities to join the tropical marine life that thrives among the corals. But there was also the lure of the wreck site of a World War II German heavy cruiser, *Prinz Eugen*, much of it accessible in the shallows. When you have spent years diving on and under countless numbers of ships and submarines, the hull of a historic German cruiser that had accompanied *Bismarck* in battles in the Atlantic was irresistible.

Prinz Eugen was transferred to the U.S. Navy as a war prize in January 1946. Its advanced sonar was removed and sent to the Sound Lab for evaluation, and the ship towed to Bikini Atoll, where it was included in (and survived) Operation Crossroads—two atomic bomb tests in July 1946. Afterwards, *Prinz Eugen* was brought into the Kwajalein atoll where it soon began to take on water, but before it could be beached, the ship rolled over. Its stern now lies above water on the shallow reef with its bow down-slope at a depth of one hundred feet. Exploring the interior of *Prinz Eugen* has long been a temptation for scuba divers, unfortunately fatal for several, and has since become off limits to recreational divers.

CAPTAIN JACK SPARROW—HUNTING FOR THE GHOSTS OF AMERICA'S PAST—(#)

An archaeologist like Dr D. K. "Kathy" Abbass can put her audience on the edge of its seat with the same nervous anticipation movie-goers experience when Captain Jack Sparrow and his motley pirate crew encounter Davy Jones and the *Flying Dutchman*, emerging from the depths of the ocean and into the mist of the giant screen.

Okay, maybe I'm being a bit dramatic here, but as the director of the Rhode Island Marine Archaeology Project (RIMAP),[135] Kathy's investigations into the rich maritime history of Rhode Island are filled with the long-lost remains of magnificent warships. One of Kathy's (and RIMAP's) goals has been identifying a famous vessel, which now lies somewhere in the shallow water off Newport, but had travelled the world under the leadership of Captain James Cook who, at least in my opinion, deserves an amount of notoriety comparable to Jack Sparrow.

Kathy's audience may be a bit more limited than Disney's, but the intrigue of the mystery and discovery is no less intense. In the mid 90s, we were approached by Kathy, her professional colleagues at the University of Rhode Island's Marine Archaeology Department, and individuals responsible for that state's submerged cultural resources. They were looking for experienced divers to join their search for British vessels, scuttled during the Revolutionary War at the approach of a French fleet, which was assembling along the Rhode Island coast.

All Navy dive teams are required to conduct and document periodic training in basic diving operations. The intent is to give teams a review of proper procedures under low-stress situations, helping make safe operations more likely when subjected to high-stress conditions. We had received some limited funding from NUWC to help cover the costs associated with this requirement, and I felt that running a series of diving operations for Kathy Abbass and RIMAP would be the best use of this funding. NUWC encourages its staff to participate in community and education outreach opportunities—what could be more fitting than surveying underwater sites associated with local maritime and naval history.[136]

During the summer of 1778, the British were in firm control of Newport. France had recently joined America's effort to gain its independence, and a fleet of warships and troop transports under Admiral, Compte D'Estaing had sailed to join George Washington and the struggling colonial army. As the fleet gathered off Rhode Island, several warships entered Narragansett Bay with the intent to test British strength in Newport, and engage the relatively small naval force within the Bay. The British, seeing the French show of force, sank a dozen or more vessels along the approaches to the town in an attempt to keep the warships out of cannon range.

Farther up the Bay, the British ran several of their ships aground, which were then burned to the waterline, to keep them from being captured. Our first experience with Kathy brought us to the site of one of these ships, HMS *Cerberus*, where we began a systematic search for the vessel's remains. One of our divers, Bruce Greenhalgh, carried an underwater camera, connected through a communications and video feed to a surface monitor, where Kathy could observe the progress of the survey and speak directly to Bruce.

Communication from a diver through his mask-mounted microphone is always grating, frequently intermittent, and often undecipherable—simple is the name of the game in Navy underwater comms. Hi-fi is not a technological priority, so when you send your voice to a lo-fi speaker, there's a reason we are trained to speak slowly and use as few words as possible. Less words means less chance of a miss-communication. When a diver encounters something unusual, or gets caught up in the excitement of a great discovery, it's not easy to engage the use of short phrases, and we revert to the exclamatory style, which most of use when telling sea stories at the local bar. "Jesus!!! . . . Do you see that?" Bruce, in a surge of excitement, swung his camera back and forth, displaying a blurred image on the topside monitor. "It's a cannon—I don't believe it—I found a fucking CANNON!!! (Constraints on foul language also revert to bar-speak.) "Hey topside . . . can you see it? It's gotta be eight feet long. Man, there's gotta be cannon balls around here somewhere."

Poor Kathy—before we began volunteering our "scientific" diving services, she had briefed us on the procedures for conducting an underwater site survey. We promised that we'd be appropriately careful when engaging the scientific method, so important in establishing the proper archaeological context of everything we discovered. But a cannon?? . . . From the Revolutionary War???? Hard to curtail a diver's enthusiasm. Then some gentle scolding from Kathy: "Now Bruce . . . please remember what I told you. You are there to record, not remove or disturb the artifacts you find. Now place a marker and measure its position relative to the datum." Our divers soon adapted to Kathy's firm hand and adherence to archaeological protocol; after all, that was the job we had signed up for.

CAPTAIN JAMES COOK

Among the vessels scuttled by the British that summer in 1778 was HMS *Lord Sandwich*, a well-worn vessel with an illustrious career under a previous name and a very famous master, Captain James Cook. Launched in 1764, the ship was soon purchased by the British Royal Navy and commissioned HMS *Endeavor* in 1768, for Cook's voyage of discovery. After returning to England, *Endeavor* was sold to a commercial enterprise. At the beginning of the American Revolution, the British chartered the vessel, renamed HMS *Lord Sandwich*, for use as a troop transport. Among the dozen or more ships scuttled, *Lord Sandwich* slowly settled into the bottom along Newport's shoreline, its superstructure disintegrating in the shallow waters, while some of its hull remained mired in the sediment.

FAST FORWARD 232 YEARS . . . AUGUST 15, 2000

"We're approaching the keel . . ." Butterflies in nervous stomachs twitched with anticipation as a video image appeared on the screen, illuminated by the camera's high intensity light. "I'm brushing away the silt . . ." a pause . . . and Kathy replies, "We can see your hand . . ."

Bruce, now fully indoctrinated in the use of fewer (and proper) words, was on the camera. He began moving his hand to sweep away sediment, which had settled over remnants of a hull exposed earlier in the day by the suction dredge. "Wait for the cloud to pass . . ." Bruce was, of course, referring to the cloud of fine-grained silt that rose in front of the camera, not about clouds in the sky; in fact, if there were clouds up there we wouldn't have cared. The sun had set over Rhode Island and darkness enveloped our divers, cautiously maneuvering over the site. But Kathy was not the only person watching the video. With hope that we were uncovering *Endeavor*, a vessel as significant to Australia's heritage as *Niña*, *Pinta* and *Santa Maria* were to American history, Kathy's audience sat in an auditorium at the National Maritime Museum in Sydney, Australia, where they could view the underwater tour via a link to the internet, which our team had established. In spite of being in a time zone on the far side of the globe, they could view in real-time, the streaming video on a large screen—the identical video that Kathy watched on her monitor at the dive site, while Paul Hundley, one of the maritime historians on site from Australia, used a cell phone to provide verbal commentary. Had we found *Endeavor*? The jury is still out, and the investigation continues.

AMERICAN SCHOOL FOR THE DEAF

Our divers have always taken pride in maintaining a visible presence in efforts associated with education outreach. Paul Mileski, one of our divers and an engineer in the Submarine Antenna Branch, was a driving force at NUWC, adapting antenna technology to the new and growing field of wireless connectivity to the internet, and the high data rate requirements of streaming video. Patrick "Pat" Gilles, who had taken a recreational diving course and was also interested in wireless technology, worked with Paul, establishing the internet connection to the Australians. But they were also instrumental in the success of another education outreach project.

Using a similar internet connection, we offered to share a view of underwater science with students at the American School for the Deaf (ASD) in West Hartford, Connecticut. Because diving primarily relies on the visual sense, where sound, smell, taste, and touch marginally influence the experience, scuba diving would appeal equally to hearing individuals and to those living in the silent world of the deaf. A unique opportunity arose in February and March 2001, during what would be our last in a series of ICECAMP (chapter 7) under-ice experiments.

We were measuring radio frequency transmission through a foot-thick layer of simulated sea ice at an outdoor freeze facility at the Army's

Cold Regions Research and Engineering Lab (CRREL) in Hanover, New Hampshire. We had cut an access hole through the ice, enabling the divers an easy entry and exit. Bruce Greenhalgh operated the underwater video, while Jack Hughes and John Wiedenheft alternated with the under-ice installation of our transmit antennas.

Paul Mileski and I took care of the topside aspects of the diving operations, while Pat Gilles set the receive antenna above the ice, and connected our two video cameras to the internet. Students, sitting in their classroom at ASD, watched video feeds on a split-screen monitor—one feed from an underwater video camera, and the second from a camera mounted above the ice. As Bruce slipped under the ice, the ASD students could watch John at work. On the other feed, they could see Paul, standing near the access hole holding a cell phone. In the question/answer setting of their classroom, the teacher relayed students' questions, expressed via American Sign Language, verbally to Paul. She then signed Paul's answers back to the kids. Taking barely an hour, the experience had a life-long impression on these kids, yet an infinitesimal impact on the progress of a week-long experiment—education outreach is well worth the effort.

Four years had passed since the New London Lab closed. Now firmly planted on the NUWC Newport waterfront, we found opportunities to participate in a variety of underwater projects. As we entered the twenty-first century, unmanned surface vehicles (USVs) and unmanned undersea vehicles (UUVs) would find their way onto—and under—our new backyard along Narragansett Bay. The EDSU continued to support the submarine towed array program, while we also sought new challenges. Sadly, that challenge would arrive in the form of a new global enemy.

Figure 69. *Above:* USS *Cole* (DDG-67) in tow after the suicide attack in 2000 by terrorists carrying explosives in a small-craft. (*Naval History and Heritage Command; Don L. Maes*) *Below: Cole* sustained significant damage to its hull, but the attack also took the lives of seventeen sailors. (*Department of Defense Photo*)

CHAPTER 9
The Global War on Terror

On September 12, 2001, I received a call from NUWC Executive Director Juergen Keil. The attack on the World Trade Center the day before had stunned everyone, and organizations large and small were rushing to provide a unified response. Law enforcement and first responders across the country took immediate action to accelerate their vigilance. All branches of the military were placed on high alert. The various national intelligence agencies scoured their data to determine how such a disaster could have occurred and if other attacks were imminent—all while the magnitude of the scene on lower Manhattan was being broadcast across the globe, minute by minute.

The phone call I received from Juergen Keil was one of many he made that day—department heads and representatives from various technical codes were being called to attend a meeting the following morning, where the threat facing our country would be discussed. These same conversations were being held throughout all of the military research agencies, where "solutions" to the threat were being solicited. Rich Russell, who worked for Juergen, would coordinate and direct any and all ideas, practical or farfetched, which would emerge from the collective energy and intellect of the Naval Undersea Warfare Center.

Throughout its history, NUWC and its predecessor organizations had all operated under the "warfare" mandate—that if there was an enemy with intent to destroy the "life, liberty, and pursuit of happiness" embodied in the Declaration of Independence, there was nothing that would stand in the way of eliminating the threat. We had faced technological adversaries that possessed what could be truly classified as weapons of mass destruction, but these historical enemies were recognizable, definable, and were themselves equally vulnerable.

Technology had been king throughout the twentieth century, and eliminating threats through technology characterized two world wars, and a Cold War where the possibility of nuclear annihilation was real. The enemy always had a national identity, and adversarial nations faced each other on a relatively equal footing.

The attack on the World Trade Center has been compared to the attack on Pearl Harbor, but beyond the element of surprise, the comparison fades. Pearl Harbor drew America into World War II. There was no doubt who the enemy was—the so-called "Axis Powers" were primarily Japan, Germany, and Italy, definable as nations at war. The antagonists wore uniforms, were members of organized military units, and fought under their national flags.

But now, the threat came from a source that this country had never confronted. As the twin towers of the World Trade Center disintegrated before our eyes, the question that frustrated the military was how to respond—but to what! Four commercial jets loaded with fuel and in the hands of hijackers had now become the weapons of choice—powerful human-directed projectiles. These were not military weapons, but had an even greater effect on the American psyche than anything a national adversary could or would devise. America was vulnerable, and in a single day this vulnerability left our entire society in shock.

The attack had been perpetrated by nineteen civilians, operating on orders from the shadows. They had slipped into this country with the intent to carry out a well-planned and executed suicide mission. There was no specific "country of origin" for this new and profound form of terrorism; this was an intensely focused manifestation of religious extremism disbursed throughout the Islamic world. The organization that soon became known across the globe as al Qaida had no specific national identity.

Within a few months, and as the site of the destruction of the World Trade Center was being cleared, President George W. Bush initiated a ground war in Afghanistan, where al Qaida and its leader Osama bin Laden had found refuge. The war was intended to root out terrorists and extremist groups from a country that had either simply looked the other way, or had willingly provided a safe haven for al Qaida's training camps, where they could plan and direct their operations.

AN UNEXPECTED THREAT

Everyone who attended that meeting with Juergen Keil on September 13, 2001, in fact all three thousand members of the NUWC staff, had focused their careers on technologies designed to keep global threats at bay. Submarine and antisubmarine warfare bore little resemblance to this new mode of warfare. Dealing with suicide bombers was not in the NUWC mission statement and some questioned whether there was anything where NUWC could make a significant contribution. That question soon found an answer.[137]

On May 24, 2002, the Cable Network News (CNN) Washington Bureau announced that the FBI had "sent a nationwide alert [through the National Law Enforcement Telecommunications System] . . . to state and local law enforcement agencies saying that it had received information about a possible threat from underwater divers." Although the CNN report mentioned that the FBI "considers the information uncorroborated and unconfirmed," the sources of information regarding the threat had come from detainees at Guantanamo and were taken seriously: "FBI sources said Friday the information relating to a potential scuba diver attack came during the continued questioning of detainees being held since their capture in Afghanistan." The CNN sources noted there were no specific targets, but that a variety of industries considered "vulnerable to that type of attack" were being notified about the potential threat; the Coast Guard also passing these concerns to the public and commercial activities within their jurisdiction.[138]

Evidence that al Qaida was considering training its members for an underwater attack continued to grow. The discovery of scuba diving manuals in an al Qaida safe-house in Afghanistan was reflected in the FBI's May 2002 warning that "various terrorist elements have sought to develop an offensive scuba diver capability."[139] These diving manuals were certainly a source of legitimate concern considering that spear fishing was not likely a sport that would be on a list of popular Afghan hobbies.

ANTICIPATING UNDERWATER ATTACKS

The newly created Department of Homeland Security (DHS) had been developing a strategy to respond to all potential modes of attack, and the increasing concern about the use of scuba divers led to their issuing the "Swimmer Attack Indicators and Protective Measures Bulletin" on August 22, 2003. Four days later, on August 26, NEWSMAX published an article describing the DHS bulletin on their web site, titled "Al Qaeda Plans Underwater Attack."[140] According to NEWSMAX, the bulletin was "issued to ship owners, port managers and maritime police organizations," advising them of "a number of incidents of suspicious activity and possible surveillance of maritime facilities . . . [and that] there is a body of information showing the desire to obtain [scuba diving] capability." The NEWSMAX article also noted that DHS "warned scuba gear operators, owners and training companies to be on the lookout for individuals or groups that have money but no visible means of support," and that DHS was also concerned about the possible use of "Swimmer Delivery Vehicles (SDVs) and Diver Propulsion Vehicles (DPVs)."

Additional concern about terrorist divers emerged from the Philippines, where Abu Sayyaf, an Islamic separatist group with ties to al Qaida, had been considering providing scuba training to their members as early as 2000—a year before 9/11—although it wasn't until 2004 when this training was discovered. In a March 2005 article titled "Next for Terrorists: Seaborne Attacks," the web site www.wnd.com provided information obtained by the Associated Press (AP) that the Philippine military had reported the kidnapping of a maintenance engineer from a resort by Abu Sayyaf. When released from captivity in 2004, the engineer said his captors had known he was a scuba instructor and wanted him to train them. A member of Abu Sayyaf, who had been caught after receiving scuba training, claimed that he had been part of an underwater operation planned for some unidentified country.[141]

It was a logical mode of attack in this part of the world, where the many island nations with ties to the West depended on their maritime commerce and infrastructure, all susceptible to underwater attack.

"A Time Bomb for Global Trade: Maritime-related Terrorism in an Age of Weapons of Mass destruction." Michael Richardson, research fellow at the Institute of South East Asian Studies, wrote this 105-page threat assessment by compiling information gained from reviewing several years of reports on al Qaida's maritime strategy. In 2002, two important al

Qaida leaders were captured; one in Indonesia was the head of operations in Southeast Asia, Omar al-Faruq who, according to Richardson, told investigators that he "planned scuba attacks on US warships in Indonesia. The site chosen was the port of Surabaya . . . the home of an important Indonesian naval base."[142]

The other captive Richardson referred to was al Qaida's "Chief of Naval Operations" Abdul al-Nasheri, caught in Yemen. The information gathered from al-Nasheri provided a disconcerting list of four modes of maritime terrorist attack. First was the use of small but fast-moving boats that could make a high speed run against a U.S. naval warship. The successful attack against USS *Cole* (DDG-67) in 2000 off Yemen (figure 69) was an example of this use of a small-craft. The second concept would employ medium-sized vessels, which would be too slow for an attack against a warship, but could pull alongside a maritime vessel or cruise liner with little danger of being suspected of launching an attack. The third was to take a small private plane from a nearby airstrip; loaded with explosives, the plane could be flown into a ship or significant maritime infrastructure.

Al-Nasheri's fourth mode of attack, of particular interest to us, was what Richardson described as the "training of underwater demolition teams to attack ships." By 2002, with information now coming from al Qaida leaders and not just a captured operative, the underwater threat gained a high level of credibility.

There was a growing realization and acceptance of al Qaida's international appeal to Islamic extremists, and their interest in considering a range of tactics, including divers. A known terrorist had been arrested in the Netherlands, having recently completed a scuba diving course. It was soon discovered that more than fifty Muslims, many of whom Dutch intelligence knew were associated with radical groups, had completed scuba training and were referred to as the "al Qaida Diving Team." Michael Richardson also mentioned the Dutch investigations into these scuba trained suspected terrorists, although Richardson indicated that as many as one-hundred-fifty Muslim men from North Africa and the Mid-East were involved.[143]

The British were no less concerned about underwater threats, particularly with these European reports of terrorists being trained to use scuba. In 2005, while preparing for the bicentennial celebration of the Battle of Trafalgar, security officials had considered the possibility of an underwater attack during a royal review of the fleet. Their concerns were noted in a report in the Times of London: "Officials fear Al Qaeda divers could attach bombs to the hulls of ships [or] detonate explosives strapped to their bodies in suicide attacks."[144]

ASYMMETRIC WARFARE

Without a "standing army" or any national identity, al Qaida and its surrogates depended on terror to spread their philosophy of hate toward Western societies. Backpacks loaded with explosives were detonated on a Spanish train and on busses in England. Suicide bombers were walking into bars and other public areas crowded with civilians. As the bombers' bodies disintegrated in the blast, the nails and ball bearings that they carried spread destruction out into the crowds. The attacks on the World Trade Center, the Pentagon, and the foiled attempt by a fourth plane over Pennsylvania were unprecedented in their scope.

When facing an overwhelming opponent, terrorist objectives all share a common theme—maximize the damage with stealth and with minimum personnel, a tactic known as asymmetric warfare. Al Qaida tactical asymmetry is characterized both by the few individuals involved and the level of technology available to these individuals. Regardless of their small numbers and their crude weapons, the terrorists are smart, dedicated, and focused on their objectives. They understand their limitations and are willing to sacrifice everything to take even a small step toward their goal. Time is on their side, and the end may not be measured in years, but in generations. In a War on Terror, the enemy's strategy is to wear down their opponent, and make the struggle too costly in dollars and human lives. While ground wars have raged on in response to 9/11, small groups of terrorist "cells" continue to plan and devise other asymmetric attacks in Europe, America, and other countries with economic ties to the West.

As the war in Afghanistan progressed, and in response to the real potential of another attack within our own borders, President Bush created the Cabinet level Department of Homeland Security (DHS) in November 2002. Three months later, on February 25, 2003, the Coast Guard was transferred from the Department of Transportation (DOT) to become the maritime security arm of DHS. This relationship would soon drive the focus NUWC would take as envisioned by Juergen Keil; after all, NUWC's mission was *undersea warfare*, and it was becoming evident that the Global War on Terror could very likely take on a maritime element—but specifically that this war would extend into this *undersea* world.

The threat was no longer from a Soviet ballistic missile submarine, where technological "symmetry" existed between us and our adversary. The "asymmetry" of the threat was now manifest in one or two scuba trained terrorists. Their target, however, might be a cruise ship or a nuclear

Figure 70. Taken in 2005, this photo shows the ex-*Saratoga* (left) and ex-*Forrestal* pierside at Naval Station Newport. These aircraft carriers represent a potential terrorist target and were the backdrop for the NUWC swimmer defense program initiated after the attack on the World Trade Center. The ex-*Forrestal* is no longer berthed at the Naval Station. (*NUWC*)

power station, or it might be a Naval vessel (figure 70) either on deployment (as was the case with USS *Cole*) or at a home base. The mode of attack could either come from an explosive laden small-craft racing to its target, or from a diver quietly approaching beneath the surface. In 2001, neither the Navy nor the Coast Guard was prepared for an al Qaida diver.

The nature of this underwater threat was soon recognized, and by 2002, both the Navy and Coast Guard pursued a similar approach to detecting and neutralizing the threat. The Navy referred to it as an Integrated Swimmer Defense (ISD) component of their Shipboard Protection System, while the Coast Guard preferred the term Integrated Antiswimmer System (IAS). The word "swimmer" was used as a generic term, referring not just to surface swimmers, but also divers using open-circuit and closed-circuit breathing systems, and potentially operating small underwater vehicles. The goal would eventually focus on a swimmer defense system applicable to both the Navy and Coast Guard. But achieving that goal depended on bringing scientists, engineers, and the military down to the waterfront.

KNOW YOUR ENEMY

This phrase used by military planners is more than simply understanding their strategic goals and operational tactics. During a ground war there is a constant anticipation of infiltration by guerilla or clandestine forces. Providing a capability to "know your enemy" becomes a responsibility of engineers who define the threat in terms that enable the development of high-tech systems for the warfighter—infrared detectors, chemical and nuclear radiation sensors, radar, and night-vision devices. The engineer measures the physical characteristics of a potential threat using human volunteer "test subjects," dressed in typical uniforms and carrying standard equipment and weapons, while conducting simulated infiltration scenarios. These measurements are then used to optimize detection and interdiction technologies. The sooner the forces on the ground can holler "who goes there," the sooner they can make the decision to pull the trigger.

When the threat slips beneath the surface, however, he becomes invisible to these above-water technologies. Again, it becomes the engineer's task to "know the enemy," but now it is the application of a technology that arose from a century of development—sonar. There is nothing unexpected about the possibility of using sonar; this technology had been designed to detect anything from icebergs to whales, submarines, schools of fish, and shipwrecks—and to enable ships to avoid becoming shipwrecks. If it exists underwater then sonar can find it. Sounds simple, but the application as an antiswimmer device is complicated.

The five sonar-based "search and destroy" steps were described in chapter 6—detect, classify, localize, track, and sink the SOB. In a wartime antisubmarine scenario, much of this process is unambiguous. The target is large, can be readily classified as a threat, and then localized and tracked for pinpoint fire control. A scuba diver is a small acoustic target, and although he moves at a relatively slow pace, detection is difficult beyond a certain range. Next, the object must be classified as a human (not a marine mammal or a small school of fish, known in the sonar world as a "false target"), then tracked as a potential threat.

Now the process takes its most difficult turn. A determination has to be made as to the diver's intent—is he truly a threat, or some sport diver that has found himself in the wrong place at the wrong time. To be effective, the diver detection sonar must be able to quickly detect and classify the target, allowing sufficient time to warn the intruder that he is in a danger zone with instructions to leave the area or come to the surface. If that fails, a decision is made to engage a non-lethal deterrent that, if he continues to ignore the warnings, can be scaled to lethal. The Coast Guard is particularly conscious of this requirement. With over 95,000 miles of coastline and over 360 ports, the likelihood is high that a sport diver, intent on finding that lobster or spearing a fish dinner, will wander into a protected area. The ability to "know your enemy" (as well knowing who is not your enemy) takes on a very significant role.

COUNTERING THE TWENTY-FIRST CENTURY THREAT

In December 2002, under Rich Russell's direction, a Memorandum of Understanding (MOU) was signed between NUWC and the Coast Guard Research & Development Center (CG-RDC), at that time located in Groton, Connecticut. While writing a document that would establish a long and close relationship, Rich solicited inputs from me and from John Cooke, NUWC's liaison at the CG-RDC. The MOU was designed to facilitate access to field engineering expertise (and enthusiasm) from those of us who thrive on challenges on and under the sea. The Coast Guard wanted a fast response from the waterfront. On February 26 2003, the day after they became part of DHS, I was in a meeting at the CG-RDC, discussing the development of a proposed antiswimmer system, which they hoped would fulfill their underwater port security (UPSec) mission. Throughout the winter and spring of 2003, the NUWC Engineering & Diving Support Unit took on a leading role in a relationship that continues to the present day.

Adaptations of several active echo-ranging sonar systems were being considered by both the Navy and Coast Guard. A series of tests had been conducted at the Naval Station North Island at Coronado, California (San Diego Bay), but with limited success—in part due to the logistical difficulties associated with operating within an active Navy base. But these systems, some cobbled together from equipment used for locating schools of fish or other underwater objects, were also based on limited knowledge of the human target. This was not a bad way to start, considering the uniqueness of the threat. New ideas often succumb to Newton's First Law of Motion, and become bogged down by the inertia of doubters and risk-evaders. For many of us, however, any ideas brought to the waterfront, cobbled together or not, created forward motion.

Developing a swimmer defense technology required a system engineering approach. NUWC was well-versed in system engineering, and became the lead Warfare Center to integrate the multiple interests within the Navy and DHS. Certainly, testing a system by simulating diver attack scenarios was important, but that system (both the hardware and the signal processing) could only be optimized with a thorough knowledge of what is referred to as target acoustics. By the spring of 2003, NUWC, and in particular the EDSU staff, had taken on the responsibility for measuring the acoustic properties of the target—a diver—and evaluating the effectiveness of multiple proposed sonar systems. The goal was developing a sonar "concept of operations" (CONOPS) for both Navy and Coast Guard applications. It was time to get to know the enemy.

DETECT AND CLASSIFY THE INTRUDER

The bottom line here is the farther away you can detect an intruder and classify him as a threat to the asset being protected (naval warship, cruise ship, nuclear power plant, hydroelectric dam), the more time your security forces will have to intervene. Swimmer defense sonar could include either (or a combination of) active echo-ranging or passive listening devices. Both types of sonar had been proposed, each requiring an understanding of different aspects of the overall acoustic characteristics of the target.

In the first case, an active sonar transmits a pulse, or a series of pulses, of sound energy. The pulses propagate through the water, strike the target, and bounce or "echo" back to the sonar. An electronic processor then evaluates the echo, or in most cases a series of echoes, to determine what the object might be. This processor uses what are called "algorithms," mathematical equations that are designed to tell, for example, whether the echoes are from a log floating just beneath the surface, a school of fish, a marine mammal (all examples of "false targets"), or possibly a scuba diver. Early detection and classification is predicated on the magnitude and quality of the echo, and is directly related to the sonar transmit frequency. It is possible to determine the optimum frequency for echo-ranging on a specific target by measuring what is called the "target strength," i.e. the ratio of the sound level of the echo to the sound level of the transmitted pulse—the more sound energy that returns as an echo, the greater will be the target strength.

For passive sonar, a hydrophone or an array of multiple hydrophones listens for sounds that might be associated with, in our case, a diver. The ocean is filled with all types of sound, some from human sources such as a distant ship's machinery and propellers, and some that come from natural sources—wind generated surface waves, fish and marine mammal vocalizations, and the sounds from tiny invertebrates called snapping shrimp—all collectively referred to as "ambient noise." The optimum passive sonar, and its decision making algorithms, is one that can distinguish from all of the ambient noise, those specific sounds attributable to a scuba diver. The unique sounds associated with a specific target are referred to as "radiated noise," and it is the uniqueness that enables a sonar system to classify the target.

The sonar designer needs precise measurements of the acoustic characteristics of a scuba diver: target strength for active echo-ranging sonar and radiated noise for passive listening sonar—otherwise it is all guesswork. For technology intended to detect a possible terrorist and where lives are at stake, there is no place for wishful thinking and "rules of thumb." Precision measurements require two things—a facility capable of scientific quality acoustic measurements and volunteers who are willing to serve as test subjects. At NUWC there is an ample availability of both.

The NUWC Acoustic Test Facility (ATF) is a 625,000 gallon pool, sixty feet long by forty feet wide by thirty-five feet deep, and is specifically designed to measure target strength and radiated noise (figure 71). The bottom and walls are lined with sound absorbing "anechoic" ("no echo") materials. Because target strength measurements rely on the ability to measure only the target echo, this anechoic material ensures that there will be no unwanted echoes from the pool walls. The sound absorbing properties also minimize ambient noise within the pool, thus maximizing the ability to measure only the radiated noise from the diver. Beginning in June 2003, we would visit the ATF on several occasions, as our involvement with swimmer defense issues escalated.

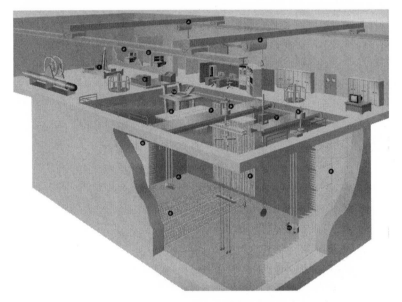

Figure 71. The NUWC Acoustic Test Facility (ATF) is used to measure the underwater acoustic properties of various objects suspended mid-depth by monofilament lines. During the swimmer defense program, those "objects" were human test subjects simulating a potential terrorist diver. (*NUWC*)

When a human is the subject of an experiment, the organization's institutional review board (IRB) monitors the safety of that test subject, based on the level of risk described in the experimental protocol. The alternative to including human test subjects means descending the slippery slope into the virtual world, where computer models must rely on assumptions about target acoustics and not on real data. Most members of the EDSU had backgrounds in acoustics and were ideally suited to design the experiments and to serve as test subjects.[145] The IRB ensured that the risk takers who volunteered to be test subjects were taking a calculated risk. I emphasize here that the NUWC IRB was incredibly supportive and fully understood the importance of our antiterrorism testing. This support was also important to the person (that would be me) designing the test and writing the experimental protocol. I was able to argue before the IRB that the risk was appropriate, and that this "aging, slightly overweight Navy diver" was also going to participate as a test subject, simulating an "aging, slightly overweight terrorist."

For all of our measurements, the diver was instructed to lie horizontally on a thin platform, suspended at mid-depth in the pool by monofilament line attached to a rotating mechanism above the pool. During the target strength measurements, this rotator changed the position of the diver in increments. At each position, a calibrated transducer transmitted a pulse toward the diver at multiple frequencies; the returning echo was then recorded on the ATF data acquisition system. Target strength was thus measured over a broad frequency range, and at positions simulating a diver facing directly at the sonar, or at multiple angles, referred to as "relative bearing" by acousticians. (Figure 72)

Figure 72. *Above:*A test subject wearing standard scuba equipment readily available to a potential terrorist diver rests on the stretcher suspended by monofilament line in the NUWC acoustic test facility. *Below:* A close-up view of another test subject and the stretcher used to maintain a consistent positioning during the acoustic testing. (*NUWC; Bruce Greenhalgh, from video frames*)

When measuring a diver's radiated noise for passive sonar, a hydrophone suspended in the ATF pool received the sounds the diver made as he inhaled and exhaled, each phase of the breathing cycle creating specific sound patterns. Comparisons were made between various types of scuba regulators readily available and commonly used by sport divers, and between test subjects with different breathing patterns.

All of our testing was bringing us closer to enabling sonar to readily and efficiently detect and classify a diver. When I presented the data, I would describe the necessity of using multiple human test subjects to accurately represent the threat . . . then mentioning to the audience that the data on one of those plots of target strength vs. target relative bearing represented the acoustic properties of that "aging, slightly overweight terrorist."

TRACK AND LOCALIZE THE INTRUDER

The CG-RDC was tasked by DHS to evaluate a specific diver detection sonar system, the components of which had been assembled by the Space and Naval Warfare Systems Center (SPAWAR), formerly the Naval Ocean Systems Center (NOSC), San Diego. This Integrated Antiswimmer System (IAS) was designed for the Navy Coastal Warfare antiterrorism and force protection (AT/FP) mission, but testing at Naval Air Station North Island (NASNI) was inconclusive. The IAS required extensive evaluation before it could be accepted by the Navy, or before the Coast Guard would consider it for their maritime homeland security mandate, and several commercial enterprises with their own prototype systems were asking for a similar evaluation.

With the escalating need for an effective deterrent, DHS put their Underwater Port Security (UPSec) swimmer defense in the hands of the CG-RDC. They, in turn, looked to NUWC for assistance—not just another opinion—and a realistic location for their IAS evaluation. With our recently signed MOU in hand, we proposed using a section of the Narragansett Bay waterfront shared by NUWC and Naval Station (NAVSTA) Newport. An area known as Stillwater Basin is bordered on the south and east by a shoreline occupied by NUWC and the Naval Station; on the north by a stone breakwater; and is open to Narragansett Bay on the west. NAVSTA operates two major piers, each nearly 1600 feet long, one of which held two decommissioned carriers, the ex-*Forrestal* and ex-*Saratoga*. This pier and its temporary occupants (the ex-*Forrestal* has since been removed) provided an ideal backdrop for swimmer defense testing—water depths were typical of that found at major ports and naval bases, and the shoreline and breakwater were representative of a perimeter where a terrorist attack could be launched.

The Coast Guard was also expanding its fast response capabilities and created Maritime Safety and Security Teams (MSST), stationed at strategic ports but with the capability of rapid deployment to a threatened location. Each MSST was mandated to include a team of Navy trained scuba divers, and each team would ultimately be responsible for operating the swimmer defense sonar that would eventually be selected. The first group of MSST divers completed their training at the Navy Diving and Salvage Training Center on May 23, 2003. Less than two weeks later they arrived on the NUWC waterfront, training with us in underwater navigation techniques in preparation for conducting simulated infiltration scenarios.

The CG-RDC, principally Rich Hansen, Ric Walker, and Scot Tripp, had prepared a test plan that would enable them to meet their IAS evaluation goals. It was our job to review and adapt their test plan to an operational test, which could be accomplished over a two-week period in June. Our responsibility was also to ensure that the IAS would be subjected to a series of realistic and repeatable infiltration scenarios. Realistic and repeatable— the necessary elements to guarantee that all diver detection systems under consideration were evaluated based on uniform performance criteria. (Figure 73)

Figure 73. *Above:* All of the swimmer defense testing included a Command and Control (C&C) tent. (*NUWC*) *Below left:* Inside C&C, a member of the Coast Guard MSST (standing) receives instruction in the system operation. (*Coast Guard Research and Development Center*) *Below right:* MSST divers install their antiswimmer sonar. (*NUWC; Bruce Greenhalgh, from video frame*)

Meeting all of the CG-RDC goals required a very substantial number of dives (and divers), more than the first graduating class of MSST divers and the NUWC EDSU could provide. There were daily limitations on the number of simulated attacks each diver could be expected to accomplish based on depth (up to 50 feet), water temperature, and the exertion required to conduct each simulated attack. One of our EDSU divers, José Arteiro, had been a Navy SEAL and was our source of information about "realism." After leaving active duty, he completed his mechanical engineering degree prior to joining NUWC, and soon found a home with the EDSU. Because we anticipated needing additional divers, José enlisted help from a nearby Navy Reserve SEAL Team.

When the MSST divers arrived on the 5th of June, they were immediately passed to José who began their training in underwater infiltration techniques. They were shown a standard combat swimmer's handheld tactical navigation board known as the TAC-100, which included a compass, depth gauge, and watch. The divers were instructed to submerge and find their way to a marker buoy 100 yards off the NUWC pier, turn around and return to the starting point—over and over and over. Proficiency at underwater navigation at a prescribed depth using a compass was essential. In anticipation of the Coast Guard tests, EDSU divers had been training throughout the spring. In addition to José, our training team included a NUWC program advisor, Lieutenant Tom Tinney, whose uncanny ability to swim in a straight line was invaluable. Tom's proficiency with a spear gun also helped supply the surf-n-turf barbecues we enjoyed on the waterfront.

The IAS included the active sonar "sound head" installed mid-water at the end of the pier, just below where a Command & Control area had been established. NUWC, CG-RDC staff, and IAS designers were on hand, while members of the MSST operated the signal processing electronics. On June 10, 2003, after two days of team training, system installation, and operational checks, the IAS was ready for its trials as a port security asset.

During a ten day evaluation, nearly one hundred simulated attacks on the ex-*Forrestal* were completed. The attacks began more than five hundred yards from the end of the NAVSTA pier, a distance that an experienced diver can cover in fifteen minutes. The swimmer defense team never knew which direction the diver would swim. An attack scenario might originate from Narragansett Bay beyond the entrance to Stillwater Basin, or from the breakwater, or from the rocky south shoreline called Coddington Point. Most dives were run either at mid depth or along the bottom. Some attacks included surface swimmers alone or simultaneously with a scuba attack, requiring the IAS to track multiple targets arriving from different directions. The IAS provided the operator with a display, which showed the track and position of the intruder as he approached the protected asset, in this case the ex-*Forrestal*. The Coast Guard supplied one of their fast response security boats, also operated by the MSST. This boat was in contact with C&C, and equipped to be vectored to the diver's location (figure 74). By the end of the evaluation, the IAS had successfully detected and tracked multiple divers, simulating a variety of attack scenarios.

1. From Coddington Cove   2. From Behind Coddington Point
3. From Narragansett Bay   4. From Behind Breakwater
5. Swimmer Defense Sonar   6. ex-*Forrestal*   7. ex-*Saratoga*

Figure 74. *Above:* Paths of simulated attack scenarios (*Aerial photo Courtesy Office of Geographic Information, Commonwealth of Massachussetts, Information Technology Division*) *Below:* During a simulated attack, a Coast Guard MSST fast response boat "interrogates" divers who have entered a protection zone. (*Coast Guard Research and Development Center*)

INTRUDER WARNING

The term "Integrated" in the acronym "IAS" refers to the multiple capabilities that have been combined in a single system to detect, classify, track, and localize the potentially hostile intruder—but "potentially" is the concern here. The possibility that an intruder has simply strayed into a restricted area is a major concern for the Coast Guard, requiring yet one more piece to be "integrated" into the IAS. On land, the intent of an intruder can readily be determined and an unambiguous verbal warning provided. When the intruder is underwater, determining intent and sending an audible warning is a much more difficult process.

The June 2003 testing included a commercially available Diver Recall System (DRS) used throughout the Navy as a one-way surface-to-diver communications system. It consists of an omni-directional transducer suspended from a surface control box, where during a typical waterfront operation the diving supervisor can either transmit high frequency tones (four blasts means return to the surface), or use the microphone to send a verbal message or warning to the diver (e.g. "stand by . . . tug boat approaching").

While the June tests demonstrated that it was effective at short ranges, the DRS could not provide an early warning to an intruder at ranges associated with the initial IAS detection. With no other options available, the DRS was included on board the MSST fast response boats, and could be used after they were vectored to the intruder's location. The desired concept of operations (CONOPS) called for the early warning capability to be in the hands of the IAS operator, potentially located at the end of a pier, and not on the response boat.

The rules of engagement, whether Coast Guard or Navy, required an effective initial warning. For the near term, the DRS would have to suffice and was provided as a component of the initial IAS deployed to operational MSSTs in 2003. The need to increase the warning notification range became a priority for a federal interagency forum known as the Technical Support Working Group (TSWG), whose mission was expediting antiterrorism technologies. The TSWG then selected the CG-RDC to coordinate the development of an underwater loudhailer that satisfied the rules of engagement. A proposal from Applied Physical Sciences Corporation (APS) in New London was selected for evaluation. The EDSU, in a partnership with the Naval Submarine Medical Research Lab (NSMRL) from the Submarine Base in Groton, was tasked to provide the testing.

In March 2005, the EDSU ran a series of prototype tests of the APS *e*LOUD system within Stillwater Basin. The encouraging results led to an extensive program the following June, involving multiple divers from the EDSU, NSMRL, and from the MSSTs, some of whom had been involved with the IAS tests two years earlier. As with all swimmer defense technology testing, the divers were considered test subjects. Because NSMRL would control the human subjects testing, the protocol was written by NSMRL, but required approval from both their Command's institutional review board, and NUWC's.

The underwater loudhailer evaluation involved the same scientific protocol used to evaluate the "intelligibility" of above water audio systems, including transmitting standardized word lists as well as specific warning phrases, e.g., "This is your final warning!" and "Surface immediately!" The *e*LOUD system met the objective of sending a warning that could be heard and understood by divers out to a range that satisfied this notification requirement.

JOINT NON-LETHAL WEAPONS DIRECTORATE

A lethal response demanded a certainty of intent—no matter how many warnings were broadcast into the water, there would always be a slight question as to the intent of a diver, heading toward some high value and potentially vulnerable asset. Both the Navy and Coast Guard had to contend with the issue of hostile intent. This question was posed to the Department of Defense Joint Non-Lethal Weapons Directorate (JNLWD), a group accustomed to dealing with technology designed to deter but not kill, including such items as Tasers, Flash Bang and other non-lethal grenades, and technologies referred to as active denial systems. The *e*LOUD underwater loudhailer became one more device in the JNLWD inventory.[146]

High intensity sound from a ship's sonar would certainly get a nearby diver's attention and could do some harm, but an SQS-53 sonar is sixteen feet in diameter and not conducive for use by a rapid response, highly mobile Coast Guard MSST. The concept of employing a high intensity sound source, however, resulted in a proposal to adapt an underwater air-impulse gun of the type used by geologists for offshore oil exploration. The concept of firing an air gun as a second level of warning was considered akin to "firing a shot across the bow."

The intensity of the sound generated when the impulse gun was fired could be controlled by the operator—a low level when the initial verbal warning had been ignored, then scaling up the intensity to provide a non-lethal but convincing level, which would bring all but the most determined intruder to the surface. Great idea, but how to test the theory? Well, you guessed it, divers were asked to volunteer to participate in an air gun test.

In another partnership between the CG-RDC, NUWC, and NSMRL, a series of experiments were designed for what the human subjects testing protocol referred to as "aversion response." Although qualitative by its very nature, divers were positioned at various distances from the air gun and asked to provide a 1 to 10 rating of their "aversion" to the sound.

Figure 75. *Above:* EDSU divers prepare for simulated attack on the ex-*Forrestal.* (L-R) Sam Carroll, David Hart, Matt Field, Jack Hughes, Vic Marolda, and the cool guy with the shades is John Wiedenheft. *Below:* Diver navigates to his intended target (*NUWC*)

These initial tests provided the final link in the detect-classify-track-locate-warn-intercept sequence. In September 2006, these same organizations ran another series of simulated attacks against the ex-*Forrestal.* As NUWC Homeland and Force Protection project

team leaders Jim Pollock and Jack Hughes recalled, these tests of "the latest version of the IAS . . . provided an opportunity for the Coast Guard to evaluate the current CONOPS for swimmer detection, classification, notification, and interdiction through various test scenarios using U.S. Navy-trained divers."[147] (Figure 75)

The protection of waterfront infrastructure was a primary focus of the Department of Homeland Security and the Coast Guard. The operational use of the IAS had been successfully demonstrated, and the CG-RDC recognized the effort of NUWC and the EDSU. In August 2003, soon after we completed the initial IAS test and evaluation, we received a letter from Captain F. A. Dutch Commanding Officer, CG-RDC, which read, in part: "The development of a swimmer detection and response capability is critical to the Coast Guard's overall Port Security mission . . . but the most important contributions came from your highly motivated and dedicated staff. The entire Engineering and Diving Support Unit was outstanding." Okay, maybe I can be accused of patting ourselves on the back by including this letter, but the EDSU took the lead from the very start.

As time went on, the various CONOPS for waterfront protection shifted to another form of infrastructure. DHS had been concerned about the vulnerability of hydroelectric dams within the interior of this country, and in October 2010, their Science and Technology division sponsored NUWC to coordinate an interagency swimmer defense demonstration at the Davis Dam in Arizona.[148] As with all previous system testing, a series of attack simulations were planned that included EDSU divers plus teams from a naval reserve unit and from the Coast Guard.

A REALITY CHECK . . . NOT A SIMULATION

"In only 13 minutes, the 213-foot vessel was on the bottom;" the opening paragraph of an article about swimmer defense systems in the October 2008 edition of NUWSCOPE provided graphic details of an underwater attack on a Sri Lankan naval ship the previous May. The following is from a web site describing terrorist activities around the world: "A piece of [the] torso of a person and diving equipment was found near the drowned Naval ship, A 520 (MV Invincible), in Trincomalee, suggesting the handiwork of a suicide bomber . . . [According to a Sri Lankan navy spokesman,] the Navy believes the suicide cadre had used a suicide jacket for the blast as only the lower part of the body was recovered."[149]

If there had been doubters about the need for a swimmer defense system, the loss of a naval vessel by a suicide bomber removed any question that this form of asymmetric warfare posed a credible threat. Although this chapter has centered on the Coast Guard and DHS, NUWC was also engaged in a parallel effort to support the Navy's antiterrorism and force protection (AT/FP) mission. Naval bases and infrastructure here in the U.S. as well as abroad were vulnerable, as were naval vessels, which could share the same fate as that Sri Lankan ship.

Through NAVSEA's Force Protection Afloat Program Office, PMS 480, NUWC was tasked to take the system engineering lead and coordinate inputs from all Navy AT/FP interests, including the several divisions of the Naval Surface Warfare Center (NSWC), the Naval Facilities Engineering Command (NAVFAC), the Office of Naval Research (ONR), and the many proposals from private industry. There were also the eventual system users—among them, the Navy Expeditionary Warfare Division (OPNAV N857) and the Program Executive Office (PEO) for Littoral and Mine Warfare. During the five years after the first IAS evaluation along the NUWC waterfront, the ex-*Forrestal* was the vessel of choice as a simulated terrorist target, not only for the Coast Guard, but also for the Navy's Integrated Swimmer Defense (ISD) system.[150] Stillwater Basin soon took on an international flavor, with swimmer detection systems brought there from British and Canadian companies (figure 76). Representatives from the Singapore Ministry of Defense were on site during one technology demonstration.

Figure 76. *Above:* One of several swimmer defense sonar systems is removed after completing its evaluation, during simulated attacks on the ex-*Forrestal* (at right). *Below:* A typical scene in the C&C tent. (*NUWC*)

Figure 77. Members of a Maritime Expeditionary Squadron make adjustments to the ISD sonar prior to installation. (*NUWC*)

Throughout 2007 and into 2008, technology demonstrations continued to show improvements in the ISD. As the intensity of the swimmer defense trials ramped up, so did the need for divers. To meet the demand, the EDSU enlisted diving support from a Navy Reserve Surge Maintenance (NR SurgeMain) unit. Lieutenant Mark Robinson, a former submarine diver and project officer assigned to NUWC, also became a member of the EDSU swimmer defense team.

It was time to subject the system to an operational evaluation, and move from the prototype to a final system, which would be introduced to the fleet. Incredibly, nearly three hundred items were eventually considered as potential elements of a final Navy ISD. Keith Bruce, also an EDSU diver, was the NUWC systems engineer responsible for consolidating all of these components into a final ISD, which would soon be subjected to its technical and operational evaluation. Keith, also the commanding officer of a Naval Reserve Maritime Expeditionary Security Squadron (MSRON), was well suited to interface with Navy units tasked to provide AT/FP security—a role similar to the MSSTs, who are responsible for the Coast Guard's Underwater Port Security (UPSec) mission under DHS.

By the end of August 2008, the first systems were shipped to the Navy Expeditionary Combat Command (NECC) and the Maritime Expeditionary Forces. But international interest in the ISD also continued to evolve. In February 2009, the Australian navy sponsored an underwater force protection demonstration in Sydney Harbor, and included participants from the US, the UK, Canada, and New Zealand. An event that would, in itself, be a deterrent to an underwater terrorist occurred when an Australian navy diver was attacked by a shark.

By the end of the decade, the Navy and NUWC had developed a full range of ISD CONOPS, providing the warfighter with another tool that evolved in response to this entirely new threat. Although a civilian scuba course is far removed from that of a military diver, everyone understood that a civilian with a determined goal can be a dangerous threat to a military target. Yet from a military perspective, a future enemy may include experienced combat swimmers who, unlike the terrorists, do have a national identity and have undergone a level of training similar to what Navy SEALs and other Special Forces divers complete. The ISD would serve the immediate need, but some future enemy combat swimmer would need to be aware that there will be a watchful eye underwater, and that the Navy's approach to interdiction might not come from the non-lethal weapons directorate.

A very small element within NUWC had combined the science that helped define and apply the acoustic vulnerability of the threat; had simulated the tactical operations of a hostile underwater intruder; had evaluated a myriad of potential systems to counter the threat; and had "system engineered" these technologies into the ISD for the Navy. This achievement was possible because these intellectual and physical risk takers were able to move ahead quickly and responsively. There were managers within NUWC who fully appreciated the nature of the threat, and stood behind those of us who pulled together along and under the waterfront.[151]

The EDSU did what it does best—interface directly with the fleet. We worked side by side with our military counterparts underwater, and because of that, we could relate to the observations and misgivings of these undersea warfighters and incorporate their recommendations (figure 77). NUWC divers had put the Integrated Swimmer Defense system into the hands of active duty expeditionary forces at the Naval Amphibious Base in Little Creek, Virginia. It is interesting to note that a half century earlier, the first Navy trained civilian divers at USN/USL had provided another cutting edge technology—a two-man submarine—to an underwater demolition team also stationed in Little Creek.

SHIT OR GET OFF THE POT

The Coast Guard (and this country) had been handed a threat that was "now"—not tomorrow. The DHS mandate to the Coast Guard was, therefore: address the problem—now! Al Qaida was training its members for scuba attacks, and the Coast Guard was determined to keep one step ahead of the threat. Maritime Safety and Security Teams were quickly established to ensure a fast response waterfront security capability, and the Navy began providing members of these teams with scuba training. When the Coast Guard looked for tools the MSSTs would need when facing a terrorist attack—not from an aircraft or a fast-moving boat, but by divers—they turned to the Navy's *Undersea Warfare* Center for assistance.

From the very beginning, the Coast Guard expected NUWC to provide a fast and efficient response. The threat assessment that the Coast Guard had in hand was immediate, and solutions had to have the same immediacy. Keeping a large research institution like NUWC focused, however, occasionally resulted in frustration. During one of our monthly meetings we sat silently, wondering why we were in this meeting and not on the waterfront. As the discussion drifted off to yet another far-fetched idea, a frustrated observer stood and proclaimed what many of us were thinking: "Excuse me . . . I'm getting a little bit upset. We have been attacked! Don't you people fucking get it? This can't be the same old shit!"

Much of the Navy's research and development effort was focused on major programs that answered threat assessments and projections a decade or more into the future; programs that required long-range planning and multi-million-dollar funding, where large numbers of engineers, contractors, and administrative personnel were involved. This new underwater threat brought on by the Global War on Terror was a call to action. Long-term proposals had to be considered, but there was a short fuse on the threat, and opinions and far-out concepts could wait. The CG-RDC understood that solutions began with real hardware—not virtual reality. Any indication that the tail was wagging the dog and the Coast Guard would have run the other way.

That almost happened early in 2003, when the Coast Guard requested an evaluation of the initial version of their Integrated Antiswimmer System. What was first proposed, however, failed to address their primary goal of subjecting the IAS to realistic simulations of attacks by terrorist divers. No one had asked the EDSU for inputs to a project totally dependent on divers. My jaw dropped when I heard about the proposal, and how far the cost estimate exceeded their budget. I called the Coast Guard IAS project manager and an hour later I was in Groton for an emergency proposal adjustment. That first test plan would have brought the IAS to the Gould Island facility, where tidal currents would limit diving operations to one or two brief periods of slack water per day—it would have taken nearly four months at Gould Island to conduct the hundred attack scenarios we eventually completed within ten days, once rational minds prevailed and the IAS evaluation shifted to Stillwater Basin and the ex-*Forrestal*.

That meeting in Groton was on February 26, 2003, the day after the Coast Guard had officially transferred to DHS. If it was responsiveness that they wanted, the EDSU would roger-up. I assured the Coast Guard that within the NUWC chain of command there were many who understood the immediacy of the problem, and that those of us who took on the challenge would do everything in our power to keep the tail from wagging the dog.

Through Juergen Keil's initiative on September 12, 2001, and Rich Russell's creation of a Memorandum of Understanding with the Coast Guard the following year, NUWC redirected a component of its undersea warfare mission onto this well defined and credible threat. Their leadership at the onset of the Global War on Terror enabled a small group of technical and physical risk takers to respond in that old fashioned way we enjoyed at USN/USL and NUSC during the Cold War. The Coast Guard's first responders on the waterfront, their MSSTs, were quickly provided with a viable swimmer defense system that continues to be improved because of their partnership with NUWC.

In spite of the overall success, there were many day to day bumps in the road. Expressing my job related frustrations in the presence of my kids, however, had consequences. Although the swimmer defense testing had been moving along at a good pace, one evening after experiencing some unnecessary snags earlier that day, I blurted out the brief but common expression at the beginning of this section that translates: "Attack the problem or get out of the way." I headed to the bathroom to ponder the issue for awhile, when my (then six-year old) daughter tapped on the bathroom door and pleaded, "Daddy! PLEASE poop or get off the potty!"

By the summer of 2005, I had decided to take my daughter's suggestion, move aside for others, and prepare to enter the company of retirees. On January 3, 2006, my family joined me for a grip-'n'-grin ceremony on the NUWC waterfront, where the dive team (my other family) and many of my other co-workers bid me farewell. After thirty-eight and a half years, nearly thirty-two as a Navy diver, I felt confident in those who would carry the responsibility of keeping the EDSU a viable contributor to the Navy. Vic Marolda was the last of us who trained in the 1970s and mentored under World War II veterans. He carried on their legacy of commitment and passed that along to any member of our dive team who joined him on the waterfront. Vic has always been a mission-focused individual, dedicated to the Navy and the submariners he ultimately served. There was no question in my mind that he would retain that focus and keep the EDSU front and center on the waterfront—we were never disappointed, and after thirty-three years as a Navy diver, Vic retired on August 31, 2012. For his outstanding service during a long career, Vic was awarded the Navy's

Superior Civilian Service Medal, the second highest award that the Navy can bestow on a civilian.

A NEW GENERATION

Changes were occurring within the Navy research and development community, and the EDSU as an organization that lived under the direction of the new NUWC would have to adapt in order to survive. One of our principal proponents in upper management, Juergen Keil, had moved on. Another champion of risk takers, Rich Russell, had retired and was heading off to complete his bucket list of adventures. I knew that Jack Hughes was the one individual who understood the changes that were taking place within NUWC—he could keep one foot firmly planted on the waterfront, while keeping the other foot firmly planted behind the scenes in upper management. Jack was respected within both worlds and could respond to the inevitable contentious issues the EDSU would face, regardless of what direction they would come from. I also encouraged the staffing of the team with individuals that would give Jack and the EDSU a secure future. I had been what was often referred to as a "crisis manager," taking on each issue as it arose and moving on to the next. But crisis management was no longer going to work; the new NUWC would require a more systematic approach, one which would be a better fit within an evolving corporate model. It was truly time for me to "poop or get off the potty," and I picked the latter.

Although we were still heavily involved with the swimmer defense testing, there was time for me to gracefully phase out of the management of the EDSU. I understood the value that a military diver brings to a civilian dive team. Every two years the Naval Safety Center reviews the operations of all Navy dive teams, both active duty and civilian. Back in New London, Senior Chief Antone "Tony" Silvia, a NUSC project advisor, was also a submarine diver who supported our team in the water, but whose insights also helped us prepare for Safety Center inspections. Recently, the EDSU has been included among active duty dive teams that, on alternate years, must complete the Navy's Diving Operational Readiness Assessment (DORA). A diver with a military background has always been an asset, and it was important to maintain this same element within the EDSU at Newport.

As I approached retirement, Keith Bruce began training as a mudpuppy and I knew we had a candidate that was organized by nature, who respected the contributions of risk takers, and who was advancing quickly through the ranks of his Navy reserve unit. In 2011, Keith, a Captain and commanding officer of MSRON 8, was deployed to the Persian Gulf, where they provided port security at the United Arab Emirates ports of Jebel Ali and Fujairah. Jack could also depend on Mike Peirson, a former active duty diver and now a long-time NUWC technician. As a member of an EOD reserve unit, Mike had deployed to the Mediterranean in 2003.[152] I also knew that when Bill Graves retired from the Navy EOD Detachment at Newport, he would join NUWC and the EDSU. Tom Fulton, a former active duty Navy diving officer, had accepted a position at NUWC, immediately heading to the EDSU office on the waterfront, where he and Keith and Mike and Bill continue to add that connectivity to the military. Our team will always attract prior active duty Navy qualified divers who have moved into a civilian position at the Center; in 2013, Andrew Elsen, electrical engineer and former submarine diver, joined NUWC and the EDSU.

For more than fifty years, the Navy could depend on a dedicated team of civilian divers with the technical backgrounds that enabled us to adapt to any underwater challenge—when I retired, a few candidates were in the mudpuppy pipeline, including Keith Bruce who qualified in 2006. David Hart and David Jasinski completed their scuba and MK-20 training in 2007, followed by Matthew Field in 2008, and Christian "Schu" Schumacher in 2009. Each of these new divers participated on the swimmer defense system development team, and also began working with Vic Marolda on submarine towed arrays. Colin Murphy completed dive school in November, 2012, adding his personal enthusiasm to our team's half-century of service to the Navy.

It was with a heavy heart that I left the EDSU back in January 2006, but I knew the quality of the people who were there to celebrate my retirement, and who would carry on the EDSU tradition of excellence through risk and commitment. Now as warfare centers adapt to changing missions and unpredictable priorities in the twenty-first century, the EDSU and other enclaves of risk takers must also adapt. Will the Navy continue to look to its civilian workforce for its first responders? We'll see.

Figure 78. Sarandos "Sandy" Traggis at sea, directing the test of a NUSC/
NL-designed sonar. (*NUSC*)

CHAPTER 10
Excellence or Mediocrity—A Choice

The pursuit of excellence and an expectation of success is the goal of any organization, whether private industry or public agency, and certainly throughout the military/industrial complex. The Naval Undersea Warfare Center sits firmly within the public trust, a legacy of excellence derived from all of its Newport and New London predecessors. As this book has tried to emphasize, success was driven by team spirit—not just a dive team—but any team of individuals driven to share the goals of creative and inventive thinkers . . . driven to find a path that converted their ideas into hardware . . . driven to take risks needed to sharpen the tip of the spear.

Yet, as the naval warfare centers evolved, the emphasis projected at all levels of management had been changing. As John Merrill and Lionel Wyld observed, "the classic laboratory role seemed to be no longer valid." They described how the merger of New London's USN/USL with Newport's NUWRES in 1970, to form the Naval Underwater Systems Center, resulted in a major restructuring within the merged Center, creating what were termed "Directorates"—the Science and Technology Directorate, the Systems Development Directorate, and the Fleet Readiness Directorate. While each was diligent and remained focused on the prosecution of their mission, the unintended consequence was what Merrill and Wyld noted as: "the tendency to compartmentalize product activities within directorates, making it difficult to transition efforts from one directorate to another." When the flow of ideas is constrained to move vertically within an organizational structure, the process is commonly referred to as stovepiping. "In 1976, a major reorganization was initiated that restructured the Center into eight product lines," a new approach that, according to Merrill and Wyld, allowed managers the "flexibility to apply the total specialized expertise in each department (the 'Product Area') to priority programs without being adversely affected by traditional organizational constraints that limited people to working on only one system or program." The goal of encouraging this "full-spectrum effort" was to create a "Center of Excellence" in submarine and antisubmarine warfare in an organization that "provided stability, corporate memory, and resident technical expertise."[153]

At the working level, however, we all continued to see difficulties emerge when attempting to efficiently enable talent and ideas to move across these product line barriers. For the policy makers at NUSC, this was a matter of growing pains within an organization that had doubled in size and was struggling to define its role. But for the rest of us in the 1970s and 1980s, it was the Cold War that mattered, and our day-to-day mission was to grab a set of travel orders and respond to the next issue. We were less concerned about what was happening on mahogany row than what was happening off the coast of Africa, or in the Mediterranean, or the Indian Ocean. We did, however, depend on our organization's leadership to believe in and support the risk taking that we all faced when asked to leave the comfort of our office.

RISK IS A TEAM EFFORT

With the end of the Cold War, and as we exited the twentieth century, the Naval Undersea Warfare Center continued to adjust to a new century and a new relevance within the Navy. The emergence of an "acquisition workforce," now gaining a greater role among the technical staff of Navy warfare centers, has brought into question the need for that "full-spectrum effort" of the field engineer. What the Navy perceives as important to maintaining "Centers of Excellence" may diminish the relevance of risk takers, and as management responds to the acquisition workforce mandate, there are potential consequences. The question that *all* organizations face will be how to walk the path toward excellence by accepting and embracing risk. Where there is risk, however, there is a potential that someone will get hurt. Those who avoid risk to eliminate that potential, take the first step along a path toward mediocrity. We live in a world where advancements in technology—not just creating the next electronic gadget—will define global leadership.

I recently ran into one of our past EDSU divers still working at NUWC. He comes from a long tradition of field engineering and continues to enjoy building and testing hardware. It really didn't surprise me when he echoed a feeling I have often heard: "I don't think management has my back any more." People will take risks, not just for the sake of risk, but for the ultimate customer—the sailors on the front line—only when there is strong aggressive leadership, and a sense that "management has my back." Otherwise, it becomes just another job. I wish I could say this individual was expressing a rare sentiment, but I feel it is becoming a national problem—not just lamenting about the good ol' days among a few of my aging peers.

No organization will last—nor retain its relevance—without the ability to blend the capabilities of individuals into a team. No matter how well that organization espouses its philosophy and its corporate model, it is ultimately the human mind and spirit that drives the machinery of success. We heard phrases that encouraged us to become a "Center of Excellence" for the "Navy After Next" . . . that we were the Navy's "Smart Buyer, Honest Broker" of warfare systems . . . that we were becoming a "Defense Acquisition Workforce." Motivation, however, does not derive from catch phrases, but from within each individual's thirst for a real goal. The pursuit of excellence must involve an engaged team, where risk is shared among everyone, and that begins at the top of the mountain.

MOVERS & SHAKERS . . .

. . . come from all levels of an organization. At the top are admirals, and captains, and civilian senior executives. They guide the Navy's contribution to a national defense strategy, defined by America's executive, legislative, and judicial arms of government. Yet there are also movers and shakers among the many teams of civilians—equally a part of the military machine—who work behind and beneath the scene to understand and supply the needs of the warfighter. This is the essence of "operations research" and what John Merrill referred to as a "slide rule strategy."[154] It is the insight that we bring back from the field, and the technology that grows from these insights, that allow those at the top of the mountain to make the best strategic decisions. But as risk takers, we derive our *esprit de corps* from the same source as our active duty brothers and sisters—the chain of command. We thrive on good leaders; do our best to avoid the other kind.

JUERGEN KEIL

I am highlighting the relationship between the dive team and past NUWC Executive Director Juergen Keil, because of his commitment to the concept of excellence through risk. Just after the New London laboratory closed and the property turned over to the Naval Facilities Command in March 1997, a new home for the Engineering and Diving Support Unit was operational on the NUWC Newport waterfront. The EDSU previously sat directly under the Officer in Charge in New London as a component of the Command Support Department, and I had tried to find a similar position for our group within the Newport organization. I met with Juergen several times in the process of creating an effective role for our engineering and diving team, and he had convinced me that to be most effective we would be assigned to the Test and Evaluation Department, a group that served all of the NUWC product lines.

The April 1997 issue of NUWSCOPE contained an article titled "Interdepartmental Teaming—Dive into it!" written by Juergen, where he announced the relocation of the EDSU, and served us up as "one particularly fine example of successful teaming within the Division." He summarized our long history of working within all of the New London mission areas, including surface ship sonar, where we had been "tasked to respond immediately to forward-deployed ships that had experienced serious degradation in sonar performance." He noted that our divers had worked "throughout the entire development of the Wide Aperture Array hull-mounted passive sonar system, . . . developed innovative procedures and specialized hardware to accomplish the block upgrade [to the TB-23 handling system] pierside, . . . led tiger teams [that] enabled the completion of the upgrades to the Fleet's fast attack submarines in record time, . . . [and] helped develop unique through-the-ice optical measurement procedures and supported baseline tests in a frozen lake in New Hampshire and beneath first-year ice in the Arctic."

In Juergen Keil, as well as many of his colleagues, we knew there were true believers at the very top of the NUWC chain of command, who recognized that innovation comes from teaming among creative individuals. We understood that encouraging risk at our level also put their careers at risk, but that the potential rewards for the Navy were worth the risk. We were confident that when push came to shove, people like Juergen "had our backs!" Without hesitation, Juergen Keil came to us in September 2001, for help with a new underwater threat; without hesitation, we stepped to the plate. What drove teams of risk takers was this commitment by leadership—good leadership. Putting their commitment into action, however, required a similar commitment throughout mid-level management. This was not always the case, whether in our new home in Newport or back in the "good ol' days" in New London.

MANAGERS

Good ones can be hard to find—that's because you keep stumbling into bad ones. After nearly thirty-nine years of federal service, I had learned to navigate our dive team through the upper echelons without stumbling too often, but when I did, I managed to land at the feet of a good one. But then in 2005, during a minor reorganization in my department, I was assigned to a new division head—much younger than me—who was of a corporate breed, with an arrogance that made him ill-equipped to manage independent thinkers. As the situation became confrontational, I recalled John Merrill's comment about the laboratory role being no longer valid in the new NUWC. I also recalled the early days of my career, listening to so many role models like Fred Deltgen, whose stories about acoustic research in Africa (see the Prologue) convinced me that I had made the perfect career choice. But those role models were gone and not being replaced. During one particularly nasty "discussion" with my latest manager, the threat of insubordination if I didn't shape up had convinced me that retirement was going to be my next career choice; after all, I had served the Navy's ASW needs for thirty-eight years and simply had no patience for this new breed.

It was obvious that I had to find an old school manager—and quickly—so I approached Lenny Cohen, coworker during the surface ship sonar days of the 1980s who had advanced into a management position. I transferred to Lenny's branch as fast as I could, where I could actively complete my final days at NUWC. Whether it was Juergen Keil or Lenny Cohen, there were many other managers and project leaders like them who encouraged risk and were fully committed to NUWC as a "Center of Excellence" for the Navy's undersea warfare mission. They understood the value that field work, including from a team of sometimes-difficult-to-manage-engineer-divers, brings to the "full-spectrum effort" described by John Merrill and Lionel Wyld.

It is the duty of a writer to use his pages to give a proper place in history to individuals who played a positive role. Hopefully, this book will show by example some of the memorable ones, as there's just not enough room to mention the many good managers who made our careers successful. You know who you are (I hope), so I apologize for describing just a few, whereas I only give a generic description of the other kind.

Among the best was Sarandos "Sandy" Traggis (figure 78), who, the reader might remember from chapter 5, would join us for post-mission debriefings at the Bank Street Café. Sandy died way too young, and the line to say goodbye at his wake stretched out past the building and down the sidewalk. He was also a role model as a family man and knew how to balance his home life with his Navy responsibilities.

Sandy had spent plenty of time "on the road," and by the time he had become a branch head, he understood the value all of his staff brought to the solution of technical issues crossing his desk. Some engineers were drawn to their cubicle and loved the ability to have a safe environment, where they could think long and hard about problems, with a chalk board (okay, so I'm from the slide rule generation) on the wall, text books on a shelf over the desk, and like-minded colleagues just around the corner.

For some of us "just around the corner" meant the Indian Ocean, or Guam, or Subic, where our colleagues were either on the fantail of a destroyer putting on a set of scuba bottles, or back in New London packing. But for Sandy, every member of his staff was equally important, and he knew that the solution to technical problems required inputs both from the field and from the cubicle. When Sandy passed away, our dive team lost someone who truly understood the need for risk takers, but who also understood that for many individuals, their lives would turn upside down if called to some God-forsaken corner of the planet. He loved his wife and kids, his Harley, a night of Rhythm and Blues, imported beer, and quality wine. So we raise our glass to Sandy: "We all enjoyed the 'great legs' of your homemade wine and we miss you—save us a bar stool in Heaven!"

SIT, FIDO, SIT! . . . BAD DOG! . . . BAD DOG!

A bad manager is, simply, the antithesis of Sandy. So I will summarize and dismiss this section quickly. When we were adding divers to our team, each candidate needed the approval of at least two levels up his chain of command, including his immediate supervisor at the branch level. These managers were required to sign an agreement (non-binding, however) that the individual would be available to support projects that fell beyond the purview of their department. Everyone understood that being a member of the dive team was a collateral duty. Each diver had to answer to his management, and be able to juggle the engineering tasks in his primary code with the commitment to support a diving operation. If there was a spirit of mutual respect between management and staff, then all was well; if the individual worked "under the thumb" in an atmosphere of distrust, then all was not well.

A diver from the submarine electromagnetics department, for example, might have been asked to support a submarine sonar project. The collateral duty assumption on our part was that the individual had accepted that he would have to take time (often on his own) to come up to speed on the technology that the diving project was being asked to support, and once the project was completed, it would be back to his full time job. We also assumed, however, that his supervisor had agreed, and understood, that there was a "greater good" issue here, and that the individual could manage both commitments.

With a need to field a complete dive team, the more advance notice I could give each diver, the easier it was for him to adjust his work load. Emergent issues for a forward deployed ship or submarine, however, required an immediate response. To meet this commitment, our dive team included several individuals with a much more defined availability from managers who understood the nature of the work. There were others, unfortunately, who worked for managers with little understanding or sympathy for any projects other than those within their own limited world.

When I called a diver who was in this situation, I tried to include him in projects with long-lead planning. I understood their short leash and would provide sufficient advanced notice, hoping that when the diver approached his manager to ask for permission to support a dive, the response would simply be:

"If the dive won't interfere with your project schedule here, then go for it . . . . Dive safe, and we'll see you when you return."

However, the abrupt, demeaning, bad-tempered response from a shortsighted, controlling, arrogant (I'll stop there) manager was more often:

"Sit, Fido, Sit! . . . Bad dog! . . . Bad dog!"

CHRISTOPHER COLUMBUS—(#)

It was probably because of an adventurous spirit (not his management skills) that this oceanic explorer was selected as the namesake of the NUSC auditorium, where the New London staff assembled for occasional "state-of-the-Laboratory" briefings. It was a place where managers could update everyone on the progress of various projects, and relate the activities of groups that had ventured into the field. But the enthusiasm of the audience was certainly related to the enthusiasm of the manager who stood on the stage—a "bad" one simply put you to sleep, while the "good" ones told great stories of their employees' latest adventures.

It was in the fall of 1981, during one of these briefings, when Tom Cummings stepped out from behind the curtain and onto the Christopher Columbus Auditorium stage—arms raised and palms up, as if welcoming his subjects to a gathering. He wore a brightly colored African caftan and pillbox cap, the standard garb of a tribal chief, accented by his robust shape, round cheeks, and grin. Over the next few minutes, Tom described the source of his latest formal wear—no suit and tie that day—in a story that may have started:

Once upon a time . . . on a dark and stormy night . . . while patrolling along the west coast of Africa, a destroyer experienced the unfortunate fate that comes from using a chart dating from World War II. The navigator hadn't noticed any indication of a sand bar just off Mauritania, so it must have been a sea monster that rose from the sand and attacked the ship's vulnerable underbelly. How serious was the wound? Someone from NUSC would have to find the answer.

I'm sure that in his younger trimmer days as a Coast Guard officer, Tom Cummings would have presented an impressive uniformed figure; but he was now a civilian, and had taken on a management position at NUSC— we were fortunate to have someone with his "at sea" background as our division head. Although I have little memory (this was three decades ago) of how Tom actually related our most recent overseas trip to his audience, I will pass on the "facts" as best I can.

USS *CONYNGHAM* (DDG-17)—A FINAL ONE-POUND STORY

I won't venture a guess as to the name of the airlines, but we were about to board a relic of commercial aviation history. It really didn't matter. We were anxious to head home.

The previous week had brought Ken Beatrice and me to a desolate Liberian waterfront, where USS *Conyngham* and a dive team from the Readiness Support Group (RSG) Norfolk were waiting. During a quick stop at the American embassy in Monrovia, we were briefed by the Navy liaison officer on the incident and its consequences, giving us the background we would soon need. Our job was to assess and photograph the damaged sonar dome, and report back to NAVSEA. That was our mission—quick in, quick out. What we had just been told, however, was that a Commodore was en route, an inquiry would be conducted on the spot, and the captain relieved of command. Our "expertise" was going to be requested, but when we contacted NAVSEA about this turn of events, we were instructed to leave the politics to the inquiry—make our inspection, leave the ship, and send the photos and a report to NAVSEA. Our orders, we were told, come from NAVSEA . . . they would deal with the commodore later.

The dive was scheduled for the following morning. With that ever-present Nikonos underwater camera in hand, we completed our damage assessment after attending to some logistical issues. As instructed, we left the ship before the inquiry began. Our return flight wasn't until the next morning, so we had an afternoon to check the sights. Not always a good idea to wander the streets of an unfamiliar country, so we hired "George," one of the teenagers that hung around the hotel, waiting to take visitors on tours. Heading to town with a friendly energetic guide, our first request was to find a local tavern. Because Ken and I both wore beards, George had to warn us that Liberians liked Americans, but we looked like Russians, and in 1981, Russians were not welcome in Liberia. So he announced our origins as soon as we entered the bar—we immediately bought a round for the house, and frowns turned to smiles.

George then took us to the local market, where we could buy a souvenir or two. We quickly picked up some local wood carvings from the vendors who lined the streets of downtown Monrovia. Walking along what might be considered the Liberian garment district, we watched ancient sewing machines convert rolls of brightly patterned fabric into traditional African clothing. That's when Ken suggested we do some shopping for Tom Cummings. There was an endless assortment of colorful choices—size X-large.

At the airport the following morning, we were ushered to a small room, each of us brought to a table where grim-faced, pistol-packing, uniformed guards inspected our baggage. These were very large dudes with very large weapons. After being informed that we didn't have the "proper papers" necessary to board the plane, and that it might take awhile to obtain the "proper papers," and even more time to get someone to sign the "proper papers," it finally occurred to us to ask what it would take to obtain the "proper papers." "Fifty dollars" was the answer. The process was simple: (1) Open your wallet. (2) Hand the guard the "proper papers." (3) Board the airplane.

The old girl was a tail dragger, maybe a vintage DC-3 or some other aging aircraft, and when we entered near the back, we had to walk uphill to find our seats. We knew this was not going to be a typical flight. The airline was a "local," stopping at several countries along the West African coast for passengers and fuel, finally arriving at Orly Airport in France.

Among the passengers was a woman carrying a wicker basket containing a chicken—a very noisy chicken. We weren't sure if it was a pet or her dinner, but throughout the flight the damned bird voiced its objections to confinement in the basket. At a brief stop in Guinea-Bissau, an elderly passenger, obviously in no condition to walk on his own, was brought aboard strapped onto a stretcher. His frequent coughing just added to the raucous chicken, and the constant babble among passengers speaking French, English, and a myriad of local dialects. The stretcher was set in the aisle with its short legs tied to adjacent passenger seats, a necessary precaution to keep the old man from sliding down the aisle.

At Orly, we had to catch a quick hop to Charles de Gaulle Airport for our flight to the U.S. I handed the film can with our damage assessment photos to an attendant, and followed the line through the security gate scanner. On the other side, I asked for the film. Her response, "Oh, my!!" was not what I expected. "As a gentleman passed through," she explained in a worried tone, "I reach out and drop in his trench coat pocket . . ."

"Who??? . . . Where??? . . ."

"I am so sorry, monsieur. I think he walked that way," pointing toward the escalator. I ran off, looking for anyone wearing a long overcoat with big pockets. But luck was on my side, and the first person I approached checked his coat and found the film. A picture may be worth a thousand words, but it would have taken a lot more than a thousand to explain how I lost the only record of damage to the sonar on a Navy destroyer, which may have bounced of a sand bar along the African coast. It was a relief to finally pass on the report to NAVSEA.

The afternoon when Tom Cummings addressed a capacity crowd at Christopher Columbus Auditorium, his intent was not to simply entertain his audience. He was, like any good manager, proud of the accomplishments of his staff, and knew that relating a moderately embellished one-pound story might inspire the same creativity in others.

COLD WAR—COLD WARRIORS

The Cold War was truly global in scope, and every continent and every ocean saw hundreds of us from USN/USL and NUSC aggressively yet quietly complete our missions, often hand in hand with our active duty brothers and sisters. We were issued a red passport, signifying our U.S. government status; it was, however, strongly suggested that when heading to an unfriendly part of the world, we should bring a standard blue tourist passport.

We were officially designated "non-combatants" within the Department of Defense, and were offered the opportunity to carry a wallet-sized card that proclaimed this status. What this would have meant to a civilian taken hostage is unknown, but identification as a non-combatant might simply have implied that our reason for being in a contested area was to support those who were, in fact, combatants. Our key to success when traveling out of the country required that we remain well under the radar. We were safer, as were our reasons for being there, with scruffy beards and old clothes, which made us look more like opportunists and vagabonds with suitcases full of contraband, than government engineers with heads full of secrets.

The monumental advances in naval capability that evolved to win the Cold War could not have happened without the total commitment of civilian scientists, supported by teams of field engineers who would return time after time to New London with real-world data. This was the same efficient machine the Sound Lab depended on in the 1950s and 1960s, when Thad Bell and his colleagues pressed forward with the Navy's SQS-26 ASW sonar; the same machine that sent teams of engineers and technicians from New London onto and under the ice in pursuit of a strategic advantage in the arctic; the same machine that maintained our technological edge throughout the decades-long Cold War. Everyone involved, from the lofty PhD down to the lowly diver, fought the Cold War with the same commitment that energized the active duty sailors and submariners we joined at sea—Cold Warriors all.

In the 1998 National Defense Authorization Act (Section 1084), Congress approved the Cold War Recognition Certificate—an award for "all members of the armed forces and federal government civilian employees who faithfully served the United States during the Cold War era, Sept.2, 1945, to Dec. 26, 1991." The legislation further recognized that "Many such personnel performed their duties while isolated from family and friends and served overseas under frequently arduous conditions in order to protect the United States and achieve a lasting peace . . . [and where] the discipline and dedication of those personnel were fundamental to the prevention of a superpower military conflict."

THE COLD WAR . . . IS IT REALLY OVER

It was a forty-six-year standoff—a nuclear holocaust averted, but punctuated by two disastrous hot wars in Korea and Viet Nam, both fought over the threat of a global infiltration of communism. While the Korean War ended in a stalemate and Viet Nam was lost, both demonstrated to the Soviets and the Communist Chinese that Western nations were willing to put up a good fight.

When Congress recognized the significant contribution of its DoD civilian workforce who served this country's security needs "under frequently arduous conditions," Congress was thanking these individuals for taking risks in order to create the military technology that won the Cold War. But the threat nuclear weapon technology brought upon the world in the 1940s remains today among volatile nations with both regional and long-range global intentions—Pakistan vs. India, Iran vs. Israel, North Korea vs. South Korea. Wherever tactical nuclear missiles are being developed, stability of regional tensions must be assured in order to avoid a return to the global conflicts that characterized the Cold War. The strategic impact that Navy research and development will have on a nuclear deterrent remains paramount, and will continue to be a dominant mission within NUWC.

THE TWENTY-FIRST CENTURY

Chapter 9 described the serious threats posed by the Global War on Terror. Our twenty-first century adversaries may now become defined by religious fundamentalism, or a race for dominance in a global economy fueled by oil. But the twenty-first century has also seen a rapid infusion of digital wireless technology into military systems. The most visible, or invisible if you are the enemy, has been the entry of the unmanned aerial vehicle, or UAV, high above the battlespace. While the UAV, most often referred to as a drone, is most effective in its role in aerial reconnaissance, they can also be deadly—mission adaptability is its strength.

The appeal of an unmanned vehicle is simple—it is unmanned. Missions that would otherwise put a person in harm's way can now be conducted from a safe distance. Wireless video now allows operators, stationed thousands of miles from the scene, to watch the progress of their UAV on a computer screen, ensuring that its objectives are met. On land, robotic devices can be sent into a dangerous situation, searching for mines or gathering intelligence within a potential battlefield before the boots hit the ground. But the adoption of unmanned vehicles is not limited to operations in the air or on land; the Navy has likewise found this technology important to its twenty-first century mission.

Enter unmanned undersea vehicles, the UUV, and unmanned surface vehicles, the USV, onto the scene at the Naval Undersea Warfare Center. In 2012, NUWC resurrected an aging building along the waterfront to create the Unmanned Antisubmarine Warfare Facility. Although NUWC had long been involved with the development of remotely operated vehicles (ROVs) and autonomous undersea vehicles (AUVs), the emphasis had shifted. Expanding the capabilities of this type of vehicle would now enable it to conduct complex ASW missions—to keep the warfighter out of the war until it was absolutely necessary. UAVs were in the sky; USVs and UUVs could serve the same role on and under the sea.

Enter the Engineering and Diving Support Unit. That first decade of the twenty-first century was a busy one for our team. The staff of the EDSU continued to serve the global strategic mission of the Navy's submarines (chapter 6), always prepared to send our divers out to the next towed array issue. After 9/11, we became intimately involved with the real potential of an underwater attack by terrorists (chapter 9). Our divers had been responsible for the operational testing of swimmer defense systems for the Department of Homeland Security, as well as the Department of the Navy. Then, as the tactical importance of the new UUVs and USVs grew more significant, NUWC became a major player in their development and in the evaluation of multiple concepts of operations (CONOPS). Unmanned vehicles and their potential missions required expertise in multiple technologies—acoustics, weapon systems, and wireless RF connectivity, to name a few—and NUWC directed a significant number of its staff to engage in the rapidly increasing role of UUVs and USVs. Waterfront savvy would be essential, and with plenty of that in our background, EDSU engineers and technicians stepped to the plate.

While Narragansett Bay and the NUWC waterfront were ideal locations for evaluating multiple system concepts, there was nothing like the real thing. The EDSU sent Mike Peirson to join a small team from NUWC who deployed to the Persian Gulf with an early version of the USV. They returned to the waterfront with first-hand knowledge of the hardships that an unmanned surface vehicle must overcome in open-ocean operational conditions. Sound familiar? It was an example of operations research—an essential ingredient in the development of an effective military system. But for operations research to be successful, an organization must be willing to embrace risk—and, of course, risk takers.

The enthusiasm for unmanned vehicles that abounds on the waterfront has been nurtured by the ease of intellectual and physical mobility among the staff. Creative people need an equally creative environment to flourish. But behind the scenes there are administrative processes that have emerged in step with the increasingly complex structure of the organization. An overemphasis on process, however, can trump progress, adding viscosity that impedes the flow of ideas and action. There are unintended consequences when an organization dedicated to research and development begins to steer a course that takes on elements of . . .

THE CORPORATE MODEL—PROCESS VS. PROGRESS

At the beginning of this chapter, I included a quote from John Merrill and Lionel Wyld: "the classic laboratory role seemed to be no longer valid." Their observation defined the overall shift from technology initiated through civilian/military research and development laboratories (e.g. USN/ USL and NUSC), to a dependence on academia and private industry. Change can be good, but with change comes a potential for that tail to wag the dog. A "corporate model" (God, I hate these MBA phrases) of an organization, whether public or private, includes the product, the physical plant where the product is created, the staffing required to create the product, and the economics associated with providing that product to a customer. I know there's more to it (I'm an engineer, not an MBA), but these are some of the basic ingredients that allow me to make a point that the processes that bind together the elements of a corporate model can be an impediment to progress.

During World War II, and a quarter century afterwards, the mandate of the Underwater Sound Lab was to provide the Navy with the best submarine and antisubmarine warfare capabilities. The physical plant, located in New London within the region known as "The Submarine Capitol of the World," included all of the laboratory space needed to carry out this mission, and access to a full spectrum of offshore facilities. The staffing consisted of a complete range of talent capable of producing unique and innovative Navy systems. While it was the taxpayer who provided the economic engine, enabling the Underwater Sound Lab to respond to the Cold War threats, the taxpayer was also the customer.

The "product" that the Sound Lab was responsible for was research and development of technology and the test and evaluation of prototypes. This effort was closely followed by the involvement of private industry, where their corporate strength was applying "best manufacturing practices" (JEEZ, another one of those MBA phrases) to build a system at minimum cost (to the taxpayer), with maximum profit (to their shareholders), but with no loss of performance (for the warfighter).

This is where I return to the concept of "risk"—intellectual, physical, and financial. The economic engine at USN/USL was based on a realization, and acceptance by the warfighter and the taxpayer, that financial risk usually follows intellectual and physical risk; but pushing the limits of science and technology depends on all three. Private industry, beholding to its shareholders, does not have the luxury of taking excessive financial risk—the corporation and their scientists and engineers have that (prepare yourself, here comes another one) "fiduciary responsibility" to put profit before science.

During the Sound Lab years from 1945 to 1970, there had been a balance, where a Navy laboratory worked hand in hand with private industry—a balance between technology and economics. During the next two decades, as Merrill and Wyld described in *Meeting the Submarine Challenge*, economics and politics within the newly created Naval Underwater Systems Center gradually moved the mission away from a laboratory environment focused on research, and created what became known as a "product line" management philosophy.

By 1992, the Soviet Union had dissolved and what we knew as the Cold War was over. NUSC became the Naval Undersea Warfare Center, and after nearly a half-century had to find a new mission within a peacetime Navy. A twenty-first-century corporate model would take the Center into what has been called a defense acquisition workforce, and with that emphasis, the "workforce" would have to switch gears and accept a new way of operating. Acceptance, however, can be tough, and there may be consequences which affect the development of new technologies for the warfighter. High on my list is the move away from field work, where the engineer is directly involved with systems on board ships and submarines—that whole concept of operations research. The exponential expansion of digital technology has tempted decision makers to avoid the cost of field work in favor of (and I cringe when I say this):

VIRTUAL REALITY—A TWENTY-FIRST CENTURY OXYMORON

Various dictionaries define "virtual" as "existing in effect though not in name or fact." In our modern, computer-dependent world, "virtual" is an adjective, which implies a realistic simulation of the real world. Taken to extremes, however, virtual reality can touch the fringe of science fiction. A twenty-first-century engineer's imagination has no bounds in the virtual world of his or her computer. The screen displays the intricacies of this imagination, with less and less influence from what lies beyond the boundaries of the chest-high cubicle walls.

Jules Verne went to great pains to incorporate 1860s submarine technology in his classic *Twenty Thousand Leagues Under the Sea*, first published in 1867. The story was set in 1863, and drew from the French submarine *Plongeur*, launched the same year. While Verne was creating his manuscript, news reports were circulating throughout Europe about the sinking of USS *Housatonic* by the Confederate submarine *Hunley*.

Horace L. Hunley was responding to the demands of an all-encompassing Civil War, where any technology that could alter its course was desperately needed. In spite of losing two crews, including Hunley himself, there appeared to have been no attempt to understand and correct the cause of the two disastrous trials, and a third crew went out on *Hunley*'s final, fateful mission. Captain Nemo and the crew of his *Nautilus*, submarine predators within a nineteenth-century fanciful ocean, lived and died in an imagined, virtual world. Lieutenant George Dixon and the *Hunley* crew,

319

however, lived and died in the real world, and in a real ocean. The concept of creating a "virtual reality" would have boggled the engineering minds of both Jules Verne and Horace Hunley.

But a century later, the complexities and lethality of submarine warfare far exceeded even the creative imagination of Jules Verne. It has been the development of high speed, high capacity computers that has tempted scientists and engineers to merge the virtual world with the real world. Military planners use computers to create a "virtual battlespace," where an unlimited variety of combat simulations can be studied. But those who create this virtual world must be scrupulous and meticulous in their understanding of the real world.

The capabilities of warfighting systems (examples include sonar, radar, communications, and weapons), and their availability to both the "good guys" and the "bad guys," can be manipulated by the computer. The "beauty" of this virtual battlespace is that the people who conceive these simulations have had long careers at sea and can bring their real world into a virtual one. The "beast" arrives when realistic expectations of the capabilities of the systems rest in the virtual imaginations of engineers who may have had no experience at sea. With increased sophistication of computer modeling, there is a temptation to avoid being cold, wet, and tired on the waterfront, in favor of the physical and mental comfort of the cubicle.

Overall, creating a computer generated virtual battlespace is a good thing, as long as users understand the limitations associated with possibly unrealistic expectations of a system's performance. Expanding the use of virtual reality depends on access to the best computational tools available. But then came:

NMCI—MEDIOCRITY, THE UNINTENDED CONSEQUENCE

The seeds of scientific and technological innovation are nurtured by providing the intellectual risk takers with tools that stimulate the growth of ideas. If the tools being provided to these individuals are inherently mediocre, then mediocrity will be the result. It's a simple concept—the intellectual music they create is only as good as the instruments available to the orchestra.

A perfect example is the implementation of NMCI (Navy Marine Corps Internet).[155] The system works fine in its intended goal to standardize connectivity within all Navy-related activities, facilitating email and internet searches, creating word documents and power point presentations, and (at the top of the list) contending with internet security concerns. For the military, and the technological machine that supports it, the importance of cyber security cannot be overstated. During the Cold War, President Ronald Reagan's "Star Wars" defense was designed to counter the missiles and satellites that defined a potential conflict in outer space—cyber space is a new battleground and NMCI was intended as one measure of defense.

So, my purpose is not to rail against NMCI, but to point out that by simplifying connectivity, the system has created an unintended flaw. Because the creators and promoters of NMCI are attempting to accomplish everything, the resulting unwieldy system sacrifices flexibility. The computer as a scientific tool requires that it be capable of being manipulated by the hands behind the keyboard. But when the scientific mind faces a wall of simplicity, climbing that wall may become an insurmountable obstacle—the result: mediocrity on one side, innovation on the far side. Truly innovative people will leave for a more intellectually stimulating environment, and the physical risk takers will follow.

In chapter 2, I described the importance of Operations Research, giving examples of engineers who accompanied the warfighters during World War II. This same type of person is with us today; these physical risk takers will supply real world data to the scientists and engineers behind the computer. But there is a caveat here—everyone involved must be equipped with the ability to perform their intended mission.

Mediocrity was not an option during World War II and the Cold War— it should not be an option today. As I watched NMCI approach, over the objections of many within NUWC, there seemed to be a difference emerging between two opposing concepts—retaining the emphasis on research and development that defined the Navy's civilian workforce prior to and during the Cold War, or becoming primarily an "acquisition" workforce. The research, development, and procurement of effective military systems can coexist in any technological organization, but the individuals responsible for each of these goals need their own tools and their own working environment; which brings us to the:

DEFENSE ACQUISITION WORKFORCE IMPROVEMENT ACT—DAWIA

Beginning in 1992, and in response to President Reagan's Packard Commission findings that Department of Defense acquisition personnel were inexperienced and undertrained, Congress passed the Defense Acquisition Workforce Improvement Act—DAWIA.[156] Keep in mind that the original intent of the Act was to improve the capabilities of DoD *acquisition* personnel—not convert its technical workforce.

In the days before DAWIA, the "smartness" that enabled the Navy to be a smart buyer came from a staff encouraged to focus on the application of scientific research. All Navy laboratories were originally charged with the responsibility to conceive and demonstrate mission essential technologies. Profitability was left to the private sector, where efficient manufacturing processes, such as Lean Six Sigma,[157] would lead to cost-effective military technology. Oversight then fell to the laboratories—the "smart buyers"—ensuring that the final product being provided to the warfighter continued to meet performance specifications. This relationship between the public and private sectors was the essence of transitioning a laboratory-designed and tested Advanced Development Model (ADM) to an industry-produced Engineering Development Model (EDM).

A great example was the procurement, installation, and sea trials of the Navy's Wide Aperture Array (see chapter 6). The acquisition process depended on the knowledge of NUSC/NL technical staff, who had been intimately involved with the WAA concept and prototype development, the system installation on USS *Augusta*, and the subsequent sea trials. The backbone behind the successful introduction of WAA into the fleet was the combined effort of the physical and intellectual risk takers. They were not burdened with becoming acquisition experts—they were the brains that provided the smartness to those individuals whose expertise was, you guessed it, *acquisition*.

As Navy research and development agencies increasingly embrace DAWIA, their scientists and engineers are increasingly required to become part of the acquisition workforce. Certainly, today's complex undersea warfare technology depends on a workforce well schooled in the acquisition process—and yes, individuals with a technical background can acquire skills as smart buyers through DAWIA classrooms. But the primary product—military technology—is created by individuals whose careers are focused on the science and not on the acquisition. Simply put, technological experts need to focus on their knowledge and skills—acquisition experts on theirs. Paraphrasing the sentiments of engineers I have discussed this with: "I spent more damn time as an 'acquisition expert' trying to 'acquire' parts than the parts were worth. I'm supposed to design the freakin' sonar . . . not buy it!"

Message received!

When human creativity becomes diffused by distractions brought on by DAWIA and other elements of the corporate model, there is a downside. As the tail begins to have more influence over the dog, energized, motivated, creative individuals whose offices had resided in the head of the dog have watched their role moving to its aft end. As Paul Mileski—friend, former EDSU diver, outstanding electrical engineer, and recent NUWC retiree—observed, these individuals have agonized over the choices they had to make in order to advance within the management hierarchy. Rather than make that choice, many have retired.

For agencies that represent the interests of the warfighter as well as the taxpayer, there needs to be a partnership between the scientific workforce and the acquisition workforce. The smartness of any agency with a commitment as a smart buyer can only be acquired through its scientists and engineers who "create" new ideas. When they continue to be creative, unburdened by DAWIA, their *technical* expertise will naturally feed credibility into the decisions and processes of acquisition experts whose focus is *acquisition*.

The technological risk takers can't disappear from the process. Future threats will require new ideas, new ideas involve risk. When facing a determined adversary, relationships between DoD research agencies and private industry must operate with exceptional efficiency—most organizations recognize that well-managed risk will work:

323

OPERATIONAL RISK MANAGEMENT

Operational risk management (ORM) was designed to allow a moderate level of decision making by individuals with sufficient knowledge and training to understand the risks associated with their specific field, and then manage them properly.[158] I was reminded recently by Paul Mileski that he had taken the required NUWC on-line training, which praised the value of ORM, but was called on the carpet by the safety department when trying to implement ORM during field testing of a high-tech Navy system. Regardless of the requirement to take the on-line training, Paul was briskly informed that "we do not use O-R-M here!" An acquisition workforce will experience few examples of operational risk (maybe carpal tunnel), hence there would be, as Paul was informed, no real need for ORM, which in reality, is intended for those who have escaped the cubicle. The Navy, however, insists that all of its dive teams take ORM training, and that it is to be used when conducting diving operations, where maintaining situational awareness is mandatory. We learn from day one at dive school that we will be conducting <u>Operations</u> with inherent <u>Risk</u> under proper <u>Management</u> . . . ORM every day.

That the judgments of risk takers will be according to ORM guidelines is an essential ingredient for success, empowering those who live and work in the field to take only calculated risks. Any organization that embraces risk must trust that managers will remove those who take unconstrained risk at their own peril—and that of their colleagues. Certainly, if an organization subscribes to ORM, there is an element of uncertainty that individuals responsible for implementing risk management will do so in a responsible manner. The tail of the dog will wag long and hard to eliminate this uncertainty, while the nose struggles to find the bone. We know, however, that when the stakes are high, instinct will survive. A bird dog will hunt quietly, alert to any sign of its quarry—the tail stops wagging and the nose takes over.

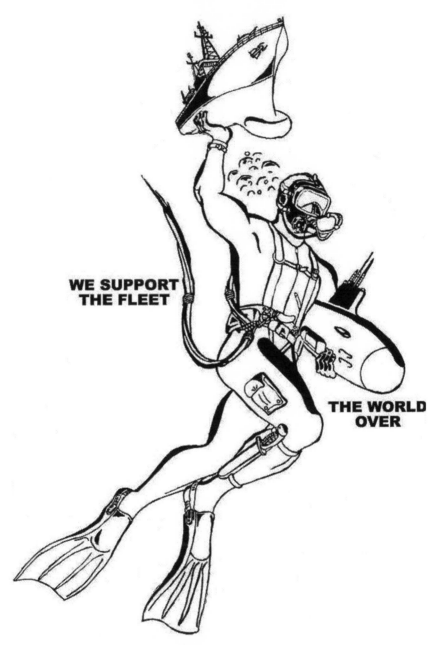

Figure 79. Our dive team logo was designed by Vic Marolda in the 1980s. Vic's original drawing depicted a diver in scuba, but in 1995 after our qualification training in enclosed space operations, Vic recreated our diver outfitted with the MK 20 surface supplied diving system. Our promise to the Navy— "We Support The Fleet...The World Over"— remains to this day. (*Victor Marolda*)

EPILOGUE

"The only easy day was yesterday."

No one said it was going to be easy. Avoiding the pitfalls of what might be referred to as trickle-down mediocrity requires diligence at all levels within *any* organization committed to the pursuit of excellence. It has been and will always be a dangerous world, where complex challenges will require complex solutions. Success depends on leadership. Leadership depends on the talent of risk takers unencumbered by the forces of mediocrity. These will be the "first responders" when technology defines future conflicts. *We need to keep an eye on the horizon—and the tough path to get there.*

Reflecting on the motivations that drove the staff of the Underwater Sound Lab and its subsequent forms in New London, there is a sense of satisfaction among the retirees who assemble every year on that Saturday in September; a satisfaction in our good fortune to have worked within an organization that contributed so much to winning the Cold War and avoiding a nuclear holocaust. Many express regrets that the laboratory atmosphere and the team spirit connecting so many disparate personalities and capabilities have been lost along the way.

Throughout the past ten chapters, I have related many "one-pound stories" from the hundreds of pounds accumulated over a long career. There is more to this book, however, than simply documenting historical events and telling a few sea stories—they have all stressed teamwork and the contributions from all levels of an organization, which ensured the success of each assignment, each mission. Ask a Navy diver if something is possible, and the response will often be "Easy day," knowing full well that it will likely *not* be an easy day. It is the dive *team*, however, that breeds confidence. The value of teamwork is embodied in the "We" on our dive team logo: "We Support the Fleet . . . The World Over" (figure 79). The diver is shown holding—"supporting"—a ship and a submarine, ensuring their operational readiness worldwide. The logo, worn for nearly three decades, is now on our team's challenge coin.

As I mentioned in the Prologue, the history of the Engineering and Diving Support Unit is no different from all of the field engineering teams from USN/USL, NUSC, and now NUWC who support the Navy's mission around the world. This epilogue celebrates what worked to create the technological exceptionalism that characterized this country during the Cold War and into the twenty-first century, and provides caution about what does not work.

WHAT WORKS: INTELLECTUAL RISK

For thousands of years, human knowledge was passed from generation to generation through verbal communication and storytelling. The listener relied on the ability to absorb the nuances of the knowledge being passed, thus dependent on the storyteller providing all of that nuanced thought. Yet there was rarely motivation to be creative—passing on knowledge was simply: "Do it this way, it has worked for hundreds of years, don't change it." Knowledge was a creation of eons of human curiosity that had evolved into a lifeless statue . . . something to admire and cherish, but any attempt to reshape it or carve a new one was deemed a capital crime—heresy. It was books that cautiously breathed life into that statue.

In spite of the punishments dealt on witches and heretics, intellectual risk took a giant leap in the seventeenth century as scientists and the scientific method arose from the shadows in what has been termed the Age of Enlightenment. Thomas Sprat (1702), in *The History of the Royal-Society of London*, defined the purpose of the Royal Society as a forum for the spread of knowledge—more specifically, scientific knowledge, then referred to as "natural philosophy." Sprat also described a shift in science from purely observational to what he called the "new Philosophers . . . who have not only disagreed from the *Ancients*, but have propos'd to themselves the right course of slow, and sure *Experimenting* . . ."[159] A new breed of natural philosophers, which included Galileo and Sir Francis Bacon, pioneered the shift from empirical to experimental science, and were an inspiration to Thomas Sprat and his contemporaries who formally established the Royal Society in 1663.

Sprat emphasized that, while science had essentially been limited to a pursuit among the intellectual and political elite, the Royal Society would now make that knowledge available to society as a whole through a scientific journal—*The Transactions of the Royal-Society*. Society members were encouraged to publish their studies in English rather than Latin. By doing this, Sprat argued, "it is not a vain or impossible Design, to endeavor the increase in *Mechanic contrivances . . .*" He encouraged his readers to "consider the *Royal Society*, and the probable effects of *Experiments*, in respect to all the *Manual Trades . . .* [and that] *the surest increase remaining to be made in Manual Arts, is to be perform'd by the conduct of Experimental Philosophy.*"[160]

So, you might legitimately ask, what does the seventeenth century have to do with a book about submarine technology and a team of divers in the twentieth century? Over the past four hundred years, human curiosity and creativity strove to find ways to explore the oceans—for science, for profit, and for new ways of waging war. Whether during the Age of Enlightenment, or the nineteenth-century industrial revolution, or the marriage of science and mechanics in the twentieth century, technological advances have always been rooted in the human mind. By the beginning of the seventeenth century, it was no longer sufficient to simply proclaim as "truth," the nature of some observed phenomenon—ideas now needed experimental verification. Truly enlightened natural philosophers would eventually put down the quill pen and walk outside. One of these individuals was Sir Edmund Halley, well known as an astronomer who had discovered the comet that carries his name. Less known, is that Halley was as intrigued by oceanography as he was by astronomy, and he ventured into the ocean in what Sprat described as "a Bell for diving under water to a great depth, wherein a man [including Halley] has continued at a considerable depth under water, for half an hour, without the least inconvenience."[161]

Throughout this book I have stressed the need for intellectual and physical risk taking, and Halley certainly possessed both traits. The Age of Enlightenment included many intellectual giants who were not comfortable with, or simply not capable of, taking the physical risks necessary to establish that experimental validation—they relied on their more adventurous peers. The same distinctions exist today. Modern "thinkers" know they can, and should, rely on risk takers to fill gaps between empirical and experimental science.

WHAT WORKS: CALCULATED PHYSICAL RISK

Risk is relative. Free-climbing with only the tips of your fingers and toes is dangerous, and for most of us exemplifies the essence of insanity. Yet even those individuals are taking calculated risks; but the calculations are based on an equation that few can understand. Some risk takers jump out of a perfectly good airplane, with the expectation that their parachute will open. During the Cold War, divers "locked-out" of a perfectly good submarine to conduct covert wire tapping missions in Soviet waters. Some divers may not be suited for saturation diving, but may be perfectly comfortable cutting a hole through six feet of ice and jumping in. In all cases, the training that risk takers receive enables each to discover his or her comfort zone.

The engineers from New London who experimented with new technologies while in pursuit of German U-boats during World War II were taking calculated physical risks. In turn, they became role models for Cold War engineers who took risks necessary to provide advanced technology to the sailors and submariners who pursued Soviet submarines. We in the Navy research and development community are civilians, but fully engaged in the military machine. Our customers are warfighters, where risk is a daily reality. Whether it is the leadership of a civilian workforce or leadership of a military unit, the acceptance and management of risk has to come from understanding (calculating) the risk and believing that risk is necessary.

So . . . where does the next generation of risk takers find their mentors, their inspiration? NUWC is filled with a technical staff consisting of incredibly talented, experienced men and women. The danger, when process places a burden on creativity, is that they will be discouraged from passing on their enthusiasm and their legacy. While the twenty-first century has been ushered in with the Global War on Terror, the future may find global threats even more dangerous than what we faced during the Cold War. *Looking beyond the here-and-now will require nurturing—not discouraging—twenty-first-century risk takers.*

In 2010 and 2011, Paul Mileski and I mentored a group of Old Saybrook [CT] High School students building a competition human powered submarine[162] for the biennial International Submarine Races (ISR),[163] held at the Naval Surface Warfare Center (NSWC) Carderock Division.[164] Fred Frese, the high school teacher Paul and I worked with, was the inspiration behind their submarine project. Fred has always challenged his students to understand calculated risk and find their limits, often reminding them: "If you're not living on the edge, you're taking up too much space." The ISR was designed to encourage creative thinking—intellectual risk taking— within a team effort. These teams converted their unique concepts into real (not virtual) hardware, and then took physical risks, operating their submarine over a timed 100-meter course. But the risk takers were not just the students who piloted their submarines; it was also the organization—in this case NSWC—that took a huge risk as the host of this incredible event.

During ISR-11 in June 2011, I had the pleasure of meeting NSWC commanding officer Captain Heidemarie Stefanyshyn-Piper, who was the perfect role model for this event. As a former Navy diver and astronaut who participated in missions aboard Space Shuttles Atlantis and Endeavour, Captain Piper personified the type of intellectual and physical risk taking that the ISR was designed to encourage. There were over two dozen teams competing in this truly international event, including entries from Canada, Mexico, Venezuela, England, France, and Oman. Most were from colleges and universities, including a team from the Naval Academy, but there were also three high schools. The nearly three hundred students who attended ISR-11 were encouraged to participate by their academic institutions, but just as important was the enthusiasm of NSWC and the several industries that sponsored the event.

High school and college students have few challenges that enable them to explore their limits—old timers like me, however, have had mentors from "the greatest generation" who offered opportunities to learn through risk. From these beginnings we gained the confidence to discover our own limits. The submarine project offered an opportunity for these young students to discover theirs, and they will enter adulthood with a unique perspective about what can be accomplished. Let's hope that farsighted organizations and industries will be there to greet them. Captain Piper made this offer to the students during the awards ceremony: "If any of you are interested in a career at NSWC . . . please contact me!" The foundation of real technical leadership is built by a career as a risk taker and the recognition that risk, failure, and finally success are the keystones of a creative organization.

WHAT WORKS: MATURITY—A BYPRODUCT OF EXPERIENCE

Success is not measured by what one or two individuals who have found their comfort zone manage to accomplish on their own. It is teamwork. But for a team to work effectively there has to be recognition (at all levels) of the difference between the destructive influence of arrogance and the constructive value of self-confidence. A young engineer filled with four years of academia may arrive on site either eager to learn or already knowing everything there is to know. When that young engineer insists that he or she has "the only solution" to a problem, the response from old timers, who designed, built, and went to sea with systems that won the Cold War, would be the same that a fresh-out-of-the-academy-know-it-all ensign receives when facing an old sea dog Chief-of-the-Boat: "With all due respect, Ensign, *Pay Attention, Dammit!*"

I spoke about this issue with Paul Mileski, who had mentored many young engineers during long trips on board submarines. Paul put it very simply: "A few days—or even better, weeks at sea—can be transformative." Classroom professors are expected to be proficient in passing on basic concepts and building blocks, and to prepare a student for taking the next step in what should be a lifetime of learning. The next "professor" that a 22-year-old fresh-out-of-college engineer might encounter could be a 22-year-old petty officer proudly wearing his "dolphins," and whose credentials are four years in the Navy—much of that underway at depth.

Paul's observations were that maturity of thought comes from time at sea—acclimating to the closed environment of a submarine; adjusting to unfamiliar sleep/work cycles; fighting sea-sickness; all while being responsible for a high-tech system that brought the engineer and the warfighter together for a critical sea test. As Paul noted, these experiences can convert arrogance into self-confidence, and build an ability to perform as a team player and a calculated risk taker. It was maturity and self-confidence that Paul carried with him during his time aboard submarines. Boat captains, as well as the crew, appreciated his honesty and resilience in the face of difficult problems.

WHAT WORKS: TEAMWORK!

While compiling this book and listening to the sea stories of so many retirees, a common thread emerged—everyone is smiling. It is not just the satisfaction over a career well spent and the enjoyment of a well-deserved retirement, these individuals smile because of the stories they relive among colleagues with whom they shared a common goal. At our reunions, former secretaries and administrative staff, draftsmen and machinists, electrical and mechanical technicians, engineers and PhDs all sit together yakking about the good ol' days and about how so much was accomplished by so few. Their voices and emails recall the camaraderie among us all. It may have taken fifty people scrambling behind the chain-link fence to send five out to sea. But all fifty had to mesh together into a team, inspired by managers who understood the importance of the mission, so that those five could hit the road.

What constitutes a "team?" Who are the members? What roles do they play? During the Cold War it was the Soviet submarine that defined a strategic threat to this country, and the Navy turned to the Underwater Sound Lab for solutions. As the issues became more clearly understood by the scientists who pondered the problem, USN/USL management looked to the resources of a staff who could convert those ideas into reality. The mission was antisubmarine warfare. The threat demanded intense and focused action, and a foundation of expertise started to gel. Managers who stepped to the plate with that essential ingredient—leadership— were responsible for creating the "team," and maintaining its focus and spirit. Scientists posed the concepts to engineers; engineers posed their ideas to technicians and machinists; soon, hardware found its way to the waterfront. Field engineers joined the "team" and brought that hardware to sea. The goal was gathering operational data that would feed back into the design, and eventually provide sailors and submariners with advanced ASW technology that was needed to meet the strategic goals of the Navy.

But the mobility of thought and action that enabled the "team" to function efficiently relied on support throughout the organization. Members of the technical "team" were joined by Sound Lab staff who handled procurements, shipped parts and pieces to remote locations, and created travel orders that sent field teams to these same God-forsaken corners of

333

the planet. The "process" involved dozens of individuals, yet each had to feel that their role included participation as "team" members, if only for the short period of time when their inputs were needed. Although the Sound Lab certainly contained some of those grumpy by-the-book individuals blinded by their love of "process," management at USN/USL understood that the role of their administrative staff was to facilitate and not hinder mobility—essential where survival of the fittest defined the successful prosecution of the Cold War. The concept of "teamwork" will evolve in *any* organization, but as Darwin discovered, evolution was not always successful.

WHAT DOESN'T WORK: SIX DEGRESS OF SEPARATION

In chapter 2, I described the need to reduce the degrees of separation between warfare system designers and the warfighter. I've had opportunities to speak with a few old retired enlisted submariners. One conversation pretty well defined their attitude. "We always worried when we heard that civilian riders were coming aboard . . . until we were told they were from the Sound Lab. That was a relief. We knew that when we were going to sea with you guys, we were in for some interesting ops. By the time we were offshore, you were just part of the crew." He was telling me that the degrees of separation had been reduced to one. Success came through shared risk, and shared risk came from teamwork—whether we were at sea on a submarine, or back at the Lab in New London.

But there were also consequences if the degrees of separation increased between an organization's leadership and its staff. In this hypothetical example of corporate America, a small start-up engineering firm provided unique and creative products for the Navy. Their fast and efficient progress was envied by a nearby larger corporation, and soon the small company was purchased by the larger one. The new management resided reasonably close to the small company, and because management still valued the product and productivity of their new acquisition, the individuals involved were encouraged to move forward with minimal interference. The profitability of the larger company was soon noticed by an industrial giant, and a hostile takeover ensued. With corporate management now residing on the west coast, its new subsidiary on the east coast had to adapt to a distant management. Decisions were now made by individuals far removed from the subsidiary, expanding the degrees of separation between the decision makers and that original engineering firm—now simply absorbed within the corporate maze.

The Sound Lab was able to move forward efficiently because the day to day operational decisions were made by managers who understood when administrative process began to impede technological progress. These decision makers were in offices just down the hall from the engineers, and readily made the correct accommodation to slow down process and speed up progress. With minimal separation between management and staff, feedback and pushback was immediate. When USN/USL became NUSC, much of that management shuttled between Newport and New London. The offices of these same managers were now sixty five miles away— in spite of the inconvenience, the engineers still had reasonable access, ensuring some degree of mobility of thought and action.

When the BRAC consolidation drew the New London Laboratory to Newport, it was expected that the proximity between leadership and staff would improve the relationship. But that expectation was not entirely realized. Decision makers who would mandate process resided in Washington, far from Newport. The day to day managers would soon have to answer first to these mandates, at the expense of responding to technological issues necessary for progress—there were simply not enough hours in the day for both. As the role of administrative process grew, exacerbated by the "regionalization" of many day-to-day activities, the expanding degrees of separation minimized feedback and pushback from staff. In chapter 10, I described how various processes can affect the creativity and motivation of intellectual and physical risk takers. The emphasis on DAWIA and NMCI; the aversion to risk, even for simple daily activities; the growing dependence on virtual reality at the expense of real reality—all are distractions that have more influence on those tasked with solving problems, than the problem solving itself.

While the goals of DAWIA, NMCI, and other administrative and infrastructure related "processes" are important and well-intentioned, their implementation can exceed their role in an organization's mission. Individuals tasked with ensuring compliance may lack the relevant experience to understand the unintended consequences, which the technical staff must endure. Once "process" becomes a mandate rather than guidance, it exists external to, not within, the structure of the team, becoming a hurdle rather than an expeditor of the mission.

There should be nothing surprising about this, nor should the solution be any more surprising—it is a return to teamwork. Managers of *any* organization need to concentrate on their true mission, managing technology and technologists. Administrative process and technological progress can move forward hand-in-hand, but only when each finds and accepts its role in the "team." When that happens, the tail of the dog will start wagging, not because the tail is in charge, but because the dog is happy.

WHAT CAN'T BE FORGOTTEN: KNOWLEDGE IS KING—BOOKS ARE ITS QUEEN

Encouraging individuals to experience the world around them leads to maturity—as the person matures so do the ideas. As the ideas mature, so does the knowledge that moves a society forward. Books express the heart and soul of knowledge—they pass on facts and figures, philosophies and fanciful stories. In all cases the authors are compelled to express ideas. Writing is truly a compulsion and a passion; this book is no exception.

Because the Cold War was a strategic endeavor, most books written on the subject covered the high-level political and military decision making. These authors, who sat near the top of the chain, correctly documented America's strategic and operational priorities. A prime example was John F. Lehman, Jr., Secretary of the Navy from 1981 to 1987, who described in his 1988 book *Command Of The Seas: Building the 600 Ship Navy*, President Ronald Reagan's naval strategy throughout his administration.[165] Lehman related the role of the President, Congress, and of course his role as SECNAV, establishing and maintaining the overall U.S. strategy of deterrence.

In 2001, as many behind-the-scenes details began to emerge, John P. Craven published *The Silent War: The Cold War Battle Beneath the Sea*.[166] Craven was appointed chief scientist of the Navy's Special Projects Office in 1959, with oversight of the Polaris missile system, later becoming head of the Deep Submergence Systems Project. Craven mentioned the use of Navy saturation divers, who were involved with intelligence gathering missions during the Cold War. These clandestine wire tapping operations by teams of Navy divers who rode and "locked-out" of submarines, which had secretly entered the Sea of Okhotsk and the Barents Sea, were described by Sherry Sontag and Christopher Drew (1998) in their book *Blind Man's Bluff: The Untold Story of American Submarine Espionage*.[167]

Few books, however, have been written by people who were assigned the task of actually doing the moving and shaking—the enlisted men who went to sea and the civilian technicians and engineers who joined them. In his book, *Stealth Boat: Fighting the Cold War in a Fast-Attack Submarine*, Gannon McHale (2008), an enlisted submariner on board USS *Sturgeon* (SSN-637) during the early 1960s, related the personal and professional lives that he and his shipmates experienced as they ventured out from the Groton submarine base and into Soviet waters.[168]

When John Merrill and Lionel Wyld published *Meeting the Submarine Challenge* in 1998, their perspective was from the point of view of scientists, program managers, and high-level management. Their monumental effort to describe the mission of NUSC, both in New London and Newport, credited the many submarine and antisubmarine warfare systems that supplied the Navy with its strategic advantage during the Cold War. But it was also important to document the foundations of ideas that led to these systems, and, for that matter, any technology. Writers who describe the evolution of scientific thought must stress that *the path travelled is as important to the next generation as the technology itself.*

Thad Bell's book *Probing the Oceans for Submarines*, at long last approved for public release and published in 2011, chronicled the effort to develop the SQS-26 surface ship sonar—the requirement defined by a fast-emerging Soviet submarine threat during the early years of the Cold War.[169] The Soviet Union was long gone, but the history of an essential technology—*and the path travelled*—written by an antisubmarine warfare pioneer, was now forever in print.

Much of our history, however, has been put into boxes. Before these boxes find their way to the shredder, the information needs to be summarized and maintained among a family of ideas and idea people. Let the details gather dust, but not the concepts. A good scientist or engineer can read the books, dust off the old details, and use a previous researcher's mistakes, successes, and frustrations as a starting point. A good example arose from the final year of World War II. Destroyers carried active echo-ranging sonar, including the British ASDIC and the U.S. Q-series, operating at frequencies above 15 KHz. These submarine hunters had become deadly at finding and destroying U-boats lurking beneath the sea. This vulnerability led the Germans to develop a counter-detection technology—a rubber-based hull coating, which made the U-boat nearly acoustically invisible, but was implemented too late to have altered the course of antisubmarine warfare. In a 1962 USN/USL report, "Sonar and Submarine Detection," Thad Bell described the German hull coating, effective at a frequency range between 9 and 18 KHz, as "capable of absorbing, under the right conditions, ninety-eight percent of the incident sound pulse."[170] With only two percent of the energy returning as an echo, the ability to detect the target was significantly reduced—the better the coating, the more difficult the detection. Modern submarines have adapted this "cloak of invisibility."

The submarine will continue to be a factor in any global conflict. Each improvement in one side of the antisubmarine equation challenges designers to improve the other side of the equation. The development of hull coatings will always be part of the equation; every piece of data, modern or early, can be a factor. Libraries that purge their past do so at great risk.

WHAT IS NEEDED: A SENSE OF HISTORY

The Cold War years in New London were dominated by scientists, and engineers, and technicians, who joined Jacques Cousteau exploring the ocean depths in his *Diving Saucer*; who participated in research expeditions to the arctic camps on ice islands T-3, CHARLIE and ARLIS II; who defined the acoustic properties of the entire Atlantic Ocean on ships and submarines, and at facilities in Bermuda, the Bahamas, and the Azores. These scientific missions were of historical importance, and each team included talented individuals from Jim Selvideo's Photo-Optics Techniques Branch, whose photo-journalistic instincts ensured that every significant detail was documented. Everyone understood the need to record these important events, but their historical value would only be appreciated in the post-Cold War decades.

When the New London Lab closed, I filled several boxes with photos and video tapes, which covered some of the Cold War projects our divers had participated in. Shortly after settling into our new home on the NUWC Newport waterfront, I began digging through these old photographs. I eventually hung some of the more memorable on the wall as reminders of that commitment to the Navy we had enjoyed in New London. It was then I learned that, as the BRAC mandated consolidation progressed, an irreversible management decision had been made to limit the amount of documentary material that would be moved to Newport. The results of that decision were that an entire archive of photographic records, covering decades of Cold War scientific research and engineering development in New London, was chopped, shredded, and disposed of. For many managers making BRAC consolidation decisions in 1996, the Cold War was only "yesterday;" the reports, the photos, and the movies were simply scenes from a typical workday. There must have been little thought about the future importance of retaining the Cold War legacy. Besides, the New London Laboratory had been permanently closed, and the future was going to reside in Newport.

In the prologue to this book I listed several projects that involved USN/USL and NUSC/NL during the Cold War, and I still cringe when I ponder that movies taken while individuals from New London were working on ice islands in the high arctic more than a half century ago are now gone. Movies taken during USN/USL research using deep ocean submersibles *Trieste*, *Alvin*, *Star III*, the Perry *Cubmarine*, and Cousteau's *Diving Saucer*—gone. Movies taken during the Sealab I project at Argus Island—gone. Movies taken during the Fishbowl project, Ocean Acre, SNAP 7-E, Colossus, Cormoran, Sanguine, Seaguard, Artemis, ANZUS Eddy, FLIP, BRASS, AFAR and MACS—all gone! How simple it would have been to archive copies of these movies, documenting the research that helped win the Cold War, and in the future, pass them on to the Naval History and Heritage Command in Washington or even to the National Archives.

I was heartened recently while researching this book, that some individuals with a sense of history had retained copies of photos taken during these early years. When, for example, Manny Finkle passed away, his collection depicting Sound Lab operations in the 1960s with Cousteau's *Diving Saucer* and other deep-ocean research was given to his son Jonathan, a few of which appear in this book. I have also located several underwater photos that "Mac" McClenny shot of *Deepstar 4000* in 1967, and of the 1971 installation of the AFAR towers in the Azores.

And now there is the Fort Trumbull State Park, a Connecticut landmark with a military history reaching back to the Revolutionary War.[171] More than a quarter of that history was dedicated to antisubmarine warfare—initially during World War I; then from the early days of World War II, and throughout the Cold War. The collections on display at the Fort Trumbull museum include a look back on these pages from its history, and where Sound Lab retirees have been helping document the work that went on behind the chain link fence a half century ago. Recently, an experimental Cold War sonar used for the BRASS II project (chapter 6),[172] which had languished behind a building at NUWC Newport, was saved from the scrap bin and shipped to Fort Trumbull. This one item, a survivor among scores of experimental devices long disposed of, exemplifies the efforts of all the Cold Warriors at USN/USL and NUSC. Preserving an important symbol of Cold War technology that arose specifically from the minds and hands of the Sound Lab has inspired participants to relate their experiences with stories and photos that will accompany the display of BRASS II.

Reminders of many similar Cold War exploits are still available in surviving copies of the weekly, and later monthly, newsletters that the Underwater Sound Lab and its successors had published. The periodic "hard copy" provided staff with brief descriptions of recent events, including the various technologies that were being developed, tested, and transitioned to the fleet. The information and accompanying photos had been selected specifically for a general readership, and sensitive technical details were excluded to allow the newsletters to find their way to the public.

The first edition of the USL Bulletin appeared on February 6, 1948, and continued uninterrupted until January 21, 1954, when the ECHO began its seventeen year run with a front-page article: "The Launching Heard

Around the World. USS NAUTILUS, the world's first atomic-powered submarine, was christened this morning . . . [We] take pride in presenting to Mrs. Dwight D. Eisenhower the first copy of the ECHO." With this first edition, the Sound Lab maintained a written legacy, defining this organization's participation in the Cold War with articles about many of the unique accomplishments of its staff.

The final edition of the ECHO was issued on March 26, 1971, soon after the merger of the Sound Lab with the Navy Underwater Weapons Research and Engineering Station (NUWRES, also abbreviated NUWS), and the establishment of NUSC, the Naval Underwater Systems Center. The merger also saw the elimination of the NUWS Narrator, and both publications were combined into the NUSCOPE with the May 1971 edition. Issued monthly, the NUSCOPE ran for twenty years, its final edition appearing in December 1991. With the creation of the Naval Undersea Warfare Center (NUWC), the publication was renamed NUWSCOPE with its first edition issued in January 1992.

After another run of twenty years, NUWC suspended the monthly hard-copy issues of NUWSCOPE with its December 2011 edition, in what was a cost cutting decision. Retirees like me no longer received our monthly issues, but we could subscribe to NUWSCOPE, which continued to be published as an on-line electronic edition. These newsletters were a reflection of not just the technologies, but of the character and "personality" of the Sound Lab, then NUSC, then NUWC. Over the years, individuals with a sense of history have retained their hard copy editions of those past publications. Copies now residing in various archives have been instrumental in providing background for this book. It was in the April 3, 1959 issue of ECHO, where I found details about Joe Gordon, the first Sound Lab engineer who became a qualified Navy diver—a person I only knew through reputation, but who represented day one of our team's half-century legacy.

Yet in 2012, the electronic version of NUWSCOPE was eliminated in favor of maintaining a continually updated, online informational link within the Center's web site. Restricted access, however, limited the outside world from a view of the Center and its staff. A hundred years from now, historians studying how this country retained its maritime strength in the twentieth and into the twenty-first century will hunt through archives for copies of these newsletters. Unfortunately, the on-line narrative of an organization whose collective research and development intellect continues to play a major role in naval history will have dissolved among the terabytes of an electronic abyss.

WHAT IS THE BOTTOM LINE: LEADERSHIP

"Good morning, Admiral . . ."

We were in the hallway at the Naval Sea Systems Command, when Stan Silverstein greeted one of the movers and shakers at the very top. It was late September, 1984, and I had just returned from the Med. We had successfully sent USS *Brumby* back to sea, avoiding a foreign port dry-docking, and I was in Washington to provide the post-repair briefing.

"Admiral, this is Roy Manstan, one of the NUSC engineers on the dive team from New London I was telling you about." Stan then described our overseas assignment to the admiral, who was very aware of the damage that had seriously affected *Brumby*'s mission. The admiral reached out, shook my hand, and expressed a simple "thank you." At that moment, there were zero degrees of separation between one of the decision makers at the top, and one of the countless field engineers being sent around the world. The Cold War was far from over. Rational and timely decision making required the integration of ideas at all levels, supported by teams who could provide a well thought-out—and immediate—response. The admiral's gratitude was genuine.

Back then, in the 1980s, I had been given the NUSC/NL Command responsibility for a small team of front line risk takers, who thrived on challenges that came from leadership at all levels during the Cold War. I was not a product line manager, and I accept that my experience and level within the organization over nearly four decades limits the perspective I bring to this history—but it is a legitimate perspective, nonetheless. Today, the Engineering and Diving Support Unit continues to serve the Navy's need for risk takers—and for those first responders when the next threat emerges.

At the Naval Undersea Warfare Center, the dive team is just one element within what is now a twenty-first-century organization of nearly three thousand DoD civilians and military advisors, plus several hundred support contractors. New sonar systems, new electromagnetic systems, new weapon systems, new targeting and fire control systems continue to be developed for the next generation submarine. The emergence of unmanned underwater and surface vehicles (UUVs and USVs) provides challenging projects along the NUWC waterfront.

Each high-tech system, each mission that NAVSEA and other Navy sponsors place within the purview of NUWC, is staffed by highly competent, energized scientists and field engineers who travel the world. NUWC carries on a legacy of maintaining global maritime superiority through innovation born a century ago at the Naval Torpedo Station in Newport and the Navy Experimental Station in New London. Anyone reading this book can trust that those who work the waterfront or work their keyboards at NUWC will continue to strive to provide the warfighter with the best technology possible.

So, here's that bottom line. When I arrived in New London in the 1960s, our management was focused on guiding technology and serving as role models to the next generation of risk takers. There was no hesitation within my chain of command when this young engineer expressed interest in the dive team. Then, on day-one of dive school, I quickly learned what it meant when a person was expected to give 110 percent. Among those of us who completed the training, that spirit has followed us throughout our careers. While this commitment to kick ass in the face of a challenge is not exclusive to dive teams, the motivation for *any* employee to continue to give 110 percent every day, whether in the cubicle or on the water, has to come from leadership. When I was asked to bring a team of divers to Africa, or to the Azores, or the Persian Gulf, I knew that those doing the asking understood the risks, having their own long list of "been there, done that" experiences. Sure . . . they may have had to get that MBA degree in order to advance up the management ladder, but the classroom was not their only source of credibility. These were leaders who understood teamwork. They had also been cold, wet, and seasick . . . had to face unfriendly, uncooperative individuals in situations far from home . . . had to find creative ways to complete their missions. They could ask me and my team of divers to go anywhere in the world, and we would respond without hesitation.

My hope is that writing this history will serve as a reminder to *any* agency or industry that managers with real-world experience make good leaders—and a reminder to those same managers, now enjoying the comfort of warm offices and a nearby coffee pot, that when this country's military strength depends on technology on and under the sea, there will be a team of field engineers bracing against a cold wind on a snow-covered pier.

———————————————

On May 31, 1974, while Chief Downey and the diving instructors stood at attention, Lieutenant Heeger presented me with the Navy scuba pin— fourteen of us were still standing that afternoon, thirty-two had started. My life changed forever that day.

On November 4, 1994, my son Dan was born, followed by Sarah on July 31, 1997, and again my life changed forever. Now with two young kids, I soon remembered that "the only easy day was yesterday."

Appendix

It is essential to acknowledge the service of every USN/USL, NUSC, and NUWC diver, listed below in the decade each joined the team—all of whom contributed to the long history of naval technology portrayed in this book.

<u>1950</u>
Catlow, James
Carey, George
Gordon, Sumner

<u>1960</u>
April, Edward
Cannan, Thomas
Fisch, Norbert
Hill, Ed
McClenny, Dennie*

<u>1970</u>
Aiksnoras, Robert
Beatrice, Kenneth
Clark, James
Fay, John
Fish, William
La Bonte, Robert*
Manstan, Roy
Marolda, Victor
Munn, Raymond
Straatveit, Nils
Sullivan, Timothy
Thibeault, Richard

<u>1980</u>
Byrne, Ross
Greenhalgh, Bruce
Hansen, Kurt
Jolie, Jeff
Murphy, Joseph
Paruszewski, Michael
Peirson, Michael*
Scheifele, Peter*
Sorrentino, Ludwig*

<u>1990</u>
Gianquinto, Paul
Hughes, John
Kaiser, Richard
Mileski, Paul
Rutkowski, Michael*
Sansone, Louis
Schmidt, Robert
Silvia, Antone*
Vincent, Harold*
Wiedenheft, John

<u>2000</u>
Arteiro, José*
Bruce, D. Keith
Carroll, Samuel
Field, Matthew
Fulton, Tom*
Graves, William*
Hart, David
Jasinski, David
McNeilly, Frank
Robinson, Mark*
Schumacher, Christian
Tinney, Tom*

<u>2010</u>
Elsen, Andrew*
Murphy, Colin

*These individuals had previously qualified as divers during their active duty service.

NOTES

Prologue

1. John Piña Craven, *The Silent War: The Cold War Battle Beneath the Sea* (New York: Simon & Schuster, 2001).

2. The term "slide rule strategy" was described in John Merrill, *Submarines, Technology, and History: Selected Articles by John Merrill* (Haverford, PA: Infinity Publishing, 2004). The chapter titled "Slide Rule Strategy" provides a historical perspective on the evolution of Operations Research, which coupled the civilian scientist with the military during World War II. The late John Merrill, whose career at the Underwater Sound Lab and its successor, the Naval Underwater Systems Center, had a keen appreciation for the history of Navy technology and wrote several books on the subject, most of which are referenced herein.

3. Roy R. Manstan and Frederick J. Frese, *TURTLE: David Bushnell's Revolutionary Vessel* (Yardley, PA: Westholme, 2010). Between 2003 and 2007, Manstan, Frese, and students in Frese's High School technical arts class created a working replica of Bushnell's *Turtle*. In 2008, the *Turtle* was brought to the Mystic Seaport Museum waterfront where Paul Mileski, David Hart, and author Roy Manstan served as test pilots during two days of operational testing; all described in the book referenced here.

4. David Humphreys, *An Essay on the Life of the Honorable Major-General Israel Putnam* (Middletown, CT: Moses H. Woodward, [1788] 1794), 111.

5. Invented by Jacques-Yves Cousteau and launched in 1959, his *Soucoupe Plongeante* was referred to by its English translation, *Diving Saucer.*

6. In 1969, Sound Lab scientists visited Lake Tanganyika as a potential site where low frequency sound attenuation could be measured over exceptional distances (the lake is 420 miles long) in fresh water for comparison to what occurs in the world's oceans. Because of political unrest and sporadic guerilla warfare in the Democratic Republic of Congo, the U.S. State Department delayed until late 1970, what became a successful scientific mission. In 1972, under Project KIWI ONE, measurements of open ocean acoustic propagation

were conducted by Laboratory scientists in the North Atlantic, South Pacific, Gulf of Mexico, and Caribbean Sea.

7. John Merrill, and Lionel D. Wyld. *Meeting the Submarine Challenge: A Short History of the Naval Underwater Systems Center.* (Washington, D.C.: United States Government Printing Office, 1997). This is a primary source for the technical and organizational history of the Naval Underwater Systems Center (NUSC) and provides a detailed timeline for the merger of the predecessor Navy research and development activities in Newport, Rhode Island and New London, Connecticut.

Chapter 1

8. My memories of Guy and Jane Williams are vivid, and I was delighted to find an article about Guy's association with the bathyscaphe *Trieste* and a photograph of his piece of the fractured *Trieste* window in the February 21, 1964, edition of the ECHO, and another article about his career in the October 21, 1966, edition.

9. Articles about the launch of *Star II* and *Star III* appeared in the April 22 and May 6, 1966, editions of the ECHO.

10. The association of Lou Maples and Walt Whitaker with the SNAP-7E project appeared in an article: "USL Plays Vital Role in Putting Nuclear Power to Use at Bottom of the Ocean," in the July 24, 1964, edition of the ECHO.

Chapter 2

11. Lieutenant Commander J. S. Barnes, USN, *Submarine Warfare: Offensive and Defensive* (New York: Van Nostrand, 1869).

12. Mark K. Ragan, *Submarine Warfare in the Civil War* (Cambridge, MA: Da Capo, 2002), 80-84.

13. Barnes, *Submarine Warfare*, 150.

14. All references to David Bushnell and his "submarine vessel" come from Roy R. Manstan and Frederick J. Frese, *TURTLE: David Bushnell's Revolutionary Vessel* (Yardley, PA: Westholme, 2010).

15. Colonel David Humphreys, *An Essay on the Life of the Honorable Major-General Israel Putnam* (Middletown, CT: Moses H. Woodward, 1794 [1st ed.

1788]), 111-117. Humphreys' description of Bushnell's *Turtle* and this quote are included in Manstan and Frese's book.

16. Descriptions and commentary about David Bushnell and his submarine by eye witnesses, including George Washington's comments, are included in Manstan and Frese, *Turtle*, see the appendices, pp. 276-310.

17. Lieutenant Francis M. Barber, *Lecture on Submarine Boats and their Application to Torpedo Operations* (Newport, Rhode Island: U.S. Torpedo Station, 1875).

18. Richard K. Morris, *John P. Holland, 1841-1914: Inventor of the Submarine* (Annapolis: United States Naval Institute, 1966), 22.

19. Barber, *Lecture on Submarine Boats*, 29.

20. http://www.isrsubrace.org

21. Rear Admiral George W. Melville, Engineer in Chief, United States Navy, "The Submarine Boat: Its Value as a Weapon of Naval Warfare," in *The Annual Report of the Smithsonian Institution for the Year Ending June 30, 1901* (Washington, DC: Government Printing Office, 1902), 717-738. (available at www.googlebooks.com)

22. John Wilkins, *Mathematical Magic; or the Wonders that may be Performed by Mechanical Geometry*, 4th ed. [1st published in 1648] (London: Ric. Baldwin, 1691), 178-190.

23. The primary source for material related to the German U-boats of both World War I and World War II comes from V. E. Tarrant, *The U-Boat Offensive 1914-1945* (Annapolis: Naval Institute, 1989), see p. 12 for these specific statistics.

24. The British Admiralty's objections to the convoy system and their use of the "thousands scheme" is discussed in Tarrant, *The U-boat Offensive*, 39-41.

25. Beginning with a subchapter heading, "The Efficacy of the Convoy," Tarrant, *The U-boat Offensive*, 66, provides detailed statistics as to how the U-boat offensive was derailed after the convoy system was instituted.

26. The history of the Navy Experimental Station comes from three sources: John Merrill, *Fort Trumbull and the Submarine* (Avon, CT: Publishing Directions,

349

2000); John Merrill, *Submarines, Technology, and History: Selected Articles by John Merrill* (Haverford, PA: Infinity Publishing, 2004); and a recently discovered archive of photographs taken during Station operations from 1917 to 1918.

27. Charles W. Domville-Fife, *Submarine Warfare of To-Day* (Philadelphia: J. B. Lippincott, 1920), 70-71.

28. For a history of Electric Boat, see Jeffrey L. Rodengen, *Serving the Silent Service: The Legend of Electric Boat* (Ft. Lauderdale: Write Stuff Syndicate, 1994).

29. I am indebted to the vast quantity of information available within the archives of the Navy Submarine Force Library and Museum related to the history of the Groton Submarine Base. http://www.ussnautilus.org/

30. For details about the research conducted at the Columbia University Division of War Research in New London, Connecticut, during World War II, see Merrill, *Fort Trumbull and the Submarine*, Chapter 3.

31. http://www.orms-today.org/orms-2-01/nps.html. The British referred to this process as Operational Research, while in the U.S. it was termed Operations Research.

32. Merrill, *Submarines, Technology, and History*, 85-99.

33. Merrill, *Fort Trumbull and the Submarine*, 52-58.

34. Prior to her fatal deployment, a team of engineers from USN/USL were at Portsmouth Naval Shipyard working with *Thresher's* prototype BQQ-1 sonar system during her post shakedown availability (PSA). Because of other onboard system priorities associated with the upcoming trials, the Sound Lab team decided to forego *Thresher's* sea trials and returned to New London— certainly the closest of all close calls.

Chapter 3

35. Captain Bond maintained a personal log of his time in the Navy, and this journal has been published in Helen A. Siiteri, ed., *Papa Topside: The Sealab Chronicles of Capt. George F. Bond, USN* (Annapolis: Naval Institute Press, 1993). One of the participants in the saturation diving tests, Bob Barth, wrote about his association with Captain Bond and his experiences as a test subject:

Bob Barth, *Sea Dwellers: The Humor, Drama and Tragedy of the U.S. Navy SEALAB Programs* (Houston: Doyle Publishing, 2000).

36. The wire-tapping operations during the Cold War are well documented in Sherry Sontag and Christopher Drew, *Blind Man's Bluff: The Untold Story of American Submarine Espionage* (New York: Public Affairs, 1998).

37. A facsimile edition was produced by the Man in the Sea Museum, Panama City Beach, Florida. The original edition is *Handbook for Seaman Gunners, Manual for Divers Prepared at the Naval Torpedo Station* (Washington: Government Printing Office, 1905).

38. Gunner George D. Stillson, *Report on Deep Diving Tests* (Washington, D.C.: Government Printing Office, 1915). Stillson's book included the text from the 1905 *Handbook for Seaman Gunners, Manual for Divers*.

39. For all of the responses, see: Stillson, *Report on Deep Diving Tests*, 168-215.

40. Robert H. Barnes, *United States Submarines* (New Haven: H.F. Associates, 1944), 72-78.

41. Commander Edward Ellsberg, *On the Bottom* (New York: Dodd, Mead & Company, 1929).

42. Information and contemporary newspaper accounts regarding Chief Fred Michels receiving the Navy Cross for service during the salvage of *S-51* were provided by Michels' grandson, EDSU diver Michael Peirson.

43. The excerpts from the 1959 Navy Diving Manual and the 1952 issue of "Diving Notes, U.S. Naval School, Deep Sea Divers" were provided by the Man in the Sea Museum, Panama City Beach, Florida. Information regarding the early use of the Aqualung during scuba training by UDT combat swimmers was from Chuck Theiss, docent at the UDT/SEAL Museum, Fort Pierce, Florida.

44. Herbert Best, *The Webfoot Warriors: The Story of UDT, the U.S. Navy's Underwater Demolition Team* (New York: John Day Company, 1962). The use of mini-subs by UDT is on pages 109-13. The illustrations are inserted between pages 96 and 97.

45. Best, *The Webfoot Warriors*, pp 136-7.

46. The "Underwater Telephone" patentees from USN/USL included Walter Wainwright and Russell Mason. The patent was filed in 1957, but was not awarded until 1967, after a decade of testing at the Lab and use by UDT. Herbert Best (1962:137) indicated that the underwater walkie-talkies had been declassified, but were still undergoing development. Although Best doesn't mention USN/USL, this system was being tested by Joe Gordon, who is shown wearing the system in the August 12, 1966, edition of the ECHO (see this book, figure 19).

47. Stillson, *Report on Deep Diving Tests*, p. 86. Simon Lake's submarine *G-1*, commissioned in 1912, included a diver lock-out hatch in the keel, near the bow. This capability was eliminated on subsequent submarines.

48. Information regarding the Medical Research Laboratory was obtained from the extensive archival material available at the Submarine Force Library and Museum, Groton, CT. http://www.ussnautilus.org/

49. Carey and Catlow's participation in the SNAP-7E project is described in the July 24, 1964, edition of the Echo. SNAP is the acronym for Systems Nuclear Auxiliary Power. There were seven of these used in various subsea applications (SNAP-7A through 7F).

50. The latest version is 12000.20B [https://www.supsalv.org/pdf/SecnavInst12000_20B.pdf] and maintains these same restrictions on civilian diving. While there are still satellite schools, the Navy Diving & Salvage Training Center (NDSTC), Panama City, Florida, is the primary school for Navy divers, and is where the EDSU continues to send its civilian candidates, see http://www.netc.navy.mil/centers/ceneoddive/ndstc/ . . . By 1980, the scuba school at the submarine base in Groton, Connecticut, had closed and transferred to NDSTC.

Chapter 4

51. W. Craig Reed, *Red November: Inside the Secret U.S.-Soviet Submarine War* (New York: Harper Collins, 2010), 73.

52. An excellent summary of the various ocean acoustic conditions that limit the ranges of active sonar can be found in Thaddeus G. Bell, *Probing the Oceam for Submarines: A History of the AN/SQS-26 Long-Range, Echo-Ranging Sonar*, 2nd Edition, 2nd Printing [Approved for Public Release] (Los Altos Hills, CA: Peninsula Publishing, 2011).

53. John Merrill and Lionel D. Wyld, *Meeting the Submarine Challenge: A Short History of the Naval Underwater Systems Center* (Washington, D.C.: United States Government Printing Office, 1997). This reference provides summaries of multiple oceanographic studies performed by USN/USL and NUSC during the Cold War, and the various acoustic ranges where scientific research was performed by these Navy laboratories.

54. For example, USS *Tigrone* (SS-419), redesignated AGSS-419 in 1963, was a major platform for USN/USL sonar research beginning in 1959. The designation "AGSS" refers to an Auxiliary Research Submarine.

55. ECHO, December 8, 1967.

56. Merrill and Wyld, *Meeting the Submarine Challenge*, 311.

57. For a description of the effects of biological reverberation on sonar, and the world-wide research to define the phenomenon, see Bell, *Probing the Oceans for Submarines*, 84-7, 101-2.

58. The USN/USL weekly newsletter ECHO ran articles about the Tudor Hill laboratory and its staff. See, for example, the August 25, 1961, edition for a description of several Sound Lab staff members, who were involved with projects in Bermuda, and the September 11, 1964, edition, which describes Fran Weigle's Tudor Hill assignment.

59. Vice Admiral James Calvert, *Surface at the Pole: The extraordinary Voyages of the USS* Skate (Annapolis: Naval Institute, 1996), 79. Francis "Fran" Weigle was one of nine civilians aboard *Skate*. His early assignments were an introduction to a long and interesting career.

60. ECHO, August 26, 1960.

61. ECHO, August 12, 1960. The activities at the Tudor Hill Lab are summarized in Merrill and Wyld, *Meeting the Submarine Challenge*, 274-7.

62. ECHO, April 10, 1959.

63. The military presence on Fishers Island during the twentieth century has been covered in exquisite photographic detail in Pierce Rafferty and John Wilton, *Guardian of the Sound: A Pictorial History of Fort H.G. Wright Fishers Island, N.Y.* (New York City: Mount Mercer, 1998).

64. John Merrill, *From Submarine Bells to Sonar: Submarine Signal Company 1901-1946* (Avon, CT: Publishing Directions, 2003), 54.

65. Pierce Rafferty, "Island History: A World War II Mystery Solved," in *The Henry L. Ferguson Museum Newsletter*, 26, 1 (Spring 2011): 12-13.

66. Gannon McHale, *Stealth Boat: Fighting the Cold War in a Fast-Attack Submarine* (Annapolis: Naval Institute, 2008), 123.

67. "Block Island Submarine," *The Fisherman*, August 5, 1993, 8.

68. Michael A. Tucchio, "Establishing Mobile Acoustic Communication System (MACS) Safety on USS Nautilus," Naval Engineers Journal, 95, 5 (Sept 1983): 71-5. http://onlinelibrary.wiley.com/doi/10.1111/j.1559-3584.1983.tb01667.x/abstract

69. At the *Nautilus* Golden Anniversary held at the Submarine Force Museum in 2004, CDR Richard Riddell, who took command of *Nautilus* off Bermuda in December, 1976, described the operation: "The [MACS] antenna would transmit an acoustic signal to a receiving submarine or surface ship well over a hundred miles away, with multiple simultaneous signal frequencies, various antenna angles, different ocean bottom types, and a variety of weather conditions. My most vivid memory of our time with MACS was the ability of the human body to adapt to the ear-splitting acoustic signals that were transmitted every few seconds. This went on for days and weeks at a time. Somehow, we learned to live with this noise—to sleep, watch movies, and even play poker on Saturday nights." http://www.ussnautilus.org/events/2004Nov17goldenyear/Riddell_lecture.shtml

70. Lieutenant Peter M. Scheifele, "Changes of Acoustical Structure in the Atlantic Bottlenose Dolphin *Tursiops truncatus (Montagu)* Relative to Changes of Environment, Preliminary Report," Naval Underwater Systems Center Technical Report 8731, January 2, 1991. (Approved for public release)

Lieutenant Peter M. Scheifele and Roy Manstan, "Definition of the Acoustical Structure of Echolocation Pulse Trains of an Atlantic Bottlenose Dolphin in Captivity," Naval Underwater Systems Center Technical Report 8729, December 28, 1990. (Approved for public release)

71. Pete retired from the Navy soon after the Aquarium testing was complete, and pursued his goal to obtain his doctorate.

72. There were slight variations among the individual clicks within each echolocation pulse train; the one shown here was selected to illustrate the general shape and duration of a single pulse.

Chapter 5

73. The primary sources for the early history of surface ship ASW sonar are John Merrill and Lionel D. Wyld, *Meeting the Submarine Challenge: A Short History of the Naval Underwater Systems Center* (Washington, D.C.: United State Government Printing Office, 1997). [See their chapter 5 "Surface Ship Sonar"], and Angela D. D'Amico and Richard Pittenger, "A Brief History of Active Sonar," Aquatic Mammals, 35, 4 (2009): 426-434.

74. Thad Bell has been an incredible source of information throughout the research for this book, both from personal communications and his book: Thaddeus G. Bell, *Probing the Ocean for Submarines: A History of the AN/SQS-26 Long-Range, Echo-Ranging Sonar*, 2nd Edition, 2nd Printing [Approved for Public Release], (Los Altos Hills, CA: Peninsula Publishing, 2011).

75. During the mid-1970s when the Navy was reclassifying many of its ships, and because Destroyer Lead (DL) vessels were outfitted with guided missiles, they were designated as either a "DDG" destroyer, or a "CG" cruiser.

76. The proposal for a Sonar Dome Rubber Window was provided to the Bureau of Ships (BUSHIPS) by B.F. Goodrich Aerospace and Defense Products, and is described in "Pressurized Bow Dome of a Cable-Reinforced Rubber Construction for use with AN/SQS-26 Sonar: Interim Report for Phase I, 1 March 1963 to 30 April 1964," Bureau of Ships, Washington, D.C., Report No. 17, 1964.

77. The tests and performance results are from Bell, *Probing the Oceans for Submarines*, chapter 7, "The Rubber Dome Window," 111-19.

78. John Merrill, *Fort Trumbull and the Submarine*, 2nd Printing (Avon, CT: Publishing Directions, 2000), 85. Chapter 4 provides an excellent summary of post-World War II surface ship sonar.

79. Soviet submarine information is from the 1979-80 and 1986-87 editions of *Jane's Fighting Ships*.

80. John F. Lehman, Jr., *Command of the Seas: Building the 600 Ship Navy* (New York: Charles Scribner's Sons, 1988), 121. See his chapter 4, "Setting the Course: Rebuilding a Naval Strategy," and chapter 5, "The Six-Hundred-Ship Navy," for an overview of the issues that Navy research and development organizations faced during the Cold War.

81. Bell, *Probing the Ocean for Submarines*, 115.

Chapter 6

82. John Merrill, *From Submarine Bells to Sonar: Submarine Signal Company 1901-1946* (Avon, CT: Publishing Directions, 2003), 10-13.

83. British patent No. 13,288 (1902) described one of the early "telephone receiver" systems installed on surface ships.

84. The suggestion that the Submarine Signal Company's underwater "sound-producing device" would be appropriate for use on submarines is found in the 1904 British patent No. 10,463, "Improved Method for Producing Sound Vibrations in Water applicable to Marine Signaling."

85. Charles W. Domville-Fife, *Submarine Warfare of To-Day* (Philadelphia: J. B. Lippincott, 1920), 77.

86. Ibid., 141.

87. Ibid., 142.

88. V. E. Tarrant, *The U-Boat Offensive 1914-1945* (Annapolis: Naval Institute, 1989). Summaries of the numbers of U-boat losses during World War I, and the modes of attack are found on page 76; and during World War II, on page 142.

89. Merrill, *From Submarine Bells to Sonar*, 57.

90. Dr. John M. Ide's ECHO article (Apr 17 and 24, 1959) also appeared in "Development of Underwater Acoustic Arrays for Passive Detection of Sound Sources," in Proceedings of the IRE [Institute of Radio Engineers], 47, 5 (May 1959): 864-6.

91. John Merrill, *Submarines, Technology, and History: Selected Articles by John Merrill* (Haverford, PA: Infinity Publishing, 2004), 132-3.

92. The development of the submarine as a hunter of other submarines can be found in Richard Compton-Hall, *Submarine versus Submarine: The Tactics and Technology of Underwater Confrontation* (New York: Orion Books, 1988).

93. John Merrill, *Fort Trumbull and the Submarine* (Avon, CT: Publishing Directions, 2000), 65-6.

94. Soviet submarine information is from the 1979-80 and 1986-87 editions of *Jane's Fighting Ships*.

95. John Merrill and Lionel D. Wyld, *Meeting the Submarine Challenge: A Short History of the Naval Underwater Systems Center* (Washington, D.C.: United States Government Printing Office, 1997), 40.

96. Thaddeus G. Bell, *Probing the Ocean for Submarines: A History of the AN/SQS-26 Long-Range, Echo-Ranging Sonar*, 2nd Edition, 2nd Printing [Approved for Public Release] (Los Altos Hills, CA: Peninsula Publishing, 2011), 36-9, 61-3. Beginning in 1959 and into the 1960s, USS *Tigrone* (AGSS-419) carried many Sound Lab acousticians who operated the BRASS II and the larger BRASS III experimental sonar.

97. Ibid., 61.

98. Merrill and Wyld, *Meeting the Submarine Challenge*, 44.

99. Much of the submarine sonar systems development history comes from: Merrill and Wyld, *Meeting the Submarine Challenge*. See, in particular, their chapter 3, "Sonar: Cornerstone of ASW."

100. The various systems carried by naval vessels can be found in editions of *Jane's Fighting Ships*.

101. Lee H. Holt, "The German Use of Sonic Listening," Journal of the Acoustical Society of America, 19, 4 (July, 1947): 678-81. Information about the GHG sonar is also from John M. Ide's article "Development of Underwater Acoustic Arrays for Passive Detection of Sound Sources," Proceedings of the IRE, 47, 5 (May 1959): 864-6, and from personal communications with Thad Bell.

102. A summary of WAA development is in Merrill and Wyld, *Meeting the Submarine Challenge*, 52-4.

103. http://www.navsea.navy.mil/nswc/carderock/pub/who/sites/seafac.aspx. The Carr Inlet range is now the Southeast Alaska Measurement Facility (SEAFAC) and has been moved to Ketchikan. The following extract from their web site describes their unique capability to conduct research with a submerged submarine:

> "The facility consists of a site to collect acoustic signatures of submerged submarines underway, and a unique site to measure acoustic signatures of motionless (static) submerged submarines with various onboard machinery secured or under unloaded operation. Acoustic signatures can be collected for a variety of speeds and operating conditions as the submarine transits back and forth between the dual bottom-mounted acoustic arrays. At the static site, suspension barges lower the submarine on cables and position it between measurement arrays to evaluate acoustic signatures of individual machinery components."

104. See chapter 2 for more of Melville's comments about submarine warfare at the turn of the twentieth century.

105. Merrill and Wyld, *Meeting the Submarine Challenge*, 45-8.

106. Norman Friedman, *The Naval Institute Guide to World Naval Weapons Systems* (Annapolis: Naval Institute, 1997), 633.

107. Stanley G. Lemon, "Towed-Array History, 1917-2003," IEEE Journal of Ocean Engineering, 29, 2 (April, 2004): 365-73.

108. The TB-33 towed array includes fiber optic technology, which is expected to improve the capability and reliability of conventional acoustic sensors used in other thin line towed arrays. Several TB-33 arrays are in the fleet, where NUWC continues to provide system expertise to several of the EDSU's more recent divers, David Jasinski, Christian Schumacher, Keith Bruce, and to Matthew Field who has since moved on as an engineer/diver for SUBMEPP at the Portsmouth Naval Shipyard. Fiber optic technology is also the basis for the hull-mounted conformal Lightweight Wide Aperture Array (LWAA). See: http://www.defenseindustrydaily.com/chesapeake-continues-work-on-tb33-sumarine-towed-arrays-02890/ Also: http://www.nrl.navy.mil/content_images/07Acoustics_Kirkendall.pdf

109. Helen Siiteri, ed., *The Sealab Chronicles of Capt. George F. Bond, USN* (Annapolis: Naval Institute, 1993), 33.

Chapter 7

110. An excellent source of information on radio communications during World War I is John Merrill, *Submarines, Technology, and History: Selected Articles by John Merrill* (Haverford, PA: Infinity Publishing, 2004), 17-32. The chapter referenced in Merrill's book first appeared in the April 1996 issue of *The Submarine Review.*

111. G. Gibbard Jackson, *The Romance of the Submarine* (London: Samson Low, Marston & Co., n.d.). Jackson's book, published about 1931, includes a number of photographs of the world's submarines during World War I with their antenna masts in place.

112. Lieutenant Commander Kenneth Edwards, *We Dive at Dawn* (Chicago: Reilly & Lee, 1941), 108-9. A photo of a carrier pigeon about to be released is on page 244.

113. For a summary of the development of submarine communications and other electromagnetic research at USN/USL and NUSC, see Chapter 7 "Submarine Electromagnetic Systems" in John Merrill and Lionel D. Wyld, *Meeting the Submarine Challenge: A Short History of the Naval Underwater Systems Center* (Washington, D.C.: United States Government Printing Office, 1997).

114. Richard Compton-Hall, *Submarine versus Submarine: The Tactics and Technology of Underwater Confrontation* (New York: Orion Books, 1988), 40.

115. Thaddeus G. Bell, *Probing the Ocean for Submarines: A History of the AN/SQS-26 Long-Range, Echo-Ranging Sonar*, 2nd Edition, 2nd Printing [Approved for Public Release] (Los Altos Hills, CA: Peninsula Publishing, 2011), 40.

116. Harvey C. Hayes, "Detection of Submarines," Proceedings of the American Philosophical Society, 59, 1 (1920): 1-47.

117. ECHO, March 9, 1962.

118. There are three reports related to Linear Chair published by the Defense Technology Information Center. The quote is from: "Preliminary Analysis of Near-Field and Far-Field Arrays for Project Linear Chair," 1977. http://books. google.com/books/about/Preliminary_Analysis_of_Near_Field_and_F. html?id=O-GltgAACAAJ

Several Navy agencies were involved with Linear Chair including NAVFAC, NSWC, and NUSC. In 2004, an engineer from NSWC received a Distinguished Service Award from the IEEE Ocean Engineering Society, for a career that included "working with NSWC's Linear Chair Program to quiet magnetic and electric signatures of submarines." See: http://www.ieee.org/organizations/society/oes/html/winter04/service_award.html

119. http://www.navsea.navy.mil/nswc/carderock/pub/who/sites/seafac.aspx. The Carr Inlet range is now the Southeast Alaska Measurement Facility (SEAFAC) and has been moved to Ketchikan. Although designed primarily for acoustic measurements (see chapter 6), the ability to suspend a submarine in a static configuration lends itself to other research initiatives.

120. By the mid-1980s, after a decade of supporting many challenging diving projects, Jim Clark and Ray Munn had both moved on with their careers at NUSC. Jim continued to support diving operations and was heavily involved with the ice diving in New Hampshire and in the arctic described in this chapter. Ray eventually completed his doctorate and later became a NUWC department head. Vic and I transferred to submarine and surface ship sonar related departments where we could pursue our field engineering careers.

121. In 1970, Dr. Mertens published *In-Water Photography - Theory and Practice* (Wiley-Interscience), one of the earliest books on underwater photography.

122. http://spie.org/x648.html?product_id=140670

123. NUWSCOPE, July 31, 1992.

124. Comb jellies are invertebrates of the phylum Ctenophora. *Balinopsis infundibulum* and *Pleurobrachia pileus* were frequently seen during the diving operations.

125. http://spie.org/x648.html?product_id=190048

126. Jacob R. Longacre, James H. Clark, Mark A. Landry, and Roy R. Manstan, "Optical propagation through sea ice," Proceedings of the Geoscience and Remote Sensing Symposium, Vol. 1 (1995): 399-401. See: http://ieeexplore.ieee.org/xpl/articleDetails.jsp?arnumber=520291

Chapter 8

127. Robert Fulton, *Torpedo War, and Submarine Explosions* (1810; facsimile reproduction, edited by Herman Hinkle, Chicago: Swallow Press, 1971). It wasn't until the end of the nineteenth century that the torpedo as we know it today became a reality, sparking worldwide interest in its history. G.-L Pesce, in his book *La Navigation Sous-Marine* (Paris: Vuibert and Nony, 1906), praised Fulton's early experiments in submarine warfare and included the illustration shown here (figure 64).

128. United States Senate, *Report of the Committee, to whom was Referred by the Senate, A Resolution to Inquire into the Expediency of Employing the Torpedo or Submarine Explosions, February 26th, 1810* (Washington City: Roger C. Weightman, 1810).

129. Lieutenant Commander J. S. Barnes, USN, *Submarine Warfare: Offensive and Defensive* (New York: Van Nostrand, 1869), 51-2, 61.

130. Beginning with the January 2009 edition of NUWSCOPE, NUWC celebrated the 140th anniversary of the Naval Torpedo Station with a series of twelve monthly articles that summarized the long history of submarine warfare development in Newport, Rhode Island. The early history can be found in a booklet: *The Naval Torpedo Station*, Compiled under the Direction of Captain Martin E. Trench USN Inspector of Ordnance in Charge and J.P. Sullivan, Chief Clerk, and by W.J. Coggeshall and J.E. McCarthy Employees of the Ordnance Department of the Torpedo Station: Training Center Press, 1920.

131. Ensign J. M. Ellicott, "The Untried Weapon," The Illustrated American, 5, 75 (July 25, 1891).

132. The timeline I have described, and that defined the transition from USN/ USL to NUSC and finally NUWC, is primarily from the book John Merrill and Lionel D. Wyld, *Meeting the Submarine Challenge: A Short History of the Naval Underwater Systems Center* (Washington, D.C.: United States Government Printing Office, 1997). The internal struggles that occurred within NUSC in New London and Newport are derived from my own recollections, from conversations with other retirees, and in particular, from Michael Pastore who shared his recollections and his unpublished manuscript, *SONAR: Cold War ASW Adventures*, covering his years as a submariner and as a civilian at USN/USL and NUSC.

133. http://spie.org/x648.html?product_id=673727

134. NUWC activities associated with the KMISS installation were detailed in the January 1997 edition of NUWSCOPE, in an article titled: "Code 38 involved in tri-service project in the Marshall Islands."

135. See their website: http://www.rimap.org

136. In 1998 (see the July 1998 edition of NUWSCOPE), NUWC created a Memorandum of Understanding with the Naval Historical Center (now the Naval History and Heritage Command) that enabled the EDSU to join RIMAP in its studies of historic wreck sites in Rhode Island waters, adding to the EDSU's commitment to community and educational outreach.

Chapter 9

137. This chapter describes the efforts of the EDSU to combat the potential threat from terrorist divers. All of the information provided in this chapter defining the threat was obtained through various internet sources available to the author in 2012 while researching this book. I thus caution the reader that information available on the internet, while in the public domain, is not necessarily a permanent record, as it is when in print.

138. http://articles.cnn.com/2002-05-24/us/scuba.terrorist.
alert_1_scuba-diver-fbi-field-offices-detainees?_s=PM:US

139. http://www.belowthewaterline.us/the-threat.html

140. http://archive.newsmax.com/archives/articles/2003/8/26/160951.shtml

141. The claims made by a member of an al Qaida-linked terrorist group in the Philippines that he had trained as a scuba diver to participate in an underwater operation were obtained from: http://www.belowthewaterline.us/the-threat.html
http://www.wnd.com/2005/03/2941

142. http://www.iseas.edu.sg

143. Details about al Qaida's maritime threat and their interest in underwater attacks, including Dutch intelligence reports of suspected terrorists receiving scuba training in the Netherlands, were obtained from: http://www.belowthewaterline.us/the-threat.html
http://abcnews.go.com/US/story?id=94074&page=1#.T8TTZNUg7IU
http://articles.latimes.com/2003/jul/31/world/fg-scuba31

144. The concerns expressed in the Times of London appeared in the web site: http://www.eaglespeak.us/2005/04/al Qaeda-divers-and-uk-navy-fleet.html

145. I worked with Harold "Bud" Vincent and Sam Carroll, both EDSU divers, and with Yadira Gilchrest, developing the experimental protocol. In addition to Bud and me, other EDSU divers who participated as test subjects included José Arteiro and Bruce Greenhalgh. Sam had graduated with his Masters degree in acoustics from the University of Rhode Island where he had been working with Bud, another of our divers who completed his doctorate.

146. http://www.jnlwd.defense.gov

147. In 2007, NUWC published two articles in NUWSCOPE: "Division's unique resources enable tests of swimmer detection systems" (January edition) and "Swimmer defense prototype system demonstrated" (November edition)

148. NUWSCOPE, January 2011. As this book was going to press, I learned that members of the EDSU were among a group receiving a Federal Laboratory Consortium Award for their participation in the NUWC Waterside Security Team. The award recognizes the development of operational systems for the protection of vulnerable facilities and critical infrastructure from water-borne threats, and the transfer of this technology to military and civilian agencies responding to the Global War on Terror. Among the many agencies benefiting from this waterside security technology are the Department of Homeland Security, the Department of the Interior, and the Army Corps of Engineers.

149. The account of the Sri Lankan naval ship can be found at: http://www.satp. org/satporgtp/countries/shrilanka/database/data_suicide_killings.htm

150. NUWSCOPE, October 2008.

151. James Pollack and John Hughes, "Swimmer Defense Initiatives," Leading Edge: Homeland and Force Protection, 6, 3 (Naval Surface Warfare Center, Dahlgren, VA., n.d.): 32-7 (approved for public release). For an overview of "swimmer defense" see: http://www.defensereview.com/underwater-detection-and-disruption-tech-being-developed-to-combat-al-qaeda

152. An article in the December 2003 edition of NUWSCOPE summarizes Mike Peirson's diving career.

Chapter 10

153. John Merrill and Lionel D. Wyld, *Meeting the Submarine Challenge: A Short History of the Naval Underwater Systems Center* (Washington, D.C.: United States Government Printing Office, 1997), 12-13.

154. John Merrill, *Submarines, Technology, and History: Selected Articles by John Merrill* (Haverford, PA: Infinity Publishing, 2004), 85-99.

155. http://en.wikipedia.org/wiki/Navy/Marine_Corps_Intranet

156. http://en.wikipedia.org/wiki/
Defense_Acquisition_Workforce_Improvement_Act

157. Lean Six Sigma was designed to improve manufacturing and industrial best practices; this process may appeal to risk-averse efficiency experts, but is the bane of make-it-happen risk takers. See: http://en.wikipedia.org/wiki/Six_Sigma http://www.novaces.com/government-defense.php

158. http://en.wikipedia.org/wiki/Operational_risk_management

Epilogue

159. Thomas Sprat, *The History of the Royal-Society of London for the Improving of Natural Knowledge.* 2nd ed. (London: for Rob. Scot, et al, 1702), 35. The use of italics in this and subsequent quotes is Sprat's.

160. Ibid., 378-89, 393.

161. Ibid., 248-9.

162. Articles about the event appeared in the March and October 2011 editions of NUWSCOPE.

163. http://www.isrsubrace.org

164. http://www.navsea.navy.mil/nswc/carderock

165. John Lehman, Jr., *Command of the Seas: Building the 600 Ship Navy* (New York: Charles Scribner's Sons, 1988).

166. John P. Craven, *The Silent War: The Cold War Battle Beneath the Sea* (New York: Simon & Schuster, 2001).

167. Sherry Sontag and Christopher Drew, *Blind Man's Bluff: The Untold Story of American Submarine Espionage* (New York: Public Affairs, 1998).

168. Gannon McHale, *Stealth Boat: Fighting the Cold War in a Fast-Attack Submarine* (Annapolis: Naval Institute, 2008).

169. Thaddeus G. Bell, *Probing the Ocean for Submarines: A History of the AN/SQS-26 Long-Range, Echo-Ranging Sonar*, 2nd Edition, 2nd Printing [Approved for Public Release] (Newport, RI: Naval Undersea Warfare Center, 2011).

170. Thaddeus G. Bell, "Submarines and Submarine Detection," USL Report No. 545, May 8, 1962.

171. www.ct.gov/dep/forttrumbull

172. The BRASS II (Bottom-Reflected Active Sonar System) followed by a much larger BRASS III was mounted on USS *Tigrone* (SS-419, later designated AGSS-419 as a sonar research submarine). Over several years, *Tigrone* carried many USN/USL engineers who recall visits to ports as diverse as Halifax, Port Canaveral, St. Croix, Bermuda, Lisbon, Gibraltar, Edinburgh, and above the Arctic Circle into the Marginal Ice Zone. A summary of the BRASS-series of experiments and their impact on Cold War sonar development is in Bell, *Probing the Ocean for Submarines*, pp. 36-9, 61-4.

INDEX

Acknowledgements

To every member of the USN/USL, NUSC/NL, and NUWC dive team—past and present—it has been your abundance of enthusiasm and team spirit spanning more than a half century that has encouraged me to tell your (our) story. With thanks for the reminders expressed at the mini-reunions we all enjoy. Whether celebrating the latest diver's return from dive school or the latest retirement ceremony; or just reminiscing over lunch on the New London waterfront with Kurt Hansen; downing a beer with Ross Byrne while perusing his photos of our arctic trip; or enjoying sea stories and a glass of wine on Vic Marolda's back porch overlooking his grape vines, there is always a constant flow of good cheer.

But it has been the retirees (and those about to retire) who kept me on track. So, my sincere thanks to past divers Ray Munn, Jim Clark, and Paul Mileski who agreed to review the entire manuscript . . . until they realized how long it would be . . . yet stayed with it to the end; and to John Wiedenheft whose nature is to ensure accuracy and attention to detail. Comments from these individuals, who always brought stability and sanity to a team of otherwise ADHD-symptomatic divers, helped build a *balanced* approach to writing this book. For the *unbalanced* content, my thanks to story-tellers Ken Beatrice, Bruce Greenhalgh and Rick Thibeault . . . and, of course, Mac.

This book, however, is not just a story about a dive team; it is about a pathway to success in an era of nuclear confrontation—the Cold War—and an organization, the U.S. Navy Underwater Sound Lab, which cleared the path and made success a priority. While many of the movers and shakers from the early days of the Cold War have passed away, I have, over the past three years, enjoyed communicating with countless retirees. The annual Sound Lab reunions bring together individuals that I hadn't seen in decades, but where even a few words spoken over a handshake would provide one more missing piece of the historical puzzle. There are hundreds of old timers who should be acknowledged here—they have enough sea stories to fill an ocean—but there are simply not enough pages available.

I cannot fail, however, to acknowledge the contributions of four of these individuals, who share an appreciation for a period in American history of which they were a part. First, my thanks to Bernie Cole who read every chapter and then began to relate stories of his own early years at the Sound Lab, and at sea. I have also enjoyed some "distance learning" from Mike Pastore, a former submariner before he became civilianized and joined the Sound Lab, now a retiree enjoying the California climate where he, too, writes about his Cold War service. My thanks to Thad Bell whose book *Probing the Oceans for Submarines*, now in its second printing, is a model for documenting a technology critical to that pathway to success in bringing down the Soviet Union. And my sincere appreciation to the late John Merrill for the several books he has published, covering a century of submarine and anti-submarine warfare history. The book *Meeting the Submarine Challenge*, which he wrote with coauthor Lionel Wyld, is no longer in print; my hope, having referenced John's writings throughout, is to encourage its reissue by the Government Printing Office.

My thanks also to the Fort Trumbull State Park and to the Customs House Museum and Archive in New London, Connecticut, where resides much of what remains of the Underwater Sound Lab historical record; and to the Naval Undersea Warfare Center Division Newport public affairs staff, and in particular editor Jane Tracy, who was able to fill in some gaps in the historical narrative missing from my own limited collection of editions of the monthly newsletter NUWSCOPE. I also want to recognize the Naval History and Heritage Command, Washington, D.C.; the Submarine Force Library and Museum, Groton, Connecticut; the UDT/SEAL Museum, Fort Pierce, Florida; and the Man In The Sea Museum, Panama City Beach, Florida, all having provided valuable historical background.

There are over one hundred illustrations in this book. Most of them are U.S. Navy photographs, many of which are accessible and in the public domain at various government web sites. The following is a list of these sources:

www.navy.mil (U.S. Navy official web site)

www.history.navy.mil (Naval History and Heritage Command)
www.defenseimagery.mil (Department of Defense)
www.archives.gov (National Archives)
www.loc.gov (Library of Congress)
www.ussnautilus.org (Submarine Force Library and Museum)
www.navsource.org . . . NavSource is a web site run by volunteers with a commitment to the preservation of naval history. This is not an official government web site, but maintains an extensive on-line archive of public domain photographs.

I have also relied on several web sites for access to historical accounts, each listed in the end notes—but web sites come and go, and information posted one year may be gone the next. So it was with caution that I have used these sites as source material, and I now remind readers that what was referenced in this book was available while researching various topics in 2012. As the digital (and digitized) word begins to overtake the printed word, and libraries offer more computer work stations for access to eBooks, there is the menace of the delete button, which can erase all traces of an era, akin to the burning in antiquity of the library of Alexandria, Egypt . . . (okay, maybe that's a bit dramatic). But whether or not this book survives in print or as an eBook, my hope is that it will add one more piece in the puzzle that will define the Cold War for future generations, who will, in turn, meet their own challenges with the same commitment and enthusiasm as we did during the twentieth century.

And finally, I want to thank my kids, Dan and Sarah, for laughing at the right times when they read some of their dad's sea stories . . . so if I didn't bore two teenagers, maybe other readers will also enjoy this history.

ABOUT THE AUTHOR

Roy R. Manstan, author with Fred Frese of *TURTLE: David Bushnell's Revolutionary Vessel*, retired from the Naval Undersea Warfare Center in 2006 where he was a mechanical engineer and diving officer for the Engineering and Diving Support Unit. Manstan, seen here emerging from a replica of Bushnell's *Turtle*, holds a bachelor's degree from Lafayette College and master's degrees from the University of Connecticut and Connecticut College. (*Jerry Roberts*)

Made in the USA
Coppell, TX
29 November 2019